C000065397

BIRDS OF INDIA
PAKISTAN, NEPAL, BHUTAN, BANGLADESH AND SRI LANKA

BIRDS OF INDIA

PAKISTAN, NEPAL, BHUTAN, BANGLADESH AND SRI LANKA

Text and Illustrations by Norman Arlott

WILLIAM COLLINS

DEDICATION

I would like to dedicate this book to Linda, who has been not only a
loving sister but also a great friend, and also to her husband Graham
and family Karen and Tristan

This edition published in 2015 by William Collins,
An imprint of HarperCollins Publishers

1 London Bridge Street
London SE1 9GF

WilliamCollinsBooks.com

First published in 2015

Text © Norman Arlott 2015
Illustrations © Norman Arlott 2015

20 19 18 17 16 15
10 9 8 7 6 5 4 3 2 1

The author asserts his moral right to be identified as the author of this work.
All rights reserved. No parts of this publication may be reproduced, stored in a
retrieval system or transmitted, in any form or by any means, electronic, mechanical,
photocopying, recording or otherwise, without the prior permission of the publishers.

A catalogue record for this book is available from the British Library.

ISBN 978-0-00-742955-4

William Collins uses papers that are natural, renewable and recyclable products made
from wood grown in sustainable forests. The manufacturing processes conform to the
environmental regulations of the country of origin.

Edited and designed by D & N Publishing, Baydon, Wiltshire
Cartography by Martin Brown

Colour reproduction by FMG
Printed and bound in India by Replika Press Pvt. Ltd

CONTENTS

ACKNOWLEDGEMENTS

Bird books take a relatively short time to paint and write, but the knowledge that enables them to be completed is gained over many, many years. I well remember that my passion started as a very young boy collecting birds' eggs (now, quite rightly, frowned upon) with my father. That passion has since been enhanced by being fortunate enough to be in the field with and inspired by some well-known and not so well-known 'birders'. I must mention the following, who have encouraged me and allowed me to pick their brains over the years: the late John G. Williams, the late Eric Hosking, the late Crispin Fisher, Robert Gillmor, the late Basil Parsons, Brian Leflay and Moss Taylor. This book could not have gone ahead without the help of the staff at the British Museum at Tring, especially Mark Adams and Robert Prŷs-Jones. Namrita and David Price-Goodfellow, Hugh Brazier and Martin Brown deserve special praise for their skill and patience in putting together the various component parts of this book. Without publishers there would not be a book, so it gives me great pleasure to thank everyone at HarperCollins, particularly Myles Archibald and Julia Koppitz. Last, but definitely not least, I must thank friends and family who have had to put up with my various mood changes whilst trying to sort out some of the more difficult aspects of putting this book together. My wife Marie probably endured more than most.

INTRODUCTION

The format of this book follows that of my Palearctic, West Indies and North American volumes. Although my brief was, predominantly, to produce an illustrated checklist (space would not allow me to produce the ultimate field guide), it is hoped that within these pages I have given a helpful nudge towards what to look for when searching for new birds, as well as providing a reminder of birds seen.

Most of the text in this book is based on the type of notes I make before embarking on a field trip to a new area, and hopefully the text and illustrations together will help to identify most birds encountered. Obviously the use of more in-depth tomes will be required for some of the trickier species (see Further Reading).

I can only hope that with this work I have been able to add to the pleasure of anticipation or memory, and perhaps even added some extra piece of knowledge about the birds of this region.

Lesser Florican

♀

♂

♀

♂

Bengal Florican

AREA AND SPECIES COVERED

Pakistan, India, Nepal, Bhutan, Bangladesh, Sri Lanka, the Andaman Islands, the Nicobar Islands and the Maldives.

I have endeavoured to include every species recorded in the region, apart from non-established introductions, and as many of the major subspecies as possible. Each has been depicted in breeding plumage, and non-breeding plumage when it differs significantly. To keep the book to a manageable size no juvenile plumages have been illustrated, although, when thought necessary and room permits, a short passage in Field Notes has been included.

I have needed to tweak the recommended order in places in order to aid plate composition; hopefully this will not cause too much aggravation.

PLATES

The abbreviations and symbols used on the plates are as follows:
♂ = male, ♀ = female, br = breeding, n-br = non-breeding.

NOMENCLATURE

I have headlined the English names that I believe are those used by most birders in the field, which means I have in many cases reverted to 'old-school' names rather than some of the more modern interpretations. Most of these 'new' names, along with other well-used ones, are included in parenthesis.

IDENTIFICATION

It is hoped that the illustrations will be all that is needed to identify a specific bird, but quite obviously with some of the trickier species more information is needed: hence the sections on Field Notes, Voice and Habitat.

FIELD NOTES: Because of the need to keep text to a minimum this section rarely mentions those aspects of a bird that should be obvious from the illustrations, e.g. wing-bars, bill shape etc. It is used mainly to point to a bird's habits or to mention facets of identification that are hidden in a standing or perched bird.

VOICE: Probably the first sign of a bird's presence. The descriptions are shown in italics. Where space has allowed I have included different interpretations of the same song. Although it is difficult to produce an accurate reproduction of bird songs or calls in the written word, this section is worth studying in order to get a feel for what is often the most important area of bird identification.

HABITAT: The main habitat preferences mentioned are those in which a species breeds; also included are wintering habitats if appropriate.

DISTRIBUTION: Mainly general, so should be read in conjunction with the maps.

DISTRIBUTION MAPS

Distribution maps (*see* pp.343–81) are shown for all species except vagrants, those that have been recently introduced and those that spend most of their time at sea. Birds that occur only on islands, including Sri Lanka, have not been mapped. They should only be used as a rough guide to where a species can be found at different times of the year. Red ▉ areas indicate where a species may be found in the summer on its breeding grounds; blue ▉ shows where it is found in winter when not breeding; and purple ▉ areas are where a species is a year-round resident.

MAP OF THE REGION

BIRD TOPOGRAPHY

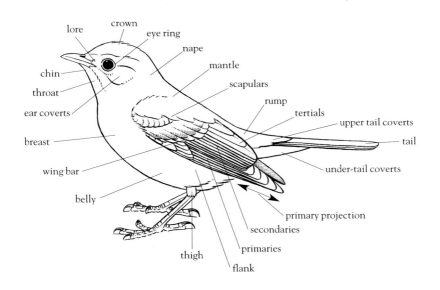

lore
crown
eye ring
nape
mantle
scapulars
rump
tertials
upper tail coverts
tail
chin
throat
ear coverts
breast
wing bar
belly
thigh
flank
primaries
secondaries
primary projection
under-tail coverts

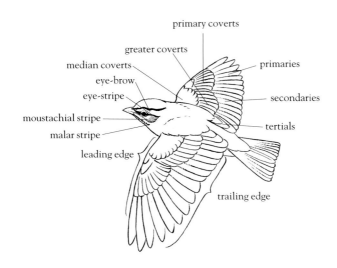

primary coverts
greater coverts
median coverts
eye-brow
eye-stripe
moustachial stripe
malar stripe
leading edge
primaries
secondaries
tertials
trailing edge

1 GEESE

1 WHITE-FRONTED GOOSE (GREATER WHITE-FRONTED GOOSE) *Anser albifrons* 64–78cm FIELD NOTES: Juvenile lacks the white at the base of the bill and has an unmarked belly. In flight shows uniform grey upperwing. VOICE: Typical goose cackling and a musical *lyo-lyok* in flight. HABITAT: Winters on wet grassland, stubble fields, lakes and rivers. DISTRIBUTION: Winters in N India, Pakistan and Bangladesh.

2 BEAN GOOSE *Anser fabalis* 66–84cm FIELD NOTES: Juvenile more scaly on back, otherwise similar to adult. VOICE: A *wink-wink* and a deep nasal *hank-hank*, also typical goose cackling. HABITAT: Winters in open country, including agricultural land. DISTRIBUTION: Vagrant, recorded in Nepal and India.

3 GREYLAG GOOSE *Anser anser* 75–90cm FIELD NOTES: In flight shows a distinctive pale grey forewing. Juvenile much as adult but more scaly with duller bill. VOICE: In flight gives a deep, honking *aahng-ahng-ung*. HABITAT: Occurs on wet grassland, agricultural land, lakes and rivers. DISTRIBUTION: Winter visitor mainly to N parts of the region.

4 LESSER WHITE-FRONTED GOOSE *Anser erythropus* 53–66cm FIELD NOTES: Juvenile lacks the white at the base of the bill and has an unmarked belly; differs from juvenile White-fronted Goose by having a yellow eye-ring, usually only visible at close range. VOICE: In flight utters a repeated, squeaky *kyu-yu-yu*. HABITAT: Wet grassland, agricultural land and lakes. DISTRIBUTION: Winter visitor to N parts of the region.

5 BAR-HEADED GOOSE *Anser indicus* 71–76cm FIELD NOTES: Juvenile has crown and hind-neck dark grey and lacks the black nape bars. VOICE: In flight utters a nasal honking. HABITAT: Breeds on high-altitude lakes and marshes, winters by large rivers and lakes, and on coastal islands of Bangladesh. DISTRIBUTION: Breeds in NW India (Ladakh), more widespread during winter.

6 SNOW GOOSE *Anser caerulescens* 65–84cm FIELD NOTES: Juvenile white phase has crown, hind-neck, back and wings grey, the latter with white fringes. Juvenile blue phase all over dark slaty-brown. VOICE: In flight gives a nasal, cackling *la-luk*, said to resemble the barking of a small dog. HABITAT: Lakeside grassland. DISTRIBUTION: Vagrant, recorded in India.

7 RED-BREASTED GOOSE *Branta ruficollis* 53–55cm FIELD NOTES: Unmistakable. Juvenile a dull version of adult. VOICE: Flight call is a squeaky, repeated *kik-yoik kik-yik*. HABITAT: Winters on pastures, crop and stubble fields. DISTRIBUTION: Doubted record of vagrancy in India.

2 SWANS, DUCKS

1 WHOOPER SWAN *Cygnus cygnus* 140–165cm FIELD NOTES: Longer-necked than Tundra Swan. Juvenile greyish-brown, slightly darker than juvenile Tundra Swan, base of bill pink. VOICE: Various honking and bugling calls. In flight gives a deep *hoop-hoop-hoop.* HABITAT: In winter occurs on wet pastures, lakes and large rivers. DISTRIBUTION: Vagrant: old records from Nepal, India and Pakistan.

2 TUNDRA SWAN (BEWICK'S SWAN) *Cygnus columbianus* 115–140cm FIELD NOTES: Shorter-necked than Whooper Swan. Juvenile greyish-brown, paler than juvenile Whooper Swan, base of bill pink. VOICE: Various honking and yapping calls. In flight utters a low *hoo-hoo.* HABITAT: Usually winters on lakes and large rivers, feeding on nearby pastures and agricultural land. DISTRIBUTION: Vagrant, recorded from India, Pakistan and Nepal.

3 MUTE SWAN *Cygnus olor* 125–155cm FIELD NOTES: Neck usually held more curved than Whooper and Tundra Swan. In flight wings make a distinctive pulsating throbbing noise. Juvenile dull brownish-grey, bill dull pinkish-grey, lacking the frontal knob. VOICE: Utters various hisses, grunts and snorts. HABITAT: Usually lakes and rivers and nearby grassy areas. DISTRIBUTION: Vagrant, recorded in Pakistan and India.

4 RUDDY SHELDUCK *Tadorna ferruginea* 61–67cm FIELD NOTES: In flight shows extensive white forewing, above and below. Juvenile much as adult female, although slightly duller. VOICE: Utters a honking *aakh* or *ah-onk,* also a repeated, trumpet-like *pok-pok-pok-pok.* HABITAT: Breeds near high-altitude swamps and lakes. Winters by lakes and rivers, has a liking for sand bars. DISTRIBUTION: Breeds in the Himalayas. Much more widespread during winter.

5 SHELDUCK (COMMON SHELDUCK) *Tadorna tadorna* 58–67cm FIELD NOTES: Appears black and white in flight due to extensive white forewing. Juvenile has white forehead, foreneck, chin and underparts, greyish scapulars, grey-brown hind-neck and face. VOICE: Male utters a thin, whistling *sliss-sliss-sliss-sliss,* female gives a rapid, nasal *gag-ag-ag-ag-ag-ak.* HABITAT: Usually breeds in burrows, tree holes or concealed hollows near coasts, lakes or rivers. Winters on mudflats and shingle banks of coasts, large rivers and lakes. DISTRIBUTION: Scattered, widespread winter visitor. Has bred in Baluchistan.

6 KNOB-BILLED DUCK (COMB DUCK) *Sarkidiornis melanotos* 56–76cm FIELD NOTES: In flight wings all dark. Juvenile has back scaled with buff fringes. Hind-neck, crown and eye-stripe brownish-black, pale buff supercilium. Underparts, foreneck and face generally pale buff. VOICE: Generally silent. During breeding season may utter grunts, hisses and whistles. HABITAT: Breeds in lowland swamps, pools and lakes in wooded country, feeding on nearby wet grassland. DISTRIBUTION: Widespread resident over much of the region.

7 WHITE-WINGED DUCK *Asarcornis scutulata* 66–81cm FIELD NOTES: In flight shows extensive white forewing. Female as male, but duller. VOICE: Generally silent, but may utter a wailing honk, ending in a nasal whistle, while in flight. HABITAT: Streams and pools in tropical forest, also in nearby open swamp areas. DISTRIBUTION: Resident in NE India and Bangladesh.

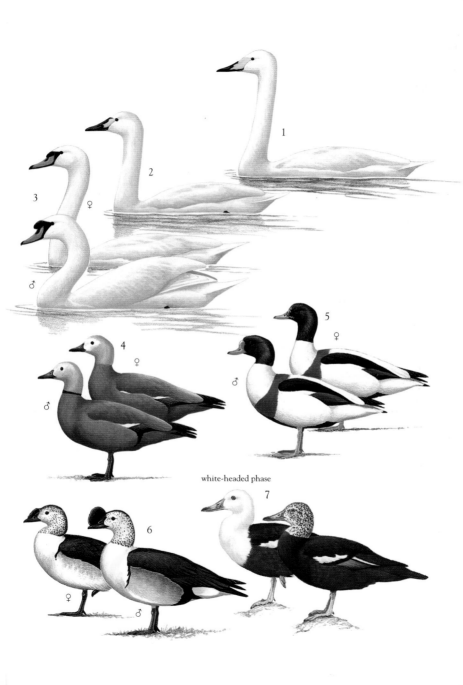

white-headed phase

3 DUCKS

1 FULVOUS WHISTLING DUCK (FULVOUS TREE DUCK) *Dendrocygna bicolor* 45–53cm FIELD NOTES: Usually occurs in small flocks, often associated with Lesser Whistling Duck. In flight wings all dark brown-black. Juvenile paler and duller. VOICE: Very vocal. In flight and when feeding or at rest utters a wader-like, whistled *k-weeoo k-weeoo*. Also gives a harsh *kee kee kee* during disputes. HABITAT: Freshwater lakes and marshes with fringing vegetation. DISTRIBUTION: Resident in NE of the region, with scattered records elsewhere.

2 LESSER WHISTLING DUCK (LESSER TREE DUCK) *Dendrocygna javanica* 38–42cm FIELD NOTES: Usually occurs in small flocks of around a dozen birds, occasionally in much larger groups. In flight shows chestnut forewing. At close range note yellow eye-ring. VOICE: In flight utters a constant thin, whistled *whi-whee*. HABITAT: Mainly freshwater pools, lakes and swamps with fringing vegetation, but may occur on wet agricultural land and coastal lagoons. DISTRIBUTION: Widespread resident over most of the region.

3 WHITE-HEADED DUCK (WHITE-HEADED STIFFTAIL) *Oxyura leucocephala* 43–48cm FIELD NOTES: Usually in small parties. Juvenile a duller version of adult female, some may show a complete brownish-black head. VOICE: Generally silent. May utter piping and rattling calls during group swimming displays. HABITAT: Lakes and brackish lagoons with fringing and submerged vegetation. DISTRIBUTION: Winter visitor to Pakistan and N India.

4 COTTON PYGMY-GOOSE (COTTON TEAL) *Nettapus coromandelianus* 30–37cm FIELD NOTES: Occurs in pairs or small parties. Regularly perches in trees. Male in flight shows white primaries with black tips and a white trailing edge to secondaries. Female primaries all black. Juvenile similar to female. VOICE: Male utters a sharp *car-car-carawak*. Female gives a weak quack. HABITAT: Vegetated freshwater lakes and pools. DISTRIBUTION: Widespread resident.

5 MANDARIN (MANDARIN DUCK) *Aix galericulata* 41–49cm FIELD NOTES: Eclipse male has pink bill, otherwise much like female. VOICE: Generally silent. HABITAT: Lakes and rivers with surrounding trees and shrubs. In winter may be on more open waters. DISTRIBUTION: Vagrant, recorded from Bangladesh, Bhutan, India and Nepal.

6 SMEW *Mergellus albellus* 38–44cm FIELD NOTES: In winter often in sexually segregated flocks. Upperwing of both sexes shows white wing-patch. VOICE: Generally silent, except during breeding season. HABITAT: Freshwater lakes, rivers and Himalayan streams. DISTRIBUTION: Winter visitor to the N of the region.

7 RED-BREASTED MERGANSER *Mergus serrator* 52–58cm FIELD NOTES: In flight both sexes show much white on the inner upperwing. VOICE: Away from breeding areas is generally silent. HABITAT: Winters on inshore and coastal waters. DISTRIBUTION: Winter visitor to Pakistan, with scattered records elsewhere.

8 GOOSANDER (COMMON MERGANSER) *Mergus merganser* 58–72cm FIELD NOTES: Inner part of male upperwing shows extensive white patch, female similar but forewing greyer. VOICE: During display male gives a twanging *uig-a*. Female utters various harsh notes. HABITAT: Breeds alongside rivers or lakes, usually with vegetated cover. Winters on lakes, rivers and coastal bays. DISTRIBUTION: Breeds in Ladakh. Winters mainly in the N of the region.

4 DUCKS

1 GADWALL *Anas strepera* 46–55cm FIELD NOTES: In flight both sexes show white secondary-patch on upperwing. Usually in small groups, and can be quite wary. VOICE: Male gives a sharp *ahrk* and also a low whistle. Female has a mechanical-sounding quack. HABITAT: Fresh waters with fringing and aquatic vegetation, less often on estuaries. DISTRIBUTION: Widespread winter visitor.

2 FALCATED DUCK (FALCATED TEAL) *Anas falcata* 48–54cm FIELD NOTES: Often found in the company of other duck species. Tends to keep near to vegetated cover. Eclipse male similar to female, but with blacker crown. VOICE: Male gives a low whistle followed by a wavering *uit-trr*. Female utters a throaty quack. HABITAT: Lakes and large rivers with emergent vegetation. DISTRIBUTION: Winter visitor, mainly to the N of the region.

3 WIGEON (EURASIAN WIGEON) *Anas penelope* 45–50cm FIELD NOTES: In flight male shows a large white patch on upperwing. Very gregarious. Grazes more than most other ducks. VOICE: Male gives a clear, whistling *wheeooo* and female a growling *krrr*. HABITAT: Wet grassland, paddyfields, marshes, lakes, rivers, coastal creeks and estuaries. DISTRIBUTION: Widespread winter visitor.

4 MALLARD *Anas platyrhynchos* 50–65cm FIELD NOTES: Often found in large flocks. Eclipse male much like female but with a dull yellow bill. VOICE: Male utters a rasped *kreep*, female a *quack-quack-quack*. HABITAT: Mainly marshes and lakes with fringe vegetation. DISTRIBUTION: Breeds in the Himalayas; otherwise winter visitor to much of the region.

5 SPOT-BILLED DUCK (INDIAN SPOT-BILLED DUCK) *Anas poecilorhyncha* 58–63cm FIELD NOTES: In flight, from above, shows large white patch on tertials and green speculum; from below shows dark primaries and secondaries contrasting with white coverts. VOICE: Calls very similar to those of Mallard. HABITAT: Well-vegetated freshwater lakes, pools and marshes DISTRIBUTION: Widespread resident.

6 CHINESE SPOT-BILLED DUCK (EASTERN SPOT-BILLED DUCK) *Anas zonorhyncha* 53cm FIELD NOTES: In flight looks plain, speculum blue. Lacks red loral spot and is more sooty-brown than Spot-billed Duck. Often regarded as the eastern race of the latter. VOICE: As Spot-billed Duck. HABITAT: Well vegetated freshwater lakes, pools and marshes. DISTRIBUTION: Frequent visitor to NE India.

7 SHOVELER (NORTHERN or EUROPEAN SHOVELER) *Anas clypeata* 44–52cm FIELD NOTES: Usually in pairs or small parties. In flight looks 'front-heavy' because of large bill. Male upperwing shows a pale blue forewing and green speculum separated by a white wing-bar; female wing duller, with thinner white wing-bar. VOICE: Usually fairly silent except during display when male utters a hollow *sluk-uk* or *g-dunk*. Female has a quacking *gak-gak-gak-ga-ga*. HABITAT: Open freshwater areas, less regular on coastal lagoons and estuaries. DISTRIBUTION: Widespread winter visitor.

8 ANDAMAN TEAL *Anas albogularis* 37–47cm FIELD NOTES: White facial markings variable: two extremes shown. In flight upperwing shows a broad white wing-bar, underwing shows white axillaries. Often considered conspecific with Sunda Teal A. *gibberifrons*. VOICE: Male utters a clear, low *preep*. Female has a loud, laughing series of quacks. HABITAT: Freshwater marshes and pools, paddyfields, mangrove swamps, coastal lagoons and estuaries. DISTRIBUTION: Resident on the Andamans.

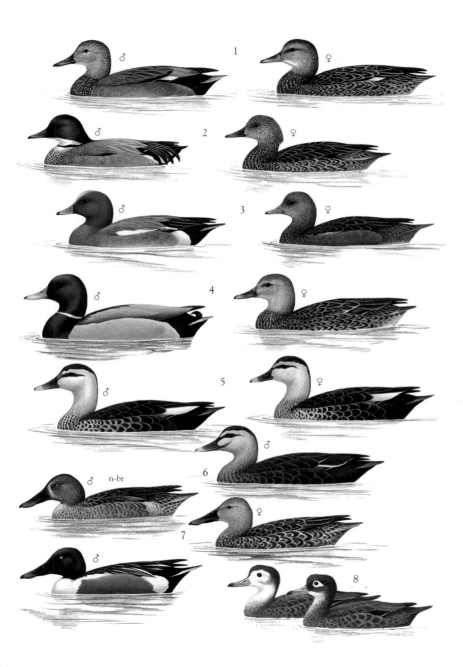

5 DUCKS

1 PINTAIL (NORTHERN PINTAIL) *Anas acuta* 51–56cm (male with tail 61–66cm)
FIELD NOTES: Long neck and tail make for an elongated look in flight. Gregarious, often in
very large flocks. VOICE: Generally silent, but male may give a mellow *proop-proop* and female
a series of weak quacks and a low croak if flushed. HABITAT: Paddyfields, freshwater marshes,
open freshwater areas, coastal lagoons and estuaries. DISTRIBUTION: Widespread winter
visitor.

2 GARGANEY *Anas querquedula* 37–41cm FIELD NOTES: Generally shy, keeps close to
aquatic vegetation. In flight, from above, male shows pale grey forewing separated from
green speculum by white wing-bar. At a distance can appear very pale-winged. Gregarious,
often in large flocks. VOICE: Generally silent, but male may be heard to give a rattling *knerek*
and female a high nasal quack. HABITAT: Freshwater lakes and marshes with extensive
vegetation, lakes and coastal lagoons. DISTRIBUTION: Widespread winter visitor.

3 BAIKAL TEAL (FORMOSA TEAL) *Anas formosa* 39–43cm FIELD NOTES: Eclipse
male shows 'shadow' of distinctive breeding facial pattern. Female similar to Teal, but
note pale loral spot. VOICE: Male utters a clucking *wot-wot-wot*. Female gives a low quack.
HABITAT: Fresh and brackish water areas. DISTRIBUTION: Uncommon winter visitor, mainly
to the N of the region.

4 TEAL (COMMON TEAL) *Anas crecca* 34–38cm FIELD NOTES: Gregarious. Rapid flight
with much twisting and turning. VOICE: Male utters a soft, high-pitched *preep-preep*. Females
rather silent, but may give a nasal *quack* when alarmed. HABITAT: Freshwater lakes and pools
with fringing vegetation, brackish marshes and estuaries. DISTRIBUTION: Widespread winter
visitor.

5 MARBLED DUCK (MARBLED TEAL) *Marmaronetta angustirostris* 39–42cm
FIELD NOTES: Secretive, difficult to locate as they forage among emergent vegetation.
In flight shows pale grey-buff secondaries and primaries, the latter having darker tips.
VOICE: Generally silent. HABITAT: Shallow freshwater and brackish lakes with developing
and border vegetation. DISTRIBUTION: Breeds in Pakistan, winters there and in scattered
locations in the rest of the region.

6 RED-CRESTED POCHARD *Netta rufina* 53–57cm FIELD NOTES: Male in eclipse
plumage has red bill, otherwise similar to female. Upperwing of both sexes shows very
pale grey flight feathers with a narrow blackish trailing edge. VOICE: Generally silent.
HABITAT: Freshwater lakes with fringing and submerged vegetation, rivers and sometimes
coastal waters. DISTRIBUTION: Widespread winter visitor.

7 PINK-HEADED DUCK *Rhodonessa caryophyllacea* 60cm FIELD NOTES: Secretive. Feeds
by both dabbling and diving. May perch in trees. VOICE: Male gives a low, weak, wheezy
whistle, female a low quack. HABITAT: Secluded marshes and pools in elephant-grass jungle.
DISTRIBUTION: Mainly the NE of the region. Probably extinct.

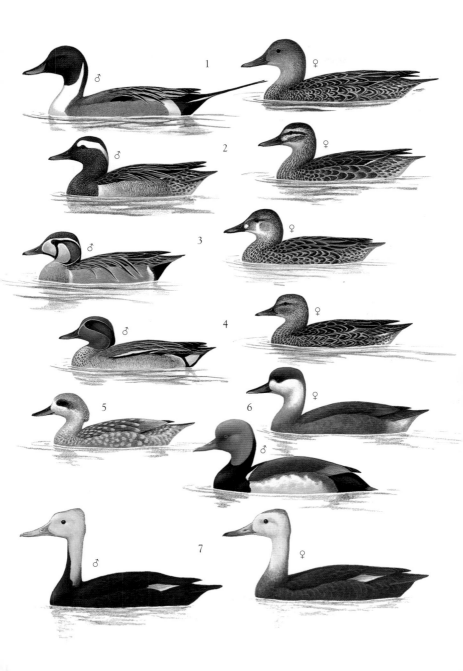

6 DUCKS

1 POCHARD (COMMON or EUROPEAN POCHARD) *Aythya ferina* 42–49cm FIELD NOTES: Gregarious, often in very large flocks. In flight shows pale grey flight feathers and darker forewing. VOICE: Generally silent. HABITAT: Large open lakes, and occasionally on rivers and coastal waters. DISTRIBUTION: Widespread winter visitor.

2 FERRUGINOUS DUCK (COMMON WHITE-EYE or WHITE-EYED POCHARD) *Aythya nyroca* 38–42cm FIELD NOTES: Rather secretive. In flight upperwing of both sexes has distinct wide white bar across all flight feathers. Underwing and large oval belly spot white. VOICE: Generally silent, but displaying male utters a soft, whistling *wheeoo* and female a harsh *gaaa*. HABITAT: Freshwater lakes and pools with surrounding and developing vegetation. In winter may occur on more open waters, rivers and coastal waters. DISTRIBUTION: Breeds in the W of the region in Baluchistan, Kashmir and Ladakh, more widespread in the winter.

3 BAER'S POCHARD (BAER'S or SIBERIAN WHITE-EYE) *Aythya baeri* 41–46cm FIELD NOTES: Usually in pairs or small groups. In flight upperwing of both sexes shows a prominent white bar on all flight feathers. VOICE: Generally silent. HABITAT: Lakes and pools with emergent and fringing vegetation, in winter also on more open lakes and marshes. DISTRIBUTION: Winter visitor, mainly to NE parts of the region.

4 TUFTED DUCK *Aythya fuligula* 40–47cm FIELD NOTES: Gregarious, often in very large numbers. In flight upperwing of both sexes shows a prominent white wing-bar on all flight feathers. VOICE: Usually silent, may give a low growl when flushed. HABITAT: Lakes, large rivers and sheltered coastal waters. DISTRIBUTION: Widespread winter visitor.

5 SCAUP (GREATER SCAUP) *Aythya marila* 40–51cm FIELD NOTES: In flight upperwing of both sexes shows a prominent white wing-bar across all flight feathers; male has a grey forewing. VOICE: Generally silent. HABITAT: Large lakes and rivers, estuaries and shallow inshore waters. DISTRIBUTION: Winter visitor, mainly to the N of the region.

6 VELVET SCOTER *Melanitta fusca* 51–58cm FIELD NOTES: In flight both sexes show prominent white secondaries. VOICE: Generally silent. In flight male may utter a loud piping and the female a harsh *braa-ah-braa-ah......* HABITAT: Inshore coastal waters, occasional on inland lakes. DISTRIBUTION: Vagrant: disputed record from Pakistan.

7 GOLDENEYE (COMMON GOLDENEYE) *Bucephala clangula* 42–50cm FIELD NOTES: In flight upperwing of male shows large white patch on inner wing, female patch crossed by two black bars. VOICE: Usually silent. HABITAT: Lakes, reservoirs and rivers. DISTRIBUTION: Winter visitor, mainly to the N of the region.

8 LONG-TAILED DUCK (OLDSQUAW) *Clangula hyemalis* 36–47cm (male with tail 48–60cm) FIELD NOTES: Often winters in sexually segregated groups. In winter facial patches sometimes very weakly coloured, which can make birds appear white-headed, and in flight both sexes show all-dark wings, contrasting with mainly white body. VOICE: Male utters a yodelling *ow-ow-owlee....caloocaloo*. Female has various weak quacks. HABITAT: Mainly coastal waters, but has occurred on inland lakes or large rivers. DISTRIBUTION: Vagrant, recorded from Pakistan, India and Nepal.

1 ♀
♂

2 ♀
♂

3 ♂
♀
♀

white-faced variety

4 ♀

white undertail variety

4 ♂
♀

5 ♂
♀

6 ♂
♀

7 ♂
♀

8 ♀ br
♀ n-br
♂ br
♂ n-br

7 GAMEBIRDS

1 NICOBAR SCRUBFOWL (NICOBAR MEGAPODE) *Megapodius nicobariensis* 43cm
FIELD NOTES: Usually in pairs or family groups. A ground forager, but will take to trees when alarmed. Juvenile lacks red facial skin or it is restricted to lores and around eye. Head and underparts rufous-brown. VOICE: A repeated, cackling *kuk-a-kuk-kuk* and a bullfrog-like *kiouk-kiouk-kok-kok-kok-kok*............ HABITAT: Dense forest undergrowth, usually near sandy beaches. DISTRIBUTION: Resident on the Nicobars.

2 SNOW PARTRIDGE *Lerwa lerwa* 38–40cm FIELD NOTES: Can be approachable. If flushed or alarmed flies rapidly downhill on whirring and clapping wings. Usually occurs in pairs or small groups. VOICE: A clear *jiju jiju jiju* that gradually quickens and rises in pitch, also a *huei huei* when flushed. HABITAT: High-altitude grassy, shrubby mountain slopes interspersed with scree and snow patches. DISTRIBUTION: Himalayan resident.

3 SEE-SEE PARTRIDGE *Ammoperdix griseogularis* 24cm FIELD NOTES: Occurs in small groups, although larger parties gather at drinking sites. When approached tends to run rather than fly. VOICE: A far-carrying, repeated *wheet-div* or *hoe-it*. When alarmed gives a rapid, piping *bwuit-bwuit-bwuit*. HABITAT: Rocky foothills with sparse vegetation. DISTRIBUTION: Resident in Pakistan.

4 TIBETAN SNOWCOCK *Tetraogallus tibetanus* 50–56cm FIELD NOTES: Shy and wary. Occurs in pairs or small parties. Often walks with tail raised and undertail-coverts fluffed out. In flight primaries and secondaries grey-brown with extensive white trailing edge to the latter. VOICE: A croaking *gu-gu-gu-gu*. Also recorded is a chuckling *chuck-aa-chuck-aa-chuck-chuck-chee-da-da-da*. HABITAT: High alpine pastures, bare or grassy mountain slopes. DISTRIBUTION: Himalayan resident.

5 HIMALAYAN SNOWCOCK *Tetraogallus himalayensis* 58–62cm FIELD NOTES: Behaviour similar to Tibetan Snowcock. In flight primaries white, tipped dark grey, secondaries brownish-grey. VOICE: A high-pitched *shi-er shi-er* and a deeper *wai-wain-guar-guar*. When disturbed utters an accelerating *kuk kuk kuk*....... HABITAT: Sparsely vegetated scree or grassy patches among or below crags on mountain slopes. DISTRIBUTION: Himalayan resident.

6 PAINTED SPURFOWL *Galloperdix lunulata* 30–34cm FIELD NOTES: Secretive, keeps to cover. When disturbed tends to run rather than fly, said to hide in holes or rock fissures if persistently pursued. VOICE: A loud, rapidly repeated *chur chur chur* and a fowl-like cackling. HABITAT: Dry, rocky areas in thornbush or bamboo thickets. DISTRIBUTION: Indian resident.

7 SRI LANKA SPURFOWL *Galloperdix bicalcarata* 30–34cm FIELD NOTES: Secretive, best located by call. Occurs in pairs or family parties. Tends to run rather than fly when disturbed. VOICE: A rising trisyllabic series of notes, *yuhuhu yuhuhu yuhuhu yuhuhu yuhuhu yuhuheeyu*, the last note lower, similar in pitch to the first. HABITAT: Undisturbed lowland and hills. DISTRIBUTION: Resident in Sri Lanka.

8 RED SPURFOWL *Galloperdix spadicea* 35–38cm FIELD NOTES: Secretive, more often heard than seen. When alarmed runs rapidly into cover. Variable: dark race *G. s. stewarti* (8b) occurs in Kerula, paler race *G. s. caurina* (8c) is found in S Rajasthan, N Gujarat and W Madhya Pradesh. VOICE: A rapidly repeated, crowing *k-r-r-r-kwek kr-kr-kwek kr-kr-kwek*. When flushed utters a harsh, cackling *kuk-kuk-kuk-kukaak*. HABITAT: Rocky foothills with scrubby bamboo thickets and dense secondary growth. DISTRIBUTION: Indian resident.

8 GAMEBIRDS

1 SZÉCHENYI'S MONAL-PARTRIDGE (BUFF-THROATED PARTRIDGE)
Tetraophasis szechenyii 50cm FIELD NOTES: In non-breeding season usually occurs in family parties of 4–12, although larger parties have been recorded. VOICE: Loud, far-carrying 2–3-note cackling interspersed with monosyllabic grating notes. HABITAT: Mountain forests. DISTRIBUTION: May occur in extreme NE of the region.

2 TIBETAN PARTRIDGE *Perdix hodgsoniae* 28–31cm FIELD NOTES: In non-breeding season occurs in small groups of 10–15 birds. Usually runs for cover rather than taking wing. Juvenile dull grey above with dark vermiculations, below dull buff with dark barring and white shaft streaks. Head shows a dull shadow of adult head pattern. VOICE: A rattling *scherrrrreck-scherrrrreck*. When flushed utters a shrill *chee chee chee chee chee chee*. HABITAT: Rocky mountain slopes and alpine meadows with scrub, descends to lower levels in winter. DISTRIBUTION: N Himalayan resident.

3 CHUKAR (CHUKAR PARTRIDGE) *Alectoris chukar* 32–34cm FIELD NOTES: Usually encountered in small parties; in cold winters large flocks have been met with. When alarmed generally runs away. VOICE: Typically a *chuck chuck chuck* or *chuck chuck chuck chuckARR chuckARR chuckARR*. When flushed often gives a repeated *wit-too-wittoo-wittoo*. HABITAT: Mountain slopes with sparse cover, semi-arid hills, grassy slopes and dry terraced cultivation. DISTRIBUTION: W Pakistan and W Himalayas.

4 BLACK FRANCOLIN *Francolinus francolinus* 33–36cm FIELD NOTES: Usually in pairs or small family groups. Very shy, keeps to cover except when 'singing'. Reluctant to fly. Juvenile a duller version of the female, underparts weakly streaked and barred on the flanks. VOICE: Generally silent apart from a strident, grating *clip gek-ge-gek gek-ge-gek* advertising call. HABITAT: Cultivated areas, grassland with bushy cover, lake edges with scrub and reeds. DISTRIBUTION: Resident in most of the N of the region.

5 PAINTED FRANCOLIN *Francolinus pictus* 31–32cm FIELD NOTES: Secretive, keeps to cover except when 'singing', which may be performed from a low perch. Reluctant to fly, if disturbed often squats in cover. VOICE: A high-pitched *click cheek-cheek-keray*, very similar to call of Black Francolin. HABITAT: Dry grassland and scrub jungle interspersed with watercourses. In Sri Lanka occurs in dry scrub and grass-covered hills. DISTRIBUTION: Resident over most of peninsular India and SE Sri Lanka.

6 GREY FRANCOLIN *Francolinus pondicerianus* 30–32cm FIELD NOTES: Variable southern birds with buff-orange throat, northern and northwestern races paler with whiter throat. Usually encountered in small groups. VOICE: Male has a rapid, repeated, strident *kat-ee-la kat-ee-la kat-ee-la*. Female gives a high-pitched, rising *tee-tee-tee*. When alarmed utters a sharp *kirr-kirr*. HABITAT: Dry grassy plains with thorn scrub, stony semi-desert and cultivated areas. DISTRIBUTION: Widespread over most of the region.

7 CHINESE FRANCOLIN *Francolinus pintadeanus* 31–34cm FIELD NOTES: Very wary, but often 'sings' from prominent perch. Juvenile like female but with barred hind-neck, indistinct eye-stripe and pale streaked upperparts. VOICE: A harsh, metallic *kak-kak-kuich ka-ka* or *wi-ta-tak-takaa*, normally repeated after lengthy pauses. HABITAT: Dry, open forest and oak scrub covered hills. DISTRIBUTION: Resident in extreme E India (Manipur).

8 SWAMP FRANCOLIN *Francolinus gularis* 36–38cm FIELD NOTES: Secretive, best located by call. Often feeds in the open early or late in the day. VOICE: A loud *kaw-care* or *ko-ko-care*, also a harsh *chuckeroo-chuckeroo-chuckeroo* preceded by a few harsh chuckles and croaks. HABITAT: Tall wet grassland, reed-beds, swamps and sugarcane fields. DISTRIBUTION: Resident in NE of the region.

9 GAMEBIRDS

1 BLOOD PHEASANT *Ithaginis cruentus* 44–48cm FIELD NOTES: Usually encountered in small groups, often tame, rarely flies. Very variable; two extremes shown, nominate from Sikkim and *I. c. kuseri* (1b) from Assam. VOICE: A repeated *chuck* or *chic*, a high-pitched, repetitive *see*, and when maintaining contact utters a loud *sree-cheeu-cheeu-cheeu* or a high trill. HABITAT: Forests or scrub at mid to high altitudes, resorts to lower forests during bad winters. DISTRIBUTION: Himalayan resident.

2 WESTERN TRAGOPAN (BLACK-HEADED TRAGOPAN) *Tragopan melanocephalus* male 68–73cm, female 60cm FIELD NOTES: Wary and skulking in dense undergrowth. When disturbed may fly up to branches of nearby tree. During display inflates bare skin of throat and horns. VOICE: A bleating, repeated *khuwah*, said to sound like a lost goat, lamb or child. In alarm gives a similar-sounding *waa waa waa*. HABITAT: Mid-altitude, oak-dominated forests with dense undergrowth, descends to lower altitudes in winter. DISTRIBUTION: Resident in W Himalayas.

3 SATYR TRAGOPAN (CRIMSON TRAGOPAN) *Tragopan satyra* male 67–72cm, female 58cm FIELD NOTES: Generally very wary and skulking when foraging in thick undergrowth, also disappears into nearby tree branches when alarmed. During display inflates bare skin of throat and horns. VOICE: A wailing *wah waah oo-ah oo-aaaa* repeated a dozen or so times. In alarm utters a quiet *wak wak*. HABITAT: High-altitude oak forests or mixed conifer and broadleaved with dense undergrowth. DISTRIBUTION: Himalayan resident.

4 BLYTH'S TRAGOPAN (GREY-BELLIED TRAGOPAN) *Tragopan blythii* male 65–70cm, female 58cm FIELD NOTES: Little known, actions and habits seem to be similar to others of the genus. Race north of the Brahmaputra, *T. b. molesworthi* (not shown), has narrower red breast-band. VOICE: During breeding season male gives a loud, moaning *ohh ohhah - ohaah ohaaah - ohaaaha - ohaaaha ohaaaha*, also a resounding *gock gock gock* or *wak wak wak*. HABITAT: Broadleaved forest with dense undergrowth. DISTRIBUTION: Resident in E Himalayas and NE India.

5 TEMMINCK'S TRAGOPAN (CRIMSON-BELLIED TRAGOPAN) *Tragopan temminckii* male 64cm, female 58cm FIELD NOTES: Wary. Often feeds in trees. During spectacular display inflates bare skin of throat, showing off a dark blue oval, spotted paler blue and surrounded by a pale blue rim with red patches. VOICE: During breeding season gives an eerie *woh - woah - woah - woah - waah - waah - waah - waah - griiiik*. HABITAT: Temperate and subalpine forests with dense undergrowth. DISTRIBUTION: Resident in E Himalayas.

6 HIMALAYAN MONAL (IMPEYAN MONAL) *Lophophorus impejanus* 64–72cm FIELD NOTES: Plumage variable both in colour of gloss on breast, from green to purple, and in amount of white on back; some have no white. Usually occurs singularly or in small, loose parties. A little less wary than others of the genus VOICE: A *kur-lieu* or *kleeh-wick*, alarm note very similar. HABITAT: Coniferous and broadleaved forest with thick understorey, venturing into alpine meadows in summer. DISTRIBUTION: Himalayan resident.

7 SCLATER'S MONAL (CRESTLESS MONAL) *Lophophorus sclateri* 64–68cm FIELD NOTES: Little known, actions said to be similar to previous species. Birds in W Arunachal Pradesh have all-white tail. VOICE: A loud, whistled *go-li*, reported to sound like part owl and part curlew. When alarmed gives a plaintive, shrill call. HABITAT: Coniferous montane forests with thick undergrowth. DISTRIBUTION: Resident in E Himalayas.

10 GAMEBIRDS

1 KALIJ PHEASANT *Lophura leucomelanos* male 63–74cm, female 50–60cm FIELD NOTES: Wary. Usually in small groups feeding early and late in the day. Roosts socially in trees. Variable plumage: shown are the nominate from W and C Nepal, *L. l. hamiltoni* (1b) from W Himalayas in Pakistan to W Nepal, *L. l. melanota* (1c) from E Nepal to W Bhutan, *L. l. lathami* (1d) from NE of the region. VOICE: At dawn and dusk gives a loud whistling chuckle or chirrup. When alarmed utters a rapid *koorchi koorchi* or *whoop-keet-keet*. HABITAT: Forests with dense undergrowth. DISTRIBUTION: Resident in the Himalayas and the NE of the region.

2 KOKLASS PHEASANT *Pucrasia macrolopha* male 56–64cm, female 52–56cm FIELD NOTES: Wary. When alarmed charges off into undergrowth. Usually encountered singly or in pairs, although larger parties sometimes occur in winter. Best observed early or late in the day foraging in grassy areas. Two extremes depicted are nominate from Uttar Pradesh and *P. m. nipalensis* (2b) from W Nepal. VOICE: Early morning call is a loud *kok-kok-kok ko-kras* or similar. When disturbed male gives a harsh *kwak kwak kwak* and female a musical *qui-quik qui-quik qui-quik*. HABITAT: Coniferous and mixed forest with thick understorey. DISTRIBUTION: W Himalayan resident.

3 TIBETAN EARED PHEASANT (HARMAN'S or ELWES'S EARED PHEASANT) *Crossoptilon harmani* 75–85cm FIELD NOTES: Generally met with in small parties, usually shy and wary. Forages in grassy areas near scrub cover. VOICE: A far-carrying, raucous *gag gag gagerah gagerah gagerah gagerah gagerah*. HABITAT: Subalpine meadows, alpine scrub and clearings in forests. DISTRIBUTION: Extreme NE of the region, although occurrence disputed.

4 CHEER PHEASANT (CHIR PHEASANT) *Catreus wallichii* male 90–118cm, female 61–76cm FIELD NOTES: Shy and wary, usually keeps close to cover. Generally encountered in pairs or small parties during winter. Roosts in rocky outcrops or in wooded gullies. VOICE: A grating, accelerating *chir-a-pir chir-a-pir chir chir chirwa chirwa*, also a series of high-pitched whistles interspersed with harsh staccato notes and short *chut* calls. HABITAT: Wooded and grassy ravines with scrub cover. DISTRIBUTION: W Himalayan resident.

5 MRS HUME'S PHEASANT *Syrmaticus humiae* male 90cm, female 60cm FIELD NOTES: Usually keeps to cover of dense bushes or grass at forest edge. Forages on the ground in small parties. VOICE: Contact calls are a loud *chuck* and a low, muttering *buk-buk-buk-buk*. Similar calls, but louder, are given in alarm, as well as a loud screech. HABITAT: Open oak and pine forest with patches of tall grass on steep, rocky hillsides. DISTRIBUTION: Resident in NE India.

6 GREY PEACOCK-PHEASANT *Polyplectron bicalcaratum* male 56–76cm, female 48–55cm FIELD NOTES: Extremely wary, creeps away through undergrowth at the first sign of alarm. Usually encountered singly or in pairs. During display male crouches and fans wings and tail, showing off ocelli. VOICE: Male utters a shrill whistled *trew-tree*, *phee-hoi* or *taa-pwi* and a guttural, raucous *qua qua qua* or *wak wak wak*, the latter also given when alarmed. HABITAT: Verdant broadleaved evergreen and semi-evergreen forest with dense undergrowth. DISTRIBUTION: Resident in NE of the region.

11 GAMEBIRDS

1 RED JUNGLEFOWL *Gallus gallus* male 65–78cm, female 41–46cm FIELD NOTES: Generally encountered in small groups, a male and several females. Best observed early morning or late afternoon, foraging beside scrub-forest tracks. Roosts socially in trees. VOICE: *Cock-a-doodle-do*, similar to the typical farmyard cockerel call, although with a more shrill and strangulated finish. Many other clucks and cackling calls are used when alarmed, feeding or making contact. HABITAT: Forest undergrowth and scrub. DISTRIBUTION: Much of the N and E of the region.

2 SRI LANKA JUNGLEFOWL (LA FAYETTE'S JUNGLEFOWL) *Gallus lafayetii* male 66–72cm, female 36cm FIELD NOTES: Best observed in early morning and late afternoon when tends to forage in the open on forest tracks. Generally wary but can be confiding where not hunted. VOICE: A loud, staccato *chick chow-chik*, the final *ik* being higher than the rest. Female utters a high-pitched, metallic *kwikukk kwikkukkuk*. Both sexes also give a harsh *clock-clock*. HABITAT: Various wooded areas, including primary and montane rainforests, scrub jungle and plantations. DISTRIBUTION: Endemic resident in Sri Lanka.

3 GREY JUNGLEFOWL (SONNERAT'S JUNGLEFOWL) *Gallus sonneratii* male 70–80cm, female 38cm FIELD NOTES: Wary, never far from cover. Usually encountered singly although occasionally seen in groups of 5–6, sometimes in very large numbers where food is abundant. Best sighted early in the morning, midday or late afternoon. Roosts socially in trees or bamboo. VOICE: A loud, staccato *kuk ka kuruk ka* or *kuck kaya kaya kuck* repeated up to five times a minute. HABITAT: Wooded areas with relatively thick understorey, scrub and bamboo thickets and overgrown or abandoned plantations. DISTRIBUTION: Resident in peninsular India.

4 INDIAN PEAFOWL *Pavo cristatus* male 180–230cm, female 90–100cm FIELD NOTES: Unmistakable. Spends much time in dense thickets, coming into the open, forest clearings, cultivated areas and water holes, in the early morning and late afternoon. Roosts at high elevation in tall trees. During display elevates and fans tail, showing off colourful ocelli. VOICE: Far-carrying, wailing *kee-ow kee-ow kee-ow* repeated several times. Also a donkey-like braying, *ka-an ka-an ka-an* usually repeated 6–8 times. When alarmed utters a *kok-kok* or *cain-kok*. HABITAT: Deciduous forest with understorey, scrub jungle, forest edges, where semi-feral also in cultivated fields and around human habitations. DISTRIBUTION: Indian resident.

5 GREEN PEAFOWL *Pavo muticus* male 180–300cm. female 100–110cm FIELD NOTES: Unmistakable. Much more timid and secretive than Indian Peafowl. Best located when calling from roost sites. Tends to forage near watercourses. During display fans and elevates tail, showing off colourful ocelli. VOICE: A trumpeting *ki-wao* or *yee-ow* usually repeated. Female utters a loud *AOW-aa AOW-aa*. When agitated utters a *tak tak ker-r-r-r oo oo ker-r-r-roo*. HABITAT: Riverine forest and nearby open country. DISTRIBUTION: Resident NE India and Bangladesh. May no longer occur.

12 GAMEBIRDS

1 QUAIL (COMMON or EUROPEAN QUAIL) *Coturnix coturnix* 16–18cm FIELD
NOTES: Shy and furtive, more often heard than seen. Usually occurs in pairs but may be in
larger numbers where food is plentiful. When flushed rises rapidly. VOICE: Male utters a
rapid *quip quip-ip* often interpreted as *wet-my-lips*; female utters a low *bree-bree*. When flushed
gives a shrill *tree-tree*. HABITAT: Open grasslands, pastures, paddy stubbles and weedy waste
areas. DISTRIBUTION: Mainly winter visitor and passage migrant, scattered resident mainly in
the N.

2 JAPANESE QUAIL (ASIAN MIGRATORY QUAIL) *Coturnix japonica* 17–19cm
FIELD NOTES: Actions and habits very similar to Quail. VOICE: A chattering *chrr-chuerrk-chrr*.
Flushed call similar to Quail. HABITAT: Grasslands and crops. DISTRIBUTION: Winter visitor
to NE (Assam), may breed in Bhutan.

3 RAIN QUAIL (BLACK-BREASTED QUAIL) *Coturnix coromandelica* 16–18cm
FIELD NOTES: Actions and habits very similar to Quail. VOICE: Male advertising call
is a high-pitched *whit-whit whit-whit whit-whit whit-whit*. Flushed call similar to Quail.
HABITAT: Open grasslands, cultivated fields, rice stubbles, plantations and sometimes
gardens. DISTRIBUTION: Widespread resident.

4 KING QUAIL (BLUE-BREASTED QUAIL) *Excalfactoria chinensis* 12–15cm FIELD
NOTES: Shy, difficult to flush, preferring to squat or run for cover. Most often observed when
running or dust-bathing on tracks. Generally occurs in pairs or family parties. VOICE: A
piping *ti-yu ti-yu ti-yu ti-yu* or *ti-ti-yu*, the last note being lower-pitched. When flushed utters
a weak *tir-tir-tir* or a sequence of sharp *cheeps*. HABITAT: Shrubby and swampy grassland,
marshes and paddyfields. DISTRIBUTION: Widespread resident away from the NW.

5 JUNGLE BUSH QUAIL *Perdicula asiatica* 17cm FIELD NOTES: Generally occurs in
parties of 6–20 birds. Often encountered dust-bathing on tracks, feeding in shrubby grassland
or walking, on well-trodden runs, to favoured watering places. Often flushed from underfoot
with an explosion of whirring wings, dropping into cover after a short flight. VOICE: A harsh
chee-chee-chuck chee-chee-chuck. Reassembling coveys utter a low, bubbling whistle, *tiri-tiri-tiri*
or *whi-whi-whi-whi-whi*. Gives a low chuckle when flushed. HABITAT: Grass areas in scrub
jungle, grassy plains and hills with rocky scrub cover. DISTRIBUTION: Resident in C and S
India and dry zone of Sri Lanka.

6 PAINTED BUSH QUAIL *Perdicula erythrorhyncha* 18cm FIELD NOTES: Actions and
habits very similar to Jungle Bush Quail. Race in E Ghats *P. e. blewitti* (not shown) generally
less richly coloured. VOICE: A pleasant *kirikee kirikee kirikee*. Reassembling coveys utter a
soft, whistled *tu-tu-tu-tu-tu-tutu-tutu-tutu*, rising in pitch. When flushed utters a Quail-
like whistle. HABITAT: Open grassy hillsides with scattered scrub near forest edge often
interspersed with cultivation. DISTRIBUTION: Resident, mainly in the W and E Ghats.

7 MANIPUR BUSH QUAIL *Perdicula manipurensis* 20cm FIELD NOTES: Best located
by call. Occurs in coveys of 5–8, usually well ensconced in tall grass but will forage in the
open early and late, attracted to fresh shoots on burnt grassland. VOICE: A softly whistled
whit-it-it-it, the notes getting progressively higher pitched, repeated 3–4 times and being
louder and higher each time. HABITAT: Moist, tall elephant-grass areas, bogs and swamps.
DISTRIBUTION: Resident in NE India.

8 ROCK BUSH QUAIL *Perdicula argoondah* 17cm FIELD NOTES: Similar to Jungle Bush
Quail. The brick-red race *P. a. salimalii* (8b) occurs in the red laterite terrain of Karnataka
and Kerala. VOICE: Similar to Jungle Bush Quail. HABITAT: Scrub-covered semi-desert plains
and thinly vegetated rocky hills. DISTRIBUTION: Resident in C and W India.

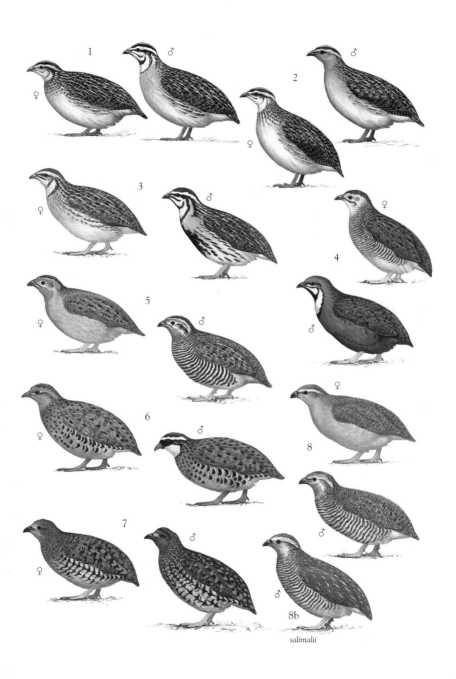

salimalii

13 GAMEBIRDS

1 HILL PARTRIDGE (COMMON or NECKLACED HILL PARTRIDGE) *Arborophila torqueola* 28–30cm FIELD NOTES: Forages in forest leaf litter in parties of 5–10. Roosts in trees, a whole covey nestling together on the same branch. Juvenile a dull version of adult, lacks rufous flank markings. VOICE: A mournful, repeated *pooo* or *pheaw* followed by a rising, whistled *do-eat do-eat do-eat do-eat*. Also duets, female uttering a *kwikwikwikwikwik* while male joins in with a series of *do-eat* calls. HABITAT: Montane oak forest mixed with laurel and rhododendron. DISTRIBUTION: Resident in the Himalayas and NE India.

2 CHESTNUT-BREASTED PARTRIDGE *Arborophila mandellii* 28–30cm FIELD NOTES: Little known, actions and habits supposed similar to Hill Partridge. VOICE: A repeated *prrreet* followed by a series of ascending *prrr prrr-er-it* calls that end in a crescendo. HABITAT: Evergreen oak and rhododendron forest with thick undergrowth. DISTRIBUTION: Resident in E Himalayas and Assam.

3 RUFOUS-THROATED PARTRIDGE *Arborophila rufogularis* 26–29cm FIELD NOTES: Actions and habits similar to Hill Partridge. Dark-throated race *A. r. intermedia* (3b) occurs E and S of the Brahmaputra River. VOICE: A far-carrying, mournful whistle, *wheeea-whu*, occasionally given in a series of 2–3 repeated 3–4 times, ascending and ending abruptly. HABITAT: Oak forest with laurel and rhododendron with thick undergrowth. DISTRIBUTION: Resident in the Himalayas, NE India and Bangladesh.

4 WHITE-CHEEKED PARTRIDGE *Arborophila atrogularis* 25–27cm FIELD NOTES: Actions and habits similar to Hill Partridge. VOICE: A far-carrying, quavering *prrrer prrrer prrrer prrrer........* ascending and accelerating and ending abruptly, often followed by a number of *wi-chu* notes. HABITAT: Bamboo and damp undergrowth in broadleaved evergreen forest. Also recorded in tea plantations, bushy grassland and scrub jungle, never far from forest edge. DISTRIBUTION: Resident in E Himalayas, NE India and Bangladesh.

5 MOUNTAIN BAMBOO PARTRIDGE *Bambusicola fytchii* 25–35cm FIELD NOTES: Usually in family parties of 5–6. Wary, feeds early morning and late evening. VOICE: A rapidly repeated, cackling *che-chiree-che-chiree chirree chirree chirree*. When flushed emits a scream. HABITAT: Various open and scrubby areas, including tall grassland in damp areas and bamboo patches. DISTRIBUTION: Resident in NE India and Bangladesh.

6 HIMALAYAN QUAIL *Ophrysia superciliosa* 25cm FIELD NOTES: Shy and elusive, keeping to thick cover. Prefers to run rather than fly when flushed. VOICE: A shrill whistle when alarmed. HABITAT: Steep hillsides with scrubby thickets and tall grass. DISTRIBUTION: W Himalayas of India. Probably extinct.

7 SMALL BUTTONQUAIL (LITTLE or COMMON BUTTONQUAIL) *Turnix sylvaticus* 15–16cm FIELD NOTES: Secretive. When alarmed prefers to run. Usually adopts a crouched posture, more upright when walking across open areas. VOICE: A low, droning *hoooo hoooo hoooo*. A low *cree cree cree*, probably given as a contact call. HABITAT: Grassland, scrub and grassy areas at edges of cultivation. DISTRIBUTION: Widespread resident, summer visitor to NW.

8 YELLOW-LEGGED BUTTONQUAIL *Turnix tanki* 15–18cm FIELD NOTES: Actions and habits similar to Small Buttonquail. VOICE: A human-like moaning hoot and a far-carrying *off-off-off*. HABITAT: Scrub, grassland, slightly marshy areas and cultivated fields. DISTRIBUTION: Widespread resident, summer visitor to NW.

9 BARRED BUTTONQUAIL *Turnix suscitator* 15–17cm FIELD NOTES: Secretive, actions and habits similar to Small Buttonquail. VOICE: A *groo groo groo drr-r-r-r-r-r-r*, said to sound like a distant motorbike; also a far-carrying *hoon-hoon-hoon*. HABITAT: Scrub, grassland and cultivated areas. DISTRIBUTION: Widespread resident.

14 DIVERS, GREBES

1 RED-THROATED DIVER (RED-THROATED LOON) *Gavia stellata* 53–69cm
FIELD NOTES: Upturned bill, usually holds head and bill noticeably upwards. Juvenile as non-breeding adult but with greyish face and neck. VOICE: Male utters a rolling, growling *oorroo-uh oorroo-uh*, female gives a slightly longer, higher-pitched *aarroo aarroo aarroo*. In flight gives a goose-like *kah kah kah kah kah*. Also utters various barking and mewing sounds. HABITAT: Lakes, rivers and shallow coastal waters. DISTRIBUTION: Vagrant, recorded from Pakistan and Nepal.

2 BLACK-THROATED DIVER (BLACK-THROATED or ARCTIC LOON) *Gavia arctica* 58–73cm FIELD NOTES: Tends to hold bill horizontally. Juvenile very similar to non-breeding adult but with slight scaling on upperparts. VOICE: A loud, mournful *clowee-cok-clowee-cok-clowee*, a snoring *knarr-knorr-knarr-knorr* and a gull-like *aaah-owww*. HABITAT: Large deep lakes and coastal waters. DISTRIBUTION: Vagrant, recorded in India.

3 LITTLE GREBE (DABCHICK) *Tachybaptus ruficollis* 25–29cm FIELD NOTES: Usually encountered in pairs or small parties. In flight shows whitish secondaries. Eye colour variable from reddish-brown to yellow-orange. Juvenile as non-breeding adult but with black streaks on face. VOICE: A high-pitched whinnying trill with various twitterings. When alarmed utters a metallic *whit whit*. HABITAT: Vegetated lakes, pond and rivers, also on more open waters including sheltered coastal waters post breeding. DISTRIBUTION: Widespread resident.

4 RED-NECKED GREBE *Podiceps grisegena* 40–50cm FIELD NOTES: Generally encountered singly or pairs. In flight upperwing shows white secondaries and forewing. Juvenile like a 'shadowy' version of adult but with black face streaks. VOICE: Wailing, braying and squeaking noises, also a grating *cherk-cherk-cherk*. HABITAT: Lakes, estuaries and sheltered coastal waters. DISTRIBUTION: Winter visitor to India and Pakistan.

5 GREAT CRESTED GREBE *Podiceps cristatus* 46–51cm FIELD NOTES: In flight upperwing shows white secondaries and forewing. Juvenile much like non-breeding adult but with black streaks on face. Prior to breeding pairs go through an elaborate water dance including 'standing on water' breast to breast carrying weed with much head-shaking. VOICE: A barking *rah-rah-rah*, also various croaks, growls and a slow nasal moaning. HABITAT: Lakes, reservoirs, rivers and sheltered coastal waters. DISTRIBUTION: Widespread winter visitor to the N of the region, breeds in parts of the NW.

6 SLAVONIAN GREBE (HORNED GREBE) *Podiceps auritus* 31–38cm FIELD NOTES: Non-breeding birds show clear white cheeks. Juvenile as adult non-breeding but with dusky marks on cheek. In flight appears like a miniature Great Crested Grebe. VOICE: A far-carrying, rattling *joarrh*, also an accelerating trill quite similar to that of Little Grebe. HABITAT: Lakes and coastal waters. DISTRIBUTION: Winter visitor to NW of the region.

7 BLACK-NECKED GREBE (EARED GREBE) *Podiceps nigricollis* 28–34cm FIELD NOTES: Steep forehead. Non-breeding adult shows dark cheeks. In flight shows white secondaries and black forewing. Juvenile a dull version of adult non-breeding with buff wash to head and neck. VOICE: A flute-like *poo-eeet* and a vibrant, trilled *tssrrrrooooeep*. HABITAT: Breeds on shallow lakes with fringing vegetation; post breeding occurs on more open waters including sheltered coastal waters. DISTRIBUTION: Breeds in Baluchistan, winters in scattered locations mainly in the N and NW of the region.

15 PETRELS, SHEARWATERS

1 CAPE PETREL (PINTADO PETREL, CAPE PIGEON) *Daption capense* 38–40cm
FIELD NOTES: Unmistakable. Flies with rapid, shallow stiff wing-beats interspersed with short glides. Follows ships and fishing boats. Normally occurs in large flocks. VOICE: Generally silent. HABITAT: Maritime. DISTRIBUTION: Vagrant, recorded from Sri Lanka.

2 BARAU'S PETREL *Pterodroma baraui* 38cm FIELD NOTES: Typical flight of the genus (generally known as gadfly petrels), beating wings to gain height followed by long glides and wide banking arcs. VOICE: Silent. HABITAT: Maritime. DISTRIBUTION: Recorded off India and Sri Lanka.

3 STREAKED SHEARWATER (WHITE-FACED SHEARWATER) *Calonectris leucomelas* 48cm FIELD NOTES: Pale-headed. Flight generally very lazy, but can be dynamic. Sometimes shows a white crescent at base of tail. VOICE: Silent. HABITAT: Maritime. DISTRIBUTION: Visitor recorded off India, Sri Lanka and the Maldives.

4 WEDGE-TAILED SHEARWATER *Puffinus pacificus* 41–46cm FIELD NOTES: Flight consists of slow wing flaps followed by short glides, more bounding flight in strong winds. Often around fishing boats. VOICE: Generally silent. HABITAT: Maritime. DISTRIBUTION: Visitor off India, Sri Lanka and the Maldives.

5 FLESH-FOOTED SHEARWATER (PALE-FOOTED SHEARWATER) *Puffinus carneipes* 40–45cm FIELD NOTES: Pale bill and feet, dark underwing. Flight consists of lazy flaps followed by long glides on stiff wings. Often follows fishing boats. VOICE: Generally silent. HABITAT: Maritime. DISTRIBUTION: Visitor off India, Sri Lanka and the Maldives.

6 SOOTY SHEARWATER *Puffinus griseus* 40–46cm FIELD NOTES: Extensive silver-white on underwing lining. Flight consists of quick wing flaps followed by a long glide. Often scavenges around fishing boats. VOICE: Generally silent. HABITAT: Maritime. DISTRIBUTION: Vagrant, recorded off Sri Lanka.

7 SHORT-TAILED SHEARWATER (SLENDER-BILLED SHEARWATER) *Puffinus tenuirostris* 41–43cm FIELD NOTES: Very similar to Sooty Shearwater, generally differs in having greyish underwing lining and shorter extension of body and tail behind wings. Flight pattern appears less graceful, more erratic than Sooty Shearwater. Often scavenges around fishing boats. VOICE: Generally silent. HABITAT: Maritime. DISTRIBUTION: Vagrant, recorded off Pakistan and Sri Lanka.

8 TROPICAL SHEARWATER *Puffinus bailloni* 31cm FIELD NOTES: Flight consists of fluttering wing-beats followed by short, low glides; in strong winds glides rise and fall. Often considered to be conspecific with Audubon's Shearwater *P. lherminieri*. VOICE: Mewing and twittering calls at breeding sites, otherwise silent. HABITAT: Breeds in burrows or crevices in rocks, otherwise maritime. DISTRIBUTION: Breeds on the Maldives, visitor off Indian coast.

9 PERSIAN SHEARWATER (ARABIAN SHEARWATER) *Puffinus persicus* 30–35cm
FIELD NOTES: Brownish wash on underwing lining. In flight wing-beats slower than Tropical Shearwater, otherwise flight pattern similar. VOICE: Generally silent. HABITAT: Maritime. DISTRIBUTION: Visitor to Pakistan, India and Sri Lanka.

16 PETRELS, STORM PETRELS

1 BULWER'S PETREL *Bulweria bulwerii* 26–28cm FIELD NOTES: Usually flies in an erratic buoyant manner, zigzagging with quick changes of height and direction. Tail wedge-shaped when fanned, which often occurs when plucking food from sea surface. Does not usually follow boats. VOICE: Generally silent. HABITAT: Maritime. DISTRIBUTION: Visitor off India, Sri Lanka and the Maldives.

2 JOUANIN'S PETREL *Bulweria fallax* 30–32cm FIELD NOTES: Flight faster, more swooping and towering than Bulwer's Petrel. Solitary. Does not usually follow boats. VOICE: Silent. HABITAT: Maritime. DISTRIBUTION: Visitor off of India and Sri Lanka.

3 WILSON'S STORM PETREL *Oceanites oceanicus* 15–19cm FIELD NOTES: Feet project beyond tail. Steady flight is fast and swallow-like. While feeding often dangles feet and 'dances' on the sea surface, when if viewed at close range yellow webs between toes can be seen. Attracted to fishing vessels. VOICE: A rapid chattering occasionally uttered while feeding. HABITAT: Maritime. DISTRIBUTION: Visitor to S and W coastal waters.

4 WHITE-FACED STORM PETREL (FRIGATE PETREL) *Pelagodroma marina* 18–21cm FIELD NOTES: Feet project well beyond tail. Forages in a series of swinging bounces, dangling feet at each bounce, when appears to walk on water. At close range yellow webs between toes can be seen. Attracted to fishing vessels. VOICE: Usually silent. HABITAT: Maritime. DISTRIBUTION: Vagrant, recorded off SW India, Sri Lanka and the Maldives.

5 BLACK-BELLIED STORM PETREL *Fregetta tropica* 20cm FIELD NOTES: Feet usually project beyond tail. Often in small groups, sometimes follows fishing vessels. Feeds by hugging the waves, legs often dangling and body swinging from side to side, bouncing breast-first into water every few seconds. VOICE: Generally silent. HABITAT: Maritime. DISTRIBUTION: Vagrant, recorded off Sri Lanka.

6 WHITE-BELLIED STORM PETREL *Fregetta grallaria* 20cm FIELD NOTES: Feet do not project beyond tail, but they may show when tail is in moult. Usually solitary, not generally attracted to boats. Feeding action similar to Black-bellied Storm petrel. VOICE: Usually silent. HABITAT: Maritime. DISTRIBUTION: Vagrant, recorded off the Maldives.

7 MADEIRAN STORM PETREL (BAND-RUMPED STORM PETREL) *Oceanodroma castro* 19–21cm FIELD NOTES: Legs do not project beyond tail. Generally encountered singly or in small groups, attracted to refuse thrown from boats. Usual flight buoyant, with quick wing-beats and low glides, recalling a small shearwater, progressing in a zigzagging manner. Sometimes flight can be erratic with tight twisting and banking moves close to the surface. When feeding, wings are held horizontally while gently foot-pattering. VOICE: Usually silent. HABITAT: Maritime. DISTRIBUTION: Vagrant, recorded off the Maldives.

8 SWINHOE'S STORM PETREL *Oceanodroma monorhis* 19–20cm FIELD NOTES: Legs do not project beyond tail. Forked tail usually held closed in flight. Flight fast and swooping with some bounding and gliding. Generally solitary, not attracted to boats. VOICE: Silent. HABITAT: Maritime. DISTRIBUTION: Visitor off India and Sri Lanka.

17 FRIGATEBIRDS, BOOBIES, TROPICBIRDS

All young frigatebird species undergo a complicated series of plumage changes before full adult plumage is gained. For fuller details see *Seabirds: an identification guide*, by P Harrison.

1 GREAT FRIGATEBIRD *Fregata minor* 86–100cm FIELD NOTES: Aggressive pursuer of other seabirds to force them to regurgitate food, also scavenges around boats. Juvenile has pale head and white belly separated by a black breast-band; the latter tends to fade as the bird ages. VOICE: Generally silent. HABITAT: Maritime. DISTRIBUTION: Visitor to the coasts of India, Sri Lanka and the Maldives.

2 LESSER FRIGATEBIRD *Fregata ariel* 71–81cm FIELD NOTES: Actions and habits similar to Great Frigatebird. Juvenile has pale head and white belly and axillaries separated by a thin, darkish breast-band; the latter fades with age as the head darkens. VOICE: Generally silent. HABITAT: Maritime. DISTRIBUTION: Visitor to the coasts of India, Sri Lanka and the Maldives.

3 CHRISTMAS ISLAND FRIGATEBIRD *Fregata andrewsi* 90–100cm FIELD NOTES: Actions and habits similar to Great Frigatebird. Juvenile much like Lesser Frigatebird but with broader black breast-band. VOICE: Generally silent. HABITAT: Maritime. DISTRIBUTION: Visitor to the coasts of India and Sri Lanka.

4 BROWN BOOBY *Sula leucogaster* 64–74cm FIELD NOTES: Feeds by plunge-diving, usually at an angle. Often gregarious. Attracted to boats. Juvenile has white areas tinged brown, bill greyish. VOICE: At breeding site male utters high-pitched whistles while female utters grunts and honks. Generally silent at sea. HABITAT: Breeds on coral atolls, otherwise maritime. DISTRIBUTION: May breed on Lakshadweep, otherwise visitor to coastal waters.

5 MASKED BOOBY (WHITE or BLUE-FACED BOOBY) *Sula dactylatra* 81–92cm FIELD NOTES: Feeds by plunge-diving, usually at a more vertical angle than other boobies. Juvenile very similar to adult Brown Booby but has paler mantle with a white collar on hind-neck, and brown of head does not extend to upper breast. VOICE: At breeding sites male utters a wheezy or piping whistle, female gives a loud honking or braying, generally silent at sea. HABITAT: Breeds on sandy atolls, otherwise maritime. DISTRIBUTION: Breeds on the Maldives and possibly on Lakshadweep, otherwise a visitor to W coastal waters.

6 RED-FOOTED BOOBY *Sula sula* 66–77cm FIELD NOTES: Action similar to Brown Booby. Variations on the dark morph include a white-tailed form and a white-headed, white-tailed form. Juvenile dark above, greyish on head, neck and underparts. VOICE: At breeding sites a harsh squawk and a guttural *ga-ga-ga-ga*.... Silent at sea. HABITAT: Breeds on coral atolls, otherwise maritime. DISTRIBUTION: Breeds on the Maldives and possibly Lakshadweep, otherwise a visitor to coastal waters.

7 RED-BILLED TROPICBIRD *Phaethon aethereus* 90–105cm FIELD NOTES: Flight pigeon-like, fluttering wing-beats followed by long glides. Feeds by hovering then plunge-diving on half-closed wings. Juvenile has yellowish bill, black nape collar and lacks elongated tail streamers. VOICE: A shrill, rasping *kee-arrr*. HABITAT: Maritime. DISTRIBUTION: Visitor to W and S coastal waters.

8 RED-TAILED TROPICBIRD *Phaethon rubricauda* 78–81cm FIELD NOTES: Actions similar to Red-billed Tropicbird. Juvenile like juvenile Red-billed but with less black on primaries, black bill and no black nape collar. VOICE: A harsh, rapid *keek-keek-keek*.... HABITAT: Breeds on cliffs, otherwise maritime. DISTRIBUTION: Possibly breeds on the Nicobars.

9 WHITE-TAILED TROPICBIRD *Phaethon lepturus* 70–82cm FIELD NOTES: Actions similar to Red-billed Tropicbird. Juvenile similar to juvenile Red-billed but lacks the black nape collar. VOICE: A squeaky *chip-chip-chip*. HABITAT: Breeds on coral atolls, otherwise maritime. DISTRIBUTION: Breeds on the Maldives, visitor to coasts of India and Sri Lanka.

18 PELICANS, DARTER, CORMORANTS

1 DALMATIAN PELICAN *Pelecanus crispus* 160–180cm FIELD NOTES: In non-breeding plumage crest smaller and bill pouch dull yellow. Juvenile brownish-grey, especially on wings. Occurs singly or in small groups, sometimes fishes cooperatively like White Pelican. VOICE: Generally silent. HABITAT: Lakes, rivers and sheltered coastal waters. DISTRIBUTION: Winter visitor, mainly to Pakistan and NW India.

2 WHITE PELICAN (GREAT WHITE PELICAN) *Pelecanus onocrotalus* 140–175cm FIELD NOTES: Bill pouch pale yellow in non-breeding plumage. Juvenile brownish on wings and neck. Highly sociable, although also met with singly or in small groups. Often fishes cooperatively, forming a semicircle to push fish into shallows, enabling each to scoop up a pouchful of fish. VOICE: At breeding sites utters various grunts and growls, in flight may give a deep croak. HABITAT: Breeds on lakes and lagoons usually with extensive fringing vegetation; post breeding also occurs on lakes, rivers and sheltered coastal waters. DISTRIBUTION: Breeds in India (Gujarat); otherwise a winter visitor, mainly to the NW.

3 SPOT-BILLED PELICAN *Pelecanus philippensis* 140cm FIELD NOTES: Non-breeding adult greyer with paler bill and facial skin. Sociable, often feeds cooperatively like White Pelican. VOICE: At breeding sites utters squeaking, barking and bleating sounds. Fishing groups may utter a deep bleating noise. HABITAT: Breeds colonially, preferring tall dead or bare trees within feeding range of large lakes, reservoirs and coastal waters. DISTRIBUTION: Breeds in S and NE India and Sri Lanka, more widespread in winter.

4 INDIAN DARTER (DARTER or SNAKE-BIRD) *Anhinga melanogaster* 85–97cm FIELD NOTES: In flight holds neck in a distinct kink. Often sits on exposed perch with wings outstretched. Non-breeding plumage is duller. Often swims with only head and neck visible. VOICE: Breeding birds utter a loud *chigi chigi chigi* and various grunts and croaks, otherwise silent. HABITAT: Inland and coastal waters, including lakes, marshes and mangroves. DISTRIBUTION: Widespread resident away from the Himalayas and extreme NE and NW.

5 CORMORANT (GREAT CORMORANT) *Phalacrocorax carbo* 80–100cm FIELD NOTES: In flight outstretched neck shows a slight kink. Often sits with wings outstretched. Juvenile dark brown above, dirty white below, greyer on the neck and breast. VOICE: At breeding colonies utters various deep guttural calls, otherwise generally silent. HABITAT: Lakes, rivers, reservoirs and coastal waters. DISTRIBUTION: Widespread resident.

6 INDIAN CORMORANT (INDIAN SHAG) *Phalacrocorax fuscicollis* 63cm FIELD NOTES: Flies with neck outstretched and held in a slight kink. Regularly perches with wings outstretched. Juvenile scaly brown above below greyish-white with flanks mottled with black. VOICE: At breeding colonies utters a sharp *kit-kit-kit-kit.....* HABITAT: Various fresh and salt waters. DISTRIBUTION: Widespread resident over much of the region.

7 PYGMY CORMORANT *Microcarbo pygmeus* 45–55cm FIELD NOTES: Flight consists of a series of rapid wing-beats interspersed with short glides, neck outstretched with a slight kink. Regularly perches with wings outstretched. Juvenile has brown upperparts, greyish-white underparts, whiter on belly, chin and throat. VOICE: Generally silent. HABITAT: Lakes, marshes and rivers with dense vegetation, may visit brackish waters post breeding. DISTRIBUTION: Vagrant, recorded from Pakistan.

8 LITTLE CORMORANT *Microcarbo niger* 51cm FIELD NOTES: Flies with neck outstretched with a slight kink. Regularly sits with wings outstretched. Juvenile has brown upperparts with slight scaling, paler below with white throat and centre of abdomen. VOICE: At breeding colonies utters various grunts, groans and roaring sounds, also a low-pitched *ah-ah-ah* and *kok-kok-kok*. HABITAT: Various fresh and salt waters. DISTRIBUTION: Widespread resident over much of the region.

19 EGRETS, HERONS

1 LITTLE EGRET *Egretta garzetta* 55–65cm FIELD NOTES: Black bill. Lores yellow, yellow-orange or reddish during onset of breeding, otherwise greyish. Often feeds by dashing to and fro with wings held open. Non-breeding adults and juveniles lack head, breast and back plumes. Breeds and roosts colonially. VOICE: Utters a harsh *aaah* or *kgarrk* during feeding disputes or when alarmed. HABITAT: Lakes, rivers, marshes, rice fields, saltpans and estuaries. DISTRIBUTION: Widespread resident over most of the region.

2 WESTERN REEF EGRET (WESTERN REEF HERON) *Egretta gularis* 55–67cm FIELD NOTES: Bill yellowish on light phase, brownish on dark phase. Intermediates occur, being grey above and grey-white below. Habits much as Little Egret. Breeds and roosts colonially. Non-breeding adults and juveniles lack head, breast and back plumes. VOICE: Utters a guttural croak during feeding disputes or when disturbed. HABITAT: Estuaries, sand coasts, mudflats and mangroves, occasionally on inland fresh waters. DISTRIBUTION: Resident, mainly on W and SE coasts.

3 PACIFIC REEF EGRET (EASTERN REEF EGRET or HERON) *Egretta sacra* 58–66cm FIELD NOTES: Breeding birds have a short inconspicuous nape crest. Dark phase shows thin white throat-streak. Shorter-legged than Western Reef Egret, especially noticeable when in crouched resting posture. Usual feeding action is lethargic, but becomes more hurried when prey is sighted. Breeds colonially. VOICE: A hoarse croak and when alarmed a harsh *arrk*. HABITAT: Rocky coasts, sandy shores and coral beds. DISTRIBUTION: Resident on the Andamans and Nicobars, visitor to Bangladesh coast.

4 INTERMEDIATE EGRET (YELLOW-BILLED or PLUMED EGRET) *Egretta intermedia* 65–72cm FIELD NOTES: During breeding bill becomes black. Non-breeding adults lack breast and back plumes. Breeds and roosts colonially. VOICE: Utters a harsh *kwark* or *kuwark* when disturbed. HABITAT: Freshwater lakes, rivers and marshes, also tidal creeks and mangrove swamps. DISTRIBUTION: Widespread resident over much of the region.

5 GREAT WHITE EGRET (GREAT EGRET) *Ardea alba* 85–102cm FIELD NOTES: While foraging walks stealthily with neck erect. Immediately prior to breeding bill is black, lores bluish and tibia pink-red. Breeds and roosts colonially. VOICE: May give a throaty croak, otherwise silent. HABITAT: Freshwater and saltwater areas. DISTRIBUTION: Widespread resident over much of the region.

6 CATTLE EGRET *Bubulcus ibis* 48–53cm FIELD NOTES: Sociable, regularly seen in parties feeding on insects disturbed by grazing animals, often perches on backs of larger animals. Breeds and roosts colonially. VOICE: At breeding sites utters a low croak, in flight may give a harsh, croaking *ruk* or *Rik-rak*, otherwise fairly silent. HABITAT: Grassland, flooded fields, paddyfields, also lake, pond and river surrounds and rubbish dumps. DISTRIBUTION: Widespread resident over most of the region.

7 CHINESE POND HERON *Ardeola bacchus* 42–45cm FIELD NOTES: In flight shows white wings and tail. Breeds in small colonies often mixed with Indian Pond Heron. VOICE: Generally silent; in flight or when flushed may utter a harsh croak. HABITAT: Various wetlands, including marshes, ponds, paddyfields, ditches, mangrove creeks and tidal mudflats. DISTRIBUTION: Resident and winter visitor, mainly NE India and the Andamans.

8 INDIAN POND HERON (PADDYBIRD) *Ardeola grayii* 42–47cm FIELD NOTES: In flight shows white tail and wings, the latter with a pale buff wash on secondaries. Non-breeding adult probably indistinguishable from non-breeding Chinese Pond Heron. VOICE: Utters a harsh squawk when flushed or in flight. HABITAT: Various wetlands, including marshes, ponds, paddyfields, ditches, mangrove creeks and tidal mudflats. DISTRIBUTION: Widespread resident over most of the region.

1

dark
phase

2

light
phase

dark
phase

3

light
phase

4

5

6

br

n-br

n-br

7

n-br

br

8

br

20 HERONS

1 HERON (GREY HERON) *Ardea cinerea* 90–98cm FIELD NOTES: Generally feeds alone, in the open. Flies with arched wings and neck drawn back, underwing-coverts grey contrasting with dark flight feathers. Often stands motionless at water's edge or on branch. Breeds and roosts colonially. Juvenile has grey neck and a dull black crown. VOICE: At breeding sites utters harsh croaks, in flight gives a harsh *frahnk*. HABITAT: Variety of inland and coastal waters, including lakes, marshes, mangroves and tidal creeks. DISTRIBUTION: Widespread resident and winter visitor.

2 GOLIATH HERON *Ardea goliath* 135–150cm FIELD NOTES: Large, man-sized, much larger than superficially similar Purple Heron. Typically feeds alone, in the open. Flies with arched wings and neck drawn back, underwing-coverts extensively purple. Juvenile a dull version of adult. VOICE: In flight gives a deep, loud *kowoorrk-kowoorrk-woorrk-work-worrk*. HABITAT: Lakes, rivers, marshes and coastal mudflats. DISTRIBUTION: Visitor or perhaps resident, mainly in NE India.

3 WHITE-BELLIED HERON (IMPERIAL HERON) *Ardea insignis* 127cm FIELD NOTES: Feeds alone or in pairs. Flies with arched wings and neck drawn back, underwing-coverts white contrasting with darker flight feathers. VOICE: A braying, croaking *ock ock ock ock urrrr*. When disturbed utters a deep croak. HABITAT: Marshes, lakes and rivers in forested areas. DISTRIBUTION: Resident in E Himalayan foothills.

4 GREAT-BILLED HERON (SUMATRAN HERON) *Ardea sumatrana* 115cm FIELD NOTES: Generally shy and wary, forages alone or in pairs. Flies with arched wings and neck drawn back, underwing-coverts grey contrasting little with flight feathers. VOICE: Occasional loud harsh croaks. HABITAT: Mangroves, tidal mudflats, estuaries, coastal swamps and beaches. DISTRIBUTION: Vagrant, disputed record from the Nicobars.

5 PURPLE HERON *Ardea purpurea* 78–90cm FIELD NOTES: More secretive than others of the genus, tends to prefer the cover of aquatic vegetation. Flies with arched wings and neck drawn back, producing a more pronounced neck bulge than Heron, underwing-coverts purplish-grey, making underwing appear all dark. Juvenile browner overall than adult, showing less prominent dark streaks on head and neck. VOICE: At breeding colonies various harsh utterances. In flight gives a similar call to Heron, but higher-pitched. HABITAT: Marshes and lakes with dense aquatic vegetation; post breeding often visits more open-water areas. DISTRIBUTION: Widespread resident.

6 STRIATED HERON (GREEN-BACKED or LITTLE HERON) *Butorides striata* 40–48cm FIELD NOTES: Often forages alone and in the same location for many days, usually among thick vegetation on the banks of rivers and ponds. Mainly crepuscular or nocturnal. Juvenile brown with pale spots on wings and dark streaking on neck and underparts. Birds from Andaman and Nicobar *B. s. spodiogaster* (6b) are darker. VOICE: When disturbed utters a harsh *kyah*. HABITAT: Mangroves, paddyfields, rivers and ponds with thick cover. DISTRIBUTION: Widespread resident over much of the region.

1

2

3

4

5

6b

spodiogaster

6

21 HERONS, BITTERNS

1 NIGHT HERON (BLACK-CROWNED NIGHT HERON) *Nycticorax nycticorax* 58–65cm FIELD NOTES: Adult unmistakable. Juvenile has back and wings dark brown spotted buff-white; head, neck and underparts pale streaked brown. Mainly crepuscular or nocturnal. Usually forages alone, but small groups may be seen flying from daytime roosts. During the day, unless feeding young, sits hunched amid the foliage of trees. VOICE: Various croaks given at breeding colonies. In flight utters a frog-like croak. HABITAT: Very varied watery areas, including marshes, lakes and rivers with extensive border vegetation; also mangroves and estuaries. DISTRIBUTION: Widespread resident over much of the region.

2 MALAYAN NIGHT HERON (TIGER BITTERN) *Gorsachius melanolophus* 49cm FIELD NOTES: Shy. Generally crepuscular or nocturnal but recorded feeding during the day. In flight shows white-tipped primaries. Juvenile has greyish upperparts densely spotted and vermiculated with white and buff underparts vermiculated and barred brown. VOICE: A deep *oo oo oo oo.....* also croaks and a rasping *arh-arh-arh*. HABITAT: Marshes and streams in dense evergreen forest. DISTRIBUTION: Resident and partial migrant in SW India, W Ghats, NE India and Nicobars; winter visitor in Sri Lanka.

3 YELLOW BITTERN (CHINESE LITTLE or LONG-NOSED BITTERN) *Ixobrychus sinensis* 30–40cm FIELD NOTES: Skulking. A crepuscular or nocturnal feeder, usually singly. In flight shows black flight feathers and tail. Juvenile buff above with dark streaking, whitish below with brownish streaks on foreneck and breast. VOICE: In flight utters a sharp *kakak kakak*. HABITAT: Vegetation surrounding marshes, lakes and flooded paddyfields. DISTRIBUTION: Widespread resident.

4 LITTLE BITTERN *Ixobrychus minutus* 33–38cm FIELD NOTES: Secretive. In flight shows black back, tail and flight feathers contrasting with buff forewing. Juvenile dull buff-brown with darker streaking above and below. VOICE: A low, repeated *hoogh* or *grook*. When flushed utters a low *ker-ak* or *ker* and when excited a loud, hoarse *eke-eke*. HABITAT: Freshwater marshes, lakes, pools and rivers with surrounding reed-beds. DISTRIBUTION: Resident mainly in the NW.

5 CINNAMON BITTERN (CHESTNUT BITTERN) *Ixobrychus cinnamomeus* 40–41cm FIELD NOTES: Secretive. Generally forages alone, mainly at dawn and dusk although reported feeding during daytime, probably when feeding young. Juvenile dark brown above with pale mottling, below buff-white heavily streaked dark brown. VOICE: A low *kwok-kwok-kwok....* Sometimes ends with two or three quieter notes. In flight utters a croak. HABITAT: Flooded paddyfields, swamps, reed-beds and overgrown ditches. DISTRIBUTION: Widespread resident.

6 BLACK BITTERN (YELLOW-NECKED or MANGROVE BITTERN) *Dupetor flavicollis* 54–66cm FIELD NOTES: Secretive, skulks in dense cover. Peak feeding time is at dusk or dawn, feeds during the day in overcast weather. Juvenile similar to female but with distinct pale feather fringes on upperparts. VOICE: In flight utters a hoarse croak. HABITAT: Dense reedy swamps. DISTRIBUTION: Widespread resident.

7 BITTERN (GREAT or EURASIAN BITTERN) *Botaurus stellaris* 70–80cm FIELD NOTES: Secretive, more often seen flying over reed-beds. Juvenile very much like adult but crown and moustachial streak brownish, less conspicuous, also upperparts less strongly marked. VOICE: Known to call when in the region, a far-carrying booming preceded by a short muffled *up-RUMBH* or *up-up-RUMBH*, repeated at short intervals. In flight gives a harsh, nasal *kau* or *krau*. HABITAT: Freshwater and brackish reed-beds. DISTRIBUTION: Widespread winter visitor.

22 STORKS

1 PAINTED STORK *Mycteria leucocephala* 93–100cm FIELD NOTES: Non-breeding adult has bare parts and plumage duller. In flight shows all dark underwing, apart from pale tips to coverts, tail black. Flies with neck outstretched. Juvenile brownish on wing-coverts, breast-band, head and neck, bill pale buff. Roosts colonially in trees or on sandbanks. VOICE: During display utters a weak 'fizzing' call along with bill-clapping, otherwise generally silent. HABITAT: Marshes, lakes, ponds, rivers and coastal mudflats. DISTRIBUTION: Widespread resident over much of the region.

2 ASIAN OPENBILL (ASIAN OPENBILL STORK) *Anastomus oscitans* 68cm FIELD NOTES: Non-breeding adult has black areas more brownish, neck and head greyish, bill grey. In flight underwing shows white coverts and black flight feathers, tail black. Juvenile brownish-grey with darker mantle. Gregarious. Breeds in colonies, often mixed with other storks and ibises. VOICE: During courtship display utters a series of hollow, nasal *hoo-hoo* calls. HABITAT: Freshwater marshes, shallow lakes, lagoons and paddyfields. DISTRIBUTION: Widespread resident over much of the region.

3 BLACK STORK *Ciconia nigra* 95–105cm FIELD NOTES: Usually encountered singly or in small parties. In flight underwing is black with a white triangle which is formed by the inner wing-coverts and axillaries, tail black. Flies with neck outstretched. Juvenile a dull version of adult. VOICE: Generally silent post breeding. HABITAT: Marshes, shallow lakes, rivers, estuaries and grasslands. DISTRIBUTION: Winter visitor and passage migrant.

4 WOOLLY-NECKED STORK *Ciconia episcopus* 75–92cm FIELD NOTES: Usually encountered singly or in small flocks, during migration often mixes with Black Storks. In flight underwing black, tail white. Flies with neck outstretched. Juvenile a dull version of adult, forehead white with dark streaks. VOICE: Generally silent except for whistling greeting calls uttered at nest site. HABITAT: Wet and dry grasslands near water and marshes, often in or near open forest. DISTRIBUTION: Widespread resident and local migrant over much of the region.

5 WHITE STORK *Ciconia ciconia* 100–115cm FIELD NOTES: In flight underwing shows white coverts and black flight feathers, tail white. Flies with neck outstretched. Occurs singly or in small parties. Juvenile like adult, but bill with an extensive black tip. VOICE: Generally silent. HABITAT: Dry or damp grasslands, including cultivations. DISTRIBUTION: Widespread winter visitor and passage migrant.

6 ORIENTAL STORK (EASTERN WHITE STORK) *Ciconia boyciana* 110–150cm FIELD NOTES: In flight similar to White Stork below, above differs by having white edges to secondaries. Flies with neck outstretched. Juvenile like adult but black areas more brown. VOICE: Generally silent. HABITAT: Marshes, wet meadows, lakes and coastal intertidal areas. DISTRIBUTION: Vagrant to NE of the region. Records disputed.

7 BLACK-NECKED STORK *Ephippiorhynchus asiaticus* 129–150cm FIELD NOTES: In flight both upperwing and underwing white with wide black band on coverts, tail black. Flies with neck outstretched. Juvenile generally brownish with white abdomen. Usually encountered singly or in small family groups VOICE: Generally silent. HABITAT: Freshwater swamps, shallow water on lakes and estuaries, all with nearby large trees. DISTRIBUTION: Widespread, although thinly spread, resident.

23 STORKS, IBISES, SPOONBILL, FLAMINGOES

1 LESSER ADJUTANT *Leptoptilos javanicus* 110–120cm FIELD NOTES: Usually seen singly or in small flocks. Generally breeds in small colonies. Flies with neck drawn back. In flight underwing shows a small white triangle in the axillary area. Juvenile a dull version of adult. VOICE: During display utters a series of high-pitched squeaks and cow-like *moos*. HABITAT: Marshes, forest pools, swamps, flood plains and drying riverbeds. DISTRIBUTION: Widespread resident, mainly in the NE.

2 GREATER ADJUTANT *Leptoptilos dubius* 120–150cm FIELD NOTES: Gregarious, often associates with vultures and kites during scavenging sorties. Non-breeding adults have wings more uniform slate-black. In flight underwing shows a small white triangle in the axillary area. Juvenile has dark brown mantle and wings, head and neck paler with greyish, downy feathering. Breeds singly or in small colonies. VOICE: At breeding sites utters various squealing and mooing sounds along with much bill clattering. HABITAT: Marshes, lakes, cultivations, drying riverbeds and rubbish dumps. DISTRIBUTION: Rare resident, mainly in the extreme NE (Assam).

3 BLACK-HEADED IBIS (ORIENTAL or BLACK-NECKED IBIS) *Threskiornis melanocephalus* 65–75cm FIELD NOTES: Usually encountered in small groups. Flies with neck outstretched. Juvenile has bare skin restricted to face, rest of neck feathered white with dark flecks. Breeds in colonies, often mixed with herons, storks and cormorants. VOICE: Generally silent, apart from strange grunts at breeding sites. HABITAT: Very varied, including marshes, wet and dry grasslands, paddyfields, saltmarshes and coastal lagoons. DISTRIBUTION: Widespread resident, mainly in W half of India.

4 GLOSSY IBIS *Plegadis falcinellus* 55–65cm FIELD NOTES: Usually encountered in small groups. Flies with neck outstretched. Juvenile plumage very similar to a dull non-breeding adult. Nests colonially. VOICE: A grunting *grru* or *graa*. Utters grunting and croaking sounds at breeding sites. HABITAT: Freshwater marshes, lakesides, rivers with surrounding vegetation, paddyfields and coastal lagoons. DISTRIBUTION: Resident and winter visitor, mainly in the W of the region.

5 RED-NAPED IBIS (BLACK IBIS) *Pseudibis papillosa* 68cm FIELD NOTES: Usually in small groups. White covert-patch often concealed when perched or walking, but very obvious in flight. Flies with neck outstretched. Juvenile dull brown, lacks the bare skin of crown and nape. VOICE: Male utters a trumpet-like call when advertising or on the wing. HABITAT: Grasslands, cultivated fields, lakesides, marsh edge and rubbish dumps. DISTRIBUTION: Widespread resident over much of the region.

6 SPOONBILL (EURASIAN or WHITE SPOONBILL) *Platalea leucorodia* 80–90cm FIELD NOTES: Sociable. Loses yellow tinges on crest and breast post breeding. Flies with neck outstretched. Juvenile similar to non-breeding adult but bill pinkish and legs paler, also black tips to primaries. VOICE: Generally silent. HABITAT: Freshwater lakes, reed swamps, coastal lagoons and mudflats. DISTRIBUTION: Widespread resident, mainly in the W of the region.

7 GREATER FLAMINGO *Phoenicopterus roseus* 120–145cm FIELD NOTES: Flies with neck outstretched and legs protruding well beyond tail. Juvenile dirty grey-brown, legs and bill grey, latter tipped darker. VOICE: In flight utters a honking *kla-ha*. Feeding flocks emit a constant, low, goose-like growling. HABITAT: Salt lakes, sea bays, less often on freshwater lakes and ponds. DISTRIBUTION: Resident (breeds in Gujarat) and winter visitor.

8 LESSER FLAMINGO *Phoenicopterus minor* 80–90cm FIELD NOTES: Flies with neck outstretched and legs protruding well beyond tail. Juvenile dirty grey-brown with black bill. VOICE: In flight utters a high-pitched *kwirrk*. Feeding flocks give a constant low murmuring. HABITAT: Saltpans and coastal lagoons. DISTRIBUTION: Breeds in Gujarat, widespread in non-breeding season.

24 VULTURES

1 LAMMERGEIER (BEARDED VULTURE) *Gypaetus barbatus* 100–115cm FIELD NOTES: Spends much time soaring, sometimes at great heights, recorded as high as 8000m. Juvenile generally dark brownish-black with a whitish patch on mantle, below ash-grey from breast to undertail-coverts. VOICE: Generally silent apart from a shrill *feeeee* uttered during aerial display. HABITAT: Mountains with sheer crags, also hunts over plains, slopes and valleys. During hard winters resorts to lower areas. DISTRIBUTION: Resident in the Himalayas and Pakistan.

2 EGYPTIAN VULTURE *Neophron percnopterus* 60–70cm FIELD NOTES: Wholly yellow-billed race *N. p. ginginianus* (not shown) occurs in Nepal and India, away from the NW. Juvenile generally dark brownish-black, some show pale fringes to wing feathers. VOICE: Usually silent. HABITAT: Mountains, open arid areas, towns, villages and rubbish dumps. DISTRIBUTION: Widespread resident over much of the region.

3 SLENDER-BILLED VULTURE *Gyps tenuirostris* 93–100cm FIELD NOTES: Slightly darker wings and mantle and greyer rump than Indian Vulture. Pale thighs often show well in flight. Juvenile has some downy white feathers on head and neck, otherwise similar to adult. VOICE: Generally silent. HABITAT: Dry open country, open forested areas, rubbish dumps. DISTRIBUTION: Resident, but declining, in the Sub-Himalayas.

4 INDIAN VULTURE (LONG-BILLED VULTURE) *Gyps indicus* 89–103cm FIELD NOTES: Whitish rump, paler undertail-coverts and darker thighs than Slender-billed Vulture. Juvenile has white downy feathers on head and neck. VOICE: Generally silent. HABITAT: Cities, towns, villages, open wooded areas and around rubbish dumps. DISTRIBUTION: Widespread, but declining, resident over much of the region.

5 GRIFFON VULTURE (GRIFFON or EURASIAN GRIFFON VULTURE) *Gyps fulvus* 95–105cm FIELD NOTES: Juvenile has all-dark bill and a brown ruff, and is darker above than adult. VOICE: At roosts or carcasses utters various hisses and grunts. HABITAT: Mountain areas and adjacent dry open plains. DISTRIBUTION: Breeds in NW, otherwise a post-breeding visitor.

6 HIMALAYAN VULTURE (HIMALAYAN GRIFFON VULTURE) *Gyps himalayensis* 115–125cm FIELD NOTES: Juvenile generally dark with pale shaft-streaks, head and neck whitish, underwing shows pale lines on coverts. VOICE: Occasionally utters whistling and clucking noises. HABITAT: High-altitude mountain areas and plains. DISTRIBUTION: Resident in the Himalayas and N Indian plain in winter.

7 INDIAN WHITE-BACKED VULTURE (WHITE-RUMPED VULTURE) *Gyps bengalensis* 75–85cm FIELD NOTES: In flight from above dark with prominent white rump. Juvenile lacks white rump and is generally dark with pale streaking on underparts, underwing with variable whitish lines on coverts. VOICE: At roosts or at carcasses utters a strident, creaky *kakakaka*. HABITAT: Open country, towns and villages. DISTRIBUTION: Widespread resident over most of the region.

8 RED-HEADED VULTURE (KING VULTURE) *Sarcogyps calvus* 85cm FIELD NOTES: Juvenile generally dull brown with white down on head, in flight shows a dull grey-white belly and white undertail-coverts. VOICE: Hoarse croaks and screams, usually given during disputes at carcasses. HABITAT: Wooded hills and open country, and near human habitation. DISTRIBUTION: Resident, mainly in the N.

9 BLACK VULTURE (EURASIAN BLACK or CINEREOUS VULTURE) *Aegypius monachus* 100–110cm FIELD NOTES: Juvenile dark brown-black, with pinkish skin on base of bill and variable patches on head and neck. VOICE: Usually silent. HABITAT: Forest areas on hills and mountains, semi-arid alpine meadows and grassland. DISTRIBUTION: Breeds in Pakistan, winters mainly in the NW of the region.

25 OSPREY, BAZAS, HONEY BUZZARD, KITES

1 OSPREY *Pandion haliaetus* 55–63cm FIELD NOTES: Feeds on fish, which is captured after hovering and a feet-first plunge to grab prey. Juvenile as adult but mantle and wing feathers fringed with pale buff. VOICE: When alarmed gives a hoarse, sharp *kew-kew-kew-kew*. HABITAT: Lakes, rivers, coastal lagoons and estuaries. DISTRIBUTION: Widespread post-breeding visitor.

2 JERDON'S BAZA *Aviceda jerdoni* 41–48cm FIELD NOTES: Hunts from a perch, making short sorties to grab prey, usually insects, lizards or frogs. Juvenile similar to adult but with dark streaks on breast and neck. VOICE: A plaintive *pee-ow*. During display utters an excited mewing *kip-kip-kip* or *kikiya kikiya*. HABITAT: Tropical and subtropical broadleaved evergreen forests. DISTRIBUTION: Resident NE and SW and Sri Lanka.

3 BLACK BAZA *Aviceda leuphotes* 30–35cm FIELD NOTES: Flies much like a crow, interspersed with level-winged glides. VOICE: A soft, quavering squeal or whistle, *tcheeoua*. HABITAT: Deciduous or evergreen tropical forest clearings or wide forest streams. DISTRIBUTION: Resident mainly in NE and S India, Bangladesh and Sri Lanka.

4 BLACK-SHOULDERED KITE (BLACK-WINGED KITE) *Elanus caeruleus* 31–35cm FIELD NOTES: Often hovers when searching for prey. In flight shows large black patch on upperwing-coverts. Upperparts of juvenile tinged brownish with pale fringes, breast and crown washed rusty. VOICE: Various calls noted including a harsh *w-eeyah*, a sharp *kree-ak* and a piping *pii-uu*. HABITAT: Grassland mixed with scattered trees or cultivations and semi-desert. DISTRIBUTION: Widespread resident over most of the region.

5 ORIENTAL HONEY BUZZARD (CRESTED HONEY BUZZARD) *Pernis ptilorhynchus* 52–68cm FIELD NOTES: Very variable, especially underparts, which range from pale with reddish bars, through rufous with slightly darker bars to almost solid black; in flight the latter also shows black underwing-coverts. Juvenile paler below with flight feathers more closely barred; tail has thinner fainter large bars. VOICE: A high-pitched *wee-wey-who* or *weehey-weehey*. HABITAT: Wooded areas. DISTRIBUTION: Widespread resident.

6 RED KITE *Milvus milvus* 60–66cm FIELD NOTES: Mainly a carrion feeder, but will take young birds, rabbits, hares, mice, voles, moles and shrews. Flight action often appears 'loose' with constant manoeuvring of tail. Juvenile very similar to adult although underparts paler. VOICE: A mewing *peee-ooo* followed by a drawn-out *peee-oooo-eee-ooo-eee-ooo-eee-ooo......* HABITAT: Forest or scattered woodland with nearby grassland or wetland, also attracted to rubbish dumps in search of carrion. DISTRIBUTION: Vagrant, recorded in India.

7 BLACK KITE *Milvus migrans* 55–60cm FIELD NOTES: Gregarious. Scavenger, often around refuse dumps. Flight action 'loose' with much twisting of tail; fork of tail often disappears when tail spread. Juvenile grey-buff below streaked dark, pale fringes to mantle and wings and dark eye-surround. *M. m. lineatus* (Black-eared Kite) (7b), Himalayan breeder and widespread northern winter visitor, is often considered a separate species. VOICE: A whinnying *pee-errrr* or *ewe-wir-r-r-r-r*. HABITAT: Mountains, urban areas including cities and towns. DISTRIBUTION: Widespread resident.

8 BRAHMINY KITE (RED-BACKED KITE) *Haliastur indus* 45–51cm FIELD NOTES: Often encountered sitting in a tall tree overlooking water, from where it swoops down to pick prey from the surface. Juvenile generally rusty-brown, mantle and wings fringed rusty-buff, underparts and head streaked rusty-buff, underwing dark with large pale patch at base of primaries, tail plain rusty-grey. VOICE: A wheezy squeal, *kyerrh*. HABITAT: Typically near water, such as lakes, rivers, marshes, flooded paddyfields, coastal lagoons, estuaries and fishing villages. DISTRIBUTION: Resident over most of the region.

1 WHITE-BELLIED SEA EAGLE *Haliaeetus leucogaster* 66–71cm FIELD NOTES: Juvenile mantle and wings brown, tail whitish with a darker subterminal band, head and underparts greyish-white, the latter with a brownish tinge, mainly on the breast. VOICE: A loud honking *kank kank kank kank........*, also a faster *ken-ken-ken-ken* and *ka ka-kaaa*. HABITAT: Typically near coastal waters. DISTRIBUTION: Resident on coasts and offshore islands.

2 PALLAS'S FISH EAGLE *Haliaeetus leucoryphus* 76–84cm FIELD NOTES: Juvenile generally dark brown, underwing shows a wide whitish bar on greater coverts and a large white patch on base of the inner primaries, tail plain dark brown. VOICE: A hoarse, barking *kwok kvok kvok*. HABITAT: Lakes, rivers, marshes and coastal waters. DISTRIBUTION: Resident in the N of the region.

3 WHITE-TAILED EAGLE (WHITE-TAILED SEA EAGLE) *Haliaeetus albicilla* 69–92cm FIELD NOTES: Juvenile generally dark brown, tail feathers dark with pale grey-white centres, bill grey, underwing shows pale axillaries and pale tips to greater coverts which form a faint bar. VOICE: A shrill *klee klee klee klee*, when alarmed a lower *klek klek klek*. HABITAT: Lakes, rivers, marshes and coasts. DISTRIBUTION: Winter visitor.

4 GREY-HEADED FISH EAGLE *Ichthyophaga ichthyaetus* 69–74cm FIELD NOTES: Juvenile brown with head, neck and underparts heavily streaked white, underwing pale buff-brown with darker trailing edge, tail with faint barring. VOICE: A squawking *kwok* or similar, harsh screams, and during display a far-carrying *tiu-weeeu*. HABITAT: Lowland forest with nearby water, lakes, rivers, coastal lagoons and sometimes near estuaries. DISTRIBUTION: Widespread resident.

5 LESSER FISH EAGLE *Ichthyophaga humilis* 64cm FIELD NOTES: Juvenile generally greyish-brown, darker on mantle and wings, underwing pale grey-brown with faint barring on flight feathers, tail grey with slightly paler base. VOICE: A plaintive *pheeow-pheeoow-pheeow* and during breeding a repeated *pheeo-pheeo*. HABITAT: Mountain and foothills in the forested margins of rapid-flowing streams, rivers and lakes. DISTRIBUTION: Resident in the Himalayas and SW India.

6 SHORT-TOED EAGLE (SHORT-TOED SNAKE EAGLE) *Circaetus gallicus* 62–67cm FIELD NOTES: Plumage variable, head and upper breast pale grey-white to blackish, underparts virtually plain to barred black and white in the darker-headed forms. Often hovers when searching for prey. VOICE: A plaintive *weeo or weeooo*, also a gull-like *woh-woh-woh*. HABITAT: Varied, including open country, scrub and semi-desert. DISTRIBUTION: Resident over much of the region.

7 ANDAMAN SERPENT EAGLE *Spilornis elgini* 51–59cm FIELD NOTES: Juvenile as adult but crown, nape and throat pale buff, ear-coverts brown. VOICE: A clear *kweep-kweep-kweep*. HABITAT: Inland forests, preferring clearings or areas with scattered trees. DISTRIBUTION: Resident on the Andaman Islands.

8 CRESTED SERPENT EAGLE *Spilornis cheela* 56–74cm FIELD NOTES: Often soaring and calling high above forest. Juvenile has underwing and underparts white, the latter with fine dark streaks the former with fine barring, upperparts grey-brown fringed pale grey. *S. c. melanotis* (8b) occurs in peninsular India; *S. c. davidsoni* (8c) occurs on the Andamans. VOICE: In flight utters a shrill *kwee-kwee-kwee-kwee-kwee-kwee-kwee*. HABITAT: Well-wooded areas. DISTRIBUTION: Resident over much of the region.

9 CENTRAL NICOBAR SERPENT EAGLE *Spilornis minimus* 41–48cm FIELD NOTES: Smaller than very similar-looking island race of Crested Serpent Eagle. Juvenile has buff fringes to crest, three dark tail bars and fainter barring on underwing. VOICE: Similar to Crested Serpent Eagle. HABITAT: Forests with nearby streams. DISTRIBUTION: Resident on the central Nicobars.

10 GREAT NICOBAR SERPENT EAGLE *Spilornis klossi* 38–42cm FIELD NOTES: Encountered mostly in forest canopy. Juvenile underwing barring less prominent and head feathers fringed buff. VOICE: Undescribed. HABITAT: Mixed evergreen forest, also on grassland and forest regeneration areas. DISTRIBUTION: Resident on Great Nicobar, Little Nicobar and Menchal.

27 HARRIERS

1 MARSH HARRIER (WESTERN or EURASIAN MARSH HARRIER) *Circus aeruginosus* 48–56cm FIELD NOTES: Generally flies close to the ground, quartering reed-beds using a series of flaps followed by a glide with wings held in a shallow V. When prey is sighted stops quickly and drops, feet-first, to capture victim. Juvenile similar to adult female but usually lacks the buff forewing and sometimes lacks the buff head markings. Melanistic morph like juvenile but tail, secondaries and inner primaries usually greyish. VOICE: Generally silent, but when alarmed may give a cackling *chek-ek-ek-ek-ek*. HABITAT: Reed-beds, grasslands, cultivated fields and saltmarsh. DISTRIBUTION: Widespread winter visitor.

2 EASTERN MARSH HARRIER (SPOTTED MARSH HARRIER) *Circus spilonotus* 47–55cm FIELD NOTES: Actions and habits similar to Marsh Harrier. Intensity of head markings variable, often leading to a black head or blackish face. Juvenile like adult male Marsh Harrier but with darker secondaries, face and tail, the latter barred black. Often considered conspecific with Marsh Harrier. VOICE: As Marsh Harrier. HABITAT: As Marsh Harrier. DISTRIBUTION: Winter visitor, mainly to the NE.

3 HEN HARRIER *Circus cyaneus* 44–52cm FIELD NOTES: Soars with wings held level or in a shallow V. Feeding technique similar to Marsh Harrier but with quicker wing-beats and shorter glides. Juvenile similar to adult female but with rufous-tinged underparts and underwing-coverts, pronounced dark crescent on ear-coverts. VOICE: When alarmed male gives a *chek-ek-ek-ek* and female a twittering *chit-it-it-it-it-et-it-et-it-et*. HABITAT: Open areas including grasslands and cultivated land, in plains and foothills. DISTRIBUTION: Winter visitor to N parts of the region.

4 PALLID HARRIER *Circus macrourus* 40–48cm FIELD NOTES: Compared to Hen Harrier has a slimmer build and more buoyant flight, with wings held in a shallow V. Hunting technique similar to Hen Harrier. Juvenile upperparts similar to adult female, underparts and underwing-coverts plain rufous; dark ear-coverts and neck are accentuated by a pale whitish collar. Inner primaries of underwing paler-tipped than on Montagu's Harrier. VOICE: When alarmed utters a rapid *chit-er chit-er chit-it-it*. HABITAT: Open country such as plains, semi-desert, grassy hills, marshes and cultivated areas. DISTRIBUTION: Widespread winter visitor.

5 MONTAGU'S HARRIER *Circus pygargus* 43–47cm FIELD NOTES: Buoyant tern-like flight, with wings held in a shallow V, helps to distinguish it from Hen Harrier. Juvenile similar to juvenile Pallid Harrier but with less noticeable pale collar, which if showing is usually more rufous; on underwing all primaries are dark-tipped compared with Pallid Harrier. VOICE: When alarmed utters a rapid *chit-er chit-er chit-it-it-it*. HABITAT: Open country, such as grasslands, cultivated areas, scrubby plains and marshes. DISTRIBUTION: Widespread winter visitor.

6 PIED HARRIER *Circus melanoleucos* 41–49cm FIELD NOTES: Usually appears heavier when in flapping flight than Pallid or Montagu's Harrier. Juvenile dark brown above with white band on uppertail-coverts; underparts, including underwing-coverts, rufous streaked darker; face pattern much as adult female. VOICE: Female utters a *chak-chak-chak-chak-chak* when alarmed. HABITAT: Open grasslands, marshes, paddyfields and stubble fields. DISTRIBUTION: Breeds in Assam, otherwise a winter visitor.

28 HAWKS

1 CRESTED GOSHAWK *Accipiter trivirgatus* 30–46cm FIELD NOTES: Usual flight consists of stiff wing-beats followed by short glides, often seen soaring high above forest canopy. The female is browner, especially on the head. Juvenile has dark mantle and wings with pale fringes, head pale rusty with dark streaks, underparts white tinged rusty with dark spots or streaks on breast and wide brownish bars on flanks with narrow brownish bars on thighs. Sri Lanka race *A. t. layardi* (not shown) is smaller and darker. VOICE: A shrill prolonged scream, *he he hehehehe*, also loud screams and deep croaks. HABITAT: Deciduous and evergreen tropical and subtropical forests, also well-wooded gardens in Sri Lanka. DISTRIBUTION: Resident, mainly in SW and NE areas and Sri Lanka.

2 SHIKRA (LITTLE BANDED GOSHAWK) *Accipiter badius* 30–36cm FIELD NOTES: Hunts from a hidden, leafy perch, taking prey, mainly lizards or birds, from trees or the ground; does not usually indulge in aerial chases after prey. Juvenile generally brown above, pale buff below with dark brown streaks on breast and brown bars on flanks, black line down centre of throat. VOICE: A piping *keeu-keeu-keeu*, also a shrill *kewick*. HABITAT: Open woodland, forest edge and wooded cultivations. DISTRIBUTION: Widespread resident over most of the region.

3 CHINESE SPARROWHAWK (HORSFIELD'S SPARROWHAWK, GREY FROG HAWK) *Accipiter soloensis* 27–35cm FIELD NOTES: Generally catches prey on the ground, usually frogs, lizards or insects. Female larger with faint barring below. Juvenile generally dark brown, head with pale streaks, underparts whitish, heavily streaked dark on breast and rusty barred on flanks; underwing shows barring on flight feathers and unmarked buff coverts. VOICE: A rapid, accelerating piping that descends in pitch. HABITAT: Woodland, often near wetlands. DISTRIBUTION: Winter visitor on the Nicobars.

4 NICOBAR SPARROWHAWK *Accipiter butleri* 30–34cm FIELD NOTES: Juvenile like a pale rusty form of juvenile Chinese Sparrowhawk. VOICE: A shrill *kee-wick*. HABITAT: Tree canopy. DISTRIBUTION: Nicobar resident.

5 BESRA *Accipiter virgatus* 29–36cm FIELD NOTES: Typical sparrowhawk hunting technique, perching inconspicuously before giving chase to avian prey. Juvenile lacks rufous flanks, otherwise much as adult female. Birds on the Andamans *A. v. abdulali* (not shown) have a grey-tawny chest, a tawny belly and grey thighs, and all underparts lack bars or streaks. VOICE: A rapid *tchew-tchew-tchew*. HABITAT: Dense broadleaved forest, more open wooded areas post breeding. DISTRIBUTION: Widespread, scattered resident.

6 JAPANESE SPARROWHAWK (JAPANESE LESSER or ASIATIC SPARROWHAWK) *Accipiter gularis* 29–34cm FIELD NOTES: Feeding actions similar to Besra. Juvenile similar to adult female but chest streaked not barred. VOICE: Harsh cries. HABITAT: Secondary forest, cultivations and residential areas. DISTRIBUTION: Winter visitor to the Andamans.

7 SPARROWHAWK (EURASIAN or NORTHERN SPARROWHAWK) *Accipiter nisus* 28–38cm FIELD NOTES: Surprises bird prey by dashing from a hidden perch or after a stealthy, twisting flight. Juvenile like adult female but with browner upperparts. Birds in the Himalayas *A. n. melaschistos* are generally darker on head, mantle and wings. VOICE: When alarmed utters a rapid *kew-kew-kew-kew-kew*. HABITAT: Wide range of open woodland, scrub forest and wooded cultivations. DISTRIBUTION: Resident and winter visitor.

8 GOSHAWK (NORTHERN GOSHAWK) *Accipiter gentilis* 48–62cm FIELD NOTES: Hunting technique similar to Sparrowhawk. Female larger and browner-grey. Juvenile generally brown above, pale buff-white below with dark streaking. VOICE: When alarmed utters a loud *kyee-kyee-kyee*. HABITAT: High-altitude coniferous forest. DISTRIBUTION: Winter visitor and possible breeder, mainly in the N and Pakistan.

29 BUZZARDS, EAGLES, HAWK-EAGLES

1 WHITE-EYED BUZZARD *Butastur teesa* 36–43cm FIELD NOTES: Sits for long periods on a prominent perch, from where it drops onto ground-based prey. Juvenile less strongly marked below, head paler with facial and throat stripes narrower or lacking. VOICE: A melancholic *pit-weer pit-weer*. HABITAT: Dry open country with scattered trees and scrub. DISTRIBUTION: Widespread resident over much of the region.

2 BUZZARD (COMMON BUZZARD) *Buteo buteo* 51–57cm FIELD NOTES: Regularly perches in the open on posts or trees. Plumage very variable. *B. b. burmanicus* (2b) is a rufous-thighed race from the Himalayas and *B. b. vulpinus* (2c) is a rufous-tailed winter visitor from the northern Palearctic. Juvenile like adult but lacks black tips to flight feathers and tail. VOICE: A mewing *peeeeoooo*. HABITAT: Open country with scattered trees. DISTRIBUTION: Resident and winter visitor.

3 LONG-LEGGED BUZZARD *Buteo rufinus* 50–65cm FIELD NOTES: Plumage variable. Three main colour morphs, medium is generally rufous. Juvenile has tail finely barred. Often encountered perched on a prominent post. VOICE: A mellow *aaah*. HABITAT: Breeds in forested hills, resorts to open country post breeding. DISTRIBUTION: Breeds in the Himalayas, winters elsewhere, mainly in the N.

4 UPLAND BUZZARD (MONGOLIAN BUZZARD) *Buteo hemilasius* 66–71cm FIELD NOTES: Plumage variable. Soars with wings held in a deeper V than Buzzard. VOICE: A prolonged mewing. HABITAT: Open areas in hills and mountains. DISTRIBUTION: Breeds in Ladakh, winter visitor to Himalayas.

5 ROUGH-LEGGED BUZZARD (ROUGH-LEGGED HAWK) *Buteo lagopus* 50–60cm FIELD NOTES: Plumage variable: race *B. l. menzbieri* (not shown) from NE Asia usually has very white head and chest. Actions much as other buzzards. VOICE: A low-pitched, cat-like *peeeooo*. HABITAT: Winters over open country. DISTRIBUTION: Vagrant, one disputed record.

6 BOOTED EAGLE *Hieraaetus pennatus* 50–57cm FIELD NOTES: Some plumage variation occurs in both morphs, especially on underwing-coverts, which can be more rufous-tinged. In head-on flight shows white 'headlights' at joint of neck and wing. VOICE: A shrill, chattering *ki-ki-ki....*, also a buzzard-like *hiyaah*. HABITAT: Forested areas with nearby open areas. DISTRIBUTION: Resident in the Himalayas and W Pakistan, widespread over much of the area post breeding.

7 RUFOUS-BELLIED EAGLE (RUFOUS-BELLIED HAWK-EAGLE) *Lophotriorchis kienerii* 53–61cm FIELD NOTES: Soars high above forest canopy, from where it makes spectacular falcon-like stoops to capture prey. Juvenile dark above and white below including underwing-coverts. VOICE: A piercing scream. HABITAT: Evergreen and moist deciduous forest. DISTRIBUTION: Resident in the Himalayas, Bangladesh, NE and SW India and Sri Lanka.

8 MOUNTAIN HAWK-EAGLE (HODGSON'S HAWK-EAGLE) *Nisaetus nipalensis* 67–86cm FIELD NOTES: May soar above forest canopy but more often concealed among leaves of a branch. Juvenile has plain buff underparts, including underwing-coverts. Race *H. n. kelaarti* (8b) from SW India and Sri Lanka is often treated as a full species. VOICE: A shrill whistled *tlueet-weet weet* and a repeated *kee-kikik*. HABITAT: Mountain and hill forests. DISTRIBUTION: Resident in the Himalayas, NE and SW India and Sri Lanka.

9 CHANGEABLE HAWK-EAGLE (CRESTED HAWK-EAGLE) *Nisaetus cirrhatus* 58–77cm FIELD NOTES: Uses concealed forest perch, from where it makes a short dash to capture prey. Juvenile has buff-white underparts and underwing-coverts. Crestless race *H. c. limnaeetus* (9b), which also has a dark morph, is from the NE of the region and the Andamans, often treated as a full species. VOICE: A series of shrill whistles. HABITAT: Forest edge and open woodland. DISTRIBUTION: Resident over much of the S and NE of the region.

burmanicus

1

2b

2b

vulpinus

2c

2

normal morph

3

dark morph

3

pale morph

4

dark morph

4

5

pale phase

6

dark phase

pale phase

6

dark phase

9b

limnaeetus

7

8b

kelaarti

7

8

9

8

9

dark morph

30 EAGLES

1 BLACK EAGLE (INDIAN or ASIAN BLACK EAGLE) *Ictinaetus malayensis*
69–81cm FIELD NOTES: Often seen soaring low over forest canopy with wings held in a
shallow V. Juvenile has head, underparts and underwing-coverts all pale streaked dark
brown. VOICE: A plaintive *kleeee-kee* or *hee-lee-leeuw*. HABITAT: Mountain and hill forests,
also mangroves in Bangladesh. DISTRIBUTION: Resident, in scattered locations, over much
of the region.

2 INDIAN SPOTTED EAGLE *Aquila (Clanga) hastata* 59–67cm FIELD NOTES: Soars
on slightly arched wings. Yellow gape extends to back of, or slightly beyond, eye. Juvenile
has pale tips to feathers of mantle and wings, less pronounced than on juvenile Spotted
Eagle. VOICE: A high-pitched laughing cackle. HABITAT: Wooded areas interspersed with
cultivation. DISTRIBUTION: Resident over much of the N.

3 BONELLI'S EAGLE *Aquila fasciata* 65–72cm FIELD NOTES: Juvenile pale rufous,
or whitish, below, including underwing-coverts, underwing primaries pale, tipped black,
secondaries slightly darker and barred dark, also a wide blackish bar formed from dark
tips on primary- and secondary-coverts, tail pale grey barred darker grey. VOICE: Generally
silent. In display utters a fluting *klu-klu-klu-kluee* or a melodious *iuh* and a long *eeeoo*.
HABITAT: Wooded country on hills and plains, desert edge and around large lakes.
DISTRIBUTION: Widespread resident.

4 SPOTTED EAGLE (GREATER SPOTTED EAGLE) *Aquila (Clanga) clanga* 59–
69cm FIELD NOTES: Soars on arched wings. Often encountered perched on riverside tree,
bush or bank. Juvenile usually has pronounced white tips to mantle and wing feathers.
VOICE: A yelping *kyak*, *kluck-kluck* or *tyuck-tyuck*. HABITAT: Near wetlands with or without
trees. DISTRIBUTION: Breeds in the NW, more widespread post breeding.

5 TAWNY EAGLE *Aquila rapax* 65–75cm FIELD NOTES: Soars with wings slightly arched.
Gape extends to middle of eye. Scavenger, often seen perched in trees near dumps or
habitations. Plumage variable, often appears scruffy. Juvenile similar to adult, but may have
pale tips to secondaries and secondary-coverts. VOICE: In breeding season utters a repeated,
barking *kowk*, otherwise generally silent. HABITAT: Open woodland, grassland, cultivation,
semi-desert and around habitations. DISTRIBUTION: Widespread resident.

6 STEPPE EAGLE *Aquila nipalensis* 67–87cm FIELD NOTES: Soars with wings arched.
Gape extends to rear of eye. Juvenile has white tips to secondaries and secondary-coverts;
underwing shows a broad white band formed by white tips to primary- and secondary-
coverts. VOICE: Generally silent. HABITAT: Wooded hills, open areas and around large lakes.
DISTRIBUTION: Widespread winter visitor, mainly to C and N of the region.

7 IMPERIAL EAGLE (EASTERN IMPERIAL EAGLE) *Aquila heliaca* 72–84cm FIELD
NOTES: Often seeks a prominent perch, on a tree or the ground, where it can easily view the
surrounding area. When soaring, wings usually held level. Juvenile paler greyish-buff with
pronounced white tips to head, mantle and wing feathers, underparts grey-buff streaked
darker. VOICE: A deep, barking *owk-owk-owk*. HABITAT: Plains, deserts and around large
wetlands. DISTRIBUTION: Winter visitor, mainly to the NW.

8 GOLDEN EAGLE *Aquila chrysaetos* 76–93cm FIELD NOTES: Spends long periods soaring
around mountain crags with wings held in a very shallow V. In flight juvenile shows large
white patches at base of primaries and outer secondaries and on base of tail. VOICE: Generally
silent, although sometimes gives a fluty whistle in flight. HABITAT: Mountains.
DISTRIBUTION: Resident in the Himalayas and Baluchistan.

pale phase

dark phase

pale phase

pale phase

dark phase

31 FALCONS

1 COLLARED FALCONET (RED-THIGHED, RED-LEGGED or RED-BREASTED FALCONET) *Microhierax caerulescens* 15–18cm FIELD NOTES: Seeks prominent exposed perch from where to make short shrike-like sorties to capture prey. Slowly pumps tail and nods head while perched. Juvenile has forehead and supercilium pale rufous, throat whitish. VOICE: A high-pitched *kli-kli-kli* or *killi-killi-killi*. HABITAT: Edges and clearings in broadleaved tropical forest. DISTRIBUTION: Resident in E Himalayas and NE Assam.

2 PIED FALCONET (WHITE-LEGGED FALCONET) *Microhierax melanoleucos* 18–20cm FIELD NOTES: Habits and actions similar to Collared Falconet. Juvenile similar to adult but with yellowish bill. VOICE: A shrill whistle, a low chattering, also hissing sounds when agitated. HABITAT: Forest edge and clearings, also recorded in tea plantations. DISTRIBUTION: Resident in E Himalayas and NE India.

3 LESSER KESTREL *Falco naumanni* 29–32cm FIELD NOTES: A social bird, migrates in flocks. Typically hovers less than Kestrel and in level flight wing-beats appear faster and shallower. White claws. VOICE: A rasping *chay-chay-chay*, usually given at roosts. When disturbed gives a trilling *keerrrl* or *kikikik*. HABITAT: Open areas including cultivations. DISTRIBUTION: Widespread passage migrant.

4 KESTREL (COMMON or EURASIAN KESTREL) *Falco tinnunculus* 31–37cm FIELD NOTES: Frequently hovers when searching for prey or sits on post or other exposed perch from which it drops onto its quarry. Usually seen singly or in pairs. Black claws. VOICE: A shrill *kee-kee-kee-kee* and a trilling *vriii*. HABITAT: Mountains slopes, hills, plains and cultivated areas. DISTRIBUTION: Resident in the Himalayas, W Pakistan, SW India and Sri Lanka, very widespread post breeding.

5 RED-NECKED FALCON (RED-HEADED MERLIN or FALCON) *Falco chicquera* 30–36cm FIELD NOTES: Often hunts in pairs with a dashing low flight. VOICE: A strident *ki-ki-ki-ki-ki*, a harsh *yak yak yak* and a screaming *tiririri tiriririeee*. HABITAT: Open country with patches of trees, cultivations and desert-edge groves. DISTRIBUTION: Widespread resident.

6 AMUR FALCON (EASTERN or MANCHURIAN RED-FOOTED FALCON) *Falco amurensis* 28–30cm FIELD NOTES: Highly manoeuvrable flight in pursuit of flying insects, also hovers. Gregarious. Communal roosts often include Lesser Kestrels. Juvenile like adult female, but head, mantle and wings brownish-grey with rufous fringes. VOICE: A shrill *kew-kew-kew* when at roost. HABITAT: Open country. DISTRIBUTION: Widespread passage migrant.

7 SOOTY FALCON *Falco concolor* 33–36cm FIELD NOTES: Hunting flight energetic with fast glides and sudden stoops. Juvenile grey on mantle and wings, crown greyish, dark around eye and moustachial streak, ear-coverts whitish with darker crescent at rear; underparts white-buff streaked dark-grey. VOICE: A loud *keee-keee-keee...*, also a plaintive chatter. HABITAT: Desert and arid coastal areas and islands. DISTRIBUTION: Summer visitor to Pakistan coast.

32 FALCONS

1 MERLIN *Falco columbarius* 25–30cm FIELD NOTES: In pursuit of prey flight is often dashing and slightly undulating with twists and turns, usually at low level. Juvenile like adult female but browner without greyish cast, and darker streaks on underparts. The pale race *F. c. pallidus* (1b) is a rare winter visitor to W Pakistan. VOICE: Generally silent away from breeding sites. HABITAT: Open country including desert scrub, cultivations and coastal areas. DISTRIBUTION: Winter visitor, mainly to the N of the region.

2 HOBBY (EURASIAN or NORTHERN HOBBY) *Falco subbuteo* 30–36cm FIELD NOTES: Fast acrobatic flier, catching prey, mainly insects and small birds, in flight. Regularly perches on isolated trees. Juvenile like adult but browner above and on head, underparts generally buff heavily streaked dark brown. VOICE: A rapid *kew-kew-kew-kew*..... HABITAT: Breeds in well-wooded areas, resorts to more open areas post breeding. DISTRIBUTION: Breeds in the Himalayas, more widespread post breeding.

3 ORIENTAL HOBBY (INDIAN HOBBY) *Falco severus* 27–30cm FIELD NOTES: Actions and habits much like Hobby. Juvenile very similar to juvenile Hobby, but upperparts darker and underparts pale rufous-buff. VOICE: A rapid *ki-ki-ki-ki*. HABITAT: Open or lightly wooded hills. DISTRIBUTION: Resident, mainly in the Himalayas and NE India.

4 SAKER (SAKER FALCON) *Falco cherrug* 45–55cm FIELD NOTES: Often encountered sitting on rocks. Usually hunts at low level; most prey, predominantly rodents, taken on the ground. Occasionally hovers or makes aerial stoops to catch birds. Juvenile is darker above and has heavier spotting below. *F. c. milvipes* (4b) is an uncommon winter visitor, mainly to the NW of the region. VOICE: A harsh *kek-kek-kek*.... HABITAT: The Indus plains and mountains and foothills in desert and semi-desert areas. DISTRIBUTION: Winter visitor, mainly in the NW.

5 LAGGAR FALCON *Falco jugger* 43–46cm FIELD NOTES: Waits on exposed perch, and when prey is sighted makes a swift low-level attack, victim taken in the air or on the ground. Juvenile like adult but crown browner and underparts heavily streaked, throat whitish. VOICE: A shrill *whi-ee-ee*. HABITAT: Arid or semi-arid open country, cultivations and sand dunes. DISTRIBUTION: Widespread resident over much of the region.

6 BARBARY FALCON *Falco pelegrinoides* 35–42cm FIELD NOTES: Prey usually taken in mid-air following a high-speed pursuit and stoop. Juvenile has brown upperparts, buff-white below streaked dark brown. Often considered conspecific with Peregrine. VOICE: A scolding *kek-kek-kek-kek*.... HABITAT: Open desert or semi-desert with rocky hills. DISTRIBUTION: Breeds in N and W Pakistan, widespread in much of the NW post breeding.

7 PEREGRINE (PEREGRINE FALCON) *Falco peregrinus peregrinator* 36–48cm FIELD NOTES: Prey captured and killed in mid-air following a fast pursuit and a high-speed stoop on closed wings. Juvenile is blackish above, buff below with dark streaking, head pattern as adult. *F. p. calidus* (7b) is a widespread post-breeding visitor from the Palearctic. Juvenile *F. p. calidus* like adult but browner, underparts whitish with dark streaking, head as adult but browner. VOICE: A loud *ka-yak ka-yak ka-yak*.... or when alarmed a shrill *kek-kek-kek*... HABITAT: Mountains and rocky hills, after breeding also found around lakes, large rivers, marshes, coastal cliffs, lagoons and mangroves. DISTRIBUTION: Widespread resident and post-breeding visitor.

pallidus

milvipes

calidus

33 CRANES

1 SIBERIAN CRANE *Grus leucogeranus* 120–140cm FIELD NOTES: Very rare. Normally the most aquatic of all cranes. In flight shows black primaries, flies with neck outstretched and legs protruding well beyond tail. Juvenile generally rusty-buff on upperparts, neck and hind-neck, underparts white. VOICE: A hollow, honking *koonk koonk* and in flight, usually when going to roost, a musical *ahooya*. HABITAT: Freshwater marshes. DISTRIBUTION: Was a regular winter visitor, in small numbers, to Keoladeo National Park, but at the time of writing no birds have been reported for eleven years. There are scattered sightings, unconfirmed, from Pakistan and other parts of India.

2 COMMON CRANE (EURASIAN CRANE) *Grus grus* 110–120cm FIELD NOTES: Gregarious, often forms large flocks post breeding. In flight, from below, shows black primaries and secondaries, flies with outstretched neck and legs protruding well beyond tail. Juvenile more brownish-grey on upperparts, neck and head, lacks adult head pattern. VOICE: A far-carrying *krooh* and a repeated, harsh *kraah*. HABITAT: Cultivated fields, lakes, marshes and river sandbanks. DISTRIBUTION: Winter visitor, mainly to the N of the region.

3 SARUS CRANE (INDIAN SARUS CRANE) *Grus antigone* 156–176cm FIELD NOTES: In flight, from below, shows black primaries, flies with outstretched neck and legs protruding well beyond tail. Juvenile has rusty head and upper neck, upperparts tinged rufous. The uncommon eastern race *G. a. sharpii* (not shown) is smaller and greyer and lacks the white collar. VOICE: A loud trumpeting. HABITAT: Watery areas such as marshes, flood plains, lakes, ponds, rivers, ditches and wet cultivations. DISTRIBUTION: Resident over most of the NC and NE of the region.

4 BLACK-NECKED CRANE *Grus nigricollis* 115cm FIELD NOTES: In flight, from below, shows black flight feathers and tail, flies with neck outstretched and legs protruding well beyond tail. Juvenile has a brownish head and upper neck and yellow-brown upper mantle and wings. VOICE: A series of loud, trumpeting honks. HABITAT: Breeds on high-altitude wetlands, reverts to lower-altitude marshes and agricultural valleys post breeding. DISTRIBUTION: Breeds in Ladakh, winters mainly in Bhutan.

5 HOODED CRANE *Grus monacha* 100cm FIELD NOTES: Often migrates alongside Common Cranes. In flight, from below, shows black flight feathers, flies with outstretched neck and legs protruding well beyond tail. Juvenile has head and neck buffish-white with a dark eye-patch. VOICE: A loud *krurrk*. HABITAT: Open wetlands, grasslands, agricultural fields, lake and river shores and paddyfields. DISTRIBUTION: Breeds in E Siberia, winters in E Asia. One disputed record from India. If it is proven that a Hooded Crane took a 'wrong turn' to spend the winter of 2011/12 in Tennessee, USA, then another 'wrong turn' of that magnitude would make an appearance in the Indian Subcontinent not so impossible.

6 DEMOISELLE CRANE *Grus (Anthropoides) virgo* 90–100cm FIELD NOTES: Gregarious, often in very large flocks during migration. In flight, from below, shows blackish primaries and secondaries, flies with neck outstretched and legs protruding well beyond tail. Juvenile has head and neck pale grey, tertials much shorter than those of adult. VOICE: Like Common Crane, but drier and higher-pitched. Juvenile utters a thin, high, rolling whistle. HABITAT: River or lake sandbanks, cultivations and desert or semi-desert areas on migration. DISTRIBUTION: Winter visitor and passage migrant mainly to the NW.

34 FINFOOT, CRAKES, RAILS

1 MASKED FINFOOT (ASIAN FINFOOT) *Heliopais personatus* 43–55cm FIELD NOTES: Very elusive, although can be quite confiding. Most active at dawn or dusk. VOICE: A high-pitched bubbling, a grunting quack and when alarmed a *keek-keek-keek*. HABITAT: Fresh or brackish water in dense forest and mangroves. DISTRIBUTION: Resident in scattered locations in the NE, primarily in the Sundarbans and Assam.

2 ANDAMAN CRAKE *Rallina canningi* 34cm FIELD NOTES: Skulking. Juvenile duller with less pronounced barring on underparts. VOICE: A deep croaking *kroop kroop* and when alarmed a sharp *chick chick*. HABITAT: Forest marshes and streams, occasionally in mangroves. DISTRIBUTION: Andaman resident.

3 RED-LEGGED CRAKE (MALAYSIAN BANDED CRAKE) *Rallina fasciata* 23–25cm FIELD NOTES: Skulker, difficult to observe or flush. Juvenile duller than adult with less pronounced barring on underparts and wings, legs brownish-yellow. VOICE: A loud *gogogogok*, a *girrr*, a nasal *pek pek pek...* and a slow descending trill. HABITAT: Reedy swamps and marshes, paddyfields and watercourses. DISTRIBUTION: Extreme NE of the region.

4 SLATY-LEGGED CRAKE (BANDED CRAKE) *Rallina eurizonoides* 27cm FIELD NOTES: Shy, often taking refuge in trees when flushed. Juvenile olive-brown above, head and neck dull ochre-brown. VOICE: A persistent *kek-kek-kek-kek....* or *ow-ow-ow-ow...* HABITAT: Forest and forest edge with marshes or wet areas. DISTRIBUTION: Resident and breeding visitor.

5 SLATY-BREASTED RAIL (BLUE-BREASTED BANDED RAIL) *Gallirallus striatus* 29cm FIELD NOTES: Very secretive. Juvenile mantle, wings and flanks like adult but paler brown, hind-neck and crown brownish, foreneck, breast and belly buffy-grey. VOICE: A sharp *terrik* or *trrrik*, which may be strung together as a 'song', also a noisy *ka-ka-ka*. HABITAT: Marshes, mangroves, paddyfields and marshy grassland. DISTRIBUTION: Widespread resident.

6 INDIAN WATER RAIL (BROWN-CHEEKED RAIL) *Rallus indicus* 23–28cm FIELD NOTES: Secretive, but feeds in the open when undisturbed. Juvenile like juvenile Water Rail but with barred undertail-coverts. VOICE: A long, clear, piping *kyu*, also a repeated, metallic, slurred *shrink shrink* call, about two per second. HABITAT: Marshes. DISTRIBUTION: Winter visitor to the NE.

7 WATER RAIL *Rallus aquaticus* 29cm FIELD NOTES: Secretive, more often seen than heard, although will feed in the open if undisturbed. Juvenile like adult but grey areas of underparts replaced with buff-grey, breast mottled brownish. VOICE: Various pig-like squeals and grunts. HABITAT: Dense reed-beds, marshes and overgrown ditches. DISTRIBUTION: Breeds in Kashmir, otherwise winter visitor to the NW.

8 CORNCRAKE *Crex crex* 27–30cm FIELD NOTES: Most active early or late, and more often heard than seen. VOICE: A monotonous dry *krek-krek-krek-krek*. HABITAT: Grasslands and cultivated areas. DISTRIBUTION: Vagrant, recorded from Pakistan, India and Sri Lanka.

9 BROWN CRAKE *Amaurornis akool* 26–28cm FIELD NOTES: Usually skulking, feeds more in the open at dawn or dusk, but runs into cover at the slightest alarm. VOICE: A long vibrating trill. HABITAT: Swamps, paddyfields, overgrown watercourses. DISTRIBUTION: Widespread over much of the region.

10 WHITE-BREASTED WATERHEN *Amaurornis phoenicurus* 28–33cm FIELD NOTES: Often seen in the open, also climbs about in bushes and trees. Juvenile is a duller grey-brown version of adult, with rear of ear-coverts, lores and forehead grey-brown. VOICE: Loud grunts, croaks and chuckles, *kru-ak kru-ak kru-ak-a-wak-wak* or *krr-kwaak-kwaak krr-kwaak-kraak....* Contact call is a *pwik pwik pwik...* HABITAT: Damp scrub, thick waterside vegetation. DISTRIBUTION: Widespread resident.

35 CRAKES, GALLINULES, COOT

1 BLACK-TAILED CRAKE (ELWES'S or RUFOUS-BACKED CRAKE) *Porzana bicolor* 20–22cm FIELD NOTES: Secretive, although will feed in the open at dawn or dusk, but at the slightest disturbance retreats into cover. Juvenile duller with brownish legs. VOICE: A rasping *waak-waak* followed by a descending trill. HABITAT: Swamp areas and paddyfields in or near forests. DISTRIBUTION: Resident in the NE of the region.

2 BAILLON'S CRAKE *Porzana pusilla* 17–19cm FIELD NOTES: Forages at dawn or dusk, close to, or in, dense cover. Short primary projection compared to Little Crake. Juvenile like adult above, whitish barred brown-grey below. VOICE: A dry fog-like rattle. HABITAT: Marshes, paddyfields, vegetation surrounding lakes and ponds. DISTRIBUTION: Breeds in Indian Himalayas, otherwise a widespread winter visitor and passage migrant.

3 LITTLE CRAKE *Porzana parva* 18–20cm FIELD NOTES: Often feeds in quite deep water and tends to swim more than other crakes. Long primary projection compared to Baillon's Crake. Juvenile similar to juvenile Baillon's Crake but appears paler below, due to less barring on foreneck and underparts. VOICE: A far-carrying, accelerating *qwek qwek qwek qwek-qwek-qwek kwa kwa-kwa-kwa....* HABITAT: Marshes and lakes with extensive, dense aquatic vegetation. DISTRIBUTION: Passage migrant and winter visitor to Pakistan and W India.

4 SPOTTED CRAKE *Porzana porzana* 22–24cm FIELD NOTES: Secretive, although will forage in the open if undisturbed. VOICE: A high-pitched, whiplash-like *whit*, also a ticking *tik-tak* and a croaking *qwe-qwe-qwe*. HABITAT: Marshes, wet meadows, reedy edges of watercourses and paddyfields. DISTRIBUTION: Widespread winter visitor.

5 RUDDY-BREASTED CRAKE (RUDDY CRAKE) *Porzana fusca* 21–23cm FIELD NOTES: Secretive, although often feeds at the edge of reed-beds. VOICE: A harsh *tewk* that often speeds up and ends with a slightly descending trill. HABITAT: Reed-beds, reedy marshes, paddyfields and vegetation by watercourses. DISTRIBUTION: Widespread resident.

6 WATERCOCK *Gallicrex cinerea* 42–43cm FIELD NOTES: Mainly a crepuscular, skulking forager, although readily swims across open water. Juvenile like adult female but with less barring below. VOICE: A long series of *kok* notes followed by a series of hollow *utumb* notes ending with a short series of *kluck* notes. HABITAT: Reed or grassy swamps, paddyfields and vegetation alongside watercourses. DISTRIBUTION: Resident, more widespread during the monsoon when birds disperse to newly created marshy land in otherwise dry low-lying areas.

7 PURPLE SWAMPHEN (PURPLE GALLINULE) *Porphyrio porphyrio* 45–50cm FIELD NOTES: Readily feeds in the open, although typically stays close to cover. Walks on floating water-plants and clambers among reeds and bushes. Juvenile duller, with small reddish shield and dull reddish bill. VOICE: Very vocal, including a series of plaintive nasal rattles ending in a crescendo, a low *chuk-chuk* and in alarm a trumpeting *toot*. HABITAT: Dense reed-beds and the fringing vegetation of lakes, ponds and rivers. DISTRIBUTION: Widespread resident.

8 MOORHEN (COMMON MOORHEN or GALLINULE) *Gallinula chloropus* 32–35cm FIELD NOTES: Usually keeps to the edge of cover. Regularly swims, with a jerky action. Juvenile dull brownish with whitish throat and faint buffish flank stripe. VOICE: A bubbling *krrrruk* or *kurr-ik* and a *kik-kik-kik* given when alarmed. HABITAT: Marshes, lakes and watercourses with surrounding emergent vegetation. DISTRIBUTION: Widespread resident and winter visitor.

9 COOT (EURASIAN or COMMON COOT) *Fulica atra* 36–38cm FIELD NOTES: Gregarious. Often feeds on waterside grass. Juvenile dull grey with white throat, foreneck, breast and belly. VOICE: Various metallic notes including a short *kow* or *kowk* and a sharp *kick*. HABITAT: Open water with fringing vegetation. DISTRIBUTION: Widespread resident and winter visitor.

36 BUSTARDS

1 INDIAN BUSTARD (GREAT INDIAN BUSTARD) *Ardeotis nigriceps* male 120cm, female 90cm FIELD NOTES: Critically endangered. Unmistakable, large and weighty. In flight shows blackish primary-, secondary- and median-coverts tipped with white, flies with neck outstretched. During display male inflates neck and struts around with tail cocked and wings drooped, calling with a deep booming moan. VOICE: Other than the display booming, utters a gruff, barked *hook*. HABITAT: Dry grassland with scattered bushes, also neighbouring open dry deciduous forest. DISTRIBUTION: Indian resident.

2 LITTLE BUSTARD *Tetrax tetrax* 43cm FIELD NOTES: In flight upperwing of male shows extensive white flight feathers apart from a black crescent formed by the tips of the primary-coverts and prominent black tips to outer primaries; female wing pattern similar but with the addition of a few dusky bars on the secondaries. Flies with neck outstretched. VOICE: When alarmed utters a low grunt. In flight wings make a sound like a squeaky bicycle, *sisisisisisisisisi.....* HABITAT: Open grasslands, rough plains, pasture and crop fields. DISTRIBUTION: Winter visitor to Pakistan and N India.

3 GREAT BUSTARD *Otis tarda* male 105cm, female 75cm FIELD NOTES: Large and weighty. Upperwing appears mainly greyish-white with darker tips to primaries and black secondaries, forewing as mantle, flies with neck outstretched. VOICE: A low bark given during disputes or when alarmed. HABITAT: Open grassland and crops. DISTRIBUTION: Vagrant, recorded from Pakistan.

4 MACQUEEN'S BUSTARD *Chlamydotis macqueenii* male 65–75cm, female 55–65cm FIELD NOTES: In flight upperwing shows large white patch on base of outer primaries, inner primaries, secondaries and primary-coverts black, the latter with whitish base patch. Flies with neck outstretched. VOICE: Generally silent. HABITAT: Semi-desert with low scrub, sandy grasslands and crop fields. DISTRIBUTION: Breeds in S Pakistan, otherwise post-breeding visitor to NW.

5 LESSER FLORICAN (LIKH) *Sypheotides indicus* male 46cm, female 51cm FIELD NOTES: Endangered. Non-breeding male like female but with whitish wing-coverts and black underwing. Male upperwing shows extensive white on coverts, female similar but much browner and whitish-buff coverts suffused with brownish feather centres. Flies with neck outstretched. During display male leaps into the air using shallow wing-beats, with neck inflated and head thrown back, and at the crest of the jump the wings are held so as to show off the white wing-patch before the bird drops to the ground to repeat the performance over and over again. VOICE: During display the male utters a loud rattling. When alarmed gives a short whistle. HABITAT: Tall dry grassland with scattered bushes and fields of cotton or millet. DISTRIBUTION: Breeds in NW India, much more widespread after breeding.

6 BENGAL FLORICAN *Houbaropsis bengalensis* male 64cm, female 68cm FIELD NOTES: Rare and declining in numbers. Upperwing of male in flight is predominantly white; female has brownish flight feathers barred dark and pale buffish wing-coverts. Flies with neck outstretched. During display the male leaps into the air, hovering momentarily at the top of the jump before gliding back to earth. VOICE: While displaying the male emits a deep hum. When alarmed utters a shrill, metallic *chik-chik-chik*. HABITAT: Tall grassy plains with scattered scrub, feeding in more open areas in the early morning. DISTRIBUTION: Resident in the NC and NE of the region.

37 SNIPES, WOODCOCK

1 JACK SNIPE *Lymnocryptes minimus* 17–19cm FIELD NOTES: Secretive, tends to wait until nearly trodden on before being flushed, flies away with less erratic movements than Snipe. VOICE: May utter a weak *gah* when disturbed. HABITAT: Marshes, flooded pastures and wet grassy areas surrounding lakes, ponds, rivers and ditches. DISTRIBUTION: Widespread post-breeding visitor.

2 SNIPE (COMMON SNIPE) *Gallinago gallinago* 25–27cm FIELD NOTES: Usually feeds close to cover. When flushed flies off in a rapid, erratic zigzagging manner. In flight shows a white trailing edge, and pale banding on underwing-coverts. During display-dives stiff outer tail feathers produce a vibrating drumming sound. VOICE: In display utters a repeated *chipper-chipper-chipper*. When alarmed gives a harsh *scaap*. HABITAT: Breeds in marshes and boggy areas, spreading to a variety of wet areas post breeding, including lakesides, flooded fields and ditches. DISTRIBUTION: Breeds in NW Himalayas; post breeding widespread over most of the region.

3 GREAT SNIPE *Gallinago media* 27–29cm FIELD NOTES: Actions usually more sluggish than Snipe. Spread tail shows extensive white on outer feathers. Underwing uniformly dark-barred, upperwing shows white wing-bars. VOICE: Utters a weak *aitch-aitch-aitch* when flushed. HABITAT: Wet pastures, marshes and swamp edges. DISTRIBUTION: Vagrant, recorded from India and Sri Lanka.

4 SWINHOE'S SNIPE (CHINESE SNIPE) *Gallinago megala* 27–29cm FIELD NOTES: At rest primaries extend beyond tertials. In flight toes project slightly beyond tail and underwing is uniformly barred. VOICE: Sometimes utters a gruff *scaap* when flushed. HABITAT: Marshes, flooded grasslands, paddyfields and less often in drier areas such as rice stubbles. DISTRIBUTION: Scattered winter visitor.

5 PIN-TAILED SNIPE (PINTAIL SNIPE) *Gallinago stenura* 25–27cm FIELD NOTES: At rest tertials overlap primaries, tail short. In flight toes project well beyond tail and underwing uniformly barred. Supercilium wider at base than in Snipe. VOICE: May utter a short, thin *scaap* when flushed. HABITAT: Very similar to Swinhoe's Snipe. DISTRIBUTION: Widespread winter visitor.

6 SOLITARY SNIPE *Gallinago solitaria* 29–31cm FIELD NOTES: When flushed zigzags away, with a heavier flight than Snipe, drops into cover quite quickly. During display-dives stiff outer tail feathers produce a bleating sound, more shrill than Snipe. VOICE: When flushed gives a harsh *kensh*. During display utters a deep *chok-a-chok-a*. HABITAT: High-altitude marshes, bogs and watercourses. DISTRIBUTION: Resident and winter visitor, mainly to the N and NE.

7 WOOD SNIPE (HIMALAYAN SNIPE) *Gallinago nemoricola* 28–32cm FIELD NOTES: Flight is direct and heavy. When flushed rarely flies far. VOICE: When flushed gives a low, croaking *chok-chok*. At breeding sites utters a nasal *check-check-check*. HABITAT: Breeds in alpine meadows and dwarf scrub; winters in wet areas in forests. DISTRIBUTION: Breeds in the Himalayas and NE India, winters in lower areas of Himalayas and on hills in S India and Sri Lanka.

8 WOODCOCK (EURASIAN WOODCOCK) *Scolopax rusticola* 33–35cm FIELD NOTES: Usually encountered when flushed or during display-flight (roding) when flies above territory with slow wing-beats giving squeaks and grunts. When flushed zigzags away through trees and then drops out of sight. VOICE: Generally silent when flushed but occasionally utters a snipe-like *schaap* or *schaap schaap*. HABITAT: Dense woodland and plantations with dry areas for nesting and nearby wetter areas for feeding. DISTRIBUTION: Breeds in the Himalayas and Pakistan hills, winters mainly in the Himalayas and S Indian hills.

38 DOWITCHERS, GODWITS, CURLEWS

1 LONG-BILLED DOWITCHER *Limnodromus scolopaceus* 27–30cm FIELD NOTES: Shorter yellow or yellow-green legs compared to Asian Dowitcher. In flight shows a white oval on lower back and a white trailing edge to flight feathers and a distinctly black and white barred tail. Juvenile like non-breeding adult but neck and breast pale rufous-buff and mantle feathers edged rufous. VOICE: A sharp *kik* or *kik-kik-kik-kik*, also a *kreeek* when alarmed. HABITAT: Various wetlands, both inland and coastal. DISTRIBUTION: Vagrant, recorded from India.

2 ASIAN DOWITCHER (ASIATIC or SNIPE-BILLED DOWITCHER) *Limnodromus semipalmatus* 33–36cm FIELD NOTES: Often associates with godwits. In flight shows whitish lower back barred and streaked dark grey, tail whitish barred darker grey. Juvenile upperparts are darkish-brown with buff fringes, neck, breast and flanks are tinged warm buff with dark streaks. VOICE: A yelping *chep-chep* or *chowp*, also a human-like, soft, moaning *kiaow*. HABITAT: Coastal wetlands. DISTRIBUTION: Winter visitor.

3 BLACK-TAILED GODWIT *Limosa limosa* 40–44cm FIELD NOTES: Gregarious. In flight shows a bold white wing-bar on upperwing, white rump and black tail. Juvenile similar to breeding adult but neck more buff, mantle feathers fringed pale buff, underparts lack barring. Eastern race *L. l. melanuroides* (not shown), which occurs in the NE, is smaller and has the chestnut areas darker and extending further down flanks, white wing-bar less pronounced. VOICE: A *kek*, *tuk* or *kip* often repeated. HABITAT: Lakes shores, grassland, mudflats and estuaries. DISTRIBUTION: Widespread winter visitor.

4 BAR-TAILED GODWIT *Limosa lapponica* 37–41cm FIELD NOTES: Gregarious, often in large flocks mixed with Black-tailed Godwits and other waders. In flight shows white from rump to mid-back, tail barred black and white, upperwing shows no wing-bar. Juvenile similar to breeding female but mantle has wider pale buff fringes. VOICE: When alarmed utters a barking *kak-kak*, a deep *kirruc* or variations of these. HABITAT: Estuaries, muddy or sandy shores. DISTRIBUTION: Winter visitor, mainly to coasts.

5 WHIMBREL *Numenius phaeopus* 40–46cm FIELD NOTES: Usually encountered in small parties, although may form larger flocks at roost. In flight shows white rump and lower back. Eastern race *N. p. variegatus* (not shown) is darker and whitish rump is strongly barred dark, often showing little contrast with rest of mantle. VOICE: A tittering, flat-toned *tetti-tetti-tetti-tet*, *bibibibibiibi* or similar. HABITAT: Coastal wetlands and nearby grassland. DISTRIBUTION: Widespread winter visitor, mainly to coasts.

6 CURLEW (EURASIAN, WESTERN or COMMON CURLEW) *Numenius arquata* 50–60cm FIELD NOTES: Usually found in small parties. In flight shows a white rump and lower back. Females slightly larger and longer-billed than males. VOICE: A far-carrying *cour-lee*, a low *whaup* and a stammering *tutututu* or *tyuywyuyu* when disturbed. HABITAT: Estuaries, mudflats, sandflats, lake edges, flooded fields and grasslands. DISTRIBUTION: Widespread winter visitor, mainly to coasts.

7 FAR EASTERN CURLEW (EASTERN or AUSTRALIAN CURLEW) *Numenius madagascariensis* 60–66cm FIELD NOTES: Shy, may mix with flocks of Curlews. In flight lacks white rump and lower back. Female slightly larger and longer-billed than male. VOICE: A far-carrying *cour-lee*, flatter-toned than Curlew. When disturbed gives a strident *ker-ker-ee-ker-ee*. HABITAT: Estuaries and beaches. DISTRIBUTION: Vagrant, recorded from Bangladesh.

39 SHANKS, SANDPIPERS

1 SPOTTED REDSHANK (DUSKY REDSHANK) *Tringa erythropus* 29–32cm FIELD NOTES: Moulting birds have non-breeding type plumage blotched with black. In flight shows white oval in centre of back. Often wades up to belly when foraging. Juvenile like non-breeding adult but with fine barring on underparts. VOICE: In flight gives a distinctive *chu-it*, when alarmed utters a short *chip*. HABITAT: Upper reaches of estuaries, coastal lagoons, lakes and marshes. DISTRIBUTION: Widespread winter visitor.

2 REDSHANK (COMMON REDSHANK) *Tringa totanus* 27–29cm FIELD NOTES: Wary, taking noisily to flight at the slightest disturbance, usually the first in a group of waders to take to the air. In flight shows a white oval in centre of back and striking white secondaries and inner primaries. Juvenile like breeding adult, but mantle and wing feathers fringed and notched with ochre-buff. VOICE: A piping *teu-hu, teu-hu-hu* or similar. When alarmed utters a loud *tli-tli-tli-tli*. During display-flight gives a musical yodelling. HABITAT: Wide variety of coastal and inland wetlands. DISTRIBUTION: Breeds in NW Himalayas, otherwise a widespread winter visitor.

3 GREENSHANK (COMMON or GREATER GREENSHANK) *Tringa nebularia* 30–35cm FIELD NOTES: Wary. Usually seen singly, but sometimes in larger flocks at roost. In flight shows white rump and back, feet project slightly beyond tail. VOICE: A ringing *chew-chew-chew* and a *kiu-kiu-kiu* given when alarmed. HABITAT: Wide variety of coastal and inland wetlands. DISTRIBUTION: Widespread winter visitor.

4 MARSH SANDPIPER *Tringa stagnatilis* 22–25cm FIELD NOTES: Wary. Usually seen singly or in scattered parties. In flight looks like a small Greenshank but feet project well beyond tail. Juvenile like non-breeding adult but upperparts browner with pale fringes. VOICE: A plaintive *keeuw* or *kyu-kyu-kyu*. When flushed utters a loud *yip*. HABITAT: Marshes, ponds, lakes, saltmarshes and estuaries. DISTRIBUTION: Widespread post-breeding visitor.

5 SPOTTED GREENSHANK (NORDMANN'S GREENSHANK) *Tringa guttifer* 29–32cm FIELD NOTES: Rare. Wary. Often wades up to belly in water. In flight shows white rump and back, tail pale grey, legs do not protrude beyond tail. Juvenile like non-breeding adult but upperparts browner with buff spots. VOICE: A piercing *keyew* and a harsh *gwark*. HABITAT: Wide variety of coastal and inland wetlands. DISTRIBUTION: Vagrant, recorded from India and Bangladesh.

6 GREEN SANDPIPER *Tringa ochropus* 21–24cm FIELD NOTES: Usually encountered singly. In flight shows a white rump and broad black bars on white tail. VOICE: A musical *tlueet-wit-wit* and a sharp *wit-wit-wit* given in alarm. HABITAT: Pools, lake edges, stream sides and ditches. DISTRIBUTION: Widespread winter visitor.

7 WOOD SANDPIPER *Tringa glareola* 19–21cm FIELD NOTES: Often found in scattered groups. In flight shows a white rump and white tail with narrow black bars. Juvenile upperparts as breeding adult but shows extensive buff spots and fringes. VOICE: A high-pitched *chiff-iff-iff* and when alarmed a *chip* or *chip-chip-chip*. HABITAT: Lakes, pools, marshes and flooded grasslands, less often on coastal waters. DISTRIBUTION: Widespread winter visitor.

8 GREY-TAILED TATTLER (POLYNESIAN, SIBERIAN or GREY-RUMPED TATTLER, GREY-RUMPED SANDPIPER) *Tringa brevipes* 24–27cm FIELD NOTES: Generally occurs singly or in loose parties, walks Common Sandpiper-like with a bobbing rear end. In flight slate-grey underwing contrasts with white belly. VOICE: In flight utters an up-slurred *tu-whip* and when alarmed a *klee, klee-klee* or *weet-eet*. HABITAT: Rocky, sandy or muddy coasts. On migration may occur on paddyfields. DISTRIBUTION: Vagrant, recorded from Bangladesh.

40 SANDPIPERS

1 COMMON SANDPIPER *Actitis hypoleucos* 19–21cm FIELD NOTES: Bobs rear end when walking. In flight, which is low with stiff, flicking wing-beats, shows white bar on upperwing. VOICE: Gives a piping *tswee-wee-wee* in flight and a *sweet-eet* when alarmed. During display-flight utters a repeated *kittie-needie*, also sometimes given on migration and after breeding. HABITAT: Breeds by upland rivers and streams; post breeding on various freshwater or saltwater wetlands. DISTRIBUTION: Breeds in NW, otherwise a widespread winter visitor.

2 TEREK SANDPIPER *Xenus cinereus* 22–25cm FIELD NOTES: Usually encountered singly or in small scattered groups, although may occur in larger groups at roosts. Often feeds in an active, dashing manner. In flight upperwing shows a wide white trailing edge. VOICE: In flight utters a rippling *du-du-du-du-du*, or a mellow *ch-du-du*. HABITAT: Estuaries, saltpans, marshes and lakes. DISTRIBUTION: Widespread post-breeding visitor, mainly to coasts.

3 BUFF-BREASTED SANDPIPER *Tryngites subruficollis* 18–20cm FIELD NOTES: Often very confiding. White underwing shows dark tips to flight feathers and primary-coverts, the latter forming a pronounced crescent. VOICE: Sometimes utters a low growling *pr-r-r-reet* in flight. HABITAT: Grasslands or dry mud surrounds of lakes and rivers. DISTRIBUTION: Vagrant, recorded from India and Sri Lanka.

4 SPOON-BILLED SANDPIPER (SPOONBILL SANDPIPER) *Eurynorhynchus pygmeus* 14–16cm FIELD NOTES: Rare. Sweeps bill from side to side while foraging in shallow water. In flight has a prominent white bar on upperwing, sides of rump white. VOICE: A rolling *preep* or a shrill *wheet*. HABITAT: Coastal lagoons and muddy coastal shores. DISTRIBUTION: Winter visitor to Bangladesh, India and Sri Lanka.

5 BROAD-BILLED SANDPIPER *Limicola falcinellus* 16–18cm FIELD NOTES: Often forages among flocks of stints. In flight upperwing shows a narrow white wing-bar, in non-breeding plumage shows a dark leading edge. VOICE: A buzzing *chrrreet* or *trreet*. HABITAT: Coastal creeks, mudflats and lagoons. DISTRIBUTION: Winter visitor.

6 GREAT KNOT (GREATER or EASTERN KNOT, GREAT SANDPIPER) *Calidris tenuirostris* 26–28cm FIELD NOTES: Usually met with in flocks, often in the company of other wader species. In flight upperwing shows a narrow white wing-bar, lower rump is white sparsely marked with dark specks, appears white, tail dark grey. Juvenile like non-breeding adult but with mantle and wing feathers fringed whitish, underparts much like breeding adult. VOICE: A low *nyut-nyut*. Also recorded is a harsh *chuker-chuker-chuker* and a soft *prrt*. HABITAT: Mainly sandy or muddy coastal shores. DISTRIBUTION: Winter visitor.

7 KNOT (RED KNOT or LESSER KNOT) *Calidris canutus* 23–25cm FIELD NOTES: Usually in small parties. In flight upperwing shows a narrow white wing-bar, lower rump is white barred blackish, appears grey. VOICE: A soft, nasal *knut*, *wutt* or *whet*. When alarmed gives a *kikkiik*. HABITAT: Sandy or muddy coastal shores. DISTRIBUTION: Winter visitor.

8 SANDERLING *Calidris alba* 20–21cm FIELD NOTES: Usually in small parties feeding along the water's edge, typically with rapid runs interspersed with quick dips to pick up prey. In non-breeding plumage upperwing shows a broad white wing-bar and a dark leading edge. Juvenile like non-breeding adult but darker above with pronounced pale fringes, giving a chequered effect. VOICE: In flight utters a *twick* or *kip*, often repeated or forming a quick trill. HABITAT: Sandy or muddy coastal shores. DISTRIBUTION: Winter visitor.

41 SANDPIPERS

1 LITTLE STINT *Calidris minuta* 12–14cm FIELD NOTES: Has a quick running-around feeding action. Sometimes shows a split supercilium, although more noticeable in juvenile plumage. In flight shows grey-sided tail. Juvenile shows prominent white 'braces' on scapulars. VOICE: A short *stit-tit*. HABITAT: Coastal mudflats, shores of lakes pools and rivers, marshes and paddyfields. DISTRIBUTION: Widespread winter visitor.

2 TEMMINCK'S STINT *Calidris temminckii* 13–15cm FIELD NOTES: Has a slow deliberate feeding action, often forages among waterside vegetation, if alarmed flees with a towering, jinking flight. At rest white-sided tail projects beyond wing. Legs yellowish. VOICE: A rapid *tirirrirrir* or a trilled *trirr*. HABITAT: Marshes, lakesides, ponds and estuaries. DISTRIBUTION: Widespread winter visitor.

3 RED-NECKED STINT (RUFOUS-NECKED STINT *Calidris ruficollis* 13–16cm FIELD NOTES: Feeding actions similar to Little Stint. If able to compare, has longer legs and slightly shorter bill than Little Stint. VOICE: A coarse *chit*, *kreep*, *creek* or *chritt*. May give a short trill when flushed. HABITAT: Mud and sandflats, coastal pools and sometimes inland wetlands. DISTRIBUTION: Winter visitor, mainly to the coasts of the NE and the Andamans.

4 LONG-TOED STINT *Calidris subminuta* 13–16cm FIELD NOTES: Regularly forages among vegetation at water's edge. When alarmed often stands upright with neck extended, if flushed flees with a towering flight with weak, fluttery wing-beats. Juvenile like juvenile Little Stint, but darker with white 'braces' even more pronounced. VOICE: A soft *prrt*, *chrrup* or *chulip*, also a sharp *tik-tik-tik*. HABITAT: Estuaries, marshes, edges of lakes and pools. DISTRIBUTION: Widely scattered winter visitor, mainly in E parts of the region.

5 DUNLIN (RED-BACKED SANDPIPER) *Calidris alpina* 16–22cm FIELD NOTES: When foraging walks quickly, interspersed with short runs, probing and pecking vigorously. In flight upperwing shows a prominent white wing-bar and white sides to rump and uppertail-coverts. Juvenile like non-breeding adult but mantle darker brown, all upperpart feathers fringed rufous-buff, breast and face tinged warm buff with dark streaks, the latter continuing onto belly and flanks. VOICE: A rasping *kreeeep*, also a low *beep*. HABITAT: Coastal mudflats, seashore, lakesides, marshes and flooded fields. DISTRIBUTION: Widespread winter visitor.

6 PECTORAL SANDPIPER *Calidris melanotos* 19–23cm FIELD NOTES: Generally confiding, if alarmed often stands upright with neck erect. In flight upperwing shows a small white wing-bar and white sides to lower rump and uppertail-coverts. VOICE: A reedy *churk* or *trrit*. HABITAT: Freshwater margins and damp grassland, less often on coastal wetlands. DISTRIBUTION: Vagrant, recorded from India and Sri Lanka.

7 SHARP-TAILED SANDPIPER (SIBERIAN PECTORAL SANDPIPER) *Calidris acuminata* 17–21cm FIELD NOTES: Usually very confiding. In flight looks very much like Pectoral Sandpiper, if seen very well white rump and uppertail-coverts show dark shaft streaks. Juvenile similar to breeding adult, but fringes of upperparts brighter rufous and breast washed rufous-buff. VOICE: A soft *wheep*, *pleep* or *trrt*, also a twittering *prrt-wheep-wheep*. HABITAT: Freshwater and coastal wetlands. DISTRIBUTION: Vagrant, recorded from Pakistan and Sri Lanka.

8 CURLEW SANDPIPER *Calidris ferruginea* 18–23cm FIELD NOTES: Regularly wades, often up to belly, in shallow water. In flight upperwing has a prominent white wing-bar and a white lower rump and uppertail-coverts. Juvenile similar to non-breeding adult but with buff fringes on upperparts and a buffish wash to breast and face. VOICE: A rippling chirrup. HABITAT: Coastal mudflats, lagoons, estuaries and saltmarshes, less often on inland lakes and marshes. DISTRIBUTION: Winter visitor.

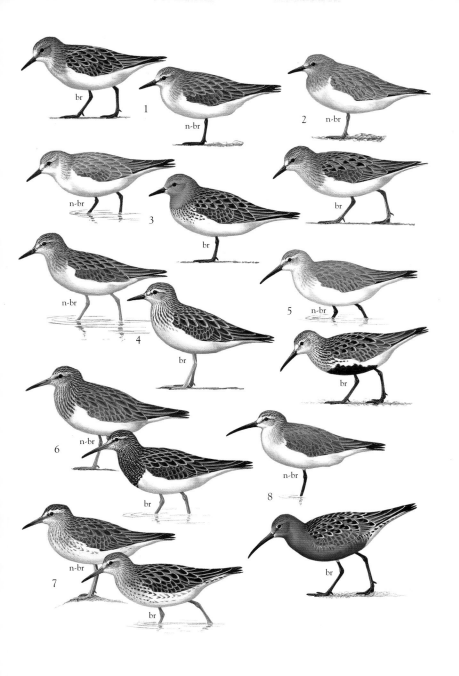

42 RUFF, TURNSTONE, PHALAROPES, PAINTED-SNIPE, JACANAS

1 RUFF (REEVE: female) *Philomachus pugnax* 26–32cm FIELD NOTES: Breeding males unmistakable, very variable. In moult males have a non-breeding type plumage splattered with dark blotches on the breast. In flight upperwing shows a narrow white wing-bar and prominent white sides to uppertail-coverts. When foraging may wade up to belly, has been known to swim and peck surface like a phalarope. VOICE: Normally silent but a shrill *hoo-ee* may be given by migrating flocks. HABITAT: Lake, pool and river margins, marshes and wet grassland, also coastal mudflats. DISTRIBUTION: Widespread winter visitor and passage migrant.

2 TURNSTONE (RUDDY TURNSTONE) *Arenaria interpres* 21–26cm FIELD NOTES: Typically forages by flicking over small stones, shells or seaweed in search of invertebrates. In flight upperwing shows white wing-bar and a white triangle on inner wing-coverts; centre of back and lower rump white, split by a black band on upper rump. VOICE: A rapid, staccato *trik-tuk-tuk-tuk*, *tuk-e-tuk* or *chit-uk*, and when alarmed a sharp *chick-ik*, *kuu* or *teu*. HABITAT: Mainly coastal, frequenting stony, rocky and sandy shores; also mudflats. DISTRIBUTION: Widespread winter visitor.

3 GREY PHALAROPE (RED PHALAROPE) *Phalaropus fulicarius* 20–22cm FIELD NOTES: Regularly forages by swimming. Short thick bill with yellowish base. In flight upperwing shows a wide white wing-bar. VOICE: In flight utters a sharp *pik*. HABITAT: On migration sometimes found on coastal pools or lakes, otherwise strictly pelagic. DISTRIBUTION: Vagrant, recorded from India and Pakistan.

4 RED-NECKED PHALAROPE (NORTHERN PHALAROPE) *Phalaropus lobatus* 18–19cm FIELD NOTES: Regularly forages by swimming. Short thin black bill. In flight upperwing shows a white wing-bar. Juvenile has upperparts much like breeding male, head pattern like non-breeding adult with a pink-buff tinge, neck and breast also tinged pink-buff. VOICE: In flight gives a short *twick*, *clip* or *kip*. HABITAT: On migration occurs on lakes, pools and coastal waters. Usually winters at sea. DISTRIBUTION: Winter visitor, mainly to offshore waters.

5 PAINTED-SNIPE (GREATER PAINTED-SNIPE) *Rostratula benghalensis* 23–28cm FIELD NOTES: Mainly crepuscular, secretive. Flies with legs dangling. VOICE: In display female utters a soft *koh koh koh*, likened to blowing across the top of an empty bottle, also various hisses and growls and a sharp *kek* when flushed. HABITAT: Marshes, flooded fields and mangroves. DISTRIBUTION: Widespread resident.

6 BRONZE-WINGED JACANA *Metopidius indicus* 28–31cm FIELD NOTES: Forages by walking on floating vegetation or wading in shallow water. Juvenile brown above, whitish below with pinkish-buff wash on neck and breast, russet cap, and dark line through eye split in front of eye by a short white supercilium, lores blackish. VOICE: A harsh grunt. When alarmed utters a wheezy, piping *seek-seek-seek*. HABITAT: Lakes and ponds with floating and emergent vegetation. DISTRIBUTION: Widespread resident.

7 PHEASANT-TAILED JACANA (WATER-PHEASANT) *Hydrophasianus chirurgus* 31–58cm FIELD NOTES: Often gregarious. Forages by walking on floating vegetation, wading in shallow water or swimming. In flight shows strikingly white wings. Juvenile similar to non-breeding adult, but feathers of upperparts have pale fringes and black necklace is less distinct. VOICE: In breeding season has a far-carrying, mewing *me-e-ou* or *me-onp*. Post-breeding flocks utter a nasal *tewn*. HABITAT: Lakes and ponds with floating and emergent vegetation. DISTRIBUTION: Widespread resident.

breeding varieties

1

1

♂

br

1

♂

n-br

2

♀

br

n-br

♀

br

1

♀

br

3

n-br

♀

br

4

n-br

♂

br

♂

br

5

♂

♀

6

7

br

n-br

43 STONE-CURLEWS, IBISBILL, CRAB-PLOVER, STILT, AVOCET, OYSTERCATCHER

1 STONE-CURLEW (EUROPEAN STONE-CURLEW, THICK-KNEE) *Burhinus oedicnemus indicus* 36–39cm FIELD NOTES: Timid. Mainly crepuscular, during the day often stands motionless in the shade, when can be hard to see against scrub or dry stony background. Greyer, larger race *B. o. harterti* (1b) occurs in the NW of the region. *B. o. indicus* is sometimes considered to be a full species, when known as Indian Thick-knee or Indian Stone-curlew. VOICE: A *cur-lee* or *churrreee*, usually given at night. HABITAT: Open stony or scrubby desert; also semi-desert and riverside scrub. DISTRIBUTION: Widespread resident.

2 BEACH THICK-KNEE (BEACH STONE-CURLEW) *Esacus magnirostris* 53–57cm FIELD NOTES: Mainly crepuscular and nocturnal, spends the day resting in shade. In flight upperwing shows grey secondaries and secondary-coverts and white inner primaries, forewing and primaries black, the latter with large white subterminal spots on three outer feathers. VOICE: A harsh, wailing *wee-loo*. When alarmed utters a weak, yapping *quip*, *peep* or a rising *quip-ip-ip*. HABITAT: Coastal shores and coral reefs. DISTRIBUTION: Resident on the Andamans.

3 GREAT THICK-KNEE (GREAT STONE-PLOVER, GREAT STONE-CURLEW) *Esacus recurvirostris* 49–54cm FIELD NOTES: Shy, mainly nocturnal or crepuscular. In flight upperwing shows black secondaries, white inner primaries with a black subterminal black bar, outer primaries black with white subterminal spots on three outer feathers, centre of wing grey, with a black bar separating it from brownish-grey forewing. VOICE: A wailing, whistled *see* or *see-ey*, also a harsh *see-eek* when alarmed. HABITAT: Shingle and rocky riverbanks, rocky beaches, estuaries and reefs. DISTRIBUTION: Widespread resident.

4 IBISBILL *Ibidorhyncha struthersii* 39–41cm FIELD NOTES: Wary. Forages and probes among the stones of riverbeds, often wades up to belly. In flight shows white bar on primaries that forms into a patch on inner feathers. Juvenile lacks the black face and has a less defined dark breast-band. VOICE: A ringing *klew-klew* and a loud, rapid *tee-tee-tee-tee*. HABITAT: Fast-flowing mountain streams and rivers with shingle beds. DISTRIBUTION: Himalayan resident.

5 CRAB-PLOVER *Dromas ardeola* 38–41cm FIELD NOTES: Adult unmistakable, wary and crepuscular. Juveniles have a greyish mantle; can look gull-like, especially when they rest on their tarsi. VOICE: A barking *ka-how ka-how* and a *kwerk-kwerk-kwerk-kwerk*. In flight utters a nasal, yapping *kirruc*. At breeding sites utters various sharp whistles such as *kew-ki-ki* and *ki-tewk*. HABITAT: Sandy coasts, estuaries, lagoons, exposed coral reefs and mudflats. DISTRIBUTION: Breeds in Sri Lanka and the Maldives, winter visitor elsewhere.

6 BLACK-WINGED STILT *Himantopus himantopus* 35–40cm FIELD NOTES: Gregarious. Crown and hind-neck pattern varies from white to slaty-grey. Juvenile has browner upperparts with buff fringes. VOICE: A sharp *kek*, a high-pitched *kikikikik* and a yelping *kee-ack*. HABITAT: Various wetlands including saltmarshes, saltpans, lakes and marshes. DISTRIBUTION: Resident in NW and Sri Lanka, winter visitor elsewhere.

7 AVOCET (PIED AVOCET) *Recurvirostra avosetta* 42–45cm FIELD NOTES: Unmistakable. Gregarious. Readily swims, upending to feed like a dabbling duck. Juvenile duller with white upperparts smudged with grey. VOICE: A melodious *kluit-kluit-kluit*. When alarmed utters a harsh *kloo-eet* or *krrree-yu*. HABITAT: Shallow saline or brackish lakes, lagoons, saltpans and estuaries. DISTRIBUTION: Breeds in NW, otherwise widespread winter visitor or passage migrant.

8 OYSTERCATCHER (EURASIAN OYSTERCATCHER) *Haematopus ostralegus* 40–46cm FIELD NOTES: In flight shows a broad white wing-bar on upperwing, white rump and black tail. Juvenile upperparts browner with pale fringes. VOICE: A sharp *kleep* or *kle-eap* and a quiet *weep*. HABITAT: Mainly coastal areas, but also frequents inland grassland and lakesides. DISTRIBUTION: Winter visitor.

44 PLOVERS

1 RINGED PLOVER (COMMON or GREAT RINGED PLOVER) *Charadrius hiaticula* 18–20cm FIELD NOTES: In flight upperwing shows a bold white wing-bar. Juvenile like dull non-breeding adult, upperparts with pale fringes. VOICE: A mellow, rising *too-lee* and a soft *too-weep* when alarmed. HABITAT: The shores of coasts, lakes and rivers. DISTRIBUTION: Widespread post-breeding visitor.

2 LITTLE RINGED PLOVER *Charadrius dubius* 14–17cm FIELD NOTES: Yellowish base to lower mandible, yellow eye-ring. In flight upperwing shows an inconspicuous white wing-bar. VOICE: A descending *pee-oo*. When alarmed utters a *pip-pip-pip*. HABITAT: Margins of lakes and rivers, marshes, mudflats and estuaries. DISTRIBUTION: Widespread resident.

3 KENTISH PLOVER *Charadrius alexandrinus* 15–17cm FIELD NOTES: Incomplete black breast-band. In flight upperwing has a white wing-bar; white sides to lower rump and tail. VOICE: A soft, clear *pit* or *pit-pit-pit-pit*. When alarmed gives a hard *prrr*, *too-eet* or *pweep*. HABITAT: Sandy shores of coasts, lakes, lagoons and saltpans. DISTRIBUTION: Breeds locally in Sri Lanka, India and Pakistan, more widespread post breeding.

4 LONG-BILLED PLOVER (LONG-BILLED RINGED PLOVER) *Charadrius placidus* 19–21cm FIELD NOTES: Yellowish base to lower mandible, dark eye-ring. In flight upperwing shows an inconspicuous white wing-bar. VOICE: A clear *pewee*, also a pleasant *tudulu*. HABITAT: Stony margins of lakes and rivers, post breeding also on paddyfields and coastal mudflats. DISTRIBUTION: Local breeder in the NW (Arunchal Pradesh), more widespread after breeding.

5 CASPIAN PLOVER (LESSER ORIENTAL PLOVER) *Charadrius asiaticus* 18–20cm FIELD NOTES: In flight upperwing shows a narrow white wing-bar, more conspicuous at the base of the primaries; toes project beyond tail. VOICE: A loud, sharp *tup*, *tyup* or *chep*. Also utters a soft, piping *tik tik tik tik*. HABITAT: Coastal mudflats. DISTRIBUTION: Post-breeding visitor to the Maldives, Sri Lanka and W coast of India.

6 LESSER SAND PLOVER (MONGOLIAN SAND PLOVER) *Charadrius mongolus* 19–21cm FIELD NOTES: Usually shows a narrow white bar on upperwing. Race *C. m. atrifrons* (6b) breeds in the Himalayas. VOICE: A short *drrit*, also a sharp *chitik* or *chiktik*. HABITAT: Breeds on mountain steppes; after breeding, occurs mainly on coasts. DISTRIBUTION: Breeds in N Himalayas, widespread on coasts post breeding.

7 GREATER SAND PLOVER (LARGE SAND PLOVER, GEOFFROY'S PLOVER) *Charadrius leschenaultii* 22–25cm FIELD NOTES: In flight upperwing shows a prominent white wing-bar; toes project beyond tail. VOICE: A soft *trrri*, also a melodious *pipruirr*. HABITAT: Coastal wetlands. DISTRIBUTION: Winter visitor.

8 ORIENTAL PLOVER (ORIENTAL DOTTEREL, EASTERN SAND PLOVER) *Charadrius veredus* 22–25cm FIELD NOTES: Powerful flight, often with erratic turns. In flight toes project beyond tail and upperwing uniform brown, although juvenile may show a slight white wing-bar. VOICE: Has trilling calls and a short, piping *klink*. In flight gives a sharp, whistled *chip-chip-chip*. HABITAT: Dry grasslands, dry areas near wetlands, also coastal mudflats and estuaries. DISTRIBUTION: Vagrant, recorded from India and Sri Lanka.

9 BLACK-FRONTED DOTTEREL (BLACK-FRONTED PLOVER) *Elseyornis melanops* 16–18cm FIELD NOTES: In flight shows pale grey central coverts contrasting with black primaries and darker grey secondaries and forewing. Juvenile has browner upperparts and lacks a complete breast-band. VOICE: A repeated, high-pitched, explosive *dip*, also a soft *tink-tink* and various clicking, buzzing and churring calls. HABITAT: Margins of fresh or brackish water. DISTRIBUTION: Vagrant in India, although record disputed.

45 PLOVERS

1 DOTTEREL (EURASIAN or MOUNTAIN DOTTEREL) *Charadrius morinellus* 20–24cm FIELD NOTES: In flight outer primary has a white shaft, which can be conspicuous. Juvenile like non-breeding adult but feather fringes brighter buff. VOICE: A soft *pweet-pweet-pweet* and a *kwip-kwip*. When taking flight may give a trilling *skeer*. HABITAT: Hills, mountains and farmland. DISTRIBUTION: Vagrant, recorded from Pakistan.

2 RIVER LAPWING (ASIAN SPUR-WINGED PLOVER) *Vanellus duvaucelii* 29–32cm FIELD NOTES: Occurs singly, in pairs or in small groups. In flight upperwing shows a broad white wing-bar contrasting with black flight feathers and grey-brown forewing; rump white and tail black. VOICE: A sharp *tip-tip* and a longer *dip-dip-to-weet*. HABITAT: Sand and shingle areas by rivers, also estuaries. DISTRIBUTION: Widespread in the NC and NE of the region.

3 LAPWING (NORTHERN LAPWING, GREEN PLOVER, PEEWIT) *Vanellus vanellus* 28–31cm FIELD NOTES: Generally encountered in pairs or small flocks. In flight from above looks black apart from white on lower rump and tips of outer primaries. Juvenile very like adult non-breeding, but with more prominent pale fringes on upperparts. VOICE: A plaintive *wee-ip* or *pee-wit*. HABITAT: Grasslands, margins of lakes and rivers, also on estuaries. DISTRIBUTION: Widespread winter visitor, mainly to the N.

4 YELLOW-WATTLED LAPWING *Vanellus malabaricus* 26–28cm FIELD NOTES: Generally occurs in pairs but may form small flocks after breeding. In flight upperwing shows a prominent white bar on secondary-coverts, contrasting with black flight feathers and brown forewing; lower rump white, tail black with white sides. Juvenile like adult, but brown crown and upperparts with pale fringes. VOICE: A plaintive *tchee-it*. When alarmed gives a *chit-oo-eet* or a sharp *whit-whit-whit*. HABITAT: Dry grasslands, open dry country, also the fringes of wetlands. DISTRIBUTION: Widespread resident, mainly India.

5 SOCIABLE PLOVER (SOCIABLE LAPWING) *Vanellus gregarius* 27–30cm FIELD NOTES: Generally occurs in small flocks. In flight upperwing secondaries and secondary-coverts white, primaries and primary-coverts black, rest of wing grey-brown, lower rump white, tail black with white sides. VOICE: A harsh *kretch* or chattering *kretch-etch-etch*. HABITAT: Dry grassland, stubble fields and scrub-desert. DISTRIBUTION: Widespread winter visitor, mainly to the W of the region.

6 GREY-HEADED LAPWING *Vanellus cinereus* 34–37cm FIELD NOTES: Normally occurs in small flocks. Flight pattern very similar to the smaller Sociable Plover. Non-breeding birds have whitish throat, neck tinged brown, black breast-band partly obscured. VOICE: A plaintive *chee-it*. When disturbed gives a rasping *cha-ha-eet* or a sharp *pink*. HABITAT: Swampy grasslands, marshland and river margins. DISTRIBUTION: Winter visitor, mainly to the NE.

7 RED-WATTLED LAPWING (RED-WATTLED PLOVER) *Vanellus indicus* 32–35cm FIELD NOTES: Occurs in pairs or small parties. In flight upperwing appears dark with a white bar on secondary-coverts; rump white, tail black. Race *V. i. atronuchalis* (7b) occurs in the NE of the region. VOICE: A shrill *did-he-do-it* or a *kree-dee-der*. When alarmed gives a sharp *trint trint trint trint*. HABITAT: Open areas such as farmland and grassland with nearby water. DISTRIBUTION: Widespread resident.

8 WHITE-TAILED PLOVER (WHITE-TAILED LAPWING) *Vanellus leucurus* 26–29cm FIELD NOTES: Usually occurs in small flocks. In flight upperwing shows brown forewing and black flight feathers split by a broad white wing-bar; tail white. VOICE: A high-pitched *pet-ee-wit pet-ee-wit* and a plaintive *pee-wick*. HABITAT: Marshes, damp grasslands and the shallows of lakes, pools and rivers. DISTRIBUTION: Breeds in Baluchistan, winters mainly in the NW of the region.

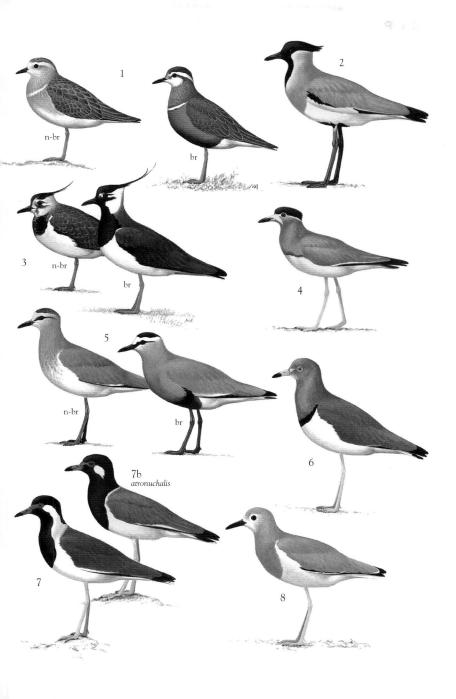

46 PLOVERS, COURSERS, PRATINCOLES

1 GOLDEN PLOVER (EUROPEAN GOLDEN PLOVER) *Pluvialis apricaria* 26–29cm
FIELD NOTES: At rest wing-tips slightly projecting or level with tail. Underwing-coverts
white. VOICE: A mellow *too-ee* or *tloo*. HABITAT: Short grassland, fields, saltmarsh and coastal
mudflats. DISTRIBUTION: Vagrant, recorded from Pakistan and India.

2 PACIFIC GOLDEN PLOVER (ASIAN or EASTERN GOLDEN PLOVER) *Pluvialis
fulva* 23–26cm FIELD NOTES: Gregarious. At rest wing-tips project beyond tail. Longer
tertials and longer legs than Golden Plover. Underwing-coverts dusky grey. VOICE: A rapid
chu-wit and drawn-out *klu-ee*. HABITAT: Coastal lagoons, mudflats, lake and river margins,
also grassland and fields. DISTRIBUTION: Widespread winter visitor.

3 GREY PLOVER (BLACK-BELLIED PLOVER) *Pluvialis squatarola* 27–30cm FIELD
NOTES: Occurs in pairs or small parties. In flight from above shows a white lower rump and
a white wing-bar. Underwing white with prominent black axillaries. VOICE: A mournful
tlee-oo-ee. HABITAT: Mainly coastal mudflats and beaches. DISTRIBUTION: Widespread winter
visitor, mainly to coasts.

4 JERDON'S COURSER (DOUBLE-BANDED COURSER) *Rhinoptilus bitorquatus*
27cm FIELD NOTES: Rare. Nocturnal, usually found in pairs or small parties. In flight
upperwing dark with a white subterminal patch on the outer primaries and a white mid-
wing-bar; rump white, tail black. VOICE: A staccato *twick-too twick-too twick-too* or *yak-way
yak-wak yak-wak*. HABITAT: Scrub jungle with bare patches. DISTRIBUTION: Local resident in
Andhra Pradesh.

5 CREAM-COLOURED COURSER (DESERT COURSER) *Cursorius cursor* 19–22cm
FIELD NOTES: Usually in pairs or small parties that forage using rapid runs interspersed
with pauses to pick up prey. In flight underwing mainly black; above buffy body and wings
contrast with black primaries. VOICE: A harsh *praak-praak*. During display gives a piping *quit
quit quit* or *quit-quit-whow*. HABITAT: Arid open desert or semi-desert, gravel plains, open
fields and saltflats. DISTRIBUTION: Resident and winter visitor in the NW of the region.

6 INDIAN COURSER *Cursorius coromandelicus* 23cm FIELD NOTES: Foraging actions as
Cream-coloured Courser. In flight above shows black primaries and inner secondaries that
contrast with the rest of the wing and body; tail grey-brown, lower rump white. VOICE: A low
gwut or *wut*. HABITAT: Less arid areas than Cream-coloured Courser. Occurs on dry fields,
stony plains and dry riverbeds. DISTRIBUTION: Widespread resident.

7 COLLARED PRATINCOLE (COMMON or RED-WINGED PRATINCOLE)
Glareola pratincola 23–26cm FIELD NOTES: Gregarious. In flight shows white trailing edge to
secondaries, white rump and deeply forked tail. Underwing shows chestnut coverts. VOICE: A
harsh *kik* or *kirrik*, also a rolling *kikik-krrik-irrik*. HABITAT: Open dry areas, areas surrounding
lakes, swamps and on coastal creeks. DISTRIBUTION: Breeds in Pakistan. Winter visitor to
India and Sri Lanka.

**8 ORIENTAL PRATINCOLE (EASTERN, EASTERN COLLARED or LARGE
INDIAN PRATINCOLE)** *Glareola maldivarum* 23–24cm FIELD NOTES: Gregarious. In
flight from above shows all-dark wings, white rump and a forked tail. Underwing-coverts
are chestnut. VOICE: A sharp *kyik*, *chik-chik* or *chet*; also a rising *trooeet* and a *ter-ack*.
HABITAT: Bare flats or fields, often near wetlands. DISTRIBUTION: Widespread resident.

9 SMALL PRATINCOLE (LITTLE, SMALL INDIAN or MILKY PRATINCOLE)
Glareola lactea 17cm FIELD NOTES: Gregarious. In flight from below shows mainly white
secondaries and inner primaries, the former with a black trailing edge; upperwing similar but
all primaries black. Tail square-ended. VOICE: A *tuck-tuck-tuck*. In flight utters a high-pitched,
rolling *prrip* or *tiririt*. HABITAT: Margins of large rivers and lakes. DISTRIBUTION: Widespread
resident.

47 SKUAS

1 POMARINE SKUA (POMARINE JAEGER) *Stercorarius pomarinus* 46–51cm FIELD NOTES: In flight wings show distinct white flash at base of primaries. The bulkiest of all the 'smaller' skuas in flight. Aggressively pursues seabirds in a bid to steal food, and has been recorded as going as far as killing the victim. Non-breeding plumage similar to breeding but with pale scalloping. Juvenile has upperparts variable from mid-brown to dark brown, barred paler; underparts paler brown, barred dark. VOICE: Generally silent. HABITAT: Coastal waters. DISTRIBUTION: Winter visitor to Pakistan, India and Sri Lanka.

2 ARCTIC SKUA (PARASITIC JAEGER) *Stercorarius parasiticus* 41–46cm FIELD NOTES: In flight wings show distinct white flash at base of primaries. Aerobatically chases and harries seabirds in an attempt to make them disgorge food. Non-breeding plumage as breeding but with pale scalloping. Juvenile very variable, from all dark brown to brown above with paler brown underparts and a whitish head; whichever form, all dark areas have pale barring. Shorter central tail projection than Pomarine or Long-tailed Skua. VOICE: Generally silent In flight may utter a nasal *gi-ooo*. HABITAT: Coastal waters. DISTRIBUTION: Winter visitor, mainly to Pakistan.

3 LONG-TAILED SKUA (LONG-TAILED JAEGER) *Stercorarius longicaudus* 48–53cm FIELD NOTES: In flight shows no, or indistinct, white flash at base of primaries. In flight often gives the impression of being heavy-chested. Less piratical than other skuas, and when indulging tends to harass terns. Juvenile very variable; similar in plumage to juvenile Arctic Skua, best told by lack of extensive white flash at base of primaries and general lighter structure. VOICE: Generally silent. HABITAT: Coastal waters. DISTRIBUTION: Vagrant, recorded from the Maldives and Sri Lanka.

4 SOUTHERN SKUA (BROWN SKUA) *Stercorarius antarcticus* 61–66cm FIELD NOTES: In flight shows prominent white flash at base of primaries. Very aggressive to other seabirds, recorded both robbing victims of their food and killing them. Juvenile has upperparts grey-brown with pale rufous spots and fringes; underparts uniform rufous, head grey-brown. VOICE: Generally silent. HABITAT: Coastal waters. DISTRIBUTION: Non-breeding visitor to India, Sri Lanka and the Maldives.

5 SOUTH POLAR SKUA (MACCORMICK'S SKUA) *Stercorarius maccormicki* 50–55cm FIELD NOTES: In flight shows prominent white flash at base of primaries. Various morphs, grading from pale to dark, all tend to lack any rufous in plumage. Juvenile similar in plumage to the respective adult morphs but with pale fringes to upperparts, bill blue with a blackish tip. VOICE: Generally silent away from breeding sites. HABITAT: Coastal waters. DISTRIBUTION: Vagrant, recorded from India, Sri Lanka and the Maldives.

48 GULLS

Given the complex plumage of young gulls (often a four-year process to get from the brown of juveniles to the grey of adults) and the lack of space, juvenile/immature plumages are not described here, and the reader should refer to books that cover this area more fully.

1 SOOTY GULL (HEMPRICH'S or ADEN GULL) *Ichthyaetus hemprichii* 43–48cm FIELD NOTES: Upperwing and underwing dark with white trailing edge. VOICE: A mewing *kaarr*, *keee-aaar*, a laughing *veeeaah ve vah veeeaah* and a high-pitched *kee-kee-kee*. HABITAT: Coasts, including harbours and ports. DISTRIBUTION: Breeds in Pakistan, winter visitor elsewhere.

2 GREAT BLACK-HEADED GULL (PALLAS'S GULL) *Ichthyaetus ichthyaetus* 57–61cm FIELD NOTES: Upperwing shows a narrow black subterminal band on white outer primaries. VOICE: A low *kyow-kyow* and a nasal *kraagh*. HABITAT: Coasts, lakes and large rivers. DISTRIBUTION: Widespread winter visitor.

3 COMMON GULL (MEW GULL) *Larus canus* 40–46cm FIELD NOTES: Upperwing shows black outer primaries with prominent white subterminal 'mirrors' on two outermost feathers. VOICE: A high-pitched laughing *ke ke ke kleeh-a...kleeeh-a...kay-a-kay-a-kay-a-kay-a ke ke*, also a yelping *keea keea*. HABITAT: Coasts, lakes and large rivers. DISTRIBUTION: Rare visitor, mainly to the N of the region.

4 CASPIAN GULL *Larus cachinnans* 52–58cm FIELD NOTES: Upperwing shows black outer primaries with large white tip to outer feather and white 'mirror' on next feather. All flight feathers tipped white. VOICE: A deep, nasal *keeah-keeah-keeah-keeah-kau-kau...* HABITAT: Coasts and inland waters. DISTRIBUTION: Winter visitor? It is possible that all records are unreliable, and that they refer to the Steppe Gull *L. heuglini barabensis*.

5 HEUGLIN'S GULL *Larus heuglini* 58–65cm FIELD NOTES: Upperwing has a white trailing edge; black outer primaries have a white subterminal 'mirror' on two outermost feathers. Slightly paler race *L. h. barabensis* (Steppe Gull) (5b) is a passage migrant and winter visitor; it is sometimes considered a full species. VOICE: A deep nasal *gagaga*. HABITAT: Coasts and inland waters. DISTRIBUTION: Winter visitor.

6 SLENDER-BILLED GULL *Chroicocephalus genei* 42–44cm FIELD NOTES: Upperwing pale grey, outer primaries white, tipped black; underwing pale grey, inner primaries darker grey, outer primaries white, tipped black. VOICE: A harsh rolling *krerr*, other notes like Black-headed Gull but lower-pitched. HABITAT: Saltwater and freshwater lakes, coasts. DISTRIBUTION: Resident in Pakistan, winter visitor elsewhere.

7 BROWN-HEADED GULL (INDIAN BLACK-HEADED GULL) *Chroicocephalus brunnicephalus* 41–45cm FIELD NOTES: Outer primaries of upperwing white with broad black tips broken by subterminal 'mirrors' on outermost feathers, underwing pattern similar. VOICE: A harsh *gek gek* or *grarhh*, a wailing *ko-yek ko-yek* and a raucous *kreeak*. HABITAT: Inland lakes and rivers, coastal waters. DISTRIBUTION: Breeds in Ladakh, winter visitor elsewhere.

8 BLACK-HEADED GULL (COMMON BLACK-HEADED GULL) *Chroicocephalus ridibundus* 37–43cm FIELD NOTES: Upperwing pale grey, outer primaries white, tipped black; underwing pale grey, inner primaries darker grey, outer primaries white, tipped black. VOICE: A high-pitched *karr* or *krreearr* and a sharp *kek-kek*. HABITAT: Coasts, lakes and rivers. DISTRIBUTION: Widespread winter visitor.

9 LITTLE GULL *Hydrocoloeus minutus* 25–30cm FIELD NOTES: Underwing dark grey, upperwing silver-grey. VOICE: A short nasal *keck* or *keck-keck-keck*. HABITAT: Coasts or nearby lagoons. DISTRIBUTION: Vagrant, recorded in India and Pakistan.

10 KITTIWAKE (BLACK-LEGGED KITTIWAKE) *Rissa tridactyla* 38–40cm FIELD NOTES: Outer primaries on upperwing and underwing are tipped black. Slightly forked tail. VOICE: A nasal wailing *kitt-i-waak kitt-i-waak*. HABITAT: Maritime. DISTRIBUTION: Vagrant, recorded in India.

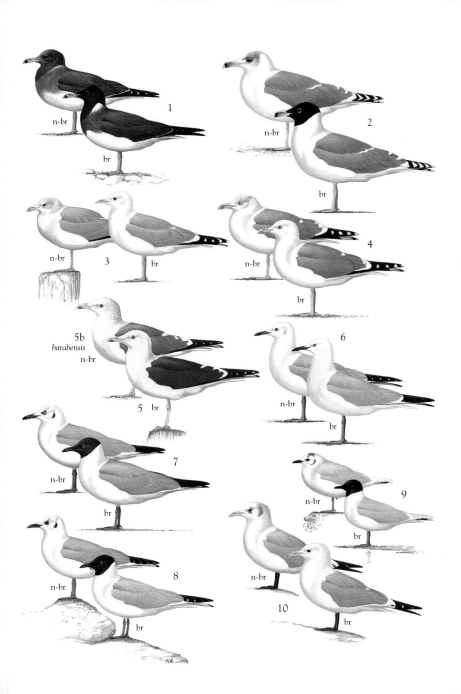

49 TERNS

1 CASPIAN TERN *Hydroprogne caspia* 47–54cm FIELD NOTES: Feeds mainly by hovering then plunge-diving, also picks from the surface of the water and sometimes harasses food from other terns and gulls. Upperwing shows grey outer primaries with darker tips, underwing shows dark outer primaries. Tail has shallow fork. VOICE: A loud, croaking *kraah, krah-krah* or *kree-ahk*. HABITAT: Coastal mudflats and creeks, saltpans and lagoons, also inland lakes, rivers and marshes. DISTRIBUTION: Breeds in Pakistan, Gujarat and Sri Lanka, winter visitor elsewhere.

2 LITTLE TERN *Sternula albifrons* 22–28cm FIELD NOTES: Very active forager, feeds by plunge-diving, preceded by prolonged hovering. Upperwing has outer pair of primaries blackish, tail deeply forked. Race *S. a. sinensis* (not shown), which occurs in Sri Lanka and parts of the W, lacks the dark outer primaries, is slightly paler grey and has longer outer tail feathers. VOICE: A rapid *kirrikikki kirrikiki*, a sharp *kik-kik* and a rasping *zr-e-e-e-p*. HABITAT: Sand bars and shingle banks on lakes, rivers and coasts. DISTRIBUTION: Resident, intercontinental migrant, more widespread post breeding.

3 SAUNDERS'S TERN (BLACK-SHAFTED TERN) *Sternula saundersi* 20–28cm FIELD NOTES: Actions and habits as Little Tern. Compared to Little Tern upperwing has three outer primaries blackish, has slightly darker grey upperparts and lacks the short white supercilium. VOICE: Like Little Tern, but a little less chattering. HABITAT: Coastal waters. DISTRIBUTION: Breeds in the NW, post-breeding visitor elsewhere.

4 GULL-BILLED TERN *Gelochelidon nilotica* 33–43cm FIELD NOTES: Feeds by hawking insects or dipping to pick prey from surface of water or ground. Flight gull-like with outer to mid primaries showing a dark grey trailing edge; rump and tail pale grey concolorous with upperparts. VOICE: A nasal *kay-did, kay-tih-did, gur-WICK, ger-erk* or *kay-vek*, also a metallic *kak-kak* and when alarmed a *kvay-kvay*. HABITAT: Fresh and brackish lakes, saltmarsh, rivers and coasts. DISTRIBUTION: Breeds in Pakistan and N India, widespread post-breeding visitor.

5 SANDWICH TERN *Thalasseus sandvicensis* 36–41cm FIELD NOTES: Feeds mainly by plunge-diving, often from a considerable height, also picks from surface of water or mud. Inner webs of outer primaries form an indistinct silver-grey wedge on upperwing; outer primaries on underwing show dusky tips. Tail deeply forked. VOICE: A grating *kikirrruk* or *kerRICK*, also a short *krik* or *krik krik*. HABITAT: Coastal waters. DISTRIBUTION: Mainly winter visitor to W coasts.

6 CRESTED TERN (GREATER CRESTED or SWIFT TERN) *Thalasseus bergii* 43–53cm FIELD NOTES: Feeds mainly by plunge-diving, but also picks from surface of water. Underwing shows dark greyish tips to outer primaries. Rump and tail pale grey, concolorous with upperparts, tail deeply forked. VOICE: A grating *krrik* or *kee-rit*, also a high-pitched *kree-kree*. HABITAT: Coastal waters. DISTRIBUTION: Resident.

7 LESSER CRESTED TERN *Thalasseus bengalensis* 36–41cm FIELD NOTES: Feeds mainly by hovering then plunge-diving. Wing pattern similar to Sandwich Tern. Rump and tail pale grey, the latter deeply forked. VOICE: A harsh *krrik-kirrik* or *kerrick*. HABITAT: Coastal waters. DISTRIBUTION: Resident.

8 RIVER TERN (INDIAN RIVER TERN) *Sterna aurantia* 38–46cm FIELD NOTES: Usually feeds by plunge-diving. In flight whitish upperwing-primaries form a conspicuous flash on outer wing. Tail deeply forked with long outer tail feathers. VOICE: In flight utters a shrill, staccato *kiuk-kiuk*. HABITAT: Large inland waters, rare on coasts. DISTRIBUTION: Widespread resident.

50 TERNS

1 BLACK-BELLIED TERN *Sterna acuticauda* 33cm FIELD NOTES: Feeds by plunge-diving and also by surface-picking from water or land. On upperwing whitish primaries contrast with grey of the rest of the wing; tail deeply forked with long outer feathers, the latter shorter in non-breeding plumage. VOICE: A clear, piping *peuo*. Also recorded is a shrill *krek-krek*. HABITAT: Large rivers and lakes. DISTRIBUTION: Widespread resident.

2 BLACK-NAPED TERN *Sterna sumatrana* 34–35cm FIELD NOTES: Feeds mainly by plunge-diving, but also by skimming low over water picking food from the surface. Outer web of outermost primary blackish, tail deeply forked with long outer tail feathers. VOICE: A sharp *tsii-chee-chi-chip* and a *chit-chit-chitrer* uttered when excited or alarmed. HABITAT: Breeds on small offshore islands, feeds in nearby coastal bays, lagoons and inlets. DISTRIBUTION: Resident on the Maldives, Andamans and Nicobars.

3 WHITE-CHEEKED TERN *Sterna repressa* 32–34cm FIELD NOTES: Feeds by plunge-diving and also by dipping to pick food from water surface. Rump and tail grey, concolorous with upperparts, tail deeply forked with long outer tail feathers. VOICE: A short *kep* or *keep*, also a rasping *kee-arrh*. HABITAT: Breeds on offshore islands, occurs off coasts post breeding. DISTRIBUTION: Breeds off the Maharashtra coast; post breeding occurs off Pakistan, W India, Lakshadweep and the Maldives.

4 COMMON TERN *Sterna hirundo* 32–39cm FIELD NOTES: Feeds mainly by plunge-diving. In flight, from below, inner primaries appear translucent. Tail deeply forked with long outer tail feathers. Dark-billed race *S. h. longipennis* (4b) probably occurs in the region. VOICE: A rapid *kye-kye-kye-kye...*, also a *kirri-kirri-kirri*. When alarmed gives a screeching *kreeeearh* or *kreee-eer* and a sharp *kik*. HABITAT: Large inland waters and on coasts. DISTRIBUTION: Breeds in Ladakh, otherwise a widespread winter visitor.

5 ARCTIC TERN *Sterna paradisaea* 33–38cm FIELD NOTES: Feeds by plunge-diving, also by picking off surface of water. In flight, from below, all primaries appear translucent. Tail deeply forked with long outer tail feathers. VOICE: A piping *pee-pee-pee* or similar, also a *prree-eh* and a rattling *kt-kt-kt-krr-kt*. When alarmed gives a high *kree-ah* or *kree-err*. HABITAT: Mainly coastal, but also on inland lakes. DISTRIBUTION: Vagrant, recorded from India.

6 ROSEATE TERN *Sterna dougallii* 33–38cm FIELD NOTES: Feeds mainly by plunge-diving, usually from a greater height than Common Tern, also by picking from the surface of the water. Tail deeply forked with very long outer tail feathers. VOICE: A rasping *kraak* or *zraaach*, also a short, soft *cher-vik*. HABITAT: Offshore islands and coastal waters. DISTRIBUTION: Resident and summer visitor, breeds on the Andamans, the Maldives, Sri Lanka and W India.

7 BRIDLED TERN (BROWN-WINGED TERN) *Onychoprion anaethetus* 34–36cm FIELD NOTES: Feeds by plunge-diving and by dipping to pick from water surface. Underwing mainly white with dusky tips to primaries and secondaries. Tail deeply forked with white outer tail feathers. VOICE: A yapping *wep-wep* or *wup-wup*. HABITAT: Rocky or sandy islands; after breeding mainly maritime. DISTRIBUTION: Breeds off the Maharashtra coast, Lakshadweep, the Andamans and the Maldives; more widespread after breeding.

8 SOOTY TERN (WIDEAWAKE TERN) *Onychoprion fuscatus* 36–45cm FIELD NOTES: Feeds mainly by dipping and picking from the surface of the water, occasionally plunge-dives. Underwing white with dusky primaries and tips to secondaries. Tail deeply forked with white outer tail feathers. VOICE: A distinctive *ker-wacki-wah, ker-wacki-wack* or *wide-awake*, also a short *kraark*. HABITAT: Rocky, stony or sandy islands; after breeding mainly maritime. DISTRIBUTION: Breeds off the Maharashtra coast, Lakshadweep and the Maldives; more widespread after breeding.

51 TERNS, SKIMMER

1 WHISKERED TERN *Chlidonias hybrida* 23–29cm FIELD NOTES: Buoyant foraging flight, regularly dipping to pick up prey from water surface, may also plunge-dive. Rump grey, paler in non-breeding plumage, tail shallowly forked. VOICE: A rasping *cherk*; also a *kek* or *kek-kek*. HABITAT: Vegetated lakes, pools and marshes; post breeding also occurs on coastal waters. DISTRIBUTION: Breeds in the N and NW, more widespread post breeding.

2 BLACK TERN *Chlidonias niger* 22–24cm FIELD NOTES: Foraging flight is buoyant with regular dips to pick up prey from water surface. Underwing pale grey. Tail and rump grey, concolorous with wings and mantle. Tail shallowly forked. In non-breeding plumage shows a black smudge at sides of breast. VOICE: A weak *kik* or *kik-kik*. Also a shrill, nasal *kyeh*, *kreek* or *ki ki ki* when alarmed. HABITAT: Vegetated lakes, ponds, marshes and estuaries. DISTRIBUTION: Vagrant, recorded in India.

3 WHITE-WINGED TERN (WHITE-WINGED BLACK TERN) *Chlidonias leucopterus* 23–27cm FIELD NOTES: Actions similar to Black Tern. Underwing-coverts black, rump white, tail pale grey and very shallowly forked. In non-breeding plumage underwing whitish with grey primaries and secondaries, and many birds have vestiges of black coverts in the form of dark lines or patches. VOICE: A harsh, high-pitched *kreek*, a soft *kek* and a rasping *kesch* or *chr-re re*. HABITAT: Vegetated lakes, pools, marshes, lagoons and estuaries. DISTRIBUTION: Widespread winter visitor.

4 BROWN NODDY (COMMON NODDY) *Anous stolidus* 38–45cm FIELD NOTES: Feeds by hovering and dipping to pick prey from water surface, may also foot-patter on water surface. Underwing-coverts slightly paler than flight feathers. Tail wedge-shaped, although can look forked during moult of central feathers. VOICE: A crow-like *kwok-kwok*, *karruuk* or *krao*. HABITAT: Breeds on islets; post breeding mainly maritime. DISTRIBUTION: Breeds in Lakshadweep and the Maldives; off other coasts post breeding.

5 BLACK NODDY (WHITE-CAPPED NODDY) *Anous minutus* 35–39cm FIELD NOTES: Feeds by hovering and dipping to pick prey from water surface, also foot-patters on the surface. Underwing-coverts brownish-black, concolorous with flight feathers. Tail wedge-shaped, may looked forked during moult of central feathers. VOICE: A distinctive *tik-tikoree* and a staccato rattle. HABITAT: Maritime. DISTRIBUTION: Vagrant, recorded from India.

6 LESSER NODDY *Anous tenuirostris* 30–34cm FIELD NOTES: Actions and habits similar to Black Noddy. Underwing-coverts dark brown, concolorous with flight feathers, tail wedge-shaped, and may appear forked when central tail feathers are moulted. VOICE: A purring *churr*, also rattling notes when alarmed. HABITAT: Breeds on islets, otherwise maritime. DISTRIBUTION: Breeds on the Maldives, visitor elsewhere.

7 WHITE TERN (FAIRY TERN) *Gygis alba* 25–30cm FIELD NOTES: Dives to the water surface to catch small fish as they leap out. Forked tail. Juvenile has tips of mantle and wing feathers tinged brownish. VOICE: A guttural *heech heech*. HABITAT: Breeds in bushes and trees on coral islands, otherwise maritime. DISTRIBUTION: Breeds on the Maldives.

8 INDIAN SKIMMER (SCISSORBILL) *Rhynchops albicollis* 38–43cm FIELD NOTES: Feeds by 'ploughing' water with lower mandible in skimming flight. In flight upperwing shows a broad white trailing edge, underwing white with dark greyish primaries. Tail forked, white with black central streak. VOICE: A nasal, yapping *kap kap kap*. HABITAT: Sandbanks on large rivers. DISTRIBUTION: Resident, mainly in the N of the region.

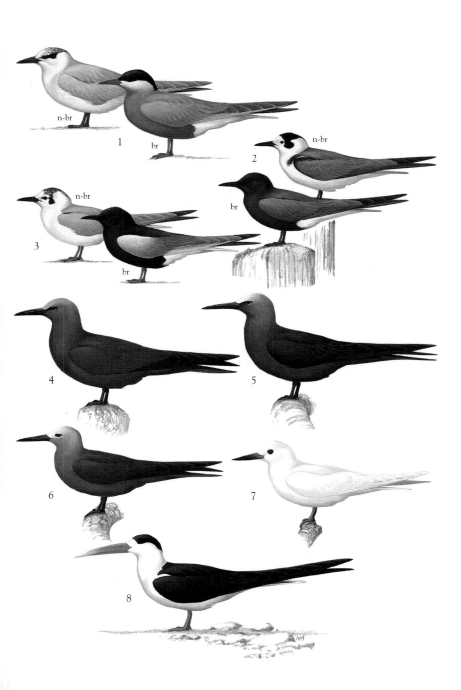

52 SANDGROUSE

1 PALLAS'S SANDGROUSE *Syrrhaptes paradoxus* 40cm FIELD NOTES: Usually flies to watering sites in the morning. In flight shows pale underwing with dark trailing edge on secondaries and long central tail feathers. VOICE: A low-pitched *cu-ruu cu-ruu cu-ou-ruu*, a rapid bubbling *kukerik-kukerik* and a sharp *tchep* or *kep*. HABITAT: Semi-desert with sparse, low vegetation, also fallow and abandoned fields. DISTRIBUTION: Vagrant, recorded in India.

2 TIBETAN SANDGROUSE *Syrrhaptes tibetanus* 40–48cm FIELD NOTES: Gregarious. Unlike most sandgrouse does not make regular watering flights. In flight upperwing-coverts sandy, contrasting with black flight feathers; underwing mainly black; long central tail feathers. VOICE: A deep, loud *guk-guk* or *caga-caga*, also a *koonk-koonk*. HABITAT: Stony or rocky areas of semi-desert or desert uplands. DISTRIBUTION: Resident in NW Nepal and Indian Himalayas.

3 PIN-TAILED SANDGROUSE *Pterocles alchata* 31–39cm FIELD NOTES: Often occurs in very large flocks. Flights to watering sites generally take place in the morning. In flight underwing-coverts white, contrasting with black flight feathers. Long central tail feathers. VOICE: A nasal *arrrh-arrrh*, a ringing *catar-catar* or *guettarr*, also a *ga-hg ga-hg arr* and an *arrk-arrk-arrk*. HABITAT: Arid and semi-arid plains with sparse vegetation. DISTRIBUTION: Winter visitor to the NW.

4 SPOTTED SANDGROUSE *Pterocles senegallus* 30–35cm FIELD NOTES: Watering flights, generally in small to large flocks, are usually made during the morning, although also in the evenings during hot weather. In flight upperwing pale sandy with dark trailing edge on primaries; underwing-coverts pale sandy-buff with dark-greyish flight feathers. VOICE: A musical *whitoo whitoo*, *wicko wicko* or *waqu waqu*. HABITAT: Desert and semi-desert with sparse vegetation. DISTRIBUTION: Breeds in Pakistan and Rajasthan, more widespread in the NW post breeding.

5 BLACK-BELLIED SANDGROUSE *Pterocles orientalis* 33–39cm FIELD NOTES: Occurs in small flocks, travels to watering sites mainly in the morning. In flight whitish underwing-coverts contrast with black flight feathers and black belly. VOICE: A bubbling *tchowrrr rerr-rerr* or *churrll-urrll-urrll*. HABITAT: Semi-desert with sparse, low vegetation and nearby dry, fallow cultivation. DISTRIBUTION: Breeds in Baluchistan, winter visitor elsewhere in the NW.

6 CHESTNUT-BELLIED SANDGROUSE *Pterocles exustus* 31–33cm FIELD NOTES: Most watering flights are made in the morning. In flight, from below, appears all dark due to black underwing and dark belly; also shows long central tail feathers. VOICE: In flight utters a chuckling *kt-arr kt-arr* or *whit kt-arr wit wit-ee-er kt-arr-arr*. HABITAT: Semi-desert with sparse vegetation, fallow fields and dry cultivations. DISTRIBUTION: Widespread resident.

7 LICHTENSTEIN'S SANDGROUSE *Pterocles lichtensteinii* 24–26cm FIELD NOTES: Mainly crepuscular or nocturnal and encountered in pairs or small groups. Underwing plain greyish-buff. VOICE: A whistling *qewheeto*, *chee-weeup* or *witch-ouuu*. HABITAT: Semi-desert, scrubby hillsides and dry rocky nullahs. DISTRIBUTION: Resident in SW Pakistan.

8 CROWNED SANDGROUSE (CORONETED SANDGROUSE) *Pterocles coronatus* 27–29cm FIELD NOTES: Watering flights usually made during the morning, in small flocks. In flight from above shows grey-buff coverts and black flight feathers; underwing has whitish coverts contrasting with dark flight feathers. VOICE: A rolling *ch-ga ch-gar-ra*. HABITAT: Arid desert areas. DISTRIBUTION: Resident, mainly in SW Pakistan.

9 PAINTED SANDGROUSE *Pterocles indicus* 28cm FIELD NOTES: Drinks after dusk, usually in pairs or small groups. In flight shows golden-yellow upperwing-coverts, underwing like Lichtenstein's Sandgrouse. VOICE: In flight utters a *chirik-chirik*. When disturbed gives a clucking *yek-yek-yek*. HABITAT: Low hills with scattered thorn-scrub, open grassy and rocky areas, firebreaks and burnt areas in forests. DISTRIBUTION: Widespread resident.

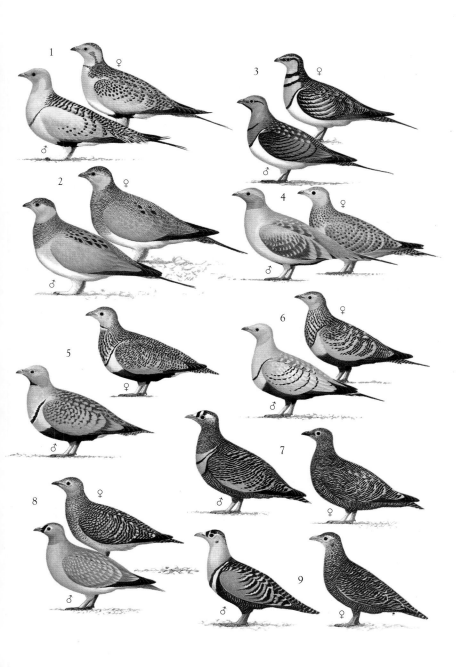

53 PIGEONS

1 ROCK DOVE (ROCK or COMMON PIGEON) *Columba livia* 31–34cm FIELD NOTES: The ancestor of feral town and city pigeons. Northern birds show a white or pale grey patch on back, southern birds are plain-backed. Tail grey with a black terminal band. Feral varieties (1b) can be very variable. VOICE: A moaning *gootr-goo gootr-goo*, *oorh* or *oh-oo-oor*, also a hurried *oo-roo-coo t coo* given during display. HABITAT: Cliffs and ruins; feral birds around human habitations, including towns and cities. DISTRIBUTION: Widespread resident.

2 HILL PIGEON (EASTERN ROCK PIGEON) *Columba rupestris* 33–35cm FIELD NOTES: Colonial, usually encountered in small flocks. Looks like a very pale version of Rock Dove with a whitish mid-band on tail. VOICE: A high-pitched, rolling *gut-gut-gut-gut*. HABITAT: Cliffs, gorges and caves in open rugged country, also in villages. DISTRIBUTION: Himalayan resident.

3 SNOW PIGEON (TIBETAN PIGEON) *Columba leuconota* 31–34cm FIELD NOTES: In flight shows a white patch on upper rump; lower rump and tail black, the latter with a white mid-band. Often feeds in the company of Hill Pigeons; post breeding may occur in large flocks. VOICE: A *hic hic cuck-cuck hic*, also a prolonged *coo-ooo-ooo*. HABITAT: High-altitude rocky cliffs, steep gorges and snow fields. DISTRIBUTION: Himalayan resident.

4 YELLOW-EYED DOVE (EASTERN STOCK DOVE, YELLOW-EYED or PALE-BACKED PIGEON) *Columba eversmanni* 29–31cm FIELD NOTES: Yellow eye-ring. In flight shows a white upper rump, two black bars on inner part of upperwing and a broad, diffuse black terminal band on tail. VOICE: A subdued *quooh quooh quooh-cuu-gooh-cuu-gooh-cuu-gooh*. HABITAT: Cultivated areas and flood plains. DISTRIBUTION: Winter visitor, mainly in the N and NW.

5 STOCK DOVE (STOCK PIGEON) *Columba oenas* 32–34cm FIELD NOTES: Most often seen in pairs or small parties. In flight shows a broad blackish terminal bar on tail and two black bars on inner part of upperwing. Juvenile duller with little or no iridescence on neck. VOICE: A low *ooo-uh* or *ooo-er*. HABITAT: Open country, cultivated areas, open woodland and forest edge. DISTRIBUTION: Vagrant, recorded in India.

6 SPECKLED WOOD PIGEON (HODGSON'S PIGEON) *Columba hodgsonii* 38–40cm FIELD NOTES: Mainly arboreal. In flight appears uniform dark grey-brown. Usually encountered in pairs or small flocks. VOICE: A deep *whock-whrroo-whrrooo*. HABITAT: Evergreen and semi-evergreen hill forests. DISTRIBUTION: Resident in the Himalayas and the extreme NE hills.

7 WOOD PIGEON (COMMON WOOD PIGEON, RINGDOVE) *Columba palumbus* 41–45cm FIELD NOTES: Encountered in small flocks; larger flocks occur post breeding. In flight, from above, shows a white crescent that stretches back from alula area. Juveniles lack the buff neck-patch. VOICE: A mellow *kookooo-koo kookooo-koo...* HABITAT: Scrub and wooded hillsides and valleys. DISTRIBUTION: Resident in Baluchistan and the Himalayas.

8 ASHY WOOD PIGEON (BUFF-COLLARED PIGEON) *Columba pulchricollis* 31–36cm FIELD NOTES: Mainly arboreal, usually occurring in pairs or small flocks. In flight appears darkish grey with a paler head. VOICE: A deep *whuoo whuoo whuoo* or *coo coo coo*. HABITAT: High-elevation, dense, broadleaved evergreen forest. DISTRIBUTION: Resident in the Himalayas and the NE Indian hills.

1b feral varieties

54 PIGEONS

1 NILGIRI WOOD PIGEON (SPOTTED WOOD PIGEON) *Columba elphinstonii* 36–42cm FIELD NOTES: Mainly arboreal, although regularly feeds on fallen fruit on the forest floor. Usually found in pairs or small parties. Female duller; juvenile also duller with neck pattern less showy and rusty fringes to wing-coverts. VOICE: A deep *who who-who-who*. HABITAT: Moist evergreen hill forests. DISTRIBUTION: Resident in the W Ghats of India.

2 SRI LANKA WOOD PIGEON *Columba torringtoniae* 33–36cm FIELD NOTES: Mainly arboreal. Female shows less grey tinge on head and neck. Juvenile generally duller and browner with purplish-grey areas more grey with rusty fringes, purple areas faintly barred black and rusty; wing-coverts with rusty fringed coverts. VOICE: A deep owl-like *hoo-hoo-hoo*. HABITAT: Mainly hill forests. DISTRIBUTION: Resident in Sri Lanka.

3 PALE-CAPPED PIGEON (PURPLE WOOD PIGEON) *Columba punicea* 36–41cm FIELD NOTES: Generally encountered in pairs or small groups. Juvenile duller, with crown, mantle and wings dull brown, the latter with rusty fringes. VOICE: A soft mew. HABITAT: Tropical and subtropical forests and nearby cultivated areas. DISTRIBUTION: Resident in E and NE.

4 ANDAMAN WOOD PIGEON *Columba palumboides* 36–41cm FIELD NOTES: Generally seen in pairs or small parties; regularly flies from island to island in search of fruiting trees. Juvenile dull brownish-grey below and brownish-black on mantle and wings, shows little or no iridescence. VOICE: A mellow, purring *crroo-crroo*. HABITAT: Dense broadleaved evergreen forests. DISTRIBUTION: Resident on the Andamans and Nicobars.

5 GREEN IMPERIAL PIGEON *Ducula aenea* 43–47cm FIELD NOTES: Usually seen in pairs or small parties, although may be in larger flocks at fruiting trees. Juvenile duller with less pronounced pink tinge to head and underparts. The race *D. a. nicobarica* (Nicobar Imperial Pigeon) (5b), found on the Nicobars and Andamans, is sometimes considered a full species. VOICE: A deep, hollow *currr-whoo*. HABITAT: Moist tropical broadleaved forest and mangroves (the latter applying mainly to *D. a. nicobarica*). DISTRIBUTION: Resident in the W Ghats, E and NE, and also Sri Lanka, the Nicobars and Andamans.

6 MOUNTAIN IMPERIAL PIGEON (MAROON-BACKED IMPERIAL PIGEON) *Ducula badia* 43–51cm FIELD NOTES: Variable. Grey-headed, brown-backed race *D. b. cuprea* (main illustration) occurs in the W Ghats, and the pink-headed, maroon-backed race *D. b. insignis* (6b) is found in the NE of the region. Usually seen in pairs or small parties. Juvenile duller, mantle and wings with rusty fringes and pale terminal tail band less distinct. VOICE: A clicking or clucking sound followed by a deep, resonant, double booming note. HABITAT: Broadleaved evergreen forest. DISTRIBUTION: Resident, W Ghats and NE of the region.

7 PIED IMPERIAL PIGEON (WHITE IMPERIAL PIGEON, WHITE FRUIT PIGEON or NUTMEG PIGEON) *Ducula bicolor* 35–42cm FIELD NOTES: Unmistakable. In flight shows black flight feathers and black terminal band on tail, contrasting with white of the rest of wings and body. Usually in flocks or small parties. Juvenile has white parts tinged greyish, and buffish fringes to most feathers. VOICE: A deep purring. Also recorded is a chuckling *hu-hu-hu* and a *cru-croo*. HABITAT: Evergreen broadleaved forest. DISTRIBUTION: Resident on the Nicobars and remote islands in the Andamans.

55 DOVES, CUCKOO-DOVES

1 TURTLE DOVE (EUROPEAN or COMMON TURTLE DOVE) *Streptopelia turtur* 26–28cm FIELD NOTES: Usually in pairs or small flocks during migration. In flight tail shows conspicuous white sides and terminal bar, contrasting with black subterminal bar, Juvenile much duller brown upperparts with buffish fringes, also lacks the black and white neck-patch. VOICE: A purring *turrrrrr turrrrrr turrrrrr.* HABITAT: Cultivated areas in dry mountain valleys. DISTRIBUTION: Vagrant, recorded from Pakistan, India and the Maldives.

2 ORIENTAL TURTLE DOVE (RUFOUS TURTLE DOVE) *Streptopelia orientalis* 30–35cm FIELD NOTES: Usually singly or in pairs, may occur in small flocks at rich feeding sites. In flight tail shows grey sides and terminal band contrasting with blackish subterminal bar. Race *S. o. meena* (2b) from the W Himalayas has tail pattern very like Turtle Dove, but is generally larger, darker and the wings and mantle appear scalier. Rusty race *S. o. erythrocephala* (2c) occurs in peninsular India. Juvenile much duller grey-brown with pale fringes on scapulars and mantle, lacks the black and white neck pattern. VOICE: A mournful *coo-cooroo-coocoo* or *gur-grugroo.* HABITAT: Open forests, open areas with scattered trees and bushes. DISTRIBUTION: Resident, more widespread post breeding.

3 COLLARED DOVE (EURASIAN COLLARED DOVE) *Streptopelia decaocto* 31–33cm FIELD NOTES: Feeds mainly on the ground. In flight shows white corners to the tail. Juvenile lacks the neck collar. VOICE: A low-pitched *koo-KOO-kook* or *koo-kooo-koo.* On landing gives a harsh *kreair* or *whaaa.* HABITAT: Open dry country with scattered trees, cultivations, groves and gardens. DISTRIBUTION: Widespread resident.

4 RED TURTLE DOVE (RED COLLARED DOVE) *Streptopelia tranquebarica* 23cm FIELD NOTES: Feeds mainly on the ground. In flight tail shows white sides and greyish-white corners. Juvenile duller, mantle and wings with buff fringes, no collar. VOICE: A deep *cru-u-u-u-u* or *groo-gurr-goo.* HABITAT: Open country with wooded or scrubby areas. DISTRIBUTION: Widespread resident.

5 LAUGHING DOVE (PALM DOVE) *Spilopelia senegalensis* 25–27cm FIELD NOTES: Generally feeds on the ground. In flight shows white corners and sides to tail. Juvenile duller with no breast markings. VOICE: A bubbling *do do dooh dooh do.* HABITAT: Scrubby hillsides and dry cultivation. DISTRIBUTION: Widespread resident.

6 SPOTTED DOVE (NECKLACE DOVE) *Spilopelia chinensis suratensis* 30cm FIELD NOTES: In flight shows white corners to dark tail. Juvenile generally sandy-brown, slightly darker above with pale fringes and no neck pattern. Race *S. c. tigrina* (6b) occurs in the NE. VOICE: A melodious *coo croo-oo croo-oo* or *coocoo croor-croor.* HABITAT: Cultivated areas, open forests and around human habitations. DISTRIBUTION: Widespread resident.

7 BARRED CUCKOO-DOVE (BAR-TAILED CUCKOO-DOVE) *Macropygia unchall* 37–41cm FIELD NOTES: Usually seen in pairs or small flocks. Acrobatically clambers around tree branches foraging for small fruits; on the ground carries tail slightly raised. Juvenile generally dark with darker barring. VOICE: A booming *croo-oom.* HABITAT: Dense broadleaved forest. DISTRIBUTION: Resident in the Himalayas and NE India.

8 ANDAMAN CUCKOO-DOVE (NICOBAR CUCKOO-DOVE) *Macropygia rufipennis* 39–40cm FIELD NOTES: Feeds on small fruits especially birds-eye chillies. Juvenile like a dull adult female but with more conspicuous barring on upperparts and neck. VOICE: A repeated, deep, subdued *o-o-o-o-ah.* HABITAT: Dense evergreen and secondary forest. DISTRIBUTION: Resident on the Andamans and Nicobars.

2b *meena*

2c *erythrocephala*

6b *tigrina*

6 *suratensis*

56 EMERALD DOVE, GREEN PIGEONS, NICOBAR PIGEON

1 EMERALD DOVE (COMMON EMERALD DOVE, GREEN-WINGED DOVE)
Chalcophaps indica 23–27cm FIELD NOTES: Usually encountered singly, in pairs or in small groups, feeding on the ground. In flight shows two white bars on black lower back. VOICE: A soft, drawn-out *tnk-hoo, hoo-hoo* or *tk-hoon*. HABITAT: Tropical and subtropical, moist broadleaved forest. DISTRIBUTION: Widespread in C and E of the region.

2 THICK-BILLED GREEN PIGEON *Treron curvirostra* 24–31cm FIELD NOTES: Usually arboreal, feeds on fruits and berries, generally in small flocks, but at rich food sites may be in large flocks. VOICE: Low-pitched, throaty whistles; also a hoarse *goo-goo* when feeding, probably a dispute call. HABITAT: Forests and well-wooded country. DISTRIBUTION: Resident in the NE.

3 POMADOUR GREEN PIGEON (SRI LANKA GREEN PIGEON) *Treron pompadora* 27–28cm FIELD NOTES: Actions and habits similar to the Thick-billed Green Pigeon. Very variable. *T. p. phayrei* (Ashy-headed Green Pigeon) (3b) occurs in the NE; *T. p. chloropterus* (Andaman Green Pigeon) (3c) is the only green pigeon on the Andamans and the Nicobars; *T. p. affinis* (Grey-fronted Green Pigeon) (3d) occurs in the W Ghats; the races depicted are treated as separate species by some authorities. VOICE: Low-pitched mellow whistles. HABITAT: Forests and well-wooded areas. DISTRIBUTION: Resident in Sri Lanka, the Andamans, Nicobars, W Ghats and the NE of the region.

4 ORANGE-BREASTED GREEN PIGEON *Treron bicinctus* 29cm FIELD NOTES: Actions and habits similar to Thick-billed Green Pigeon. May mix with other green pigeon species at trees with a large fruit crop. VOICE: A modulated, mellow whistle, also a croaking note and a chuckling call. HABITAT: Forests and well-wooded country. DISTRIBUTION: Resident in the Himalayas, hills of India, Bangladesh and Sri Lanka.

5 PIN-TAILED GREEN PIGEON *Treron apicauda* 28–32cm FIELD NOTES: Acrobatic, parakeet-like feeding actions. Generally habits much as other green pigeons. VOICE: A deep, musical *oou ou-ruu oo-ru ou-rooou*; also recorded is a mellow, whistled *ko-kla-oi-oi-oi-oilli-illio-kla*. HABITAT: Evergreen broadleaved hill forests. DISTRIBUTION: Resident in the NE.

6 YELLOW-FOOTED GREEN PIGEON (COMMON GREEN PIGEON) *Treron phoenicopterus* 33cm FIELD NOTES: Actions and habits similar to other green pigeons. *T. p. chlorigaster* (6b) occurs in India south of the Gangetic Plain. *T. p. phillipsi* (not shown) from Sri Lanka is like the latter but duller and smaller. VOICE: Melodious whistling notes. HABITAT: Forests, fruiting trees in cultivations, gardens and parks. DISTRIBUTION: Widespread resident.

7 WEDGE-TAILED GREEN PIGEON (SINGING GREEN PIGEON) *Treron sphenurus* 30–33cm FIELD NOTES: Actions much as others of the genus, although less gregarious. VOICE: A series of musical whistling or fluting notes, also a curious grunting. HABITAT: Subtropical and temperate broadleaved forest. DISTRIBUTION: Resident in the Himalayas and the NE of the region.

8 NICOBAR PIGEON (HACKLED, WHITE-TAILED or VULTURINE PIGEON)
Caloenas nicobarica 40cm FIELD NOTES: Usually feeds at dawn or dusk, mainly on the ground on fallen fruit. Female has smaller cere, shorter hackles and browner upperparts. Juvenile lacks hackles and is generally brownish-black, including tail. VOICE: Usually silent, although recorded as uttering a short, soft cooing and giving a pig-like grunting during disputes. HABITAT: Dense broadleaved, evergreen forest. DISTRIBUTION: Resident on the Nicobars and Andamans.

1

2

3d
affinis ♂ ♀

3c
chloropterus

4

♂ ♂ 3b
phayrei

3

5

6b
chlorigaster

6

7

8

♀ ♂

♀ ♂

♀ ♂

♀ ♂

♀ ♂

57 HANGING PARROTS, PARAKEETS

1 VERNAL HANGING PARROT (INDIAN HANGING PARROT) *Loriculus vernalis* 14cm FIELD NOTES: Sleeps hanging upside-down, like a bat. Usually encountered in pairs or small parties, presence generally indicated by squeaking calls, feeding mainly on fruit and berries. Juveniles have a greyish wash on face, and red rump is mixed with odd green feathers. VOICE: A squeaking *chi-chi-chee chi-chi-chee chi-chi-chee...* given in flight or when foraging. HABITAT: Broadleaved evergreen and deciduous woodlands. DISTRIBUTION: Resident on the Andamans, Nicobars and SW and SE India and the NE of the region.

2 SRI LANKA HANGING PARROT *Loriculus beryllinus* 14cm FIELD NOTES: Actions and habits similar to Vernal Hanging Parrot. Feeds on fruit, seeds, flowers and nectar. Juvenile generally green, lacking the red crown. VOICE: Similar to Vernal Hanging Parrot. HABITAT: Wooded country, groves, plantations and gardens. DISTRIBUTION: Resident in Sri Lanka.

3 RING-NECKED PARAKEET (ROSE-RINGED PARAKEET) *Psittacula krameri* 37–43cm FIELD NOTES: Usually in small flocks, although large flocks occur at rich food sources or roosts. Feeds on fruit, seeds and cereals. Flight fast and direct. Juvenile like adult female but yellower, may show an indistinct collar. *P. k. borealis* (not shown), occurring in the N of the region, has an all-red bill. VOICE: A screeching *kee-a* or *kee-ak*. HABITAT: Open woodland, groves, parks and gardens. DISTRIBUTION: Widespread resident.

4 ALEXANDRINE PARAKEET *Psittacula eupatria* 53–58cm FIELD NOTES: Occurs in small flocks, with larger concentrations at rich food sources and roosts. Feeds on fruit, seeds, cereals and fleshy parts of plants. Flight slower and more laboured than Ring-necked Parakeet. VOICE: A hoarse screaming *kii-e-rick*, *keeak* or *kee-ah*. HABITAT: Well-wooded areas and plantations. DISTRIBUTION: Widespread resident.

5 LORD DERBY'S PARAKEET (DERBYAN PARAKEET) *Psittacula derbiana* 46–50cm FIELD NOTES: Gregarious, often encountered while flying strong and fast above forest canopy. Food includes fruit, seeds and ripening crops. Juvenile duller with a green head. VOICE: A high-pitched shrill whistle; also a long, raucous, metallic cry. HABITAT: Coniferous and mixed mountain forests. DISTRIBUTION: Resident in the extreme NE (Arunachal Pradesh), although this is disputed by some authorities.

6 GREY-HEADED PARAKEET (FINSCH'S PARAKEET, EASTERN SLATY-HEADED PARAKEET) *Psittacula finschii* 36–40cm FIELD NOTES: Head paler grey, upperparts with a slightly yellower wash and bluish tail separate this species from the very similar Slaty-headed Parakeet, which was originally considered conspecific. Food includes fruit, grain and plant parts. Flight swift and agile, especially when flying among trees. Female lacks the maroon shoulder-patch. Juvenile has greenish head, probably not distinguishable from Slaty-headed Parakeet. VOICE: A loud, shrill *sweet sweet swit*. HABITAT: Hill forests. DISTRIBUTION: Resident in the NE of the region.

7 SLATY-HEADED PARAKEET (HIMALAYAN PARAKEET) *Psittacula himalayana* 39–41cm FIELD NOTES: Dark head, greener upperparts and yellow-tipped tail distinguish this species from the very similar Grey-headed Parakeet. Flight is agile and swift, especially when flying through trees. Feeds on fruit and seeds. Female lacks the maroon shoulder-patch. Juvenile has a greenish head, probably not separable from juvenile Grey-headed Parakeet. Often considered conspecific with Grey-headed Parakeet. VOICE: A high-pitched *scree-scree* and a drawn-out *wee...eenee*. HABITAT: Woodland and cultivated areas with large trees. DISTRIBUTION: Himalayan resident.

58 PARAKEETS

1 PLUM-HEADED PARAKEET *Psittacula cyanocephala* 33–37cm FIELD NOTES: Generally occurs in small parties, but found in much larger flocks where food is plentiful. Food variable: includes fruit, seeds, buds and fleshy parts of plants. Flight quick and agile, particularly when threading through trees. Juvenile has a green head with a yellow-orange forehead. Hybrid '*intermedia*' (probably a cross between this species and Slaty-headed Parakeet) was originally thought to be a full species known as Intermediate or Rothschild's Parakeet. VOICE: A high-pitched *tooi-tooi*. HABITAT: Forests, well-wooded areas and cultivations. DISTRIBUTION: Widespread resident.

2 BLOSSOM-HEADED PARAKEET *Psittacula roseata* 30–36cm FIELD NOTES: Actions and habits similar to Plum-headed Parakeet. Juvenile has a green head. VOICE: Similar to Plum-headed Parakeet. HABITAT: Open forests and well-wooded country. DISTRIBUTION: Resident in the NE of the region.

3 MALABAR PARAKEET (BLUE-WINGED PARAKEET) *Psittacula columboides* 36–38cm FIELD NOTES: Usually encountered in small parties; flight fast and agile. Feeds on grain, seeds and fruits. Juvenile like adult female but with an indistinct collar. VOICE: A coarse *che-chwe*. HABITAT: Tropical evergreen and moist deciduous forest, secondary growth, discarded plantations, nearby cultivations. DISTRIBUTION: Resident in W Ghats.

4 LAYARD'S PARAKEET (EMERALD-COLLARED or SRI LANKAN PARAKEET) *Psittacula calthropae* 29–31cm FIELD NOTES: Usually encountered in good-sized flocks on the edge or in open areas of woodlands. Flight swift and agile. Food includes fruit, fleshy parts of plants and nectar. Juvenile generally green, including head, which may show an indistinct collar. VOICE: A harsh, chattering scream. HABITAT: Forest edges and clearings, plantations and gardens. DISTRIBUTION: Resident in Sri Lanka.

5 NICOBAR PARAKEET (BLYTH'S PARAKEET) *Psittacula caniceps* 56–61cm FIELD NOTES: Occurs singly, in pairs or in small parties. Rests in foliage at the tops of trees when not feeding, where best located by noisy calls. Feeds mainly on the ripe fruit of *Pandanus*. VOICE: Wild screeching notes uttered while at rest or in flight, transcribed as a crow-like, raucous *kraan....kraan*. HABITAT: Tall forest. DISTRIBUTION: Resident on Great and Little Nicobar.

6 ROSE-BREASTED PARAKEET (RED-BREASTED or MOUSTACHED PARAKEET) *Psittacula alexandri* 33–38cm FIELD NOTES: Usually occurs in small parties, with much larger flocks where food is plentiful. Food includes fruit, seeds, crops, buds, flowers and nectar. Juvenile generally green with a greyish-brown tinge to the head. VOICE: A short, nasal *kaink*, repeated by several birds when disturbed. HABITAT: Moist deciduous forest, secondary growth and plantations. DISTRIBUTION: Resident in the Himalayas, the Andamans and the NE of the region.

7 LONG-TAILED PARAKEET (PINK or RED-CHEEKED PARAKEET) *Psittacula longicauda* 40–48cm FIELD NOTES: Recorded as appearing in vast flocks, especially when attracted to a rich food source. Food includes fruit, seeds and flowers. Juvenile has a pale green face. Greener race *P. l. nicobarica* (7b) occurs on the Nicobars. VOICE: A loud, screeching *kee-ah*. HABITAT: Forests, mangroves, cultivations and gardens. DISTRIBUTION: Resident on the Nicobars and Andamans.

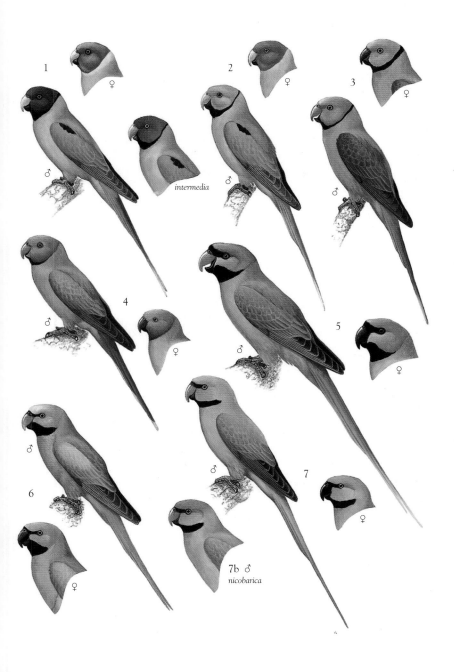

1

2

intermedia

3

4

5

6

7

7b ♂
nicobarica

59 CUCKOOS

1 LARGE HAWK-CUCKOO *Hierococcyx sparverioides* 38–40cm FIELD NOTES: Secretive, keeps to the foliage of trees, best located by call. Juvenile barred brown and rufous above, tail barred black and rufous. VOICE: A shrill, screaming *pi-pee-ha... pi-pee-ha* often transcribed as '*brain-fe-ver*', that increases in speed and pitch leading to a frenetic climax. HABITAT: High-elevation open forests, especially of oak. DISTRIBUTION: Breeds in the Himalayas and the NE of the region. Scattered post-breeding records from peninsular India.

2 COMMON HAWK-CUCKOO *Hierococcyx varius* 33cm FIELD NOTES: Arboreal. Juvenile barred brown and rufous above; white below, spotted and barred blackish. Race *H. v. ciceliae* (not shown) in Sri Lanka is darker above with more rufous streaking on throat. VOICE: A monotonous, screeching, high-pitched *wee-piwhit... wee-pwhit....* that becomes even more frenetic than that of the Large Hawk-Cuckoo. HABITAT: Wooded country, groves and gardens. DISTRIBUTION: Widespread resident.

3 HODGSON'S HAWK-CUCKOO *Hierococcyx fugax* 28–30cm FIELD NOTES: Arboreal, skulking, usually low down, moves higher when calling. Juvenile has dark grey upperparts barred rufous and fringed whitish; white below, barred and streaked dark grey. VOICE: A shrill, insistent *gee-whizz... gee-whizz ... gee-whizz... gee-whizz....* HABITAT: Broadleaved evergreen and moist deciduous forest. DISTRIBUTION: Resident or summer visitor in the NE.

4 CUCKOO (COMMON or EURASIAN CUCKOO) *Cuculus canorus* 32–34cm FIELD NOTES: Often perches horizontally with tail cocked and wings drooped. Juvenile has conspicuous white nape-patch, otherwise similar to rufous female, although some are more grey, with pale fringes on upperparts and dark barring on throat and breast. VOICE: Male gives a far-carrying *cuck-oo*, and when agitated a harsh *gowk gowk gowk*. Female delivers a bubbling *puhuhuhuhuhuhuhuhu*. HABITAT: Forests and well-wooded country. DISTRIBUTION: Breeds in the N and in scattered locations elsewhere. Scattered winter records.

5 HIMALAYAN CUCKOO (ORIENTAL CUCKOO) *Cuculus saturatus* 30–32cm FIELD NOTES: Only safely separated from Cuckoo by voice, although underparts more buff-tinged, with slightly broader barring, and a darker mantle. Juvenile has underparts more broadly barred, otherwise not reliably distinguished from Cuckoo. VOICE: A distinctive, resonant *poo-poo-poo*, also a muted hoopoe-like *poo-poo poo-poo poo-poo poo-poo*. HABITAT: Forests, forest clearings and open woodland. DISTRIBUTION: Breeds in the Himalayas and the NE of the region. Winter visitor to the Andamans and Nicobars.

6 INDIAN CUCKOO *Cuculus micropterus* 33cm FIELD NOTES: Occurs in the foliage of tree canopy. Compared to Cuckoo, generally darker grey-brown above, with more widely spaced barring on underparts and a broad blackish subterminal band on tail. Juvenile barred brown and white on head, neck and underparts; mantle and wings grey-brown with whitish fringes. VOICE: A loud, persistent whistle, transcribed as *crossword puzzle* or *one more bottle*. HABITAT: Deciduous, evergreen and secondary forests. DISTRIBUTION: Resident or summer visitor over much of the region apart from the NW.

7 LESSER CUCKOO (SMALL CUCKOO) *Cuculus poliocephalus* 26cm FIELD NOTES: Note small size and widely spaced barring on underparts. Action and habits similar to Indian Cuckoo. VOICE: A loud, cheery *pretty-peel-lay-ka-beet*, often given in flight above tree canopy. HABITAT: Broadleaved and pine forest and well-wooded country. DISTRIBUTION: Breeds in the Himalayas and the NE, passage migrant elsewhere on the mainland, winters in Sri Lanka.

8 BANDED BAY CUCKOO *Cacomantis sonneratii* 24cm FIELD NOTES: Frequents bare treetop branches. Calls with tail depressed. Juvenile similar to adult, but with pale fringes to upperparts and less pronounced dark ear-coverts. VOICE: A shrill *pi-pi-pew-pew*. HABITAT: Forests and wooded country. DISTRIBUTION: Resident.

1

2

3

4

normal

rufous
morph

♀

♀

rufous
morph

♂

rufous morph

♀

5

♂

♀

6

♂

7

rufous
morph

♀

♂

8

60 CUCKOOS

1 PLAINTIVE CUCKOO *Cacomantis merulinus* 23cm FIELD NOTES: Mainly arboreal. Restless forager among the foliage at the top of trees, sometimes making sallies after flying insects or dropping to the ground to collect prey. VOICE: A mournful *tay...ta...ta*, also a repeated *tay... ta... tay*. HABITAT: Forest and wooded country. DISTRIBUTION: Resident, mainly in the NE.

2 GREY-BELLIED CUCKOO *Cacomantis passerinus* 23cm FIELD NOTES: Actions and habits very similar to Plaintive Cuckoo. VOICE: A clear *pee-pipee-pee...pipee-pee*. HABITAT: Open woodland, secondary forest, bush, scrub and cultivated areas. DISTRIBUTION: Summers in the N, widespread resident or winter visitor in peninsular India and Sri Lanka.

3 ASIAN EMERALD CUCKOO (ORIENTAL EMERALD CUCKOO) *Chrysococcyx maculatus* 18cm FIELD NOTES: Favours the branches and foliage in the tree canopy. Active forager, often making aerial sallies to capture flying insects. Flight is fast and direct, very parrot-like. Juvenile much like adult female, but feathers of mantle and wings with rufous-buff fringes. VOICE: A loud, descending *kee-kee-kee*, also a *chweek* given in flight. HABITAT: Mainly dense evergreen forest. DISTRIBUTION: Summer visitor to the N and NE, winter visitor on the Andamans and Nicobars.

4 VIOLET CUCKOO *Chrysococcyx xanthorhynchus* 17cm FIELD NOTES: Little recorded of habits, presumed to be similar to Asian Emerald Cuckoo. Juvenile similar to juvenile Asian Emerald Cuckoo, but upperparts more barred and fringed rufous-buff. VOICE: A loud, sharp, repeated *tee-wit*, often uttered in flight; also a descending trill *seer-se-seer seeseeseesee*. HABITAT: Secondary evergreen forest, forest edge and orchards. DISTRIBUTION: Resident or summer visitor in the NE.

5 DRONGO-CUCKOO (ASIAN or INDIAN DRONGO-CUCKOO) *Surniculus lugubris* 25cm FIELD NOTES: Sluggish movements. Arboreal, occurs in the foliage of tree canopy; uses a bare treetop branch when calling, when tends to perch more horizontally with wings drooped. Juvenile dull black with whitish spots on all feather tips. Some authorities separate square-tailed Sri Lankan birds *S. lugubris* from the fork-tailed Indian form *S. dicruroides*. VOICE: A rising *pip-pip-pip-pip-pip-pip*. HABITAT: Forests, well-wooded areas, plantations and orchards. DISTRIBUTION: Resident in the S and Sri Lanka, summer visitor to the Himalayas and the NE.

6 KOEL (COMMON, ASIAN or INDIAN KOEL) *Eudynamys scolopaceus* 40–43cm FIELD NOTES: Unobtrusive, usually keeps to dense foliage, first sighting is generally of a bird flying silently from tree to tree. Juvenile blackish with white tips to mantle and wing feathers and variable white barring below. VOICE: A shrill *ko-el ko-el ko-el ko-el* that increases in scale and pitch before ending abruptly; also a bubbling *koel koel koel koel...* HABITAT: Open woodlands, forest edge, scrub, orchards and gardens. DISTRIBUTION: Widespread resident.

7 JACOBIN CUCKOO (PIED CUCKOO) *Clamator jacobinus* 34cm FIELD NOTES: Mainly arboreal, often perches in the open. In flight shows a white patch at the base of primaries. Juvenile like adult, but browner above. VOICE: A loud, fluting *piu piu pee-pee piu pee-pee-piu*. When alarmed utters a harsh *chu-chu-chu-chu*. HABITAT: Open woodland, bushes, groves and gardens. DISTRIBUTION: Widespread summer visitor, resident in the S and Sri Lanka.

8 CHESTNUT-WINGED CUCKOO (RED-WINGED CRESTED CUCKOO) *Clamator coromandus* 46cm FIELD NOTES: Shy, usually hidden among foliage in tree canopy, although regularly forages in low vegetation in search of insects. Juvenile duller with rufous fringes on mantle feathers. VOICE: A harsh *chee-ke-kek* and a hoarse whistle. HABITAT: Broadleaved forest, scrub and bush jungle. DISTRIBUTION: Breeds in the NE, winters in the S and Sri Lanka.

61 MALKOHAS, COUCALS

1 BLUE-FACED MALKOHA *Phaenicophaeus viridirostris* 39cm FIELD NOTES: Usually seen singly or in pairs, quietly but actively foraging in thickets. Weak flier, generally only takes to the wing when travelling from one thicket to another. VOICE: A low, croaking *kraa*. HABITAT: Secondary woodland, thorn-scrub and bush. DISTRIBUTION: Resident in peninsular India and Sri Lanka.

2 GREEN-BILLED MALKOHA *Phaenicophaeus tristis* 38cm FIELD NOTES: Skulking, forages in dense thickets. Best located when flying, weakly, from one thicket to another. VOICE: A frog-like croaking *ko ko ko ko*; also utters a peculiar chuckle when flushed. HABITAT: Dense broadleaved forest and thickets. DISTRIBUTION: Resident in E and NE India, Bangladesh and the Himalayas.

3 RED-FACED MALKOHA *Phaenicophaeus pyrrhocephalus* 46cm FIELD NOTES: Arboreal, works its way through foliage, usually in the company of other species, hopping from branch to branch, before fluttering across to the next tree to carry on the process. Juvenile has a much smaller dull red face-patch, whitish streaks on head and throat and dull brownish-black upperparts. VOICE: Usually silent, although may utter some short yelping whistles and a low *kra* or *kok*. HABITAT: Dense forest. DISTRIBUTION: Resident in Sri Lanka.

4 SIRKEER MALKOHA *Taccocua leschenaultii* 42cm FIELD NOTES: Feeds mainly on the ground; sometimes forages in shrubs and small trees by clambering among twigs or hopping from branch to branch. Juvenile as adult, but has dark streaking on head, throat, breast and mantle, the latter and wing feathers with rufous fringes. VOICE: Generally silent, but may utter a sharp *kek-kek-kek-kerek-kerek*. HABITAT: Dry deciduous secondary forest, scrub and bush, thorn and grass jungle and dry stony hillsides. DISTRIBUTION: Widespread over most of the region.

5 GREATER COUCAL *Centropus sinensis* 48cm FIELD NOTES: Skulks in vegetation or walks with tail held horizontally when searching for food. Flight weak and clumsy. Juvenile has brownish-black head and underparts narrowly barred white, upperparts rufous barred dark brown, tail black with white bars. *C. s. parroti* (Southern Coucal) (5b) occurs over much of peninsular India and Sri Lanka, considered by some authorities to be a full species. VOICE: A deep, descending then rising *hoop-hoop-hoop-hoop-hoop-hoop*. HABITAT: Scrub, tall grassland, thickets, waterside vegetation and gardens. DISTRIBUTION: Widespread resident.

6 BROWN COUCAL (ANDAMAN COUCAL) *Centropus andamanensis* 45–48cm FIELD NOTES: Actions and habits similar to Greater Coucal. Juvenile like adult but finely barred above and below. VOICE: A rapid, deep *hoop-hoop-hoop-hoop-hoop* which starts weakly and slowly, increasing in intensity before ending abruptly. HABITAT: Forests, cultivations, mangrove swamps and gardens. DISTRIBUTION: Resident on the Andamans.

7 LESSER COUCAL *Centropus bengalensis* 31–33cm FIELD NOTES: Actions and habits much like Greater Coucal. Juvenile a duller version of non-breeding adult. VOICE: A deep *whoot-whoot whoot-whoot kurook kurook kurook......* which increases in tempo and descends in pitch. HABITAT: Tall grassland, reed-beds and thickets. DISTRIBUTION: Resident in the NE and the SW.

8 GREEN-BILLED COUCAL *Centropus chlororhynchos* 43–46cm FIELD NOTES: Secretive, actions similar to Greater Coucal. Juvenile much like adult but with a darker bill. VOICE: A deep *hoop-poop-pooop*, the last note lower in pitch, also a short *hu-hu* and a *chewkk*. HABITAT: Humid, tall, evergreen forest with dense undergrowth, usually of bamboo or rattan cane. DISTRIBUTION: Resident in Sri Lanka.

1 BARN OWL *Tyto alba* 33–35cm FIELD NOTES: Appears strikingly white in flight. Nocturnal, although readily hunts during daylight. Buff race *T. a. deroepstorffi* (Andaman Barn Owl) (1b) occurs on the Andamans, considered by some authorities to be a full species. VOICE: A shrill, hoarse *shrrreeeeee*, also various chuckling, snoring and hissing sounds. HABITAT: Cultivations and around habitations. DISTRIBUTION: Widespread resident.

2 GRASS OWL (EASTERN GRASS OWL) *Tyto longimembris* 32–38cm FIELD NOTES: Crepuscular and nocturnal. In flight, from above, shows a pale ochre patch at the base of the primaries, contrasting with the dark primary-coverts. VOICE: Similar to Barn Owl. HABITAT: Open grassland and tall grass jungle. DISTRIBUTION: Resident over much of the region, away from the NW.

3 ORIENTAL BAY OWL *Phodilus badius* 29cm FIELD NOTES: Nocturnal. Hides in tree hollows during the day. Flight rapid. Darker-backed race *P. b. assimilis* (Sri Lanka Bay Owl) (not shown) occurs in SW India and Sri Lanka. VOICE: A series of whistles, eerie and with an upward inflection. HABITAT: Dense evergreen and broadleaved forest; also, in the SW, mangrove edge. DISTRIBUTION: Resident in the NE, SW and Sri Lanka.

4 SNOWY OWL *Bubo scandiacus* 53–66cm FIELD NOTES: Usually crepuscular, although may forage during daylight. Flight rapid and agile when chasing prey. VOICE: A booming *goo goo*. When alarmed male gives a cackling *kre-kre-kre*, the female a loud mewing or whistling. HABITAT: Open country. DISTRIBUTION: Vagrant, recorded from Pakistan.

5 DUSKY EAGLE-OWL *Bubo coromandus* 58cm FIELD NOTES: Usually in pairs. During the day hides in the shady areas of trees. VOICE: A deep, hollow *WO Wo wo-o-o-o-o*. HABITAT: Dense foliaged trees near water. DISTRIBUTION: Widespread resident.

6 SPOT-BELLIED EAGLE-OWL (FOREST EAGLE-OWL) *Bubo nipalensis* 63cm FIELD NOTES: Generally nocturnal. Hides in the shade of forest trees during daylight. Juvenile generally white, with dark barring on crown, neck, mantle, wings and underparts. VOICE: A deep *hoo....hoo* and a rising and falling mournful scream. HABITAT: Dense broadleaved woodland. DISTRIBUTION: Resident in the NE, SW and Sri Lanka.

7 EAGLE-OWL (EURASIAN EAGLE-OWL) *Bubo bubo* 56–66cm FIELD NOTES: Usually nocturnal or crepuscular. Rests during the day in the shade of a tree or in a rock fissure. Darker race *B. b. bengalensis* (Indian Eagle-Owl) (7b), resident over most of the region away from the north, is often considered a full species. VOICE: A deep *whooh-tu* or *woo-hoooo*, the latter uttered by *B. b. bengalensis*. HABITAT: Cliffs, rocky areas, woodlands and semi-desert. DISTRIBUTION: Widespread resident.

8 SHORT-EARED OWL *Asio flammeus* 37cm FIELD NOTES: Generally active during daytime. Hunts by quartering low over vegetation, often hovers before pouncing on prey. In flight outer primaries appear dark-tipped compared to Long-eared Owl. VOICE: Generally silent, may give various barking notes. HABITAT: Open country with scattered bushes, scrubby hillsides and semi-desert. DISTRIBUTION: Widespread winter visitor.

9 LONG-EARED OWL *Asio otus* 35–37cm FIELD NOTES: Generally nocturnal. During the day rests on a shady branch close to tree trunk, also on the ground under a bush or grass tussock. In flight outer primaries show four or five dark bars. VOICE: A drawn-out *hoo hoo hoo hoo hoo......* When alarmed utters a barking *ooack ooack ooack*. HABITAT: Stunted trees, poplar plantations and tall grasslands. DISTRIBUTION: Mainly a winter visitor to the NW.

deroepstorffi

bengalensis

63 OWLS

1 BROWN FISH OWL *Ketupa zeylonensis* 50–57cm FIELD NOTES: Crepuscular and nocturnal. From a perch swoops on fish, scooping them up with talons. VOICE: A deep *boom boom* or *boo-o-boom*, a subdued *hu-who-hu* and a harsh *we-aaah*. HABITAT: Tree-lined rivers and watercourses. DISTRIBUTION: Widespread resident.

2 TAWNY FISH OWL *Ketupa flavipes* 61cm FIELD NOTES: Crepuscular and nocturnal. Captures fish in talons by swooping from waterside perch. VOICE: A deep *whoo-hoo* and a cat-like mewing. HABITAT: Dense broadleaved forest by rivers and streams. DISTRIBUTION: Resident in the Himalayas and the NE.

3 BUFFY FISH OWL *Ketupa ketupu* 38–44cm FIELD NOTES: Mainly nocturnal. Catches fish in talons by swooping from a perch, by walking along river shore or by wading in shallow water. VOICE: A loud, monotonous *kootookookootook......*, also a ringing *pof pof pof*, a musical *to-whee to-whee* and various hisses, mews and shrieks. HABITAT: Forested streams and mangroves. DISTRIBUTION: Resident in the NE.

4 MOTTLED WOOD OWL *Strix ocellata* 40–48cm FIELD NOTES: Mainly nocturnal. During the day rests in trees in the shade of thick foliage. VOICE: An eerie, quavering *whaa-aa-aa-aa-ah*, also a mellow hoot and an occasional harsh screech. HABITAT: Open woodland, thick foliaged trees on village outskirts and groves. DISTRIBUTION: Resident in peninsular India.

5 TAWNY OWL *Strix aluco* 37–39cm FIELD NOTES: Nocturnal. During the day rests among the foliage on a branch near a tree trunk. Browner race *S. a. nivicola* (Himalayan Wood Owl) (5b) from the NE and the Himalayas is sometimes considered a full species; it also occurs in a rufous form. VOICE: A haunting *hoooo.....hu huhuhu hoooooo*, also an *oo-oo* and a shrill *kewick*. HABITAT: Forests of oak, pine and fir. DISTRIBUTION: Resident in the Himalayas, NW and NE.

6 BROWN WOOD OWL (HIMALAYAN BROWN OWL) *Strix leptogrammica indranee* 47–53cm FIELD NOTES: Nocturnal. Very shy, rests during the day in dense tree foliage. Larger, whiter-faced race *S. l. newarensis* (6b) occurs in the Himalayas. VOICE: A low hollow *tok tu-hoo tok tu-hoo*, also eerie shrieks and chuckles. Himalayan race utters a pigeon-like *to-hooh*. HABITAT: Dense forest. DISTRIBUTION: Resident in the Himalayas, the E and W Ghats, the NE and Sri Lanka.

7 HUME'S OWL (HUME'S TAWNY OWL) *Strix butleri* 35–38cm FIELD NOTES: Nocturnal. Perches prominently on rocks or posts. VOICE: A soft *hoooo hoo-u-hoo-u*. HABITAT: Arid mountains and gorges in rocky desert with nearby water and trees. DISTRIBUTION: Vagrant, recorded from W Pakistan coast, though record is disputed.

8 BROWN HAWK-OWL *Ninox scutulata lugubris* 27–33cm FIELD NOTES: Crepuscular and nocturnal. Shortly before dusk recorded as hunting insects in the manner of a nightjar. Tends to use the same perch over a prolonged period. Birds in the W Ghats and Sri Lanka are darker; fully dark race *N. s. obscura* (Hume's Hawk-Owl) (8b) from the Andamans is sometimes considered a full species. VOICE: A soft *oo...ok oo...ok oo...ok*. HABITAT: Forests and well-wooded areas. DISTRIBUTION: Widespread resident.

9 ANDAMAN HAWK-OWL *Ninox affinis* 25cm FIELD NOTES: Little known; recorded hawking moths, so presumably actions and habits are much like Brown Hawk-Owl. Birds on the Nicobars *N. a. isolata* have the rufous markings on underparts more diffuse, and are sometimes considered to be a race of Brown Hawk-Owl. VOICE: A loud *craw*. HABITAT: Forest, secondary woodland and mangroves. DISTRIBUTION: Resident on the Andamans and Nicobars.

newarensis

obscura

64 SCOPS OWLS

1 ANDAMAN SCOPS OWL *Otus balli* 19cm FIELD NOTES: Nocturnal, very little else known. More often heard than seen. VOICE: A loud, abrupt *hoot....hoot-curroo*. HABITAT: Trees in semi-open areas, cultivations and around human habitations. DISTRIBUTION: Resident on the Andamans.

2 MOUNTAIN SCOPS OWL *Otus spilocephalus* 17–21cm FIELD NOTES: Nocturnal. Hunts beneath the canopy, reported as keeping close to the ground. Roosts during the day in tree hollows. VOICE: A far-carrying *plew-plew*, *too-too* or *tunk-tunk*. HABITAT: Dense evergreen broadleaved montane forest. DISTRIBUTION: Resident in the Himalayas and the NE.

3 NICOBAR SCOPS OWL *Otus alius* 19–20cm FIELD NOTES: Actions and habits unknown. VOICE: A repeated, melancholic, rising *ooo-m*. HABITAT: Coastal forest. DISTRIBUTION: Resident on the Nicobars.

4 SERENDIB SCOPS OWL *Otus thilohoffmanni* 17cm FIELD NOTES: Nocturnal. Roosts on a horizontal branch among dead leaves, which act as camouflage. VOICE: A hollow *whoor-u*, repeated at 20-second intervals. HABITAT: Dense rainforest. DISTRIBUTION: Resident in Sri Lanka.

5 SCOPS OWL (EURASIAN or COMMON SCOPS OWL) *Otus scops* 19–20cm FIELD NOTES: Nocturnal. Roosts on a branch up against tree trunk, in thick foliage or in tree hollows. More often heard than seen. VOICE: A monotonous, plaintive *tyuu*, repeated about every three seconds. HABITAT: Juniper forest, scrub in dry rocky hills and valleys. DISTRIBUTION: Summer visitor in N and W Pakistan; post breeding occurs in S Pakistan and NW India.

6 ORIENTAL SCOPS OWL (EASTERN or ASIAN SCOPS OWL) *Otus sunia* 18–21cm FIELD NOTES: Nocturnal. Grey morph virtually indistinguishable from Scops Owl, apart from call. Rufous morphs much brighter than rufous morph of Scops Owl; the race on the Nicobars, *O. s. nicobaricus* (not shown), can be fully rufous and lacks any markings except for white scapular spots. VOICE: A toad-like *wuk-tuk-tah*, *wut-chu-chraaii* or similar. HABITAT: Forests and around habitations. DISTRIBUTION: Widespread resident.

7 PALLID SCOPS OWL (BRUCE'S, STRIATED or PALE SCOPS OWL) *Otus brucei* 21cm FIELD NOTES: Nocturnal, although recorded hunting before dusk and during the day. Roosts in rock crevices, tree hollows or among thick foliage. VOICE: A hollow, low-pitched *boo...boo...boo...* given at about one-second intervals. HABITAT: Open areas with scattered trees and bushes, rocky foothills in semi-desert. DISTRIBUTION: Resident in Pakistan, post-breeding visitor elsewhere.

8 INDIAN SCOPS OWL *Otus bakkamoena* 20–24cm FIELD NOTES: Nocturnal. Daytime roost is often on a branch close to the trunk or in a tree hollow. Only reliably separated from the very similar Collared Scops Owl by call. Pale race *O. b. deserticolor* (8b) occurs in S Pakistan. VOICE: A subdued, frog-like *wuk* or *whut*, repeated at four- to six-second intervals. HABITAT: Forests and well-wooded areas, groves and trees around human habitations, also riverine forest in the dry parts of Pakistan. DISTRIBUTION: Widespread resident S of the Himalayas.

9 COLLARED SCOPS OWL *Otus lettia* 23–25cm FIELD NOTES: Often considered conspecific with Indian Scops Owl. Actions and habits similar; only reliably separated by call. VOICE: A soft, downward inflected *buuo*, repeated every twelve to 20 seconds; also utters a chattering when alarmed. HABITAT: Forests and well-wooded areas. DISTRIBUTION: Resident in the Himalayas and NE of the region.

1   rufous morph   grey morph

2   rufous morph   grey morph

3

4

5   rufous morph   grey morph

6   rufous morph

7

grey morph

8   grey morph

8b

deserticolor

9   grey morph   rufous morph

65 OWLS, OWLETS

1 COLLARED OWLET (COLLARED PYGMY OWL) *Glaucidium brodiei* 16–17cm
FIELD NOTES: Crepuscular and diurnal. Bold, fierce hunter, taking birds as large as itself. Has eye-like markings on rear of head. VOICE: A mellow, bell-like *hoo hoo-hoo hooo* or *toot-tootoot-toot*. HABITAT: Open hill forests. DISTRIBUTION: Resident in the Himalayas and NE of the region.

2 ASIAN BARRED OWLET (BARRED or CUCKOO OWLET) *Glaucidium cuculoides* 22–25cm FIELD NOTES: Mainly diurnal. Often seen in the open, perched on a bare branch or tree stump. Rufous race *G. c. rufescens* (2b) occurs in the NE. VOICE: A bubbling, whistled *wowowowowowowowo* and a loud *hooloo hooloo hooloo kok kok chiurr*. HABITAT: Open forests of pine, oak and rhododendron, also subtropical and tropical evergreen jungle. DISTRIBUTION: Resident in the Himalayas and NE of the region.

3 CHESTNUT-BACKED OWLET *Glaucidium castanotum* 19cm FIELD NOTES: Diurnal, occurs in branches at the top of tall trees, shy and wary. VOICE: A slow, far-carrying *kRaw kRaw kRaw kRaw kRaw*. HABITAT: Dense forests. DISTRIBUTION: Resident in Sri Lanka.

4 JUNGLE OWLET *Glaucidium radiatum* 20cm FIELD NOTES: Mainly crepuscular, also recorded hunting during the daytime. Roosts amid leafy branches or in tree hollows. Darker and more rufous race *G. r. malbaricum* (4b) occurs on the Malabar coastal strip. VOICE: A loud *kao....kao....kao kao-kuk kao-kuk kao-kuk....* that quickens then fades at the end; also a monotonous *cur-cur-cur-cur-cur-ur*. HABITAT: Open tropical and subtropical forest. DISTRIBUTION: Widespread resident.

5 TENGMALM'S OWL (BOREAL OWL) *Aegolius funereus* 24–26cm FIELD NOTES: Rare. Nocturnal. Sit-and-wait hunter, sits for a few minutes before moving on to another nearby perch, then goes through the waiting process again. Most prey, mainly small mammals or birds, captured within ten metres of perch. VOICE: A soft, rapid *po-po-po-po-po-po-po....*, also a nasal *kuwake* and a *chiak*. HABITAT: Subalpine scrub. DISTRIBUTION: Resident in the NW.

6 FOREST OWLET *Heteroglaux blewitti* 23cm FIELD NOTES: Rare. Diurnal. Frequently perches on prominent bare branches. VOICE: A loud, mellow *uwwww* or *uh-wuwww*, also a hissing *shreeee* or *kheek* and a rising and falling series of *kwaak* notes. HABITAT: Moist deciduous jungle and fairly open dry deciduous forest, predominated by teak. DISTRIBUTION: Resident in the hills of NC India.

7 LITTLE OWL *Athene noctua* 21–23cm FIELD NOTES: Mainly crepuscular, but regularly seen perched on posts and telephone wires or hunting during daylight. VOICE: A clear *KEE-ew* repeated every few seconds, also a barking *werro-werro*. HABITAT: Cliffs and ruins in semi-desert regions. DISTRIBUTION: Resident in the Himalayas, Baluchistan and W Pakistan.

8 SPOTTED LITTLE OWL (SPOTTED OWLET) *Athene brama* 19–21cm FIELD NOTES: Nocturnal and crepuscular, although often seen abroad in daylight. Generally roosts within hollows or foliage of trees. Paler race *A. b. indica* (8b) occurs in N and C India. VOICE: A harsh, screeching *chirurrr chirurrr chirurrr* interspersed with, or followed by, a *cheevak cheevak cheevak*; also a rapid *kuerk-kuerk-kuerk*, said to sound like fighting cats. HABITAT: Around cultivations and habitations. DISTRIBUTION: Widespread resident.

1   grey morph   rufous morph

2   2b *rufescens*

3

4   4b   *malbaricum*

5

6

7

8   8b *indica*

66 FROGMOUTHS, NIGHTJARS

1 SRI LANKA FROGMOUTH *Batrachostomus moniliger* 23cm FIELD NOTES: Nocturnal. Sits, immobile, even on a close approach. Little else recorded on action and habits. VOICE: A soft, rapid *kooroo kooroo kooroo*, also various chuckles and croaks. HABITAT: Dense secondary growth in tropical and subtropical evergreen forests. DISTRIBUTION: Resident in the W Ghats and Sri Lanka.

2 HODGSON'S FROGMOUTH *Batrachostomus hodgsoni* 22–27cm FIELD NOTES: Nocturnal. Little recorded on actions and habits. VOICE: A soft *gwaa gwaa gwaa....*, also a long, rising, then descending, whistle. HABITAT: Subtropical evergreen forest. DISTRIBUTION: Resident in E Himalayas and the NE.

3 GREAT EARED NIGHTJAR *Lyncornis macrotis* 40cm FIELD NOTES: Crepuscular and nocturnal. Hunts above forest clearings. VOICE: A wailing *pee-wheeoo wheeoo wheeoo*. HABITAT: Evergreen and moist deciduous forest. DISTRIBUTION: Resident in the W Ghats and the NE.

4 NIGHTJAR (EUROPEAN NIGHTJAR) *Caprimulgus europaeus* 26–28cm FIELD NOTES: Mainly nocturnal. In flight, male shows white spots on outer primaries and white tips to outer tail feathers. VOICE: A prolonged churring. HABITAT: Rocky slopes with scattered bushes. DISTRIBUTION: Summer visitor, mainly to the NW.

5 JUNGLE NIGHTJAR *Caprimulgus indicus* 28–32cm FIELD NOTES: Nocturnal. In flight, male displays white spots on outer primaries and white tips to outer tail feathers; female wing and tail spots buff-tawny. Dark race *C. i. jotaka* (Grey Nightjar) (5b) occurs in the N and NE and is often considered a full species. VOICE: A slow *fwick-m fwick-m fwick-m...* *C. i. jotaka* utters a rapid *tuk tuk tuk tuk.......* HABITAT: Forest clearings and scrubby slopes. DISTRIBUTION: Widespread resident.

6 EGYPTIAN NIGHTJAR *Caprimulgus aegyptius* 24–26cm FIELD NOTES: Nocturnal. Shows a pale underwing. VOICE: A rapid purring that slows towards the end. HABITAT: Semi-desert. DISTRIBUTION: Summer visitor to SW Pakistan.

7 SYKES'S NIGHTJAR *Caprimulgus mahrattensis* 23cm FIELD NOTES: Nocturnal. Male in flight shows white spots on outer primaries and white tips to outer tail feathers; female wing and tail spots smaller and more buff. VOICE: A soft, even *churr*. HABITAT: Mainly semi-desert with thorn-scrub. DISTRIBUTION: Resident in the NW, more widespread post breeding.

8 ANDAMAN NIGHTJAR *Caprimulgus andamanicus* 28cm FIELD NOTES: Crepuscular and nocturnal. Flight pattern as Large-tailed. VOICE: A weak, rapid *tyuk tyuk tyuk.....* HABITAT: Open forest and open country with scattered trees. DISTRIBUTION: Resident on the Andamans.

9 JERDON'S NIGHTJAR *Caprimulgus atripennis* 28cm FIELD NOTES: Crepuscular and nocturnal. Flight pattern similar to the much larger Large-tailed. VOICE: A liquid, tremulous *ow-r-r-r-r*. HABITAT: Forest edge. DISTRIBUTION: Resident, peninsular India and Sri Lanka.

10 LARGE-TAILED NIGHTJAR *Caprimulgus macrurus* 33cm FIELD NOTES: Crepuscular and nocturnal. In flight, male shows white spots on outer primaries and extensive white tips to outer tail feathers. VOICE: A resonant *tok tok tok......* HABITAT: Forest edge. DISTRIBUTION: Resident in the E and NE.

11 INDIAN NIGHTJAR *Caprimulgus asiaticus* 24cm FIELD NOTES: Crepuscular and nocturnal. Flight pattern similar to Nightjar. Often squats in the middle of dusty tracks. VOICE: A far-carrying *chuck-chuck-chuck-chuck-k-k-k-roo*. In flight gives a *quit-quit*. HABITAT: Wooded country and scrubland on plains and foothills. DISTRIBUTION: Widespread resident.

12 SAVANNA NIGHTJAR (ALLIED or FRANKLIN'S NIGHTJAR) *Caprimulgus affinis* 23cm FIELD NOTES: Crepuscular and nocturnal. In flight male shows white patch on outer primaries and white sides to tail. Observed drinking by flying low over pools and dipping to scoop up water, much like swallows. VOICE: A repeated *chweep*, *chwip* or *dheet*, given mainly in flight. HABITAT: Open woodland, scrubby hillsides and grassland with rocky outcrops. DISTRIBUTION: Widespread resident.

67 SWIFTS

1 GLOSSY SWIFTLET (WHITE-BELLIED or BEAVAN'S SWIFTLET) *Collocalia esculenta* 10cm FIELD NOTES: Tame and gregarious, regularly flies in and around human habitations. Banking and gliding flight, interspersed with fluttering, bat-like, wing-beats. From below shows white belly, contrasting with darker throat and breast. VOICE: A sharp twitter. HABITAT: Around human habitations. DISTRIBUTION: Resident on the Andamans and Nicobars.

2 INDIAN SWIFTLET *Aerodramus unicolor* 12cm FIELD NOTES: Gregarious, often in huge numbers at cave roosts. Typical banking and gliding flight, interspersed with bat-like fluttering wing-beats. VOICE: A twittering *chit-chit-chit* given at roosts, also a harsh tern-like call note. HABITAT: Rocky hills, scrub and dry forest with nearby cliffs. DISTRIBUTION: Resident in SW and Sri Lanka.

3 HIMALAYAN SWIFTLET *Aerodramus brevirostris* 13–14cm FIELD NOTES: Regularly seen in flocks flying over forests; also noted around mountain peaks and ridges. Flight as Indian Swiftlet. VOICE: A twittering *chit-chit*, also a low rattle. HABITAT: Over wooded valleys in mountainous areas. Roosts in caves. DISTRIBUTION: Resident in the Himalayas and the NE of the region.

4 EDIBLE-NEST SWIFTLET *Aerodramus fuciphagus* 12cm FIELD NOTES: Flight actions as Indian Swiftlet. Grey rump sometimes indistinct. VOICE: A loud, metallic *zwing*. HABITAT: Habitations, cultivations, plantations and mangrove swamps. Roosts in caves. DISTRIBUTION: Resident on the Andamans and Nicobars.

5 WHITE-RUMPED SPINETAIL *Zoonavena sylvatica* 11cm FIELD NOTES: Usually seen in small groups, hawking insects over forests. Underparts whitish, contrasting with dark breast and throat. VOICE: In flight gives a twittering *chick-chick*, also transcribed as *swicky-sweezy*. HABITAT: Broadleaved evergreen and moist deciduous forests. DISTRIBUTION: Resident in the Himalayas, SW and NE India.

6 WHITE-THROATED NEEDLETAIL (NEEDLE-TAILED SWIFT) *Hirundapus caudacutus* 19–20cm FIELD NOTES: Flight is fast and powerful. In flight, from below, underparts show a white throat and a white horseshoe-shaped area from undertail to flanks. Juvenile has less clear-cut white throat, black streaking on white of flanks and dark fringes to white undertail-coverts. VOICE: A weak, high-pitched twittering. HABITAT: Forages over cliffs and ridges, forests, vegetated hills and river valleys. Roosts on cliffs or trees. DISTRIBUTION: Summer visitor to the Himalayas and NE India.

7 SILVER-BACKED NEEDLETAIL *Hirundapus cochinchinensis* 20cm FIELD NOTES: Usually encountered in small groups, flying fast and powerfully over forests. In flight underparts like White-throated Needletail, except throat dark brownish-grey, although some can be slightly paler brownish-grey. Juvenile has dark fringes to white undertail-coverts. VOICE: A soft, rippling *trp-trp-trp-trp-trp*. HABITAT: Forests and forested hills. DISTRIBUTION: Resident in the Himalayas and the NE of the region.

8 BROWN-BACKED NEEDLETAIL (BROWN-THROATED SPINE-TAILED SWIFT) *Hirundapus giganteus* 23–25cm FIELD NOTES: White lores, underparts much as Silver-backed Needletail, but throat darker. Typical powerful and fast flight when hawking insects over forests and grassy hilltops, usually in small groups. In evenings comes to drink at pools or rivers, scooping up water in flight. Juvenile has dark fringes to white undertail-coverts. VOICE: In flight utters a rippling trill, like White-throated Needletail, but slower; also a squeaky, repeated *cirrwiet* and a thin *chiek*. HABITAT: Broadleaved evergreen and moist deciduous forests, forest clearings and grassy hilltops. Roosts, colonially, in tree hollows. DISTRIBUTION: Resident in the SW, NE and Sri Lanka.

68 SWIFTS, TREESWIFT

1 ALPINE SWIFT *Tachymarptis melba* 20–22cm FIELD NOTES: Usually seen in small scattered flocks, flying fast and powerfully, although less agile and with slower wing-beats than *Apus* swifts. VOICE: A high-pitched, twittering *trihihihihihihihih.....*, or *trrr-tititititititititi.....* HABITAT: Mountains, cliffs, old habitations, may forage over virtually any habitat. Roosts in cliff crevices. DISTRIBUTION: Local resident and summer visitor.

2 SWIFT (COMMON or EUROPEAN SWIFT) *Apus apus* 16–17cm FIELD NOTES: Generally in small parties. Flight is fast and powerful, with rapid wing-beats interspersed with long high-speed glides. Forked tail not always apparent during fast direct flight. VOICE: A screaming *srreeee*. HABITAT: Mainly mountains, but may forage over virtually any habitat. DISTRIBUTION: Mainly summer visitor to the NW and Himalayas.

3 PALLID SWIFT (MOUSE-COLOURED SWIFT) *Apus pallidus* 16–17cm FIELD NOTES: Very difficult to separate from Swift. If seen well note blunt wing-tips, larger whitish throat and paler secondaries. VOICE: A screaming, disyllabic *srreeeu, sreih, cheeu-eet* or *churr-ic*. HABITAT: Coastal areas. DISTRIBUTION: Winter visitor to coastal Pakistan.

4 DARK-RUMPED SWIFT (DARK-BACKED SWIFT) *Apus acuticauda* 17cm FIELD NOTES: Does not appear to forage far from breeding cliffs, although noted feeding above nearby forests. Belly can look very pale in strong light, contrasting with darker undertail. VOICE: A high-pitched *tsee-tsee*. HABITAT: Rocky cliffs and gorges. DISTRIBUTION: Summer visitor and resident in the NE.

5 FORK-TAILED SWIFT *Apus (leuconyx) pacificus* 17–18cm FIELD NOTES: Forages over forests and open hilltops. Underparts similar to Dark-rumped Swift, but with prominent whitish throat. Some authorities treat the subcontinent birds as a separate species, using the name Blyth's Swift *A. leuconyx*. VOICE: A high-pitched *skree-ee-ee*. HABITAT: Mountains, foraging above forests. DISTRIBUTION: Breeds in the Himalayas and the NE, with scattered winter records in the S.

6 HOUSE SWIFT *Apus nipalensis* 15cm FIELD NOTES: Slightly forked tail. Often considered conspecific with Little Swift, although the latter is paler with square-ended tail. Actions and habits similar to Little Swift. VOICE: A shrill whickering scream. HABITAT: Towns, cities and mountain areas. DISTRIBUTION: Resident in the Himalayas and the NE of the region.

7 LITTLE SWIFT *Apus affinis* 12–13cm FIELD NOTES: Square-ended tail, looks more rounded when spread. Fluttering bat-like flight combined with short glides. From below appears black with prominent white throat. VOICE: A high-pitched rippling trill and a rapid *siksiksiksiksik...* HABITAT: Habitations, ruins, cliffs and ravines. DISTRIBUTION: Widespread resident.

8 ASIAN PALM SWIFT *Cypsiurus balasiensis* 13cm FIELD NOTES: Slim. Flight agile and rapid, with fluttering wing-beats and short glides. VOICE: A trilling *te-he-he-he-he* or *tititee*. HABITAT: Open country and cultivations, but generally with nearby palms. DISTRIBUTION: Widespread resident.

9 CRESTED TREESWIFT (CRESTED SWIFT) *Hemiprocne coronata* 23–25cm FIELD NOTES: Readily perches on branches and occasionally wires. In flight tail often held in a spike, which can make it appear like a large version of the Asian Palm Swift. Juvenile whitish below, scalloped with dark grey, upperparts and wings with white fringes. VOICE: In flight utters a harsh *whit-tuck whit-tuck* or *ti-chuck ti-chuck*. HABITAT: Well-wooded areas of deciduous forests. DISTRIBUTION: Widespread resident.

69 TROGONS, HOOPOE, ROLLERS

1 MALABAR TROGON *Harpactes fasciatus* 29–31cm FIELD NOTES: Hard to see; generally the first indication of a presence is the call. Sits upright on a branch or tree stump, from where it makes short sallies to capture flying insects; feeds until well after sunset, often tagging on to mixed-species flocks. Black-headed race *H. f. malabaricus* (1b) occurs in the W and E of India. VOICE: A throaty, musical *cue-cue-cue....* also a low, rolling *krr-r-r-r* when alarmed. HABITAT: Dense forests, preferably with an abundance of bamboo. DISTRIBUTION: Resident in Sri Lanka and the W and E of India.

2 RED-HEADED TROGON *Harpactes erythrocephalus* 31–35cm FIELD NOTES: Actions and habits similar to Malabar Trogon. Juvenile similar to adult female, but lower breast, belly and flanks buffish-white. VOICE: A descending *tyaup tyaup tyaup tyaup tyaup*, also a chattering croak given when alarmed. HABITAT: Dense broadleaved evergreen forest. DISTRIBUTION: Resident in the NE of the region.

3 WARD'S TROGON *Harpactes wardi* 35–38cm FIELD NOTES: Actions typical of the genus: sits very still, often hidden, with occasional sallies to catch winged insects. VOICE: A mellow, rapid *klew klew klew klew...* also a harsh *whirrur*. HABITAT: Evergreen montane forest. DISTRIBUTION: Resident in the NE.

4 HOOPOE (COMMON or EURASIAN HOOPOE) *Upupa epops* 26–32cm FIELD NOTES: Unmistakable, even in flight, where it gives the impression of a giant butterfly. When agitated or alighting crest is fanned. Forages mainly on the ground, usually singly or in pairs. VOICE: A low *hoop-hoop-hoop* or *poop-poop-poop*. When alarmed gives a harsh *schaahr*. HABITAT: Open country with scattered trees, cultivations and around villages. DISTRIBUTION: Mainly a widespread resident.

5 ROLLER (EUROPEAN ROLLER) *Coracias garrulus* 30–32cm FIELD NOTES: Generally uses a prominent perch such as a post, bare branch or overhead wires, from where it pounces on prey. During display indulges in an acrobatic rolling and diving performance. Juvenile duller, especially on head and breast. VOICE: A short *rack*, a chattering *rack rack rack rackrak-ak* and a screeching *aaaarrr* given in warning. During display utters a loud rattling *ra-ra-ra-ra-raa-raa-aaaaaa aaaaar*. HABITAT: Open country with scattered trees, open woods and cultivations. DISTRIBUTION: Breeds in the NW, migrant elsewhere.

6 INDIAN ROLLER *Coracias benghalensis* 30–34cm FIELD NOTES: Actions and habits similar to Roller; also recorded taking fish from water surface or plunging much like a kingfisher. In flight shows a bright pale blue patch on primaries. Juvenile is a dull version of adult with heavier streaking on breast and throat. The much darker race *C. b. affinis* (6b) occurs in the NE. VOICE: A harsh *chak-chak-chak*. During display-flight gives various cackling and screeching calls. HABITAT: Open country with trees and bushes, cultivations, parkland and large gardens. DISTRIBUTION: Widespread resident.

7 DOLLARBIRD (ORIENTAL DOLLARBIRD, RED-BILLED or BROAD-BILLED ROLLER) *Eurystomus orientalis* 25–28cm FIELD NOTES: Often perches on the topmost branches of tall dead trees, from where acrobatic sallies are made after flying insects. In flight shows a large pale blue patch on base of primaries. Juvenile duller with dusky pink bill. VOICE: A fast *krak-kak-kak-kak* and a hoarse *chak*. HABITAT: Forest edges and clearings. DISTRIBUTION: Resident in the Himalayas, the NE and SW, Sri Lanka and the Andamans.

70 KINGFISHERS

1 BLYTH'S KINGFISHER (GREAT BLUE KINGFISHER) *Alcedo hercules* 22cm
FIELD NOTES: Dives after fish from a low concealed perch. Female has orange-red base to lower mandible. VOICE: In flight gives a loud *pseet*. HABITAT: Streams and small rivers in dense tropical and subtropical forests. DISTRIBUTION: Resident in the NE.

2 KINGFISHER (COMMON or RIVER KINGFISHER) *Alcedo atthis* 16–17cm FIELD NOTES: Often first sighted as a blue flash flying low along a river uttering its high-pitched call. Regularly uses a prominent perch from where it plunge-dives after small fish. Female has orange-red base to lower mandible. Birds from S India and Sri Lanka A. *a. taprobana* (not shown) are bluer on upperparts. VOICE: A penetrating, high-pitched *tseee* or *tseee ti-ee ti-ee ti-tee*; when disturbed utters a harsh *shrit-it-it*. HABITAT: Rivers, streams and ponds, in winter also in mangroves and estuaries. DISTRIBUTION: Widespread resident.

3 BLUE-EARED KINGFISHER *Alcedo meninting* 17cm FIELD NOTES: Tends to fish from a low shady perch overhanging a forest stream. Juvenile has orange ear-coverts, dusky tips to breast feathers and a black bill with a whitish tip. VOICE: A high-pitched, shrill *seet*; also thin, shrill contact calls. HABITAT: Streams in dense forests. DISTRIBUTION: Resident in the NE, SW, Sri Lanka and the Andamans.

4 ORIENTAL DWARF KINGFISHER *Ceyx erithaca* 14cm FIELD NOTES: Perches low in vegetation or on rocks, from where fish or insect prey is taken from water or the ground. Old records of rufous form (4b) from Andamans and the Nicobars may be erroneous; this was often treated as a full species *C. rufidorsa*. VOICE: A high-pitched shrill or a soft *tsriet-tsriet*. HABITAT: Shady streams or ponds in damp broadleaved forests. DISTRIBUTION: Summer visitor to the NE, resident in SW India, Bangladesh, Sri Lanka, the Andamans and the Nicobars.

5 BROWN-WINGED KINGFISHER *Pelargopsis amauroptera* 35cm FIELD NOTES: Azure rump conspicuous in flight. Usually perches high in mangroves, feeds on fish and crabs. VOICE: A harsh *chak-chak-chak-chak-chak* and a mournful, whistled *chow-chow-chow*. HABITAT: Mangroves, tidal rivers and creeks. DISTRIBUTION: Resident on NE coasts.

6 STORK-BILLED KINGFISHER *Pelargopsis capensis* 35cm FIELD NOTES: Sits quietly, fairly concealed, on waterside branch. Plumage variable: greyish-headed race *P. c. osmastoni* (6b) occurs on the Andamans; blue-backed race *P. c. intermedia* (6c) is found on the Nicobars. VOICE: A shrieking *ke-ke-ke-ke*, also a pleasant *peer peer peer*. HABITAT: Shady waters in well-wooded country. DISTRIBUTION: Widespread resident.

7 RUDDY KINGFISHER *Halcyon coromanda* 25cm FIELD NOTES: Shy and secretive. Juvenile duller with dark bill. VOICE: A high-pitched, descending *tititititititi*, also a soft trilling. HABITAT: Watercourses in dense evergreen forests, also mangrove swamps. DISTRIBUTION: Resident in the NE and the Andamans.

8 WHITE-BREASTED KINGFISHER (WHITE-THROATED or SMYRNA KINGFISHER) *Halcyon smyrnensis* 27–28cm FIELD NOTES: Often encountered far from water. In flight shows a large pale blue patch at base of primaries. VOICE: A rapid, trilling *kililili....*, also a cackling *chake ake ake-ake-ake-ake* given as bird takes flight. HABITAT: Very cosmopolitan, including roadside trees, plantations, forest edge, freshwater and coastal wetlands. DISTRIBUTION: Widespread resident.

9 BLACK-CAPPED KINGFISHER *Halcyon pileata* 28cm FIELD NOTES: Shy, but perches on exposed branches or overhead wires. In flight shows prominent white patches at base of primaries. VOICE: A ringing, cackling *kikikikikiki*. HABITAT: Mainly coastal wetlands, also on rivers. DISTRIBUTION: Resident.

71 KINGFISHERS, BEE-EATERS

1 COLLARED KINGFISHER (MANGROVE or WHITE-COLLARED KINGFISHER) *Todiramphus chloris humii* 23–25cm FIELD NOTES: Conspicuous, bold and noisy, especially early in the day. Buffy-bellied race *T. c. davisoni* (1b) occurs on the Andamans; buff-eyebrowed race *T. c. occipitalis* (1c) is found on the Nicobars. VOICE: A harsh *krerk-krerk-krerk-krerk*. HABITAT: Coasts, mangrove swamps, tidal creeks; forest edge on the Andamans. DISTRIBUTION: Resident in E and W India, Bangladesh, the Andamans and the Nicobars.

2 PIED KINGFISHER *Ceryle rudis* 25cm FIELD NOTES: Usually encountered in pairs or small parties. Regularly hovers and dives to catch fish. *C. r. travancoreensis* from the SW (not shown) is darker above. VOICE: A noisy *kwik-kwik* or *chirruk-chirruk*, also a high-pitched *TREEtiti TREEtiti*. HABITAT: Lakes, rivers and ponds, also estuaries, tidal creeks and coastal lagoons. DISTRIBUTION: Widespread resident.

3 CRESTED KINGFISHER *Megaceryle lugubris* 41–43cm FIELD NOTES: Unmistakable. Shy, usually in pairs perched on rocks or branches in or beside a river pool. VOICE: A loud *ping*, also deep croaks and raucous grating notes. When disturbed utters a loud *kek*. HABITAT: Fast-flowing rivers and streams in mountain forests. DISTRIBUTION: Resident in the Himalayas and the NE of the region.

4 BLUE-BEARDED BEE-EATER *Nyctyornis athertoni* 31–34cm FIELD NOTES: Catches insects in flight, but also recorded foraging by clambering about in trees searching for insects. VOICE: A gruff *gga gga ggr gr* or *kor-r-r kor-r-r*. HABITAT: Edges and clearings of dense broadleaved forest. DISTRIBUTION: Resident in the SW, E, NE and the Himalayas.

5 LITTLE GREEN BEE-EATER (GREEN BEE-EATER) *Merops orientalis* 22–25cm FIELD NOTES: Darts from wire or branch to capture flying insects; also recorded using the backs of cattle as a moving perch. Roosts communally in trees, huddled together on a branch. Juvenile duller and lacking the black throat-band. Chestnut-headed race *M. o. ferrugeiceps* (5b) occurs in the NE. VOICE: A quiet, trilling *trrr trrr trrr trrr*; also a sharp *ti-ic* or *ti-ti-ti* given when alarmed. HABITAT: Open country with scattered trees, semi-deserts and grazing land. DISTRIBUTION: Mainly a widespread resident.

6 BLUE-CHEEKED BEE-EATER *Merops persicus* 27–31cm FIELD NOTES: Usually in pairs or small groups. Typical bee-eater action, sallying from exposed branch or wire to chase after winged insects, gracefully circling back to same or nearby perch after capture. Juvenile duller, lacks elongated tail feathers. VOICE: A rolling *diririp*, a mellow *tewtew* and when alarmed a sharp *dik-dik-dik*. HABITAT: Sandy areas with scrub and scattered trees, usually near water. DISTRIBUTION: Summer visitor to the NW.

7 BLUE-TAILED BEE-EATER *Merops philippinus* 23–26cm FIELD NOTES: Actions and habits similar to Blue-cheeked Bee-eater. Juvenile like juvenile Blue-cheeked Bee-eater but with a blue tinge to tail, uppertail-coverts and rump. VOICE: Similar to Blue-cheeked Bee-eater. HABITAT: Wooded country, near water. DISTRIBUTION: Summers in the N, winters in the S, Sri Lanka and the Andamans.

8 CHESTNUT-HEADED BEE-EATER (BAY-HEADED BEE-EATER) *Merops leschenaulti* 18–20cm FIELD NOTES: Typical bee-eater feeding actions, but usually perches at the top of trees. Birds from the Andamans *M. l. andamanensis* (8b) have a chestnut mask. VOICE: A *pruik* or *churit*. HABITAT: Near water in deciduous forests. DISTRIBUTION: Resident in the SW, NE, Sri Lanka and the Andamans.

9 BEE-EATER (EUROPEAN BEE-EATER) *Merops apiaster* 27–29cm FIELD NOTES: Actions much as Blue-cheeked Bee-eater. VOICE: A liquid, repeated *prruip*, *threep* or *kruup*. HABITAT: Open country, cultivations with scattered trees, near water. DISTRIBUTION: Summer visitor to the NW, winters in Sri Lanka.

1
humii

1b
davisoni

1c
occipitalis

2

3

5b
ferrugeiceps

5

6

4

8

8b
andamanensis

9

7

72 HORNBILLS

1 INDIAN GREY HORNBILL (GREY or COMMON GREY HORNBILL) *Ocyceros birostris* 50cm FIELD NOTES: Usually encountered in pairs or small parties, often in the company of mynas, green pigeons and bulbuls. Feeds mainly in trees, but descends to the ground to pick up fallen fruit or search for insects. In flight shows white tips to all flight feathers and outer tail feathers. Juvenile like adult, but mainly yellow bill lacks a casque; also lacks white tips to flight feathers. VOICE: A shrill *wheeee*, also a cackling *k-k-k-ka-e* and a rapid, piping *pi-pi-pi-pi-pipipieu-pipipieu-pipipieu*. HABITAT: Deciduous woodland, open thorn forest with scattered fig trees, cultivations and gardens. DISTRIBUTION: Widespread resident.

2 MALABAR GREY HORNBILL *Ocyceros griseus* 45cm FIELD NOTES: Generally occurs in pairs or small groups of 6–20, often in the company of other fruit-eating birds. In flight shows white tips to primaries and outer tail feathers. Juvenile like adult female, but bill smaller and wing and mantle feathers fringed rufous-buff. VOICE: A raucous cackling *kyah kyah kyah*, also a maniacal, laughing *waa...waa...wa-wa-wa-wa*. HABITAT: Evergreen and deciduous forest, usually near watercourses; also plantations and gardens. DISTRIBUTION: Resident in the W Ghats.

3 SRI LANKA GREY HORNBILL *Ocyceros gingalensis* 45cm FIELD NOTES: Arboreal, forages mainly in the foliage, below the canopy; may form small groups at fruiting trees. In flight shows white tips on primaries and white outer tail feathers. Juvenile has a smaller yellowish bill. VOICE: A loud *kaa...kaa...ka-ka-ka-ka* or *kuk...kuk-kuk-kuk ko ko kokoko*. HABITAT: Evergreen forest and deciduous woodland, plantations and gardens. DISTRIBUTION: Resident in Sri Lanka.

4 MALABAR PIED HORNBILL (INDIAN PIED HORNBILL) *Anthracoceros coronatus* 65cm FIELD NOTES: Generally occurs in small parties, but much larger flocks encountered at rich feeding sites which may include other hornbill species and fruit-eating birds. Mainly arboreal, but often descends to the ground to feed on fallen fruit or search for insects. In flight shows prominent white tips to all flight feathers and white outer tail feathers. Juvenile has smaller bill and casque. VOICE: Various loud, shrill squeals and raucous cackles. HABITAT: Evergreen forest edge, open forests, plantations and fruiting trees around villages. DISTRIBUTION: Resident in the W Ghats, E India and Sri Lanka.

5 ORIENTAL PIED HORNBILL (ASIAN or NORTHERN PIED HORNBILL) *Anthracoceros albirostris* 55–60cm FIELD NOTES: Usually encountered in small groups; bigger flocks may form post breeding. Mainly arboreal, foraging in the foliage of trees, although will descend to the ground to feed. In flight shows prominent white tips to flight feathers and large white tips to outer tail feathers. Juvenile has smaller bill and casque. VOICE: Various loud squeals and raucous cackles. HABITAT: Evergreen forest edge, open deciduous forest, woodland and plantations. DISTRIBUTION: Resident over much of the N and E of the region.

73 HORNBILLS

1 GREAT HORNBILL (GREAT INDIAN or GREAT PIED HORNBILL) *Buceros bicornis* 95–105cm FIELD NOTES: Usually encountered in pairs or small groups; may gather in larger flocks at fruiting trees or at communal roosts. Mainly arboreal, although may descend to the ground to pick up fallen fruit. In flight shows white tips to flight feathers, a buff-white wing-bar and white tail with a black subterminal band. Juvenile lacks casque, it taking up to five years to mature. VOICE: A loud, reverberating *tok…. tok…. tok*; also a loud *ger-onk*, uttered in flight, and various hoarse grunts, barks and roars. HABITAT: Mature broadleaved forest. DISTRIBUTION: Resident in the Himalayas, the NE and the W Ghats.

2 BROWN HORNBILL (AUSTEN'S or WHITE-THROATED BROWN HORNBILL) *Anorrhinus austeni* 60–75cm FIELD NOTES: Mainly arboreal, encountered in small, noisy, restless flocks, often accompanied by Oriental Pied Hornbills and other fruit-eating birds. In flight males show white tips to primary feathers and outer tail feathers. Juvenile similar to male, but with pale fringes to wing-coverts and pink orbital skin. VOICE: A high-pitched yelp, also loud croaks, chuckles and screams. HABITAT: Broadleaved evergreen forest. DISTRIBUTION: Resident in the NE.

3 RUFOUS-NECKED HORNBILL *Aceros nipalensis* 90–100cm FIELD NOTES: Usually seen in pairs or small groups feeding in the tops of trees or flying across forested valleys. Generally arboreal, although may descend to the ground to pick up fallen fruit. In flight shows white tips to outer primaries and a white-tipped tail. Juvenile has greyish bill with faint, or no, dark markings. VOICE: A short repeated bark, said to resemble the noise made by an axe striking a sapling; also various loud roars, croaks or cackles. HABITAT: Dense evergreen and deciduous hill forest. DISTRIBUTION: Resident in the NE.

4 NARCONDAM HORNBILL *Rhyticeros narcondami* 45–50cm FIELD NOTES: Generally encountered in small parties, with larger groups occurring in fruiting trees. Juvenile has smaller bill and lacks a casque. The only hornbill on Narcondam Island, with a population of around 300 birds. VOICE: A cackling *ka-ka-ka-ka-ka*. HABITAT: Mature undisturbed forest with large trees. DISTRIBUTION: Resident on Narcondam Island in the Andamans.

5 WREATHED HORNBILL *Rhyticeros undulatus* 75–85cm FIELD NOTES: Generally in pairs or small parties, and in larger groups where food is plentiful or at communal roosts. Forages mainly in the canopy, although will descend to the ground to collect fallen fruit or take small animals. Juveniles lack the wreathed casque and bill markings, both of which develop in the first year, gaining a new wreath each subsequent year. VOICE: A very loud, breathless *kuk-KWEHK*. HABITAT: Tropical evergreen forest. DISTRIBUTION: Resident in the NE of the region.

74 BARBETS

1 WHITE-CHEEKED BARBET (SMALL GREEN BARBET) *Megalaima viridis*
23cm FIELD NOTES: Usually encountered in pairs or small parties; also occurs in mixed foraging flocks, when can be aggressive to other species. Often climbs trunks and branches like a woodpecker. Juvenile like a dull adult, with obscured breast markings. VOICE: A trilling *prrr-rrr* followed by a series of *tu-kowt* notes leading to shorter *t-kot* notes; also utters a *tot-tot tot-tot*. HABITAT: Forest and woodland, plantations, parks and gardens. DISTRIBUTION: Resident in the S and SW.

2 YELLOW-FRONTED BARBET *Megalaima flavifrons* 21cm FIELD NOTES: Usually seen in pairs or small parties; in fruiting trees occurs in larger flocks, often accompanied by other fruit-eating species. Juvenile duller. VOICE: An ascending, rolling *kowowowowowo* leading to a repeated *kuiar kuiar kuiar*, also transcribed as a fast *towowowowo* followed by a series of *toowo* or *too-ka-o* notes. HABITAT: Hill forests, tree plantations and well-wooded gardens. DISTRIBUTION: Resident in Sri Lanka.

3 GOLDEN-THROATED BARBET *Megalaima franklinii* 23cm FIELD NOTES: Forages in the middle storey, gregarious when feeding in fruiting trees. VOICE: A continuing trill or a trill followed by a *tuk...tuk...tuk...*, a *tu-kee...tu-kee...tu-kee...*, or a *too-ka-weel...too-ka-weel...too-ka-weel....*; the follow-on notes may be interspersed with a trill. Also recorded are a monotonous *pukwowk pukwowk pukwowk* and a wailing *peeyu peeyu*. HABITAT: Montane forest, moist deciduous or evergreen. DISTRIBUTION: Resident in the Himalayas and the NE of the region.

4 BLUE-THROATED BARBET *Megalaima asiatica* 23cm FIELD NOTES: Actions and habits similar to the White-cheeked Barbet. Juvenile has head pattern less well defined and red crown mixed with green and black feathers. The variable *rubescens* morph (4b) occurs in the NE of the region. VOICE: A rapid, harsh *took-a-rook took-a-rook*. HABITAT: Evergreen and deciduous mountain forests, plantations and gardens. DISTRIBUTION: Resident in the Himalayas and the NE.

5 BLUE-EARED BARBET *Megalaima australis* 17cm FIELD NOTES: Typically occurs in pairs or small parties, with much larger groups attracted to fruiting trees. VOICE: An endlessly repeated *tk-trrt tk-trrt*, *koo-turr koo-turr* or *too-rook too-rook*, also various grating notes and a throaty whistled *teeow teeow...* HABITAT: Dense broadleaved evergreen forest. DISTRIBUTION: Resident in the NE of the region.

6 COPPERSMITH BARBET (CRIMSON-BREASTED BARBET) *Megalaima haemacephala* 17cm FIELD NOTES: Generally found in pairs or small parties, with very large groups occurring in fruiting trees, where often accompanied by other fruit-eating species. Juveniles lack the red markings. VOICE: A monotonous, metallic *tuk tuk tuk tuk tuk.....* HABITAT: Lightly wooded areas, plantations and well-wooded gardens. DISTRIBUTION: Widespread resident.

7 CRIMSON-FRONTED BARBET *Megalaima rubricapillus* 17cm FIELD NOTES: Usually found in pairs or small parties; bigger groups, mixed with other fruit-eating species, occur in fruit-laden trees. Juveniles lack the red markings and rest of head markings are much subdued. VOICE: A slow *pop pop pop....*, also a rapid *popo-popo-popo-pop-po*. HABITAT: Open wooded areas. DISTRIBUTION: Resident in Sri Lanka.

8 MALABAR BARBET *Megalaima malabarica* 17cm FIELD NOTES: Actions and habits similar to Crimson-fronted Barbet. Juveniles green with traces of red on head and throat. Originally considered conspecific with Crimson-fronted Barbet. VOICE: Like Coppersmith Barbet, but softer and quicker, transcribed as *tik tik tik tik tik.....*, *tunk tunk tunk tunk....* or *poop poop poop poop....* HABITAT: Moist evergreen forest; also fig trees in coffee plantations. DISTRIBUTION: Resident in the W Ghats.

75 BARBETS, HONEYGUIDE, WRYNECK, PICULETS

1 GREAT BARBET (GIANT BARBET) *Megalaima virens* 32–35cm FIELD NOTES:
Usually seen singly or in small parties, with bigger groups where trees are in fruit. When
not feeding sits motionless in the topmost branches. Juvenile is duller with a greener head.
VOICE: A mournful *piho piho piho*, a rapid *tuk tuk tuk* and a harsh *karr-r*. HABITAT: Deciduous
and evergreen mountain forests and well-wooded areas. DISTRIBUTION: Resident in the
Himalayas and the NE of the region.

2 BROWN-HEADED BARBET (LARGE GREEN BARBET) *Megalaima zeylanica* 25–
28cm FIELD NOTES: Actions typical of the genus, usually seen singly or in small groups, with
larger groups, mixed with other fruit-eating species, in trees laden with fruit. Duller race M.
z. inornata (2b) occurs in W India. VOICE: A monotonous *kutroo kutroo kutroo....* or *kutruk
kutruk kutruk....* HABITAT: Broadleaved forests, wooded areas, plantations and trees around
habitations. DISTRIBUTION: Widespread resident.

3 LINEATED BARBET (GREY-HEADED BARBET) *Megalaima lineata* 25–30cm
FIELD NOTES: Variable: dark and light forms shown. Juvenile has less prominent streaking
on breast. Actions and habits similar to Brown-headed Barbet. VOICE: A monotonous
kotur kotur kotur.... or a trill then a long series of *poo-tok* notes. HABITAT: Moist deciduous
forests, light secondary forest, plantations, roadside trees and well-wooded gardens.
DISTRIBUTION: Resident in the Himalayas and the NE of the region.

4 YELLOW-RUMPED HONEYGUIDE *Indicator xanthonotus* 15cm FIELD NOTES: Feeds
mainly on beeswax. May gather in numbers at exposed bees' nests, will also sit motionless
on topmost branches of trees before making clumsy flycatcher-like sallies after insects.
Plainer race *I. x. radcliffi* (4b) is said to occur in the W Himalayas, but no records have been
forthcoming for many years. VOICE: Various calls, including a quiet *weet*, a chipping *tzt* and
a *chaenp-chaenp*, all appear to be recorded while on the wing. HABITAT: Mixed forests and
wooded gorges, near cliffs with Giant Rock Bee colonies. DISTRIBUTION: Resident in the
Himalayas and the NE of the region.

5 WRYNECK (EURASIAN WRYNECK) *Jynx torquilla* 16–17cm FIELD NOTES:
Generally shy. Feeds mainly on the ground, often with tail slightly raised. Flight low and
moderately undulating. VOICE: A plaintive *quee-quee-quee-quee*. When alarmed utters a hard
teck. HABITAT: Breeds in open forests; post breeding found in open scrub and cultivations.
DISTRIBUTION: Breeds in the NW, winters over most of the region.

6 SPECKLED PICULET (SPOTTED PICULET) *Picumnus innominatus* 10cm FIELD
NOTES: Presence usually revealed by persistent tapping while searching for food; agile
forager, even hanging upside-down to poke in crevices; also flies or hovers in pursuit of
flushed prey. Often joins mixed-species feeding parties. VOICE: A high-pitched *ti-ti-ti-
ti-ti* and a squeaky *sik-sik-sik*. Drums on bamboo or dead branch with a persistent *brr-r-r
brr-r-r....* HABITAT: Bamboo and low bushes in moist deciduous and semi-evergreen forest.
DISTRIBUTION: Resident in the Himalayas, Bangladesh, SW, E and NE India.

7 WHITE-BROWED PICULET (HIMALAYAN RUFOUS PICULET) *Sasia
ochracea* 9–10cm FIELD NOTES: Agile and restless forager, with regular, loud tapping
of branches; often part of mixed-species parties. VOICE: A short, sharp *chi*, also a fast,
high-pitched trill *chi-rrrrrrrra or ti-iiiii*. A loud, tinny drumming, generally on bamboo.
HABITAT: Mixed semi-evergreen and deciduous secondary growth with bushes and bamboo.
DISTRIBUTION: Resident in the NE of the region.

1

2b *inornata*

2

dark form

3

pale form

4 *radcliffi* 4b

♀ ♂
6

♀
7

5

♂

76 WOODPECKERS

1 PALE-HEADED WOODPECKER *Gecinulus grantia* 25–27cm FIELD NOTES: Noisy, usually encountered singly or in pairs. Forages on bamboo, trees, fallen logs and sometimes on the ground. VOICE: An accelerating, nasal *chaik-chaik-chaik-chaik* or *kweek kwek-kwek* that is repeated four or five times. When alarmed gives a rattling *kereki kereki*. Drums with fast steady rolls. HABITAT: Bamboo jungle, mixed bamboo and secondary forest. DISTRIBUTION: Resident in the NE of the region.

2 RUFOUS WOODPECKER *Micropternus brachyurus* 25cm FIELD NOTES: Usually seen in pairs, digging at tree ant nests or foraging on fallen logs and termite nests; also recorded feeding on fruit. VOICE: A high-pitched *kenk kenk kenk*. Drumming said to sound like a stalling motorcycle engine, *bdddd-d-d-d-d*. HABITAT: Secondary jungle mixed with bamboo. DISTRIBUTION: Resident in the Himalayas, W, E and NE India, Bangladesh and Sri Lanka.

3 HEART-SPOTTED WOODPECKER *Hemicircus canente* 16cm FIELD NOTES: Squeaky calls often give away bird's presence. Generally encountered singly or in pairs searching among the thin branches at the top of tall trees; often part of mixed-species feeding parties. VOICE: A squeaky, *nasal ki-yew, ch-yew* or *chirrick*, also a high-pitched *kee-kee-kee-kee*. Drumming is weak and infrequent. HABITAT: Broadleaved forests, bamboo and coffee plantations. DISTRIBUTION: Resident in the hills of W, E and NE India.

4 BROWN-CAPPED WOODPECKER (BROWN-CAPPED PYGMY WOODPECKER) *Dendrocopos nanus* 13cm FIELD NOTES: Forages on smaller branches in the tops of tall trees; also has a liking for the lower woody stems of shrubs. Often part of mixed-species flocks. Dark-headed race *D. n. gymnopthalmos* (4b) occurs in Sri Lanka. VOICE: A rapid *kikikiki*. A soft, far-carrying drumming. HABITAT: Light and secondary forest, bamboos and trees near cultivations and around villages. DISTRIBUTION: Widespread resident.

5 GREY-CAPPED WOODPECKER (GREY-CAPPED PYGMY WOODPECKER) *Dendrocopos canicapillus* 14–16cm FIELD NOTES: Forages in the tops of trees, bushes and saplings, favouring outer branches and twigs. Agile, often hanging upside-down. VOICE: A soft *cheep, pic* or *tzit*, a *chip-chip* and a squeaky *ki-ki ki ki rrr*.... Drumming muted. HABITAT: Semi-evergreen open forests and cultivations. DISTRIBUTION: Resident in the Himalayas and the NE of the region.

6 BROWN-FRONTED WOODPECKER *Dendrocopos auriceps* 19–20cm FIELD NOTES: Forages in trees and bushes, often part of mixed-species feeding flocks. VOICE: A squeaky *chick* or *peek*, also a *chitter-chitter-chitter-r-r-rh* or *cheek-cheek-cheek-rrr*. Drums for long periods. HABITAT: Open temperate and pine forest, groves and gardens. DISTRIBUTION: Resident in the Himalayas and the NW.

7 FULVOUS-BREASTED WOODPECKER *Dendrocopos macei* 18–19cm FIELD NOTES: Favours tall trees, where usually encountered singly, in pairs or in small parties. Birds on the Andamans also occur in lower bushes. Spot-breasted birds on the Andamans, *D. m. andamanensis* (7b), are considered by some authorities to be a separate species. VOICE: A sharp *tchick*, also a *pik-pik* or *chik-it-chik-it*. Birds on the Andamans utter a staccato *chu-ik*. Drumming is weak, with short rolls. HABITAT: Open forest and forest edge. DISTRIBUTION: Resident in the Himalayas and the NE.

8 STRIPE-BREASTED WOODPECKER *Dendrocopos atratus* 21–22cm FIELD NOTES: Red on nape and more boldly streaked underparts help to distinguish this from the very similar Fulvous-breasted Woodpecker. VOICE: An explosive *tchick* and whinnying rattle. HABITAT: Open pine and oak forests and stunted trees on mountain slopes. DISTRIBUTION: Resident in the NE.

gymnopthalmus 4b

andamanensis 7b

77 WOODPECKERS

1 YELLOW-CROWNED WOODPECKER *Dendrocopos mahrattensis* 17–18cm FIELD
NOTES: Forages mainly in the crowns of trees or on trunks, usually singly or in pairs; also
accompanies mixed-species feeding parties. Race *D. m. pallescens* from the N and NW (not
shown) has paler head markings, larger white markings on mantle, often a complete white
rump, and less distinct streaks on underparts. VOICE: A feeble *peek*, sharp *click-click*, and
a rapid, repeated *kik-kik-kik-r-r-r-h*. HABITAT: Open woodland, desert scrub, plantations,
roadside and waterside trees, cultivations and gardens. DISTRIBUTION: Widespread resident.

2 RUFOUS-BELLIED WOODPECKER *Dendrocopos hyperythrus* 20–25cm FIELD
NOTES: Mainly arboreal. Sometimes joins mixed-species feeding flocks. Juvenile has dark
streaking on throat, buffy-rufous below with darkish barring. VOICE: A reeling *chit-chit-chit-r-
r-r-r-h* and a fast *ptikitititititit* when alarmed. Drums in short fading rolls. HABITAT: Subtropical
and temperate forests. DISTRIBUTION: Resident in the Himalayas and the NE of the region.

3 CRIMSON-BREASTED WOODPECKER *Dendrocopos cathpharius* 17–19cm FIELD
NOTES: Usually forages low down in trees and bushes, also favours dead trees. Race *D.
c. pyrrhothorax* (3b) has a prominent red breast-spot; it occurs in the NE, south of the
Brahmaputra River. VOICE: A loud, repetitive *chip* or *tchick*, also a short, rapid, descending
rattle. HABITAT: Broadleaved forests. DISTRIBUTION: Resident in the Himalayas and the NE
of the region.

4 DARJEELING WOODPECKER *Dendrocopos darjellensis* 25cm FIELD NOTES: Forages
from ground to tree canopy, sometimes in mixed-species flocks. Juveniles lack the ochre
patch on side of neck. VOICE: A rattling *di-di-di-d-ddddddt*, low *puk puk*, and when alarmed a
tsik tsik tsik... HABITAT: High-altitude forest and open woodland. DISTRIBUTION: Resident in
the Himalayas and the NE of the region.

5 GREAT SPOTTED WOODPECKER *Dendrocopos major* 24cm FIELD NOTES: Forages
mainly in the upper branches of trees; agile, often clinging tit-like to extricate prey.
Juvenile duller with a red crown and pinkish ventral area. VOICE: A high-pitched *kik*
or soft *chik*. Drumming loud, rapid and far-carrying. HABITAT: Oak and pine forests.
DISTRIBUTION: Resident in the NE Indian hills.

6 SIND WOODPECKER *Dendrocopos assimilis* 20–22cm FIELD NOTES: Forages among
tree branches, often low down, on fallen trees and fence posts etc. Juvenile duller, vent area
pinkish. VOICE: An explosive *ptik* a weak *chir-rir-rirrh-rirrh* and a rapid, repeated *wicka toi-whit
toi-whit toi-whit*. HABITAT: Riverine forests, thorn-scrub, roadside trees and tree plantations.
DISTRIBUTION: Widespread resident in Pakistan.

7 HIMALAYAN WOODPECKER *Dendrocopos himalayensis* 23–25cm FIELD NOTES:
Mainly arboreal, usually encountered singly or in pairs; sometimes joins mixed-species
feeding parties. Black mark below and behind eye often lacking, isolated or indistinct.
Juvenile duller, vent pinkish. Whiter race *D. h. albescens* (7b) occurs in the NW Himalayas.
VOICE: A sharp *kit*, a rapid high-pitched *chissik-chissik* and a fast *tri tri tri tri......* Drums in short
bursts. HABITAT: Dense mountain forests. DISTRIBUTION: Resident in W Himalayas.

78 WOODPECKERS

1 WHITE-BELLIED WOODPECKER *Dryocopus javensis* 40–48cm FIELD NOTES: Usually encountered singly, in pairs or in small groups of 4–6 birds foraging in tall trees, on or near the ground, with a liking for dead trees, stumps, fallen logs and leaf litter. Flight crow-like, with leisurely, deliberate wing-beats, when white rump and underwing-coverts are prominent. VOICE: A laughing *kek-kek-kek-kek-kek....* or *kiau-kiau-kiau-kiau...* Also a single loud, sharp *kiyow*, *kyah* or *keer*. Drumming is loud and accelerating, lasting about two seconds. HABITAT: Forests and light secondary forest with tall trees. DISTRIBUTION: Resident in the E and W Ghats.

2 ANDAMAN WOODPECKER *Dryocopus hodgei* 38cm FIELD NOTES: Usually seen in pairs or loose parties. Actions and habits similar to White-bellied Woodpecker. VOICE: A loud, chattering *kuk-kuk-kuk* that ends with a whistled *kui*, also a loud, sharp *kik-kik-kik*. Drumming is loud and far-carrying. HABITAT: Evergreen, open forest. DISTRIBUTION: Resident on the Andamans.

3 LESSER YELLOWNAPE *Picus chlorolophus* 25–28cm FIELD NOTES: Usually found in pairs. Regularly appears in mixed-species feeding flocks that include woodpeckers, drongos and other insectivorous birds. Often feeds on the ground on ants and termites. Race occurring in peninsular India, *P. c. chlorigaster* (3b) has underparts more white-spotted than barred and a red crown; the race in Sri Lanka, *P. c. wellsi* (not shown), is somewhat similar, but smaller and darker. VOICE: A loud, mournful *peee-ui*, *pee-a* or *pee-oow*. HABITAT: Forest, secondary growth, plantations and well-wooded gardens. DISTRIBUTION: Resident in the NE, the Himalayas, much of peninsular India and Sri Lanka.

4 GREATER YELLOWNAPE *Picus (Chrysophlegma) flavinucha* 33–34cm FIELD NOTES: Often encountered in small loose groups foraging on trunks and branches of trees, also on the ground, searching for ants, termites and grubs. VOICE: A loud, plaintive *pee-u... pee-u...* also a metallic *chenk* and. When disturbed a rich, laughing *kwek-kwek-kwek-kwek...* HABITAT: Mixed evergreen and deciduous forest also forest edge and clearings. DISTRIBUTION: Resident in the NE and the Himalayas.

5 GREY-HEADED WOODPECKER (GREY-FACED or BLACK-NAPED WOODPECKER) *Picus canus* 25–26cm FIELD NOTES: Regularly forages on the ground in search of ants, termites and grubs. In flight shows a yellowish rump. Birds from the E Himalayas are slightly yellower below and more bronze-golden above. VOICE: A musical, repeated *peeek peeek peeek peeek peeek* that fades at the end. When alarmed utters a chattering *kyakyakyak*. HABITAT: Temperate and moist subtropical forests. DISTRIBUTION: Resident in the Himalayas and the NE.

6 STREAK-BREASTED WOODPECKER *Picus viridanus* 30cm FIELD NOTES: Regularly forages on the ground in search of ants. In flight shows a dull yellow-green rump. In original records misidentified as Laced Woodpecker *P. vittatus*. VOICE: A *tcheu-tcheu-tcheu-tcheui*, an explosive *kirrr* and a squirrel-like *kyup*. HABITAT: Mangroves. DISTRIBUTION: Resident in the Bangladesh Sundarbans.

7 STREAK-THROATED WOODPECKER (LITTLE SCALY-BELLIED WOODPECKER) *Picus xanthopygaeus* 30cm FIELD NOTES: Generally solitary. Spends a lot of time foraging on the ground. In flight shows a yellow rump. VOICE: A sharp *queemp*, otherwise rather silent. HABITAT: Open deciduous, semi-evergreen and mixed bamboo forests, secondary growth and plantations. DISTRIBUTION: Widespread resident.

8 SCALY-BELLIED WOODPECKER *Picus squamatus* 35cm FIELD NOTES: Feeds on trees and also on the ground. In flight shows yellow rump. VOICE: A ringing, melodious *klee-guh kleeguh* or *kuik-kuik-kuik*, also utters a high-pitched *kik* or a drawn-out, nasal *cheenk*. HABITAT: Mixed woodland, open country with tall trees, scrub, orchards and groves. DISTRIBUTION: Resident in the NW and the Himalayas.

3b ♂

chlorigaster

3 ♂

♀

1 ♂

♀

♂

4 ♀

♂

2

♀

♀

5 ♀

6 ♂

♀

7 ♀

8 ♀

♂

79 WOODPECKERS

1 HIMALAYAN FLAMEBACK (HIMALAYAN GOLDENBACK) *Dinopium shorii* 30–32cm FIELD NOTES: Actions as most woodpeckers: clings to trunks and branches tapping at tree in a search for insects and grubs; also forages on the ground. Often forms part of mixed-species feeding parties, and often associates with Greater Flameback where the two ranges overlap. VOICE: A rapid, tinny *klak-klak-klak-klak-klak*. HABITAT: Mature deciduous and semi-evergreen forests. DISTRIBUTION: Resident in the Himalayas, locally elsewhere in the E and NE.

2 COMMON FLAMEBACK (COMMON GOLDENBACK) *Dinopium javanense* 28–30cm FIELD NOTES: Generally seen in pairs. Actions similar to Himalayan Flameback. VOICE: Similar to Himalayan Flameback, but faster and higher-pitched. HABITAT: Moist deciduous and evergreen forest. DISTRIBUTION: Resident in SW India and Bangladesh.

3 LESSER FLAMEBACK (BLACK-RUMPED FLAMEBACK or LESSER GOLDENBACK) *Dinopium benghalense* 26–29cm FIELD NOTES: Usually encountered in pairs or family parties; also forms part of mixed-species feeding groups. Both sexes of the Sri Lanka race *D. b. psarodes* (3b) have crimson upperparts. VOICE: A laughing *kyi-kyi-kyi* and strident *kierk*. HABITAT: Open woodland, light forest, open country with trees, groves, plantations and well-wooded gardens. DISTRIBUTION: Widespread resident.

4 GREATER FLAMEBACK (GREATER GOLDENBACK) *Chrysocolaptes lucidus* 33cm FIELD NOTES: Often found with Himalayan Flameback or in mixed-species foraging flocks. Tends to prefer large trees, working up from lower trunk in jerky spurts and spirals. The Indian form of this widespread woodpecker is now often treated as a separate species *C. guttacristatus*, as is the Sri Lanka form *C. stricklandi* (4b), both sexes of which have crimson upperparts. VOICE: A single *kik* and a monotonous metallic *di-di-di-di-di-di* or similar. HABITAT: Deciduous and semi-evergreen forests and well-wooded areas. DISTRIBUTION: Resident in the Himalayas, E and W India, the NE and Sri Lanka.

5 WHITE-NAPED WOODPECKER (BLACK-BACKED or BLACK-RUMPED WOODPECKER) *Chrysocolaptes festivus* 29cm FIELD NOTES: Usually encountered singly, in pairs or in small parties. Feeds on tree trunks and also on the ground, where it tends to favour areas of bare, burnt earth. VOICE: A rattling, repeated *kwirri-rr-rr-rr-rr*, higher-pitched than calls of other flamebacks. HABITAT: Deciduous forest, foothills with scrub and scattered trees. DISTRIBUTION: Widespread resident, mainly in India.

6 BAY WOODPECKER (RED-EARED BAY WOODPECKER) *Blythipicus pyrrhotis* 27–30cm FIELD NOTES: Generally seen in pairs. Feeds low down on trunks, stumps and fallen logs. VOICE: A loud, laughing rattle *chake chake chake chake*, which increases in tempo while dropping in pitch. When disturbed utters a chattering *churra-cha-churra-cha-churra*. HABITAT: Dense evergreen forest and nearby secondary growth with bamboo. DISTRIBUTION: Resident in the Himalayas and the NE.

7 GREAT SLATY WOODPECKER (HIMALAYAN GREAT SLATY WOODPECKER) *Mulleripicus pulverulentus* 51cm FIELD NOTES: Regularly encountered in small parties, flying from one forest patch to another in a loose follow-my-leader fashion. Climbs trunks and branches of tall trees, although also noted on small trees and saplings. VOICE: A single loud *dwot*, said to sound somewhere between the bleating of a goat and the barking of a dog. In flight utters a cackling *woikwoikwoikwoik*. HABITAT: Large trees in moist deciduous and evergreen forests, overgrown clearings with scattered tall trees. DISTRIBUTION: Resident in the Himalayas and the NE.

80 PITTAS, BROADBILLS, WHISTLER

1 EARED PITTA (PHAYRE'S PITTA) *Hydrornis phayrei* 22cm FIELD NOTES: Forages on the ground, in leaf litter and among rotting logs, progressing in short hops, although said to be more static than others of the family. VOICE: A whistled *wheeow-whit*. When alarmed utters a dog-like whine or yelp. HABITAT: Broadleaved evergreen and mixed deciduous forest and bamboo. DISTRIBUTION: Vagrant, recorded from Bangladesh, although this record is disputed.

2 BLUE-NAPED PITTA (NEPAL PITTA) *Hydrornis nipalensis* 22–25cm FIELD NOTES: Feeds on the ground, moving by way of short hops, stopping to turn over leaves or dig for food. Juvenile generally dark brown with dark buff spots above and below; belly and vent white. VOICE: A sharp *chow-whit*, *uk-wuip* or *ip-wuiip*. HABITAT: Broadleaved evergreen forest, usually near water. DISTRIBUTION: Resident in the Himalayas and the NE.

3 BLUE PITTA *Hydrornis cyaneus* 22–24cm FIELD NOTES: Forages on the ground, recorded scratching, chicken-like, at the ground when searching for food. Juvenile like a very dull female; mantle, crown and wings brown, underparts blotched and streaked brown; dull buff supercilium and dark eye-stripe. VOICE: A liquid *pleoow-whit*. HABITAT: Damp ravines and scrubby undergrowth in evergreen and bamboo forests. DISTRIBUTION: Resident in the NE.

4 HOODED PITTA *Pitta sordida* 19cm FIELD NOTES: Feeds on the ground, often perches on vines or branches while singing. Juvenile duller, underparts dirty-buff and lacking red vent. VOICE: A loud *whew-whew*. HABITAT: Damp deciduous and broadleaved evergreen forest. DISTRIBUTION: Summers in the Himalayas and the NE.

5 INDIAN PITTA *Pitta brachyura* 19cm FIELD NOTES: Feeds on the ground, and when alarmed often sits quietly on low branches or creepers with only a wagging tail giving away its presence. Juvenile duller; lacks red vent. VOICE: A whistled *wheet-tieu*, *wieet-piyou* or *pree-treer*. HABITAT: Light deciduous and evergreen forests with thick undergrowth. DISTRIBUTION: Resident, summers in the N, winters in the S.

6 MANGROVE PITTA *Pitta megarhyncha* 20cm FIELD NOTES: Forages on muddy areas around mangrove roots and nearby drier ground. Juvenile duller, with crown barred blackish. VOICE: A loud *tae-laew* or *wieuw-wwieuw*. HABITAT: Mangroves. DISTRIBUTION: Resident on the Sundarbans.

7 LONG-TAILED BROADBILL *Psarisomus dalhousiae* 28cm FIELD NOTES: Regularly encountered in small loose parties, moving from tree to tree; foraging by gleaning or making short sallies after flying insects. Juvenile duller and lacks the blue crown. VOICE: A loud, sharp *tseeay-tseeay-tseeay-tseeay.....*, or *pseew-pseew-pseew-pseew-pseew....* HABITAT: Broadleaved evergreen and semi-evergreen forest. DISTRIBUTION: Resident in the Himalayas and the NE.

8 SILVER-BREASTED BROADBILL *Serilophus lunatus* 18cm FIELD NOTES: Forages in pairs or small groups. Finds prey by gleaning from branches or leaves; also by making short aerial sallies after flying insects. VOICE: A soft, musical *chir-r-r*; also a squeaky *ki-uu*. HABITAT: Mixed tropical evergreen, semi-evergreen and bamboo secondary forest. DISTRIBUTION: Resident in the NE.

9 MANGROVE WHISTLER (GREY THICKHEAD) *Pachycephala cinerea* 17cm FIELD NOTES: Unobtrusive. Gleans prey from trunks and branches, also makes short fly-catching sallies. Juvenile warmer brown with rusty edges to wing-coverts and secondaries, the latter often appearing as a rusty wing-patch. VOICE: A rising, clear whistle; repeated three or four times. HABITAT: Mangroves. DISTRIBUTION: Resident on the Sundarbans and Andamans.

81 CROWS

1 CHOUGH (RED-BILLED CHOUGH) *Pyrrhocorax pyrrhocorax* 38cm FIELD NOTES: Sociable, forming very large winter flocks that forage on pastures or crop fields, often in association with Alpine Choughs. Juvenile less glossy with dull brownish-yellow bill. VOICE: A far-carrying *chee-aw, chaow, chi-ah* or similar. HABITAT: Mountains, alpine pastures and cultivations. DISTRIBUTION: Resident in the Himalayas and the mountains of W Pakistan.

2 ALPINE CHOUGH (YELLOW-BILLED CHOUGH) *Pyrrhocorax graculus* 38cm FIELD NOTES: Regularly encountered in flocks, usually at higher elevations than Chough; often scavenges around climbing camps; generally fairly tame. VOICE: A descending, thin *sweeeoo*, a rippling *preep* and a rolling *churr*. HABITAT: High mountains, mountain pastures and cultivations. DISTRIBUTION: Resident in the Himalayas and the mountains of W Pakistan.

3 JACKDAW (EURASIAN or WESTERN JACKDAW) *Corvus monedula* 34cm FIELD NOTES: Generally encountered in flocks, regularly associates with other crows and starlings. VOICE: An abrupt, repeated *chjak*, also a low, drawn-out *chaairurr* accompanied by a *chak*. HABITAT: Damp meadows, pastures and cultivated areas. DISTRIBUTION: Resident in the NW of the region.

4 HOUSE CROW (INDIAN HOUSE CROW) *Corvus splendens* 40cm FIELD NOTES: Bold, very sociable. Birds in the NW have a paler, more pronounced hind-neck. VOICE: A flat, dry *kaaa-kaaa*. HABITAT: Villages, towns and cities, often common around ports; also in cultivated areas. DISTRIBUTION: Widespread resident.

5 ROOK *Corvus frugilegus* 47cm FIELD NOTES: Baggy thighs compared with other crows. Juveniles have face feathered. Usually in large flocks accompanied by Jackdaws and House Crows. VOICE: A dry *kraah* and a higher-pitched *kraa-a*. HABITAT: Pastures and cultivations. DISTRIBUTION: Winter visitor to the NW of the region.

6 CARRION CROW *Corvus corone* 49cm FIELD NOTES: Shy, usually in pairs or small groups. Hooded Crow *C. c. cornix* (6b), which occurs as a winter visitor, is often regarded as a full species. VOICE: A vibrant *kraaa*, often repeated; sometimes utters a hollow *konk-konk*. HABITAT: Open country, cultivated areas and upland habitations. DISTRIBUTION: Resident and winter visitor to N Pakistan and NW India.

7 LARGE-BILLED CROW *Corvus macrorhynchos* 41–49cm FIELD NOTES: Usually seen singly, in pairs or in small parties. Eastern Jungle Crow *C. m. levaillanti* (7b) which occurs in the NE, and the Indian Jungle Crow *C. m. culminatus* (7c), which is widespread over much of the region away from the northern mountains and the NE, are often considered to be full species. VOICE: A hoarse *kyarrh kyarrh* or *kyearh kyearh*. Eastern birds utter a distinctive *nyark nyark*. HABITAT: Various, including wooded areas, open country and near habitations. DISTRIBUTION: Widespread resident.

8 RAVEN (COMMON or NORTHERN RAVEN) *Corvus corax* 51–69cm FIELD NOTES: Wary. Usually seen singly, in pairs or in larger groups where food is plentiful. In flight shows a distinct wedge-shaped tail. The browner, smaller, Punjab Raven *C. c. laurencei* (8b) occurs in Pakistan and NW India and is often considered a full species. VOICE: A deep, hollow *pruk-pruk-pruk*, also various other croaks and a guttural rattle. HABITAT: From lowland desert to rocky areas above the tree line. DISTRIBUTION: Resident in Pakistan, NW India and the Himalayas.

9 BROWN-NECKED RAVEN *Corvus ruficollis* 53cm FIELD NOTES: Wings reach tip of tail (fall slightly short on Raven). VOICE: A dry, rising *aarg-aarg-aarg* and an abrupt croak. HABITAT: Desert and semi-desert. DISTRIBUTION: Resident in S Pakistan.

7b
levaillanti

7c
culminatus

7

6b
cornix

8b
laurencei

8

9

1 JAY (EURASIAN JAY) *Garrulus glandarius bispecularis* 34cm FIELD NOTES: Often wary; harsh alarm calls are usually the first sign of its presence, although can be quite bold and inquisitive. In flight shows a prominent white rump. In winter regularly forms large flocks of 20 or more, often accompanied by other jays and treepies. VOICE: A harsh *skaaaak-skaaaak*, also a weak *piyeh*. HABITAT: Temperate, mixed forests of oak, chestnut, pine, rhododendron etc. DISTRIBUTION: Resident in the Himalayas and the NE.

2 LANCEOLATED JAY (BLACK-THROATED or BLACK-HEADED JAY) *Garrulus lanceolatus* 33cm FIELD NOTES: Actions similar to Jay, usually less wary, often recorded feeding on scraps around houses in isolated villages and camps. In winter often a member of feeding parties which include Jays and Gold-billed Blue Magpies. In flight shows a pinkish-buff rump. VOICE: A dry *skaaaak*, thinner than similar call of Jay. HABITAT: Montane forests. DISTRIBUTION: Resident in the Himalayas and the NW of the region.

3 MAGPIE (EURASIAN or BLACK-BILLED MAGPIE) *Pica pica* 45cm FIELD NOTES: Usually in pairs or small parties. Forages mainly on the ground; rests in trees, on rocks or on buildings. Western birds show a white rump; those in the E have a black rump. VOICE: A chattering *chack-chack-chack-chack-chack....*, also an enquiring *ch-chack* and a squealing *keee-uck*. HABITAT: Cultivated upland valleys and around villages with orchards and groves. DISTRIBUTION: Resident in the NW mountain areas, in the Himalayas in Bhutan and N India.

4 SRI LANKA BLUE MAGPIE *Urocissa ornata* 42–47cm FIELD NOTES: Rare and endangered. Mainly a bird of the tree canopy, moving through forests in noisy small parties and regularly foraging in a tit-like acrobatic style. VOICE: Very varied: includes a far-carrying *chink-chink* or *cheek-cheek*, a rasping *crakrakrakrak* and a loud *whee-whee*. HABITAT: Dense evergreen broadleaved forests. DISTRIBUTION: Resident in Sri Lanka.

5 GOLD-BILLED MAGPIE (YELLOW-BILLED BLUE MAGPIE) *Urocissa flavirostris* 63cm FIELD NOTES: Usually in pairs or small parties; forages in trees and on the ground and is regularly a member of mixed-species flocks. Generally wary, but recorded feeding on human food scraps in and around isolated hill stations and villages. VOICE: A wheezy *bu-zeep-peck-peck-peck pop-unclear pu-pu-weer* and a high-pitched *clear-clear*. HABITAT: Deciduous and mixed mountain forests. DISTRIBUTION: Resident in the Himalayas and NE India.

6 BLUE MAGPIE (RED-BILLED BLUE MAGPIE) *Urocissa erythrorhyncha* 66cm FIELD NOTES: Social, mainly arboreal, regularly forages in the canopy of fruiting trees; also recorded feeding on food scraps around mountain hill stations. VOICE: Very varied, including a piercing *quiv-pig-pig*, a soft, repeated *beeee-trik* and when alarmed a rapid *penk-penk-penk-penk*. HABITAT: Broadleaved forests in foothills. DISTRIBUTION: Resident in the Himalayas and the NE of the region.

7 GREEN MAGPIE (COMMON GREEN MAGPIE) *Cissa chinensis* 37–39cm FIELD NOTES: Inconspicuous, presence usually given away by its whistled calls. Generally forages low down in shrubbery or in forest understorey; post breeding forms small flocks which often join with mixed-species feeding flocks. VOICE: A loud *peep-peep* or *kik-wee*; also a rich, squealing whistle. HABITAT: Tropical and subtropical evergreen forest, with a liking for bamboo thickets and shrubbery along watercourses. DISTRIBUTION: Resident in the Himalayas and the NE of the region.

83 TREEPIES, NUTCRACKER, GROUNDPECKER

1 RUFOUS TREEPIE (INDIAN TREEPIE) *Dendrocitta vagabunda* 46–50cm FIELD NOTES: Usually encountered in pairs or small parties, with much larger groups where food is plentiful; also joins other species to feed in fruiting trees. Juvenile has a brown head and upper breast. VOICE: A flute-like *ko-ki-la* often mixed with a harsh rattle; also utters a variety of harsh metallic and mewing notes. HABITAT: Open wooded areas, cultivations, parks and gardens. DISTRIBUTION: Widespread resident.

2 GREY TREEPIE (HIMALAYAN TREEPIE) *Dendrocitta formosae* 36–40cm FIELD NOTES: Regularly found in small parties. Forages mainly in trees but will descend to feed on the ground; often forms part of mixed-species flocks. Juvenile duller, with less black on chin and forehead. VOICE: A loud, rapid *klok-kli-klok-kli-kli*; also a variety of short harsh and musical calls. When alarmed gives a Magpie-like chatter. HABITAT: Deciduous mountain forests, usually open and near scrub or cultivation. DISTRIBUTION: Resident in the Himalayas, E Ghats and the NE of the region.

3 WHITE-BELLIED TREEPIE (SOUTHERN TREEPIE) *Dendrocitta leucogastra* 48cm FIELD NOTES: Generally an arboreal forager; often encountered among mixed-species feeding parties, especially those containing Greater Racket-tailed Drongos. VOICE: Often mimics the calls of the Greater Racket-tailed Drongo; also utters a throaty *chuff-chuff-chuff* and various other creaking, quacking, clicking and dove-like calls. HABITAT: Humid evergreen hill forest and secondary growth. DISTRIBUTION: Resident in the W Ghats and SE India.

4 COLLARED TREEPIE (BLACK-FACED or BLACK-BROWED TREEPIE) *Dendrocitta frontalis* 38cm FIELD NOTES: Arboreal; forages in small parties in dense forest. Recorded making fly-catching sorties much like a drongo. VOICE: Little recorded; said to have typical range of treepie calls. HABITAT: Dense mixed humid evergreen forests with bamboo thickets. DISTRIBUTION: Resident in the Himalayas and the NE of the region.

5 ANDAMAN TREEPIE *Dendrocitta bayleii* 32cm FIELD NOTES: An arboreal forager, usually in pairs or small parties although big groups of 20 or more are not unusual. Tags on to mixed-species feeding parties, especially those containing Andaman Drongos. VOICE: Little recorded; said to have various harsh and melodious notes. HABITAT: Dense evergreen forests. DISTRIBUTION: Resident on the Andamans.

6 NUTCRACKER (SPOTTED NUTCRACKER) *Nucifraga caryocatactes* 32–35cm FIELD NOTES: Usually shy and wary. Mainly arboreal, although will descend to feed on nuts dropped on the forest floor. First sightings are often of birds flying lazily from one treetop to another, generally in pairs or small parties although at times in much bigger groups. The race occurring in the NW, *N. c. multipunctata* (Large-spotted Nutcracker) (6b) is sometimes regarded as a full species. VOICE: A dry *kraaaak*, often repeated to form a discordant rattle; also utters a weak *zhree*. HABITAT: Coniferous forests. DISTRIBUTION: Resident in the Himalayas and the mountains of NW Pakistan.

7 HUME'S GROUNDPECKER (HUME'S GROUND-JAY, GROUND TIT) *Pseudopodoces humilis* 19cm FIELD NOTES: Looks and acts much like a wheatear; bounces along and when at rest flicks wings and tail. Usually shy and wary but can become very confiding, especially around human settlements. Juvenile has weak dark barring on throat and breast. Recent research suggests that this species is in fact a member of the tit family, and it is increasingly referred to as *Parus humilis*. VOICE: A short *chip* followed by a rapid, whistled *cheep-cheep-cheep-cheep*. HABITAT: Open grassy steppe and plains with scattered boulders and bushes, above the tree line. DISTRIBUTION: Resident in the Himalayas.

84 WAXWING, HYPOCOLIUS, ORIOLES

1 WAXWING (BOHEMIAN WAXWING) *Bombycilla garrulus* 16cm FIELD NOTES: Gregarious, occurring in small to large parties; can be quite confiding. Flight starling-like. Juvenile duller with shorter crest; lacks the black throat. VOICE: A shivering, trilled *sirrrr*; feeding flocks utter a low twittering. HABITAT: Open areas with fruiting trees and bushes. DISTRIBUTION: Vagrant, recorded from Pakistan, India and Nepal.

2 GREY HYPOCOLIUS *Hypocolius ampelinus* 23cm FIELD NOTES: Gregarious, usually occuring in small parties or larger groups of up to 20. Forages in bushes and sometimes drops to the ground to pick up insect prey. VOICE: Various mewing and whistling notes, a low, harsh *chirr* and a continuous *kirrrkirrrkirrr*. HABITAT: Semi-desert with scattered scrub and palm groves. DISTRIBUTION: Winter visitor to S Pakistan and Gujarat.

3 BLACK-HOODED ORIOLE *Oriolus xanthornus* 25cm FIELD NOTES: Generally arboreal, encountered singly, in pairs or small parties; attracted to fruiting trees. Juvenile has duller head with forehead and eye-ring yellow; throat and upper breast whitish, streaked black. VOICE: A melodious fluty whistled *why-you* or *why-you-you*, often interspersed with harsh *cheeahs* and *kwaaks*. HABITAT: Open broadleaved forest, well-wooded areas, cultivations, groves, parks and gardens with trees. DISTRIBUTION: Widespread resident.

4 BLACK-NAPED ORIOLE *Oriolus chinensis* 27cm FIELD NOTES: Arboreal, usually stays hidden in foliage; attracted to fruit-bearing trees. Juvenile has diffuse black line through eye; throat, breast and flanks streaked with black. VOICE: A liquid, fluty *luwee - wee - wee-leeow*, or similar; also a harsh scolding whistle. HABITAT: Broadleaved woodlands. DISTRIBUTION: Resident on the Andamans and Nicobars, winter visitor to India and Bangladesh.

5 SLENDER-BILLED ORIOLE *Oriolus tenuirostris* 25cm FIELD NOTES: Actions and habits similar to Black-naped Oriole. Juvenile as juvenile Black-naped Oriole. VOICE: A drawn-out *wheeow* or a liquid *chuck tarry-you*, also a high-pitched *kich* and a cat-like *miaow*. HABITAT: Open well-wooded country. DISTRIBUTION: Breeding and winter visitor in the NE.

6 GOLDEN ORIOLE (EURASIAN GOLDEN ORIOLE) *Oriolus oriolus* 24cm FIELD NOTES: Arboreal, often stays hidden in foliage. Juvenile much like adult female but with a dark brown bill. VOICE: A mellow, fluty *weela-weeoo*, also a harsh *kweeaahk* and a fast *gigigigigi*. HABITAT: Open, well-wooded country. DISTRIBUTION: Vagrant records from India, Pakistan and Sri Lanka.

7 INDIAN GOLDEN ORIOLE *Oriolus kundoo* 25cm FIELD NOTES: Mainly arboreal, attracted to fruiting trees, and often a member of mixed-species feeding parties that may include jungle babblers, drongos and flycatchers. Juvenile similar to adult female but bill dark brown. VOICE: Very similar to Golden Oriole. HABITAT: Open woodland, groves, cultivations and urban gardens with large trees. DISTRIBUTION: Resident in C and NE areas, summer visitor to the N and NW, winter visitor in the S and E.

8 MAROON ORIOLE *Oriolus traillii* 27cm FIELD NOTES: Arboreal, keeps to the top of trees; generally singly or in pairs and often in the company of drongos, minivets and nuthatches. Juvenile brown above and whitish below with dark streaking. VOICE: A harsh *kee-ah* followed by a rich, fluty *pi-lo-lo*. HABITAT: Moist deciduous and evergreen forest. DISTRIBUTION: Resident in the Himalayas and the NE of the region.

85 CUCKOOSHRIKES, TRILLER, FLYCATCHER-SHRIKE, FANTAILS

1 LARGE CUCKOOSHRIKE *Coracina macei* 30cm FIELD NOTES: On landing, flicks wings alternately. Generally occurs in treetops, in pairs or loose parties. Race *C. m. nipalensis* (1b) occurs in the Himalayan foothills and the NE of the region. VOICE: A loud whistled *tee-treee* or *ti-eee*, often uttered while flying from tree to tree. HABITAT: Open wooded country, cultivations with tall trees, groves and plantations. DISTRIBUTION: Widespread resident.

2 BAR-BELLIED CUCKOOSHRIKE *Coracina striata* 26cm FIELD NOTES: Keeps to the tops of trees, often part of mixed-species feeding parties. VOICE: A clear whinnying *kliu-kliu-kliu-kliu* and a grating *gree-ew gree-ew*. HABITAT: Forests. DISTRIBUTION: Resident on the Andamans.

3 BLACK-WINGED CUCKOOSHRIKE *Coracina melaschistos* 24cm FIELD NOTES: Arboreal. Sometimes hovers in front of leaves to glean insects, when white patch under each wing may be conspicuous. VOICE: A slow, descending *twii-twii-weeo-weeow*. HABITAT: Open woodland, riverine bamboo and groves. DISTRIBUTION: Breeds in the Himalayas and the NE, winters elsewhere in the region.

4 BLACK-HEADED CUCKOOSHRIKE *Coracina melanoptera* 18cm FIELD NOTES: Usually seen singly, pairs or in small parties; regularly part of mixed-species feeding flocks. Race *C. m. sykesi* (4b) occurs away from the NW of India. VOICE: A mellow whistling followed by a rapid, repeated *pit-pit-pit*. HABITAT: Broadleaved forest and secondary growth. DISTRIBUTION: Widespread, breeds in N and C areas, resident in parts of the S, the NE and Sri Lanka, elsewhere an inter-region migrant.

5 PIED TRILLER *Lalage nigra* 18cm FIELD NOTES: Forages in low scrubby undergrowth. VOICE: A nasal *chaka-chevu*, a rattling *wheek chechechecheche-chuk*. HABITAT: Forest edges and secondary growth. DISTRIBUTION: Resident on the Nicobars.

6 BAR-WINGED FLYCATCHER-SHRIKE *Hemipus picatus* 15cm FIELD NOTES: Makes fly-catching sallies from habitually used perches. Race *H. p. capitalis* (6b) occurs in the Himalayas. VOICE: A sharp *chisik* or *chir-up*; also a high-pitched trilling. HABITAT: High open forests, forest edge, secondary forest and bamboo strands. DISTRIBUTION: Resident in the hills and mountains over most of the region.

7 YELLOW-BELLIED FANTAIL *Chelidorhynx hypoxantha* 13–14cm FIELD NOTES: Restless. Often part of mixed-species feeding flocks. Tail often held erect and fanned. VOICE: A feeble trill; also a thin, high *sip-sip*. HABITAT: Mixed forests. DISTRIBUTION: Resident in the Himalayas and the NE.

8 WHITE-THROATED FANTAIL *Rhipidura albicollis* 17cm FIELD NOTES: Restless forager, often working up and down main tree trunk or nearby branches. Makes fly-catching sallies. Tail often fanned and held erect. VOICE: A descending *tut-tut-tut-sit-sit-sit-sit*; also a sharp *cheep* or *chuck*. HABITAT: Forests, wooded areas and secondary growth. DISTRIBUTION: Resident in the Himalayas, E and NE of the region.

9 WHITE-SPOTTED FANTAIL *Rhipidura albogularis* 17cm FIELD NOTES: Actions and habits as White-throated Fantail. VOICE: As White-throated Fantail but slower. HABITAT: Wooded country and secondary forest. DISTRIBUTION: Resident over much of peninsular India.

10 WHITE-BROWED FANTAIL *Rhipidura aureola* 17cm FIELD NOTES: Generally encountered singly, in pairs or in small parties. Forages, restlessly, low down in bushes and undergrowth and is often part of mixed-species feeding flocks. Makes fly-catching sallies. Often holds tail erect and fanned. VOICE: A rising then descending series of tinkling notes, transcribed as *chee-chee-cheweechee-vi*; also a harsh *chuck-chuck*. HABITAT: Forests, wooded areas, areas with scattered trees and groves. DISTRIBUTION: Widespread resident.

86 MINIVETS

1 ROSY MINIVET *Pericrocotus roseus* 20cm FIELD NOTES: Tends to be more sluggish than other minivets, often sits quietly at the top of a tree. VOICE: A squeaky, whistling *whiririri-whiririri-whiririri*. HABITAT: Deciduous and evergreen forest, wooded country and gardens. DISTRIBUTION: Resident in the Himalayas and the NE, winter visitor elsewhere.

2 SWINHOE'S MINIVET *Pericrocotus cantonensis* 20cm FIELD NOTES: Forages in the canopy, often found in mixed-species feeding flocks. VOICE: A metallic trill. HABITAT: Evergreen and deciduous forests, forest edge and open woodland. DISTRIBUTION: Vagrant, recorded from Bangladesh.

3 ASHY MINIVET *Pericrocotus divaricatus* 18cm FIELD NOTES: Forages in the outer branches of tree canopy, makes short fly-catching sallies, when white patches show. VOICE: A jangling metallic trill, often uttered in flight. HABITAT: Woodland and forest edge. DISTRIBUTION: Winter visitor, widespread isolated records.

4 SMALL MINIVET *Pericrocotus cinnamomeus* 16cm FIELD NOTES: Active, flits about among foliage in search of insects, also makes short fly-catching sallies; often part of mixed-species feeding flocks. Plumage variable, race with redder underparts *P. c. vividus* (4b) occurs in the C Himalayas, NE India and Bangladesh. VOICE: A constantly repeated, thin, drawn-out *tswee-swee*. HABITAT: Foothill forests, scrub jungle, acacia and subtropical dry woodland. DISTRIBUTION: Widespread resident.

5 WHITE-BELLIED MINIVET *Pericrocotus erythropygius* 15–16.5cm FIELD NOTES: Usually found in pairs or small parties; generally forages low down. Regularly perches on bushes or long grass, from where it drops to the ground to pick up prey; may also hover over grassland before dropping onto insects. VOICE: A soft *tchip* or *tsip-i-sip*; also various sweet, high-pitched notes such as *thi, tuee, chi, tschi* and *tchu-it*. HABITAT: Open, dry scrub, grassland and savannah with scattered trees. DISTRIBUTION: Resident, mainly in N and C India.

6 SCARLET MINIVET (ORANGE MINIVET) *Pericrocotus flammeus* 20–22cm FIELD NOTES: Gleans insects from foliage, also hovers or makes short sallies to capture flying insects. Forages mainly in the tree canopy; a regular member of mixed-species feeding flocks. Birds from the N, *P. f. speciosus* (not shown), sometimes treated as a separate species, are larger and redder. VOICE: A piercing *sweep-sweep-sweep-sweep* or *weep-weep-weep-wit-wip*. HABITAT: Forests and wooded areas. DISTRIBUTION: Widespread over much of the region.

7 GREY-CHINNED MINIVET *Pericrocotus solaris* 17–19cm FIELD NOTES: Actions and habits much as Scarlet Minivet. VOICE: A thin, repeated *tzee-zip* and a slurred *swirrrrit*; also a soft *trip* and a stronger *trii-ti*, often uttered while foraging. HABITAT: Montane forests. DISTRIBUTION: Resident in the Himalayas and the NE.

8 SHORT-BILLED MINIVET *Pericrocotus brevirostris* 19cm FIELD NOTES: Forages among foliage, usually in pairs or as part of mixed-species feeding flocks. VOICE: A distinctive, thin, whistled *tsuuuit*; also a dry *tup*. HABITAT: Deciduous and evergreen forests, forest edge and secondary growth. DISTRIBUTION: Resident in the Himalayas and the NE.

9 LONG-TAILED MINIVET *Pericrocotus ethologus* 20cm FIELD NOTES: Forages mainly in the tree canopy, gleans or hovers in front of foliage to take insects; also makes short fly-catching sallies. VOICE: A sweet, rolling, repeated *prrr wi* and *prrr i*; also a thin, sibilant *swii-swii swii-swii-swii*. HABITAT: Forests and well-wooded areas. DISTRIBUTION: Breeds or is resident across the N of the region, winters S to C India.

87 DRONGOS

1 BLACK DRONGO *Dicrurus macrocercus* 30cm FIELD NOTES: Uses a prominent perch from which it makes fly-catching sallies. Captures prey in the air or pounces on insects on the ground; attracted to areas where grazing animals disturb insects. VOICE: A harsh *ti-tui*, and *cheece-cheece-chichuk*; during the breeding season pairs often participate in noisy duets. HABITAT: Light hill forest, open wooded country and cultivations. DISTRIBUTION: Widespread resident.

2 ASHY DRONGO *Dicrurus leucophaeus* 30cm FIELD NOTES: Makes fly-catching forays from the tops of trees. Birds from the E and NE, *D. l. hopwoodi* (2b), are paler; the distinctive race *D. l. salangensis* (2c) is a rare vagrant. VOICE: A harsh *cheece-cheece-chichuck* followed by a querulous *kil-kil-kil-kil* or *tililili*. HABITAT: Forests and well-wooded country. DISTRIBUTION: Breeder and resident across the N and NE, much more widespread in winter.

3 CROW-BILLED DRONGO *Dicrurus annectans* 28cm FIELD NOTES: Keeps to tall undergrowth and lower tree branches, makes fly-catching sallies from hidden perch. VOICE: Loud, musical whistles and chirrs. HABITAT: Moist deciduous and evergreen forests. DISTRIBUTION: Breeds in the Himalayan foothills and the NE, winters in the NE.

4 BRONZED DRONGO *Dicrurus aeneus* 24cm FIELD NOTES: Arboreal, often frequents the same area over a long period; a regular member or mixed-species feeding groups. VOICE: Loud, clear musical whistles. HABITAT: Clearings and edges of moist broadleaved forests; also bamboo jungle and plantations. DISTRIBUTION: Resident in E and W Ghats, the Himalayan foothills, and the NE of the region.

5 WHITE-BELLIED DRONGO *Dicrurus caerulescens* 24cm FIELD NOTES: Makes fly-catching sallies from the tops of trees; often a member of mixed-species parties. Dark-bellied race *D. c. leucopygialis* (5b) occurs in Sri Lanka. VOICE: Three or four pleasant whistling notes, similar to Black Drongo but less harsh. HABITAT: Clearings and edges of open forest and well-wooded areas. DISTRIBUTION: Widespread resident.

6 GREATER RACKET-TAILED DRONGO *Dicrurus paradiseus* 30cm; including tail, up to 65cm FIELD NOTES: Gleans insects from foliage or flowers; also makes fly-catching sallies. Regular member of mixed-species parties. Race *D. p. grandis* (6b) occurs in the N and NE of the region. VOICE: A monotonous *kit-kit-kit-kit*, mainly given pre-dawn. Regularly mimics other bird calls. HABITAT: Broadleaved, bamboo and secondary forest. DISTRIBUTION: Widespread resident.

7 SRI LANKA CRESTED DRONGO *Dicrurus lophorinus* 34cm FIELD NOTES: Actions as Greater Racket-tailed Drongo. VOICE: Explosive mix of fluty, bell-like and grinding notes; also a nasal *urdle-eee* or a quicker *urd-lee*. Often mimics calls of other species. HABITAT: Wet-zone forests. DISTRIBUTION: Resident in Sri Lanka.

8 LESSER RACKET-TAILED DRONGO *Dicrurus remifer* 25cm; including tail, up to 40cm FIELD NOTES: Arboreal. Makes swooping sallies in pursuit of flying insects. VOICE: A range of loud metallic, musical whistles; mimics the calls of other species. HABITAT: Moist broadleaved forest. DISTRIBUTION: Resident in the Himalayas and the NE.

9 SPANGLED DRONGO (HAIR-CRESTED DRONGO) *Dicrurus hottentottus* 32cm FIELD NOTES: Arboreal, attracted to flowering trees; feeds mainly on nectar. VOICE: A loud *chit-wiii* and single *wiii* calls. HABITAT: Moist broadleaved forest. DISTRIBUTION: Resident in the Himalayas, the W and E Ghats and the NE.

10 ANDAMAN DRONGO *Dicrurus andamanensis* 32cm FIELD NOTES: Arboreal. Often clings to trunks, woodpecker-like, when searching for insects: also makes fly-catching sallies. VOICE: A variety of sharp metallic notes. HABITAT: Forests. DISTRIBUTION: Resident on the Andamans.

1

2

2b

2c

hopwoodi

salangensis

3

6b
grandis

4

5

5b

leucopygialis

8

6

7

9

10

88 MONARCH, PARADISE FLYCATCHER, IORAS, FAIRY-BLUEBIRD, LEAFBIRDS

1 BLACK-NAPED MONARCH *Hypothymis azurea* 16cm FIELD NOTES: Actively gleans insects from foliage; also hovers or makes aerial sallies to capture prey. Race *H. a. tytleri* (1b) occurs on the Andamans; race *H. a. ceylonensis* (1c) occurs in Sri Lanka. VOICE: A high-pitched, rasping *sweech-which* or *che-chwe*. When alarmed utters a *sweech-which-which*. HABITAT: Evergreen or mixed deciduous forest, secondary jungle and plantations. DISTRIBUTION: Widespread resident.

2 ASIAN PARADISE FLYCATCHER *Terpsiphone paradisi* 20cm; male with tail 45cm FIELD NOTES: Generally hunts from a perch in the lower part of tree canopy; usually in pairs or as part of a mixed-species feeding party. VOICE: A clear rolling *chu-wu-wu-wu-wu-wu...*, also a loud *chee-tew*, a harsh *tst*. When mobbing utters a *weep-poor-willie- weep-poor-willie*. HABITAT: Open forests, bushes, groves and gardens. DISTRIBUTION: Widespread resident.

3 COMMON IORA *Aegithina tiphia* 14cm FIELD NOTES: Forages, acrobatically, in the canopy. Race *A. t. multicolor* (3b) occurs in extreme S India and Sri Lanka; race *A. t. humei* (3c) occurs in C India. VOICE: A two-toned *we-e-e-tu*; also a *chee-chit-chit-chit* call note and a piping *tu-tu-tu-tu*. HABITAT: Open forests, forest edge, scrub jungle and cultivations. DISTRIBUTION: Widespread resident.

4 MARSHALL'S IORA *Aegithina nigrolutea* 14cm FIELD NOTES: Actions similar to Common Iora. VOICE: A slurred *tchoo-tchoo*, followed by a loud, metallic *chee-tchoo-tchoo-tchee* or *chee-cho-chi-choo*; other calls include a *wheeti wheeti*, *twsee-ku-kee* and a *tswee-twsee-tee-dik*. HABITAT: Thorny acacia, scrubby groves and sheesham woodland. DISTRIBUTION: Resident in N and C India and Sri Lanka.

5 ASIAN FAIRY-BLUEBIRD *Irena puella* 25cm FIELD NOTES: Generally encountered in treetops, keeps on the move, hopping from branch to branch and flying from tree to tree. VOICE: A percussive, liquid *weet-weet be-quick peepit whats-it*, usually repeated every few seconds. In flight utters a sharp *chichichichik*. HABITAT: Evergreen and moist deciduous forests. DISTRIBUTION: Resident in the Himalayan foothills, NE, S and W India, Bangladesh, the Andamans and the Nicobars.

6 JERDON'S LEAFBIRD *Chloropsis jerdoni* 20cm FIELD NOTES: Forages in trees, searching, acrobatically, for insects, fruit and nectar; often part of mixed-species feeding flocks. VOICE: A random, varied combination of whistles, buzzing and rich sharp notes. HABITAT: Open forests, secondary growth, orchards and wooded gardens. DISTRIBUTION: Resident over peninsular India and in Sri Lanka.

7 BLUE-WINGED LEAFBIRD *Chloropsis cochinchinensis* 20cm FIELD NOTES: Actions and habits similar to Jerdon's Leafbird. VOICE: Various sweet musical notes; mimics other species. HABITAT: Deciduous and evergreen forests in damp, hot valleys; also in groves. DISTRIBUTION: Resident in the NE.

8 GOLDEN-FRONTED LEAFBIRD *Chloropsis aurifrons* 19cm FIELD NOTES: Acrobatic forager in the thick foliage of trees. Race *C. a. insularis* (8b) occurs in far SW India and Sri Lanka. VOICE: A musical *swich-chich-chich-weee*; also a repeated *tzik* and a *chup-chaw*. Mimics the calls of other species. HABITAT: Broadleaved forests and secondary growth. DISTRIBUTION: Resident in NE, W, E, S and parts of C India, Bangladesh, the Himalayas and Sri Lanka.

9 ORANGE-BELLIED LEAFBIRD *Chloropsis hardwickii* 20cm FIELD NOTES: Forages in tree foliage, acrobatically probing flowers for nectar and leaves for insects. VOICE: Said to have the sweetest songs of all the leafbirds. Various ringing and melodious calls recorded, including a soft *tilu-tilu-tilu-tilu-ti* a low *tp-tp-tp-tp-tp* and a *tshiwatshishi-watshishi-watshishi* and a loud, rapid, repeated *ti-ti-tsyi*. HABITAT: Broadleaved forests. DISTRIBUTION: Resident in the Himalayas and the NE.

1b ♂
tytleri

♀

rufous
morph

♀

1c ♂
ceylonensis

1

♂

2

♂

multicolor
3b

3

♂

♀

4

♂

♂

♀

3c
♂

humei

♂

white
morph

♀

8

8b
insularis

5

♀

6

♂

♀

7

♂

9

♂

♀

1 RED-BACKED SHRIKE *Lanius collurio* 17cm FIELD NOTES: Usually perches prominently on bush tops or other vantage points from where it can pounce on insects or small vertebrates. In flight shows a grey rump and white bases on outer tail feathers. Juvenile duller with barring above and below. VOICE: A harsh *shack* or *shak-shak*; also a harsh *churruck-churruck*. HABITAT: Dry country with bushes, also cultivation edges. DISTRIBUTION: Passage migrant in the NW.

2 BROWN SHRIKE *Lanius cristatus* 18cm FIELD NOTES: Actions similar to Red-backed Shrike. Juvenile has upperparts, from forehead to tail, barred dark. Greyer race *L. c. lucionensis* (2b) is a winter visitor to Sri Lanka, the Andamans and the Nicobars. VOICE: A harsh *chr-r-r-ri*. HABITAT: Forest edge, scrub and open cultivation. DISTRIBUTION: Widespread winter visitor.

3 LONG-TAILED SHRIKE *Lanius schach* 24cm FIELD NOTES: Noisy, restless and aggressive, recorded robbing other birds of food; otherwise actions much as Red-backed Shrike. In flight shows white bases to primary feathers and a rufous rump. Juvenile generally dull greyish-brown barred above and dark brown below. Black headed race *L. s. tricolor* (3b) occurs in the Himalayas. Birds of peninsular India and Sri Lanka have much less rufous on the scapulars. VOICE: A metallic warble that often contains mimicry of other birds' calls and songs; also utters a harsh *tchick*, a buzzing *grennh* and a coarse *rrrre*. HABITAT: Open wooded country, cultivations and gardens. DISTRIBUTION: Widespread resident.

4 RED-TAILED SHRIKE (TURKESTAN SHRIKE) *Lanius phoenicuroides* 17cm FIELD NOTES: Actions and habits similar to Red-backed Shrike. Recently split from Isabelline Shrike. VOICE: A babbling and warbling that contains harsh and melodious whistles; also a harsh grating call. HABITAT: Open dry scrub. DISTRIBUTION: Breeds in Baluchistan, also occurs as a migrant in the NW.

5 ISABELLINE SHRIKE (RUFOUS-TAILED SHRIKE) *Lanius isabellinus* 17cm FIELD NOTES: Actions and habits similar to Red-backed Shrike. Juvenile like an adult female, but with heavier scaling below and some scaling on upperparts. VOICE: Calls and song similar to Red-tailed Shrike. HABITAT: Arid areas with scattered bushes and scrub. DISTRIBUTION: Winter visitor, mainly to the NW.

6 BAY-BACKED SHRIKE *Lanius vittatus* 18cm FIELD NOTES: Territorial, often occupying the same prominent perches day after day. Actions similar to Red-backed Shrike. In flight shows white rump, white patches at base of primaries and white outer tail feathers. Juvenile duller with much dark barring above. VOICE: A pleasant loud warble interspersed with mimicry of other birds' calls; also a scolding *chur-r* or *chee-urr*. HABITAT: Open dry country with scattered trees and scrub. DISTRIBUTION: Widespread resident.

7 GREY-BACKED SHRIKE (TIBETAN SHRIKE) *Lanius tephronotus* 22cm FIELD NOTES: Usually seen singly, or in widely separated pairs; feeding actions much as Red-backed Shrike. In flight shows a rufous rump. Juvenile duller with dark barring above and below. VOICE: A prolonged, subdued, melodious warble interspersed with mimicry of others birds' calls; also harsh grating calls, typical of the genus. HABITAT: Forest clearings, high-altitude open scrub; winters in lower-altitude scrub and cultivations. DISTRIBUTION: Resident and winter visitor in the Himalayas and the NE.

8 BURMESE SHRIKE *Lanius collurioides* 20cm FIELD NOTES: Confiding, usually easy to approach; feeding actions as Red-backed Shrike. Juvenile duller with dark barring above and below. VOICE: Sweet, with musical and grating notes. HABITAT: Open woodland, forest edge, secondary growth and cultivations. DISTRIBUTION: Passage migrant in the NE.

90 SHRIKES, WOODSHRIKES, WOODSWALLOWS

1 LESSER GREY SHRIKE *Lanius minor* 20cm FIELD NOTES: Uses prominent perch from where to pounce on prey; although tends to hover and pounce more than other shrikes. In flight shows white patch on primaries and white outer tail feathers. Juvenile brownish-grey above with dark bars. VOICE: A babbling chatter that includes mimicry; also a harsh *kerrib-kerrib*. HABITAT: Open semi-desert and cultivation with scattered bushes. DISTRIBUTION: Vagrant, recorded from India.

2 GREAT GREY SHRIKE (NORTHERN SHRIKE) *Lanius excubitor* 24cm FIELD NOTES: Perches prominently, often using the same vantage point for long periods; feeds mainly on small vertebrates. In flight shows large white patches on base of primaries that extend onto base of secondaries and white outer tail feathers. VOICE: A ringing *shreeee*; also a repeated, nasal *shack*. HABITAT: Open country with scattered trees, bushes or scrub. DISTRIBUTION: Vagrant, recorded from Pakistan and India.

3 SOUTHERN GREY SHRIKE *Lanius meridionalis* 25cm FIELD NOTES: Feeding actions similar to Great Grey Shrike. In flight shows extensive white patches on base of primaries and on outer tail feathers. Pale-billed race *L. e. pallidirostris* (3b) occurs in W Pakistan. VOICE: A repetition of two melodious notes, the second higher-pitched, often interspersed with a long subdued warble; also a harsh *tscheee*. HABITAT: Semi-desert scrub, open thorn bush and cultivation edge. DISTRIBUTION: Widespread over much of the region.

4 WOODCHAT SHRIKE *Lanius senator* 18cm FIELD NOTES: Typical shrike, using mainly a perch-and-pounce feeding method. In flight shows white on rump, primary bases and outer tail feathers. VOICE: A rattling *trr-trr-trr*, a *gek-gek-gek*, a short *crex* and a *kwikwik*. HABITAT: Open woodland, woodland edge and scrubby country. DISTRIBUTION: Vagrant, recorded from Pakistan.

5 LARGE WOODSHRIKE *Tephrodornis virgatus* 23cm FIELD NOTES: Usually encountered in small parties, actively foraging in treetops, hopping from branch to branch in search of insects; occasionally makes aerial sallies after flying insects. Post breeding may be found in larger flocks, often in association with other species. *T. v. sylvicola* (Malabar Woodshrike) (5b) occurs in S and W India and is treated by some as a full species. VOICE: A musical, repeated *kew-kew-kew-kew*; also various harsh notes and mellower *tra-a-a* and *thul thull*. HABITAT: Evergreen forest, open deciduous secondary growth and various well-wooded areas. DISTRIBUTION: Resident in the Himalayan foothills, E, S, W and NE India and Bangladesh.

6 COMMON WOODSHRIKE *Tephrodornis pondicerianus* 18cm FIELD NOTES: Occurs in pairs or small parties, foraging among foliage; sometimes takes invertebrate prey from the ground or during aerial sallies. *T. p. affinis* (Sri Lanka Woodshrike) (6b) occurs in Sri Lanka and is treated as a full species by some authorities. VOICE: A plaintive *weet-weet* followed by a quick *whi-whi-whi-whee*; also soft trills during breeding season. HABITAT: Light deciduous woodland, secondary growth, scrub and wooded gardens. DISTRIBUTION: Widespread resident.

7 ASHY WOODSWALLOW *Artamus fuscus* 19cm FIELD NOTES: Gregarious; groups often perch on bare treetop branches, wires or palm leaf-stalks, from where they make aerial sallies to capture flying insects. VOICE: A harsh *chek-chek-chek* or *chake-chake-chake*; the latter sets off and finishes a pleasant twittering song that is given during the breeding season. HABITAT: Open wooded country with nearby palms. DISTRIBUTION: Resident, mainly in the E, SE, NE and S of the region.

8 WHITE-BREASTED WOODSWALLOW *Artamus leucorynchus* 19cm FIELD NOTES: Actions similar to Ashy Woodswallow. VOICE: Similar to Ashy Woodswallow. HABITAT: Open wooded country, forest clearings and plantations. DISTRIBUTION: Resident on the Andamans.

1 ♀ n-br

♂ br

2

3

3b
pallidirostris

4 ♀

♂

5 ♀

♂

5b
sylvicola

♀

6

6b
affinis

7

8

91 ROCK THRUSHES, WHISTLING THRUSHES

1 ROCK THRUSH (COMMON or RUFOUS-TAILED ROCK THRUSH) *Monticola saxatilis* 20cm FIELD NOTES: Usually wary. Generally forages on the ground, although sometimes feeds in trees or makes short aerial sorties to capture flying insects. Frequently wags tail. VOICE: A series of soft, clear melodic phrases; also a low *chak-chak* and a clear *diu*. HABITAT: Open rocky hillsides. DISTRIBUTION: Breeds in Baluchistan; migrant in the NW.

2 BLUE ROCK THRUSH *Monticola solitarius* 20cm FIELD NOTES: Forages on the ground, or drops on prey from low perch; sometimes makes aerial sorties after flying insects. Rufous-bellied race M. *s. philippensis* (2b) occurs as a vagrant. VOICE: A loud, fluty, melodic *tju-sri - tjurr-titi - wuchi - trr-trrt-tri*; may also include some mimicry. Also utters a deep *chak-chak*, a plaintive *see* and a *wit-wit*. HABITAT: Barren rocky hills and steep hillsides; during the winter occurs in a wider range of rocky locations including cliffs, rocky seashore, quarries and old habitations. DISTRIBUTION: Breeds in the NW, otherwise a widespread winter visitor.

3 CHESTNUT-BELLIED ROCK THRUSH *Monticola rufiventris* 23cm FIELD NOTES: Forages mainly on the ground, occasionally makes fly-catching sorties from high branches. VOICE: A pleasant warble and a whistled *fweeeur-fweet*, usually delivered from a treetop; also utters a *quock*, a coarse *quach* and a shrill *tick*. HABITAT: Open moist forests on steep, rocky hillsides. DISTRIBUTION: Resident in the Himalayas and the NE.

4 BLUE-CAPPED ROCK THRUSH *Monticola cinclorhynchus* 17cm FIELD NOTES: Mainly arboreal, picks insects off trunks and branches; also feeds on the ground among leaf litter. VOICE: A fluty *tew-li-di - tew-li-di - tew-li-di* or *tra-trr-treee-treea...*, usually given from the topmost branch of a tree or during a song-flight. HABITAT: Open pine and oak forests and rocky grass-covered slopes with scattered trees; winters in moist forest and well-wooded areas. DISTRIBUTION: Breeds in the Himalayas, winters mainly in the W Ghats.

5 SRI LANKA WHISTLING THRUSH *Myophonus blighi* 20cm FIELD NOTES: Very shy and elusive; forages on the ground, usually at the edge of streams. VOICE: A rich mixture of tinkling, chortling and buzzing notes; also a down-slurred buzzy *sriii* or *sriii-sriii* often preceded by a shrill warbling series. HABITAT: Near fast-flowing streams in dense mountain forests. DISTRIBUTION: Resident in Sri Lanka.

6 MALABAR WHISTLING THRUSH *Myophonus horsfieldii* 25cm FIELD NOTES: Forages on the ground or in shallow water at the edge of streams; readily perches in trees. VOICE: A series of rambling, rich, mournful whistles; also a high-pitched, descending *kree-ee*. HABITAT: Rocky hill streams in forests, secondary growth and plantations; also noted on forest paths or in gardens. DISTRIBUTION: Resident in the hills of W and C India.

7 BLUE WHISTLING THRUSH *Myophonus caeruleus* 33cm FIELD NOTES: Feeding actions much like a Blackbird. Generally seen feeding from rocks in strong-flowing streams, dipping to collect food from water surface. VOICE: A disjointed string of melodious, high-pitched, human-like whistles; sometimes includes mimicry. Calls include a far-carrying *tzeet-tze-tze-tzeet* or *tzeet-tzuit-tzuit-zuit* and a shrill *skree*. HABITAT: Broadleaved evergreen and mixed deciduous forest; often in gorges and ravines. DISTRIBUTION: Resident in the Himalayas and in the NE and NW of the region.

1 DARK-SIDED THRUSH *Zoothera marginata* 25cm FIELD NOTES: Very shy. Often forages in moist stream beds. VOICE: A thin whistle. Calls include a low *chuck* and when alarmed a high-pitched *pit-pit-pit*. HABITAT: Dense forest with nearby streams. DISTRIBUTION: Resident in the Himalayas and NE of the region.

2 PLAIN-BACKED THRUSH *Zoothera mollissima* 26cm FIELD NOTES: Feeds mainly on the ground. Generally shy and unapproachable. VOICE: Variable, rich musical phrases. Calls include a thin *chuck* and a rattling alarm. HABITAT: Rocky alpine areas with juniper and dwarf rhododendron; winters in lower areas. DISTRIBUTION: Resident in the Himalayas and the NE of the region.

3 LONG-TAILED THRUSH *Zoothera dixoni* 27–28cm FIELD NOTES: Secretive, feeds on the ground in thick vegetation. VOICE: Often begins with a *w-t-it* followed by a slow, slurred *wu-ut - cheet-sher - wut-chet-shuur* interspersed with twitters and *too-ee* phrases. HABITAT: Dense forests above or along the tree line; winters in lower-altitude thick forest or open areas with bushes. DISTRIBUTION: Resident in the Himalayas and the NE of the region.

4 SRI LANKA THRUSH *Zoothera imbricata* 24cm FIELD NOTES: Forages low down, mainly on the ground. VOICE: A series of eight or more single, rich whistles. Calls include a high-pitched, repeated *tchiss*. HABITAT: Dense moist forest. DISTRIBUTION: Resident in Sri Lanka.

5 SCALY THRUSH *Zoothera dauma* 27cm FIELD NOTES: Mainly a ground forager in thick cover. Birds in the W Ghats *Z. d. neilgherriensis* (5b) often regarded as a full species. VOICE: Repeated slow phrases, sometimes interspersed with low squeaks and twitters. Calls include a soft *tsi* and a drawn-out *tzeep*; when alarmed utters a *chuck-chuck*. HABITAT: Forests and well-wooded areas in winter. DISTRIBUTION: Summers in the Himalayas and W Ghats; Himalayan birds winter further south.

6 LONG-BILLED THRUSH *Zoothera monticola* 28cm FIELD NOTES: Shy and retiring ground forager in thick cover. VOICE: A melancholic series of plaintive whistles. When alarmed utters a loud *zaaaaaaa*. HABITAT: Thick undergrowth in dense high-altitude fir forest; winters at lower levels. DISTRIBUTION: Resident in the Himalayas and the NE of the region.

7 SPOT-WINGED THRUSH *Geokichla spiloptera* 23cm FIELD NOTES: Best located while singing. Retiring, keeps to the cover of thick vegetation. VOICE: A variable, rich series of short whistled phrases. Contact call is a soft *tzseee*. HABITAT: Undergrowth in dense rainforest. DISTRIBUTION: Resident in Sri Lanka.

8 PIED THRUSH *Geokichla wardii* 22cm FIELD NOTES: Shy when breeding, less so post breeding. Forms small flocks during migration. Feeds on the ground and in fruiting trees. VOICE: A short, repeated two-note warble. Call is a sharp, spitting *ptz-ptz-ptz-ptz*. HABITAT: Broadleaved forest and secondary growth. DISTRIBUTION: Breeds in the Himalayas, winters mainly in S India and Sri Lanka.

9 ORANGE-HEADED THRUSH *Geokichla citrina* 20–23cm FIELD NOTES: Shy; may form into small flocks post breeding. Figure (9b) shows the distinctive peninsular race *G. c. cyanota*; birds from the Andamans *G. c. andamanensis* and the Nicobars *G. c. albogularis* (not shown) lack the white in the wing. VOICE: A loud, clear series of lilting phrases. Calls include a soft *chuk* and a screeching *kreeee*. HABITAT: Moist, shady areas in forests. DISTRIBUTION: Fairly widespread resident, summer visitor in the Himalayas.

10 SIBERIAN THRUSH *Geokichla sibirica* 22cm FIELD NOTES: Secretive, feeds on the ground or in trees when in fruit. VOICE: A weak *tseee*, a soft *zit* and a gruff squawk when alarmed. HABITAT: Forests. DISTRIBUTION: Winter visitor to the NE and the Andamans.

typical underwing pattern of *Zoothera* and *Geokichla* thrushes

1

2

3

4

5

5b

neilgherriensis

6

7

8 ♀ ♂

9b ♂
cyanota

9 ♀ ♂

10 ♀ ♂

93 THRUSHES

1 KESSLER'S THRUSH (WHITE-BACKED THRUSH) *Turdus kessleri* 28cm FIELD NOTES: Gregarious; may be found among parties of Black-throated or Dusky Thrushes. VOICE: A soft *squack*, a low *dug-dug*, a high-pitched *swi-swi-swi-swi* and harsh chuckles. HABITAT: Open shrubby areas; also potato fields and orchards. DISTRIBUTION: Winter visitor to E Himalayas.

2 CHESTNUT THRUSH *Turdus rubrocanus* 24–28cm FIELD NOTES: Generally perches in the tops of trees. Feeds on the ground and in trees and bushes. Race *T. r. gouldii* (2b) occurs in E Himalayas and the NE of the region. VOICE: Short warbled phrases repeated up to eight times. Calls include a *chuck-chuck* and a rapid *kwik-kwik kwik-kwik*. HABITAT: Breeds in conifer and mixed forests with ground cover; winters in open wooded areas and orchards. DISTRIBUTION: Resident and winter visitor in the Himalayas and the NE of the region.

3 WHITE-COLLARED BLACKBIRD *Turdus albocinctus* 28cm FIELD NOTES: Generally wary; more sociable post breeding. Forages on the ground or in fruiting bushes and trees. Juvenile lacks the white collar; generally brown above with ochre tips to wing feathers, ochre below with dark brown spotting. VOICE: A series of mellow, descending whistles, *tew-i-tew-u-tew-o* or similar. Call is a throaty *tuck-tuck-tuck*. HABITAT: Various forests with good ground cover. DISTRIBUTION: Resident in the Himalayas and the NE of the region.

4 BLACK-BREASTED THRUSH *Turdus dissimilis* 23cm FIELD NOTES: Forages on the ground and also in fruiting trees and bushes. VOICE: A sweet lilting series of short-spaced notes. Calls include a thin *seeee* and a resounding *tuc tuc tuc*. HABITAT: Breeds in oak and conifer forest, broadleaved evergreen forest and secondary growth. Post breeding also occurs in scrub jungle and mangroves. DISTRIBUTION: Resident in NE India; winters south to Bangladesh.

5 INDIAN BLACKBIRD *Turdus simillimus* 25cm FIELD NOTES: Forages on the ground and in fruiting trees. Pale race *T. s. nigropileus* (5b) occurs in W, C, and SE India. Dark race *T. s. kinnisii* (5c) occurs in Sri Lanka. VOICE: Loud and melodious with much mimicry. *T. s. kinnisii* has a long series of warbling whistles. Call is a *kack-kack*. HABITAT: Moist forest and wooded ravines. DISTRIBUTION: Resident in the hills of peninsular India and Sri Lanka.

6 GREY-WINGED BLACKBIRD *Turdus boulboul* 29cm FIELD NOTES: Generally shy. May form small winter flocks, which often include White-collared Blackbirds. VOICE: Rich and melodious, usually consisting of a soft opening note followed by four high notes descending in tone. Calls include a *chuck-chuck*, a *chook-chook* and a *churi* contact note. HABITAT: Moist broadleaved forest of oak and rhododendron with thick cover, conifer forest clearings and dry scrub on hillsides. DISTRIBUTION: Resident in the Himalayas; winter visitor in N India.

7 TIBETAN BLACKBIRD *Turdus maximus* 26–29cm FIELD NOTES: Forages on the ground; attracted to soft areas at the edge of melting snow. VOICE: A series of phrases that includes rapid metallic notes, squeaks, wheezy sounds, guttural caws and a pure whistle. Calls include a low *chut-ut-ut* and a harsh *chak-chak-chak-chak*. HABITAT: Subalpine rocky grassy slopes with dwarf juniper; winters at lower levels. DISTRIBUTION: Resident in NW Himalayas; winter visitor in the rest of the Himalayas.

8 BLACKBIRD (COMMON or EURASIAN BLACKBIRD) *Turdus merula* 27cm FIELD NOTES: Forages on the ground and in fruiting trees. VOICE: Rich, clear, fluty notes that merge into short, continuous phrases. Calls include a drawn-out *seee* and a low *chuck-chuck-chuck*. HABITAT: Woodland and thickets. DISTRIBUTION: Winter visitor to Pakistan.

94 THRUSHES

1 TICKELL'S THRUSH *Turdus unicolor* 21cm FIELD NOTES: Feeds mainly on the ground. In winter sometimes forms loose flocks. VOICE: Song is a weak, monotonous series of phrases. Calls include a loud *juk-juk*, a chattering, decelerating *juh juk-juk juk*, also a short, high buzz. HABITAT: Breeds in mixed forests with clearings, open broadleaved woodland, groves and orchards; winters in groves and well-wooded areas. DISTRIBUTION: Summers in the Himalayas; winters in S and E India.

2 GREY-SIDED THRUSH *Turdus feae* 23cm FIELD NOTES: Shy, mainly a ground feeder. In winter sometimes associates with Eyebrowed Thrush. VOICE: A thin *zeee*. HABITAT: Montane forest, slightly lower-level forest in winter. DISTRIBUTION: Winter visitor to the NE.

3 EYEBROWED THRUSH *Turdus obscurus* 22cm FIELD NOTES: Forages on the ground and in fruiting trees and bushes. Often associates with other thrushes. VOICE: A soft *chuk*, a hard *tack-tack*, a *shree* and a *dzee* given in flight. HABITAT: Open forests. DISTRIBUTION: Winter visitor, mainly to the NE of the region.

4 BLACK-THROATED THRUSH *Turdus atrogularis* 26cm FIELD NOTES: Gregarious; forages on the ground and in bushes. VOICE: Calls include a thin *seet*, a squeaky *qui-kwea* and a throaty chuckling when alarmed. HABITAT: Grassy scrubby hillsides, forest edge and cultivations. DISTRIBUTION: Winter visitor to the N of the region.

5 RED-THROATED THRUSH (RUFOUS-THROATED THRUSH) *Turdus ruficollis* 25cm FIELD NOTES: Forages mainly on the ground and in low bushes. Often associates with other thrush species. VOICE: Calls include a hoarse, high *kwee-kweek*, a *skrie-kri-kriek kukukukuk sweeseek* and a thin *tseep* uttered in flight. HABITAT: Forest, forest edge, cultivations and fields with scattered trees. DISTRIBUTION: Winter visitor in the Himalayas and the NE.

6 DUSKY THRUSH *Turdus eunomus* 23cm FIELD NOTES: Forages mostly on the ground, but also in fruiting bushes and trees. VOICE: Calls include a low staccato *chuck* and a rhythmic *chek-chek-chek*. HABITAT: Hillside scrub, sparse woodland, grassy areas with scattered trees. DISTRIBUTION: Winter visitor to the Himalayas and the NE of the region.

7 SONG THRUSH *Turdus philomelos* 23cm FIELD NOTES: Forages mostly on the ground; specialises in feeding on snails, which are usually smashed on stones or rocks. In flight shows ochre underwing-coverts. VOICE: Clear, repeated phrases. Calls include a *sip* or *zip* and a loud *chick* when alarmed. HABITAT: Open woodland with extensive undergrowth. DISTRIBUTION: Vagrant, recorded from Pakistan and India.

8 MISTLE THRUSH *Turdus viscivorus* 27cm FIELD NOTES: Feeds on the ground, and also in fruiting trees and bushes. In flight shows white underwing-coverts. VOICE: Clear, far-carrying, fluted phrases. Calls include a harsh rattle and a *tuck-tuck-tuck*. HABITAT: Open conifer forest, juniper shrubberies, rocky areas with stunted junipers and orchards; winters around forest edges and grassy slopes. DISTRIBUTION: Resident in W Himalayas and NW of the region.

9 FIELDFARE *Turdus pilaris* 25cm FIELD NOTES: In winter usually found in large flocks. In flight shows white underwing-coverts. VOICE: Calls include a harsh *chak-chak* a nasal *tseee* and a *chetchetchetje* when alarmed. HABITAT: Open areas with scattered bushes; also orchards. DISTRIBUTION: Vagrant, recorded in India.

95 SHORTWINGS, CHATS

1 GOULD'S SHORTWING *Heteroxenicus stellatus* 13cm FIELD NOTES: Mouse-like as it forages among tangled roots and fallen branches. VOICE: A high-pitched, undulating *tssiu - tssiu - tssiu - tssiu - tssiu - tsitsitsiu....* When alarmed utters a *tik-tik.* HABITAT: Rhododendron, bamboo, juniper and subalpine forest. DISTRIBUTION: Resident and breeding visitor in the Himalayas.

2 RUSTY-BELLIED SHORTWING *Brachypteryx hyperythra* 13cm FIELD NOTES: Skulking. Forages on the ground in thick undergrowth. VOICE: A *tu-tiu* that leads into a fast warble of slurred notes. HABITAT: Dense thickets and forest undergrowth. DISTRIBUTION: Resident in E Himalayas.

3 LESSER SHORTWING *Brachypteryx leucophris* 13cm FIELD NOTES: Often holds tail erect while foraging among dead leaves on the forest floor. Males of the race *B. m. carolinae* (not shown), which occurs in the extreme NE, are browner, looking much like females. VOICE: A single note followed by a melodious, sibilant warble with a jumbled finish of buzzy and rich melodious notes. Calls include a thin whistle and a harsh *tack.* HABITAT: Dense, damp undergrowth in broadleaved forest. DISTRIBUTION: Resident in the Himalayas and the NE of the region.

4 WHITE-BROWED SHORTWING *Brachypteryx montana* 14cm FIELD NOTES: Skulking; forages on the ground, acting much like a Robin. VOICE: Song starts slowly with a few single notes, then speeds to a plaintive babble and ends abruptly. HABITAT: Damp shady forests with undergrowth; also in ravines with dense brush. DISTRIBUTION: Resident in the Himalayas and the NE of the region.

5 WHITE-BELLIED BLUE ROBIN *Myiomela albiventris* 15cm FIELD NOTES: Forages on the ground. VOICE: A series of beautiful phrases consisting of rich slurred whistles and buzzy notes. Calls include a high-pitched whistle and a loud chatter. HABITAT: Wet areas of undergrowth in forest patches and densely wooded ravines. DISTRIBUTION: Resident in S Kerula and W Tamil Nadu areas of India.

6 NILGIRI BLUE ROBIN *Myiomela major* 15cm FIELD NOTES: Secretive; forages on the ground. VOICE: A short jumble of whistles, twangy buzzes and harsh notes. Calls include a harsh rattle and an indrawn whistle. HABITAT: Undergrowth in sheltered woods. DISTRIBUTION: Resident in the S Karnataka and Nilgiri Hills of S India.

7 RUFOUS BUSH ROBIN (RUFOUS-TAILED SCRUB ROBIN) *Cercotrichas galactotes* 16cm FIELD NOTES: Forages mainly on the ground. VOICE: Song involves rich and varied ringing notes. Calls include a hard *tek-tek.* HABITAT: Dry scrub jungle. DISTRIBUTION: Breeds in W Pakistan, migrant elsewhere.

8 NIGHTINGALE (COMMON NIGHTINGALE) *Luscinia megarhynchos* 16cm FIELD NOTES: Very skulking; forages on the ground or in low cover. VOICE: Calls include a deep *grrrr* and a harsh *tucc-tucc.* HABITAT: Thick undergrowth and thickets. DISTRIBUTION: Vagrant, recorded from Pakistan.

9 WHITE-TAILED RUBYTHROAT (HIMALAYAN RUBYTHROAT) *Luscinia pectoralis* 15cm FIELD NOTES: Secretive, although often more exposed when singing. Regularly cocks tail while foraging on the ground. Birds from N Kashmir *L. p. tschebaiewi* (9b) have a white moustachial streak. VOICE: Song is a complex series of shrill, undulating, warbling trills and twitters. Calls include a *tchuk* and a *siiii-siiii* when alarmed. HABITAT: Scrub and bushes in subalpine forest; winters at lower elevations in dense scrub and marshy grassland. DISTRIBUTION: Resident in the Himalayas; moves to lower slopes post breeding.

10 SIBERIAN RUBYTHROAT *Luscinia calliope* 15cm FIELD NOTES: Shy; forages mainly on the ground. VOICE: A *chak-chak* and a whistled *ee-uk.* HABITAT: Thick undergrowth, bushes and long grass or reeds. DISTRIBUTION: Winter visitor, mainly to the NE.

96 CHATS

1 BLUETHROAT (RED-SPOTTED BLUETHROAT) *Luscinia svecica* 14cm FIELD NOTES: Forages on the ground or in low cover. Chestnut tail bases often 'flash' as bird flits into cover. VOICE: Vigorous with a bell-like *ting-ting-ting* and a throaty *torr-torr-torr-torr*; often mimics other birds or insects. Calls include a *tucc-tucc*, a croaky *turrc-turrc* and a plaintive *hweet*. HABITAT: Breeds in waterside scrub; winters in scrub and tall grass. DISTRIBUTION: Breeds in NW Himalayas; widespread winter visitor.

2 FIRETHROAT *Luscinia pectardens* 14cm FIELD NOTES: Skulks in thick cover; often flicks tail as it forages on the forest floor. VOICE: Song is varied, with loud, long sweet notes repeated several times; often includes some mimicry and harsh notes. Calls include a throaty *tok*. HABITAT: Broadleaved forest, bamboo and dense scrub. DISTRIBUTION: Vagrant, recorded from India.

3 INDIAN BLUE ROBIN *Luscinia brunnea* 14cm FIELD NOTES: Forages on the ground or in low growth; runs rapidly and flicks wings and tail. VOICE: A few introductory whistles followed by a short, sweet jumble of hurried phrases. Calls include a high-pitched *tsee* and when alarmed a hard *tuk-tuk*. HABITAT: Dense undergrowth in forests; winters in forested ravines in wet undergrowth along streams. DISTRIBUTION: Breeds in the Himalayas and NE India; winters in the NE, S and Sri Lanka.

4 SIBERIAN BLUE ROBIN *Luscinia cyane* 14cm FIELD NOTES: Shivers tail while foraging on the ground or in low cover; said to run and hop around like a small crake. VOICE: Calls include a subdued *tak*, a louder *se-ic* and when alarmed a *chuck-chuck-chuck*. HABITAT: Forest undergrowth, thickets and bamboo brakes. DISTRIBUTION: Vagrant, recorded from India and Nepal.

5 GOLDEN BUSH ROBIN *Tarsiger chrysaeus* 15cm FIELD NOTES: Forages on the ground or in low cover; often holds tail cocked. VOICE: A wispy *tse-tse-tse-tse-tse-chu-r-r* or similar. Calls include a croaky *trrr* and a scolding *chirik-chirik*. HABITAT: Scrub above the tree line, thickets on boulder-covered alpine slopes and forest undergrowth. DISTRIBUTION: Resident in the Himalayas and the NE hills.

6 RED-FLANKED BLUETAIL (HIMALAYAN BLUETAIL or ORANGE-FLANKED BUSH ROBIN) *Tarsiger cyanurus* 14cm FIELD NOTES: Forages on the ground and in low cover. The slightly brighter race that breeds in the Himalayas *T. c. rufilatus* (not shown) may be split and be known as Himalayan Bluetail. VOICE: Song a soft, weak *churrh-cheee* or similar. Calls include a deep croaking *tack-tack*. HABITAT: Forest understorey and bushes in forest clearings. DISTRIBUTION: Breeds in the Himalayas; winter visitor or vagrant (nominate race) elsewhere in India.

7 WHITE-BROWED BUSH ROBIN *Tarsiger indicus* 15cm FIELD NOTES: Forages on or near the ground in thick cover. VOICE: A rapidly repeated, sharp, bubbling *shri-de-de-dew...shri-de-de-dew*. Calls include a sweet *heed* or *tuit-tuit*, a croaking *churr* and a clucking *tukukukukukukuk*. HABITAT: Mixed subalpine forest. DISTRIBUTION: Resident in the Himalayas and the NE of the region.

8 RUFOUS-BREASTED BUSH ROBIN *Tarsiger hyperythrus* 13cm FIELD NOTES: Forages on or near the ground, where it often adopts an upright stance. VOICE: A lisping warble, *zeew-zeew-zeew...* Calls include a low *duk-duk-duk-tseak*. HABITAT: Forest-edge bushes and streamside vegetation. DISTRIBUTION: Resident in the C and E Himalayas; winters in NE Indian hills.

9 ROBIN (EUROPEAN ROBIN) *Erithacus rubecula* 14cm FIELD NOTES: Generally wary. Forages on the ground or in low cover. VOICE: Melodic warbling and trilling phrases. Call is a hard *tick* or *tick-tick-tick-tick*. HABITAT: Woodland scrub and bushes. DISTRIBUTION: Vagrant, recorded from Pakistan.

97 CHATS

1 REDSTART (COMMON REDSTART) *Phoenicurus phoenicurus* 15cm FIELD NOTES: Usually sits in cover, only showing when flying out to feed. Regularly shivers tail. VOICE: A weak *hooeet* followed by a weak melancholic warbling. Calls include a *hooeet* and a harsh *tchak*. HABITAT: Semi-arid or arid areas with scattered scrub. DISTRIBUTION: Spring migrant, mainly in the NW.

2 HODGSON'S REDSTART *Phoenicurus hodgsoni* 15cm FIELD NOTES: Chases insects in short sallies from a rock or branch perch; in taller trees often acts like a flycatcher. VOICE: Song consists of short phases with tinny tinkly notes. Calls include a *prit* and a *trr* or *tschrrr*, the latter given when alarmed. HABITAT: Tree-lined stony riverbeds, open scrub jungle and cultivated areas with bushes. DISTRIBUTION: Winter visitor to the Himalayas and the NE of the region.

3 DAURIAN REDSTART *Phoenicurus auroreus* 15cm FIELD NOTES: Forages in trees and bushes, often in the manner of a flycatcher. Shivers tail. VOICE: Song is a series of cheerful, whistled notes. Calls include a *wheep*, and a soft *tac-tac* that is preceded by a series of soft whistles. HABITAT: Bushy areas and cultivations. DISTRIBUTION: Winter visitor to the NE of the region.

4 BLACK REDSTART *Phoenicurus ochruros rufiventris* 15cm FIELD NOTES: Flits from low perch to catch insects from the ground or catches flying insects by making short aerial sallies. Greyer-crowned race *P. o. phoenicuroides* (4b) occurs in W Himalayas. VOICE: Song is a rapid warble, interspersed with a rattle, and ending with a rushed burst of ringing notes. Calls include a *tsip*, a *tucc-tucc* and, when alarmed, a *tititicc*. HABITAT: Tibetan steppe; winters in plantations and cultivations. DISTRIBUTION: Summers in the Himalayas; widespread over the whole region post breeding.

5 EVERSMANN'S REDSTART (RUFOUS-BACKED REDSTART) *Phoenicurus erythronotus* 15cm FIELD NOTES: Drops from a rock or twig to capture insects. Flicks tail up and down. VOICE: A whistled *few-weet* and a croaking *gre-er*. HABITAT: Dry scrub areas on hills and valleys. DISTRIBUTION: Winter visitor to the NW.

6 BLUE-FRONTED REDSTART *Phoenicurus frontalis* 15cm FIELD NOTES: Descends from a rock or branch to capture insects. Flicks tail up and down. VOICE: Song similar to Black Redstart, but less wheezy. Calls include a *tic* and, when alarmed, a repeated *ee-tit - ti-tit*. HABITAT: Subalpine scrub; winters in bushes and open forest. DISTRIBUTION: Resident in the Himalayas; uses lower elevations in winter.

7 WHITE-THROATED REDSTART *Phoenicurus schisticeps* 15cm FIELD NOTES: Restless, often feeds in a flycatcher-like manner. VOICE: A series of dry trilled phrases, usually accelerating towards the end. Call is a drawn-out *zieh* followed by a rattling note. HABITAT: Thick scrub in subalpine, park-like, conifer forests; descends to lower elevations in winter. DISTRIBUTION: Resident and winter visitor in the Himalayas.

8 GÜLDENSTÄDT'S REDSTART (WHITE-WINGED REDSTART) *Phoenicurus erythrogastrus* 18cm FIELD NOTES: Rather shy, but showy during quivering-wing display-flight, when white wing-patches are prominent. VOICE: A series of clear notes, followed by a burst of short, wheezy notes. Call is a hard *tik* or *tek*. HABITAT: High-altitude boulder-strewn slopes, rocky meadows often near water, forced to lower elevations during severe weather. DISTRIBUTION: Himalayan resident and winter visitor.

98 CHATS

1 BLUE-CAPPED REDSTART *Phoenicurus coeruleocephala* 15cm FIELD NOTES: Drops to ground, or makes aerial sallies to capture insects. Shakes tail. VOICE: Loud, fast, high-pitched, ringing jingles. Calls include a *tik-tik* and, when alarmed, a piping *tit-tit-tit*. HABITAT: Open montane forests with rocky slopes; winters in lower-altitude open forest and scrubby areas. DISTRIBUTION: Resident in the Himalayas.

2 ORIENTAL MAGPIE-ROBIN *Copsychus saularis* 20cm FIELD NOTES: Confiding; usually conspicuous but can become more secretive in the non-breeding season. VOICE: Varied musical warbling, alternating with churrs and sliding whistles. Calls include a clear rising whistle. When alarmed issues a harsh *che-e-e-h*. HABITAT: Open forests, groves, parks and gardens. DISTRIBUTION: Widespread resident.

3 WHITE-RUMPED SHAMA *Copsychus malabaricus* 25cm FIELD NOTES: Retiring; usually forages on the ground or in low cover. Uses wings to make a clicking sound when flying across open ground. Birds on the Andamans *C. m. albiventris* (3b) considered by some authorities to be a full species. VOICE: Rich, melodious phrases; has a harsh scolding alarm call; also utters a musical *chir-chur* or *chur-chi-churr*. HABITAT: Forest undergrowth. DISTRIBUTION: Resident over much of the NE, the W Ghats, Sri Lanka and the Andamans.

4 INDIAN ROBIN *Saxicoloides fulicatus* 16cm FIELD NOTES: Confiding; hops or runs with tail regularly carried erect or well over back. Brownish-backed race *S. f. cambaiensis* (4b) occurs in the N and NW. VOICE: A repeated *wheech* or a harsh *chu-r - chu-r*. Song is a short, high-pitched, cheery warble. HABITAT: Dry stony foothills with scrub, cultivation edges, in and around human habitations. DISTRIBUTION: Widespread resident.

5 WHITE-CAPPED REDSTART (WHITE-CAPPED WATER REDSTART)
Chaimarrornis leucocephalus 19cm FIELD NOTES: Sits on rocks in or close to water; continuously flicks tail. VOICE: A plaintive *tseeit-tseeit*. Song is a weak undulating whistle. HABITAT: Mountain streams and rivers; moves down-river in winter. DISTRIBUTION: Resident in the Himalayas and the NE.

6 PLUMBEOUS REDSTART (PLUMBEOUS WATER REDSTART) *Rhyacornis fuliginosa* 14cm FIELD NOTES: Makes sallies from rock or low branch to capture insects. Continuously wags tail up and down and opens it, scissor-like. VOICE: A sharp *ziet-ziet* or a threatening *kree*. Song is a rapid jingle. HABITAT: Fast-flowing streams and rivers. DISTRIBUTION: Resident in the Himalayas and the NE.

7 WHITE-BELLIED REDSTART *Hodgsonius phoenicuroides* 19cm FIELD NOTES: Retiring; forages mainly on the ground. Tail often held vertically and spread. VOICE: A *chuck* and, when alarmed, a *tsiep-tsiep-tk-tk* or *tck-tck-sie*. Whistled song is often transcribed as *he-did-so*. HABITAT: Subalpine thickets; winters at lower elevations in dense low scrub or undergrowth. DISTRIBUTION: Breeds in the Himalayas; winters in the Himalayas and the NE.

8 WHITE-TAILED ROBIN *Myiomela (Cinclidium) leucura* 18cm FIELD NOTES: Shy; forages in dark thickets. Often spreads tail, revealing white tail base. There is a white neck-spot that is usually concealed. VOICE: A low *tuc*. Song consists of clear, liquid, separated phrases. HABITAT: Dense undergrowth in moist montane forest. DISTRIBUTION: Resident in the Himalayas and the NE.

9 BLUE-FRONTED ROBIN *Cinclidium frontale* 19cm FIELD NOTES: Forages in low cover and probably on the ground. VOICE: A series of short melodious phrases. Calls include a harsh buzzy *zschwick* when alarmed, and a shrill *shraak*. HABITAT: Densely vegetated gulleys in montane primary broadleaved evergreen forest. DISTRIBUTION: Resident in E Himalayas.

3b *albiventris*

4b ♂
cambaiensis

99 FORKTAILS, GRANDALA, COCHOAS

1 LITTLE FORKTAIL *Enicurus scouleri* 12–14cm FIELD NOTES: Constantly wags tail up and down, also rapidly opens and closes it in a scissor-like movement. Juvenile browner and lacks the white forehead. VOICE: A loud, thin *ts-youeee*. HABITAT: Mountain streams, rivers and waterfalls. DISTRIBUTION: Resident in the Himalayas and the NE.

2 BLACK-BACKED FORKTAIL *Enicurus immaculatus* 20–25cm FIELD NOTES: Forages among rocks or along the water's edge, constantly wagging tail. VOICE: A hollow *huu* often followed by a shrill *zeee*, also a squeaky *weeng*. HABITAT: Fast-flowing waters, with uncovered rocks, in damp dense forests. DISTRIBUTION: Resident in the Himalayan foothills and the NE.

3 SLATY-BACKED FORKTAIL *Enicurus schistaceus* 22–25cm FIELD NOTES: Hops or flits from rock to rock in search of prey. Sways tail slowly up and down. Flight is undulating, much like a wagtail. VOICE: A mellow *cheet* and a metallic *teenk*. HABITAT: Fast-flowing rocky streams in damp forests or cultivations. DISTRIBUTION: Resident in the Himalayas and the NE.

4 WHITE-CROWNED FORKTAIL *Enicurus leschenaulti* 25–28cm FIELD NOTES: Forages on rocks or along the water's edge; when disturbed often disappears into nearby forest cover. VOICE: Song is an elaborate series of sweet high-pitched whistles. Calls include a harsh *tssee* or *tssee-chit-chit-chit*. HABITAT: Fast-flowing rocky streams and rivers in dense evergreen forest. DISTRIBUTION: Resident in E Himalayan foothills and hills of the NE.

5 SPOTTED FORKTAIL *Enicurus maculatus* 26–27cm FIELD NOTES: Actions and habits much as Slaty-backed Forktail. Juvenile browner and lacking the white forehead. VOICE: A sharp, creaky *cheek-chik-chik-chik-chik* and a shrill, rasping *kreee* or *tseek*. HABITAT: Rocky streams in dense mountain forests; winters at lower elevations and often on wider watercourses. DISTRIBUTION: Resident in the Himalayas and the NE.

6 GRANDALA *Grandala coelicolor* 19–23cm FIELD NOTES: Forages mainly on the ground; posture much like a rock thrush. Winter flocks act starling- or wader-like, wheeling and circling around before dropping onto the top branches of trees or onto cliffs. VOICE: A ringing *tji-u*. Song is a subdued *tju-u tiu-u ti-tu tji-u*. HABITAT: Alpine meadows, bare rocky areas above the tree line and open forests. DISTRIBUTION: Resident in the Himalayas.

7 GREEN COCHOA *Cochoa viridis* 25–28cm FIELD NOTES: Forages in trees and undergrowth, and on the ground, frequently in pairs or small groups. Juvenile has similar wing pattern to adult but body is generally dark brown with ochre spotting, crown whitish with dark barring. VOICE: Song is a pure, thin monotonous whistle, higher and more even than that of the Purple Cochoa. Calls include a harsh note and a short, thin *pok*. HABITAT: Dense, moist broadleaved evergreen forest, often near streams. DISTRIBUTION: Resident in the Himalayas and the NE.

8 PURPLE COCHOA *Cochoa purpurea* 25–28cm FIELD NOTES: Secretive. Generally arboreal, feeding in fruiting trees, but will also forage on the ground. Juvenile has similar wing and head pattern to adult female, but body is generally dark brown with ochre scaling below and ochre spotting above. VOICE: A thin *sit* or *tssri*, a chuckling *nyerr* and a soft, high *pink-pink-trrrrew*. Song is a pure whistled *peeeee* or *peeee-you-peeee*. HABITAT: Dense, humid, broadleaved evergreen forest. DISTRIBUTION: Summer visitor to the Himalayas and the NE.

100 STONECHATS, ROCK CHAT

1 STOLICZKA'S BUSHCHAT (WHITE-BROWED BUSH CHAT) *Saxicola macrorhynchus* 15cm FIELD NOTES: Actions much like Siberian Stonechat, although tends to spend more time hopping on the ground. In flight white tail-base pattern looks like that of a wheatear. VOICE: A sharp *chip-chip* and a deep *prupp prupp*. Song is a low musical *twitch-chhe chee chee*. HABITAT: Sandy, semi-desert scrubland. DISTRIBUTION: Resident in the NW.

2 HODGSON'S STONECHAT (WHITE-THROATED BUSH CHAT) *Saxicola insignis* 15cm FIELD NOTES: Actions much as Siberian Stonechat, although may forage more on the ground. VOICE: A metallic *tek-tek*. HABITAT: Tall riverside vegetation and cane fields. DISTRIBUTION: Winter visitor to the N plains.

3 WHITE-TAILED STONECHAT (WHITE-TAILED BUSH CHAT) *Saxicola leucurus* 12–14cm FIELD NOTES: Actions and habits very similar to Siberian Stonechat. VOICE: Song is a series of lark-like phrases, consisting of rapid, scratchy squeaky notes and ending on a high slurred note. Calls include a short *peep-chaa*, a hard dry *kek-kek-kek* and warning *pseep*. HABITAT: Tall grassland and reeds. DISTRIBUTION: Resident in the N, mainly on the plains.

4 SIBERIAN STONECHAT *Saxicola maurus* 13cm FIELD NOTES: Sits atop a prominent perch, flicking wings and tail, with frequent sallies to capture insects from on or near the ground; at times makes flycatcher-like aerial sallies to catch flying insects. Various races occur in the region: the nominate race breeds in the NW; *S. m. indicus* (4b) is resident, moving away from breeding areas in the NW and C Himalayas; *S. m. przewalskii* (4c), with rufous underparts, is a winter visitor to the N and NE. VOICE: A *chak* or *wheet* often combined as *wheet-tak-tak*. Song is a thin scratchy warble, often given in a short song-flight. HABITAT: Open country with bushes; winters in scrub, reed-beds and cultivations. DISTRIBUTION: Breeds in the N and W, much more widespread in winter.

5 GREY BUSH CHAT *Saxicola ferreus* 15cm FIELD NOTES: Actions and habits much as Siberian Stonechat. VOICE: A *prrei* and when alarmed utters a repeated *zee-chunk* or *tic-tic-brzeeee*. Song consists of a short feeble trill ending with a rolling whistle. HABITAT: Open scrubby and bush-covered hillsides. DISTRIBUTION: Resident; breeds in the Himalayas and the NE, winters south to the N plains.

6 PIED STONECHAT *Saxicola caprata* 13–14cm FIELD NOTES: Actions similar to Siberian Stonechat. VOICE: A repeated, plaintive *chep-chep-hee* or *chek-chek-trweet* and scolding *chuh* when alarmed. Song is a brisk, whistled *chip-chepee-chewee-chu*. HABITAT: Stony hillsides with low scrub, open country with scattered bushes, tall grass and reeds, cultivated fields and tamarisk growth. DISTRIBUTION: Widespread resident.

7 JERDON'S BUSH CHAT *Saxicola jerdoni* 15cm FIELD NOTES: Actions and habits very similar to those of Siberian Stonechat. VOICE: Song comprises a series of sweet, clear, mellow warbled phrases, often ending with a trilled flourish. Calls include a high, nasal, down-slurred *heeew*, a short, plaintive, high-pitched *chirr* or *chit-churr* and when alarmed a high, dry, rapid ticking. HABITAT: Tall grassland in the Himalayan foothills and the NE Indian plains. DISTRIBUTION: Resident, mainly in the NE.

8 BROWN ROCK CHAT *Cercomela fusca* 17cm FIELD NOTES: Drops from a low perch to capture prey from the ground. Has habit of flexing legs and spreading and raising tail. VOICE: A short whistled *chee*, a mournful down-slurred *pseeu* and a harsh *tchk-tchk-tchk* when alarmed. Song consists of a sweet thrush-like warbling HABITAT: Low rocky hills, sandstone cliffs and old buildings. DISTRIBUTION: Resident in NE Pakistan and NC India.

101 WHEATEARS

1 WHEATEAR (NORTHERN WHEATEAR) *Oenanthe oenanthe* 14.5–15.5cm FIELD NOTES: Forages in a stop-start fashion, little runs interspersed with short stops to pick up prey or to look around; regularly flicks wings and wags tail. In flight shows white rump and white outer tail bases. VOICE: A hard *chak* and a *wheet*; often combined as *wheet-chak-chak*. HABITAT: Open areas, managed grassland and cultivated fields. DISTRIBUTION: Passage migrant, mainly in the NW.

2 EASTERN PIED WHEATEAR (VARIABLE WHEATEAR) *Oenanthe picata* 15cm FIELD NOTES: Sings from a prominent perch or in flight. In flight shows white rump and outer tail bases. Three colour morphs occur: nominate, *O. p. opistholeuca* (2b) and *O. p. capistrata* (2c). VOICE: A loud *chek-chek*. Song is scratchy, consisting of low-pitched *chott* notes, whistles, chirrups and trills. HABITAT: Arid boulder-covered hills with scattered vegetation; winters in stony desert foothills and cultivated areas. DISTRIBUTION: Breeds in Baluchistan and N and W Pakistan; winter visitor, mainly to the NW.

3 PIED WHEATEAR *Oenanthe pleschanka* 14.5cm FIELD NOTES: Forages on the ground, also makes short vertical sallies after flying insects. In flight shows white rump and outer tail bases, outer tail feathers dark-edged. White-throated form '*vittata*' (3b) is uncommon. VOICE: A harsh *zack-zack* or *chep-chep* and a *psyiep*. Song is a repeated buzzy, trilling phase with much mimicry. HABITAT: Stony lowlands with scattered small trees. DISTRIBUTION: Breeds and a passage migrant in the NW.

4 FINSCH'S WHEATEAR *Oenanthe finschii* 15cm FIELD NOTES: In flight shows extensive white rump and large area of white on outer tail bases. VOICE: A harsh *chak-chak*. HABITAT: Dry stony foothills and arid semi-desert plains. DISTRIBUTION: Winter visitor to Baluchistan.

5 DESERT WHEATEAR *Oenanthe deserti* 14–15cm FIELD NOTES: Wary, often perches in low vegetation. Usually sings from the top of a bush. In flight shows white rump and mainly black tail. VOICE: A low *chuck*, a whistled *peeeeoo* and a *trrr*. Song is a descending *swee-you*, occasionally interspersed with rattles or trills. HABITAT: Arid areas with scattered scrub. DISTRIBUTION: Breeds in the NW Himalayas; winters in the NW.

6 RED-TAILED WHEATEAR *Oenanthe chrysopygia* 14.5cm FIELD NOTES: Wary, often runs for cover. In flight shows a chestnut rump and outer tail bases. VOICE: A low *thrrr-thrr-thrr*. Song is a loud warble with much mimicry. HABITAT: Dry rocky slopes, often with nearby streams; winters in semi-desert areas with scattered scrub. DISTRIBUTION: Breeds in Baluchistan; winters in the NW.

7 ISABELLINE WHEATEAR *Oenanthe isabellina* 17cm FIELD NOTES: Often has a very upright stance. Jerky emphatic tail-wagging. In flight shows white rump and outer tail bases. VOICE: A piped *weep* or *dweet*, a high-pitched *wheet-whit* and a quiet *cheep*. Song loud with various croaks, whistles and mimicry. HABITAT: Plains and plateaux with sparse vegetation; winters in sandy semi-desert. DISTRIBUTION: Breeds in Pakistan; winter visitor to the NW.

8 HOODED WHEATEAR *Oenanthe monacha* 17.5cm FIELD NOTES: In flight shows extensive white rump and tail. Often makes prolonged aerial pursuit of insects. VOICE: A harsh *zack* and a low *wit-wit*. Song is a sweet medley of whistles and thrush-like notes. HABITAT: Barren desert. DISTRIBUTION: Resident in SW.

9 HUME'S WHEATEAR *Oenanthe albonigra* 17cm FIELD NOTES: Shows extensive white rump and outer tail bases. VOICE: A whistled *triki-treet* or *trooti-trooti-tree* and a harsh *chack-chack*. Song is a cheerful, rising *chew-de-dew-twit*. HABITAT: Barren rocky slopes with sparse vegetation. DISTRIBUTION: Resident in the NW.

1

♂

♀

n-br

br
♂

br

2

♀

2c
capistrata
♂

♂

2b
opistholeuca

3b
♀

♂

3

♂

'vittata'
dark-
throated
form
♀

pale-throated
form
♀

4

♂

♀

n-br
7

♀

5

♂

6

♂
br

8

♂

♀

9

NA

102 FLYCATCHERS

1 GREY-HEADED FLYCATCHER (GREY-HEADED CANARY FLYCATCHER)
Culicicapa ceylonensis 12–13cm FIELD NOTES: Returns to the same perch after making aerial sallies after flying insects. Often forms part of mixed feeding parties post breeding. VOICE: A soft *pit - pit - pit*, a clear *kitwik*, a *kui-whi-whi* and a quiet *chichictrr*. Song is a sweet, clear whistle, transcribed as *tyissi-a-tyi* or similar. HABITAT: Forests and wooded ravines. DISTRIBUTION: Breeds in the Himalayas, the hills of India, Bangladesh and Sri Lanka; more widespread in winter.

2 NICOBAR JUNGLE FLYCATCHER *Rhinomyias nicobaricus* 15cm FIELD NOTES: Catches insects in flight, also forages on the ground and in the lower canopy and bushes. VOICE: Harsh churrs. Song is a loud, rich, rapid series of descending whistles, *fee-tee tuu-tee fuu trrr*. HABITAT: Forests, scrub and mangroves. DISTRIBUTION: Resident on the Nicobars; vagrant on the Andamans.

3 SPOTTED FLYCATCHER *Muscicapa striata* 14cm FIELD NOTES: Fly-catching sallies take the bird out in a sweeping circle, returning to its favoured perch, or one nearby. VOICE: A squeaky *zeee* or *chick*; utters a *zee-zucc* when agitated. Song consists of a series of squeaky notes, often with lengthy intervals between phrases. HABITAT: Juniper and open forests, especially pine. DISTRIBUTION: Breeds in NW India and Pakistan; more widespread as a passage migrant in the NW.

4 DARK-SIDED FLYCATCHER (SIBERIAN or SOOTY FLYCATCHER) *Muscicapa sibirica* 13cm FIELD NOTES: Makes darting sorties after flying insects, much like Spotted Flycatcher. VOICE: A tinkling *chi-up-chi-up-chi-up*. Song is a series of repetitive thin notes combined with trills and whistles. HABITAT: Open conifer forest and oak forest clearings. DISTRIBUTION: Breeds in the Himalayas.

5 BROWN FLYCATCHER (ASIAN BROWN FLYCATCHER) *Muscicapa latirostris* 13cm FIELD NOTES: Crepuscular; feeding actions similar to Spotted Flycatcher. VOICE: A short thin *tzi*, a soft *churr* and a soft, rattling *tze-te-te-te-te*. Song is a faint, squeaky, melodious warble. HABITAT: Deciduous and mixed woodland, plantations and groves. DISTRIBUTION: Breeds in the Himalayas and hills of C and W India; widespread in peninsular India and Sir Lanka in winter.

6 RUSTY-TAILED FLYCATCHER (RUFOUS-TAILED FLYCATCHER) *Muscicapa ruficauda* 14cm FIELD NOTES: Unobtrusive, forages in trees, snapping up insect prey while flitting from branch to branch. VOICE: A *tee-peup tee-peup*. When alarmed utters a plaintive, ceaselessly repeated *peup* followed by a soft *churr*. Song consists of three or four loud, clear notes repeated at short intervals. HABITAT: Mixed coniferous broadleaved forest; winters in evergreen broadleaved forest. DISTRIBUTION: Breeds in the Himalayas; winters mainly in SW India.

7 BROWN-BREASTED FLYCATCHER *Muscicapa muttui* 14cm FIELD NOTES: Secretive. Frequents low vegetation from where it makes short sallies to catch flying insects. VOICE: Song is feeble but pleasant. Calls include a soft low note which is uttered while rapidly vibrating half-open wings. HABITAT: Dense thickets in broadleaved evergreen forest and riverside forests in Sri Lanka. DISTRIBUTION: Breeds in the NW and winters in the SW and Sri Lanka.

8 FERRUGINOUS FLYCATCHER *Muscicapa ferruginea* 12.5cm FIELD NOTES: Retiring; actions much like Spotted Flycatcher. VOICE: A soft trilling *si-si-si*. Song is probably a high-pitched *tsit-tittu-tittu*. HABITAT: Broadleaved or fir forest and dense mixed jungle. DISTRIBUTION: Breeds in the Himalayas and the NE.

9 WHITE-GORGETED FLYCATCHER *Anthipes monileger* 11.5–13cm FIELD NOTES: Occurs low down in dense undergrowth; captures insects by making short aerial sallies or from the ground. Race *A. m. leucops* (9b) occurs in the NE. VOICE: A scolding, rattling short whistle. Song consists of a weak high-pitched whistle. HABITAT: Thick forest undergrowth and bamboo. DISTRIBUTION: Resident in the Himalayas and the NE.

9b
leucops

103 FLYCATCHERS

1 YELLOW-RUMPED FLYCATCHER *Ficedula zanthopygia* 13cm FIELD NOTES: Forages in the foliage of trees and undergrowth, often making short sallies after flying insects. VOICE: A dry rattling *tr-r-r-rt*. HABITAT: Forests and undergrowth along rivers and streams; also coastal scrub and mangroves. DISTRIBUTION: Vagrant, recorded from India and Sri Lanka.

2 SLATY-BACKED FLYCATCHER *Ficedula hodgsonii* 13cm FIELD NOTES: Sallies after flying insects from tree-canopy perch; occasionally takes insects from the ground. VOICE: Song is a ripple of descending, whistling notes. Calls include a hard *tchat* and a rattled *terrht*. HABITAT: Damp broadleaved forest, shrubberies and bamboo. DISTRIBUTION: Winter visitor to the Himalayas and the NE.

3 RUFOUS-GORGETED FLYCATCHER *Ficedula strophiata* 14cm FIELD NOTES: Flits and spreads tail when agitated, showing white tail sides. Forages mainly in undergrowth or low down in trees. VOICE: A low *tik-tik* or *pink*, and a croaking *churr* when alarmed. Song is a spirited *tin-ti-ti*. HABITAT: Dense or open forests, thick secondary scrub and forest edge. DISTRIBUTION: Resident in the Himalayas and the NE.

4 RED-BREASTED FLYCATCHER *Ficedula parva* 11.5– 12.5cm FIELD NOTES: Forages among foliage with occasional aerial sorties after flying insects, when white outer tail bases are prominent. VOICE: A *chick* or *chick-chick*, also a rattled *serrrt*. HABITAT: Open forest, secondary growth, orchards and urban trees. DISTRIBUTION: Widespread winter visitor and passage migrant.

5 TAIGA FLYCATCHER (RED-THROATED FLYCATCHER) *Ficedula albicilla* 11– 12cm FIELD NOTES: Actions and female colouring very similar to Red-breasted Flycatcher, with which it is often thought to be conspecific. VOICE: A buzzing *drrrrt* or *trrrr*. HABITAT: Open forests and scrub at the edge of cultivations. DISTRIBUTION: Widespread winter visitor.

6 KASHMIR FLYCATCHER *Ficedula subrubra* 13cm FIELD NOTES: Actions similar to Rufous-gorgeted Flycatcher. VOICE: A sharp *chack*, a subdued, harsh *purr* and a dry rattle. Song is a rising twitter. HABITAT: Deciduous forests; winters in plantations, forest edge and gardens. DISTRIBUTION: Breeds in the NW; winters in Sri Lanka and SW India.

7 LITTLE PIED FLYCATCHER *Ficedula westermanni* 11.5cm FIELD NOTES: Forages in treetops, constantly on the move; also makes short sallies after flying insects. VOICE: A mellow *tweet*. Song is a thin, high *pi-pi-pi* followed by a rattling *churr-r-r-r-r*. HABITAT: Dense evergreen forest; winters in open woodland, orchards and reed-beds. DISTRIBUTION: Resident in the Himalayas and the NE.

8 ULTRAMARINE FLYCATCHER *Ficedula superciliaris* 12cm FIELD NOTES: Forages in the foliage of low trees and bushes. Race *F. s. aesigma* (8b) occurs in C and E Himalayas and NE India. VOICE: A soft *tick* and a low rattling *trrrt*. Song is a repeated *chi-chi-purr*. HABITAT: Open mixed forests, also orchards and gardens in winter. DISTRIBUTION: Breeds in the Himalayas, resident in the NE and a widespread winter visitor.

9 SNOWY-BROWED FLYCATCHER *Ficedula hyperythra* 11cm FIELD NOTES: Forages low down in scrub and thickets, or runs about on the ground much like a shortwing. VOICE: A thin *sip* and an up-slurred *seep*. Song is a wheezy, shrill *tsit-sit-si-sii tsi-sii-swrri* or *tsi-sit-i*. HABITAT: Dense montane forest with thick undergrowth. DISTRIBUTION: Resident in the Himalayas and the NE.

10 SLATY-BLUE FLYCATCHER *Ficedula tricolor* 12–13cm FIELD NOTES: Secretive; forages in undergrowth and lower tree branches, also takes insects from the ground. Race *F. t. cerviniventris* (10b) occurs in the hills of the NE. VOICE: An *ee-tik* and a rapid *ee-tick-tick-tick-tick*. Song is a three-note whistle, *zieth-ti-zietz*. HABITAT: Evergreen mountain forests, shrubberies and forest edge; in winter also in reed-beds and tall grass. DISTRIBUTION: Resident in the NE, summer visitor in the Himalayas.

104 FLYCATCHERS, NILTAVAS

1 SAPPHIRE FLYCATCHER *Ficedula sapphira* 11cm FIELD NOTES: Forages in undergrowth and trees; occasionally picks food from the ground or makes aerial sallies after flying insects. VOICE: A low, rattled *tit-tit-ti*. Song consists of several high-pitched notes followed by a series of short rattles. HABITAT: Evergreen broadleaved forests. DISTRIBUTION: Resident in E Himalayas and the NE.

2 BLACK-AND-ORANGE FLYCATCHER *Ficedula nigrorufa* 11cm FIELD NOTES: Forages in shady undergrowth. VOICE: Calls include a low *pee* and a *zit-zit* when alarmed. Song is a high, insect-like *chiki-riki-chiki*. HABITAT: Evergreen hill forests (sholas) with dense undergrowth, damp riverine thickets and plantations. DISTRIBUTION: Resident in the W Ghats.

3 VERDITER FLYCATCHER *Eumyias thalassinus* 16cm FIELD NOTES: Makes aerial sallies after flying insects from an exposed perch on trees, wires or buildings. VOICE: A *tze-ju-jui*. Song is a pleasant trilled *pe-tititi-wu-pititi-weu*. HABITAT: Open forests, forest clearings and edge, groves and gardens. DISTRIBUTION: Breeds in the Himalayas and the NE; widespread in the region post breeding.

4 DULL-BLUE FLYCATCHER *Eumyias sordidus* 15cm FIELD NOTES: Forages low down in trees or undergrowth, also on the ground. VOICE: A series of four or five *chip* notes. Song is a series of mournful, down-slurred warbling notes. HABITAT: Edges of forest and plantations, also well-wooded areas and large gardens. DISTRIBUTION: Resident in Sri Lanka.

5 NILGIRI FLYCATCHER *Eumyias albicaudatus* 15cm FIELD NOTES: Forages in bushes and trees with occasional aerial sallies after flying insects. VOICE: A series of *chip* notes. Song is a rambling, mournful warble of about eight notes. HABITAT: Evergreen hill forest, plantations, forest edge and clearings, thick streamside vegetation. DISTRIBUTION: Resident in the W Ghats.

6 LARGE NILTAVA *Niltava grandis* 21cm FIELD NOTES: Skulks and flits about in low bushes, occasionally feeds on the ground. Less agile than most flycatchers. VOICE: A scolding, nasal *djuee*. Song is a whistled, ascending *whee-whee-wip tee-ti-tree*. HABITAT: Dense, moist submontane and montane broadleaved forest. DISTRIBUTION: Resident in the Himalayas and the NE.

7 SMALL NILTAVA *Niltava macgrigoriae* 13cm FIELD NOTES: Forages in shady undergrowth and bushes, regularly making sallies after flying insects. VOICE: Calls include a high-pitched *see-zee* and various metallic scolding and churring notes. Song is a high-pitched rising and falling *twee-twee-ee-twee*. HABITAT: Forest edges and clearings, bushes along tracks; in winter also occurs in dense reeds and tall grass with scattered trees. DISTRIBUTION: Resident in the Himalayas and the NE.

8 RUFOUS-BELLIED NILTAVA *Niltava sundara* 18cm FIELD NOTES: Unobtrusive. Sits on a low perch from where darting sallies are made after flying insects; also drops to the ground to capture prey. Constantly flicks and spreads tail. VOICE: A rasping *zi-i-i-f-cha-chuk*, a hard *tic*, a thin *see* and a soft *chacha*. HABITAT: Undergrowth and bushes in broadleaved evergreen or mixed forests. DISTRIBUTION: Resident in the Himalayas and the NE.

9 VIVID NILTAVA *Niltava vivida* 17.5cm FIELD NOTES: Forages on the large branches of the middle or upper storey of trees; also makes aerial sallies after flying insects. VOICE: A whistled *yiyou-yiyou*. Song consists of slow, mellow, whistles interspersed with some scratchy notes, transcribed as *beu-wii-riu-chrt-trrt-heu-wii-tiu-wii-u.......* HABITAT: Broadleaved evergreen or mixed forests. DISTRIBUTION: Resident in the NE.

105 FLYCATCHERS

1 WHITE-TAILED FLYCATCHER *Cyornis concretus* 18cm FIELD NOTES: Forages low down in undergrowth or lower branches of trees; often spreads tail to reveal white panels. VOICE: Song is a variable series of penetrating and sibilant whistles. Calls include a soft *pweee* and a harsh *scree*. HABITAT: Dense forest, often near streams. DISTRIBUTION: Resident in the NE.

2 WHITE-BELLIED BLUE FLYCATCHER *Cyornis pallipes* 15cm FIELD NOTES: Forages in thick undergrowth with occasional sallies after flying insects. At rest often lifts and spreads tail. VOICE: A low *tsk-tsk*. Song is a rambling, faltering series of unmelodious squeaky and slurred notes. HABITAT: Undergrowth in dense broadleaved evergreen forest and patches of dense or tangled hillside vegetation. DISTRIBUTION: Resident in the W Ghats.

3 PALE-CHINNED FLYCATCHER (PALE-CHINNED BLUE FLYCATCHER)
Cyornis poliogenys 14cm FIELD NOTES: Forages from undergrowth to the canopy. Birds in the E Ghats, '*vernayi*' (3b), may be a hybrid with Tickell's Blue Flycatcher. VOICE: A grating rattle and a repeated *tik*. Song is a loud, rising and falling series of high-pitched notes, often interspersed with chuckling and harsh notes. HABITAT: Open forests; in winter also occurs in open country with scrub. DISTRIBUTION: Resident in the Himalayas, E India and the NE of the region.

4 PALE BLUE FLYCATCHER *Cyornis unicolor* 18cm FIELD NOTES: Makes aerial sorties after flying insects; also forages in the middle and upper canopy of trees. VOICE: A soft *tr-r-r-r* given when alarmed. Song is rich and melodious, very thrush-like. HABITAT: Moist primary and secondary broadleaved forest and bamboo. DISTRIBUTION: Resident in the NE and summer visitor to the Himalayas.

5 HILL BLUE FLYCATCHER *Cyornis banyumas* 14cm FIELD NOTES: Unobtrusive; hawks insects from a low perch. VOICE: A hard *tac* and a scolding *trrt-trrt-trrt*. Song similar to Tickell's Blue Flycatcher, but descends overall. HABITAT: Dense humid forest with abundant undergrowth. DISTRIBUTION: Winter visitor or resident in the NE.

6 LARGE BLUE FLYCATCHER *Cyornis magnirostris* 15cm FIELD NOTES: Probably similar to Hill Blue Flycatcher, with which it was once considered conspecific. VOICE: Unrecorded. HABITAT: Evergreen forests. DISTRIBUTION: Breeds in E Himalayas.

7 TICKELL'S BLUE FLYCATCHER *Cyornis tickelliae* 14cm FIELD NOTES: Forages from undergrowth up to forest middle levels, regularly making sallies to capture flying insects. VOICE: A harsh *tac* or *kak*, a *tik-tik* and a sharp, churring *trrt-trrt*. Song consists of a short metallic trill of 6–10 notes, firstly descending and then ascending. HABITAT: Open dry forest and wooded areas. DISTRIBUTION: Widespread resident in India and Sri Lanka.

8 BLUE-THROATED BLUE FLYCATCHER *Cyornis rubeculoides* 14cm FIELD NOTES: Forages low down in undergrowth; regularly makes aerial sallies to capture flying insects. VOICE: A soft *tac* or *check* and when agitated a harsh *trrt* or *trrt-trrt*. Song similar to Tickell's Blue Flycatcher but more trilling, higher-pitched and more rapid. HABITAT: Dense undergrowth in dry broadleaved evergreen and mixed deciduous forests. DISTRIBUTION: Breeds in the Himalayas, resident in the NE; winters in the NE, SW and Sri Lanka.

9 PYGMY BLUE FLYCATCHER *Muscicapella hodgsoni* 10cm FIELD NOTES: Very active forager in foliage of trees and scrub; also makes aerial pursuits after flying insects. VOICE: A feeble *tsip* and a low *churr*. Song is a high-pitched *tzit-che-che-che-ckeeee*. HABITAT: Dense broadleaved forest and secondary scrub. DISTRIBUTION: Resident in the Himalayas and the NE.

106 STARLINGS

1 SPOT-WINGED STARLING *Saroglossa spiloptera* 19cm FIELD NOTES: Usually in tree canopy, feeding on insects, fruit and nectar; often forms large flocks alongside other starling species. VOICE: Noisy chattering, an aggressive *chek-chek-chek* and a soft *chik-chik*. Song consists of a musical warbling and dry discordant notes. HABITAT: Open hill forest. DISTRIBUTION: Breeds in the Himalayan foothills; winters in the NE.

2 WHITE-FACED STARLING *Sturnornis albofrontatus* 19–22cm FIELD NOTES: Arboreal; usually forages in the tree canopy. VOICE: A high down-slurred *cheewp, cheow* or *chirp*. Song said to be soft and sweet. HABITAT: Rainforest and adjacent fruiting trees. DISTRIBUTION: Resident in Sri Lanka.

3 WHITE-HEADED STARLING *Sturnia erythropygia* 19–22cm FIELD NOTES: Gregarious; forages in trees and shrubs. Birds on the Andamans have paler buff undertail and a greyish rump. VOICE: Song is a mess of discordant musical, snarling, snorting, squeaky and rattling notes intermingled with mimicry of other bird species. HABITAT: Forest clearings, forest edge, secondary woodland and open cultivated and grassland areas. DISTRIBUTION: Resident on the Nicobars and the Andamans.

4 CHESTNUT-TAILED STARLING *Sturnia malabarica* 20cm FIELD NOTES: Forages mainly in trees. Race *S. m. blythii* (4b) occurs in SW India, race *S. m. nemoricola* (4c) in the NE. VOICE: Song is a series of short hard notes, low squeaky churrs; the same notes are also given in rapid subdued outbursts. Calls include short buzzes and whistles. HABITAT: Open woodland and open country with scattered trees. DISTRIBUTION: Resident in the NE and SW, summers in W and C Himalayas; more widespread in winter.

5 BRAHMINY STARLING *Sturnia pagodarum* 21cm FIELD NOTES: Forages mainly on the ground, often in the company of cattle; also feeds in fruiting and flowering trees. VOICE: Various croaking and chattering notes and short grating churrs when alarmed. Song is short, a nasal slurr followed by a bubbling yodel; also includes mimicry. HABITAT: Open deciduous forests, thorn-scrub, cultivations and around human habitations. DISTRIBUTION: Widespread resident.

6 WHITE-SHOULDERED STARLING *Sturnia sinensis* 17–18cm FIELD NOTES: Arboreal; usually gregarious. VOICE: A soft *preep* uttered in flight and a harsh *kaar*. HABITAT: Open country, scrub and urban areas. DISTRIBUTION: Vagrant, recorded from India and Nepal.

7 CHESTNUT-CHEEKED STARLING *Agropsar philippensis* 16–18cm FIELD NOTES: Mainly arboreal; usually in flocks. VOICE: When excited utters an *airr* or *tshairr*; when alarmed gives a penetrating *tshick*; flight call is a melodious *chrueruchu*. HABITAT: Open mixed deciduous woodland, cultivations and urban parks. DISTRIBUTION: Vagrant, recorded from India.

8 DAURIAN STARLING *Agropsar sturninus* 17cm FIELD NOTES: Gregarious, mainly arboreal. VOICE: Flight call is a soft *prrp*. HABITAT: Open deciduous woodland, thickets and groves. DISTRIBUTION: Vagrant, recorded from Pakistan, India, Nepal and Sri Lanka.

9 ROSE-COLOURED STARLING (ROSY STARLING) *Pastor roseus* 21cm FIELD NOTES: Gregarious. Juvenile pale grey-brown above, dirty buff below; wings dark brown-black; bill pale yellowish. VOICE: Flocks emit a constant chatter; flight calls described as short and harsh or a clear *ki-ki-ki*. HABITAT: Open country, wooded areas including orchards. DISTRIBUTION: Widespread passage migrant and winter visitor.

10 STARLING (COMMON or EUROPEAN STARLING) *Sturnus vulgaris* 22cm FIELD NOTES: Gregarious. Mainly forages on the ground. Juvenile grey-brown above, slightly paler below, bill dark. VOICE: Song is a medley of clicks, creaks, chirrups and warbles, interspersed with drawn-out whistles and mimicry. Calls include a harsh *tcherrr*, a hard *kyik* and a grating *schaahr*. HABITAT: Damp grasslands, cultivations and around urban habitations. DISTRIBUTION: Breeds in the NW; widespread winter visitor, mainly across the N of the region.

4b
blythii

4c
nemoricola

1

2

3

4

5

6

7

8

9

10

n-br

br

107 STARLINGS, MYNAS

1 ASIAN PIED STARLING (PIED MYNA) *Gracupica contra* 23cm FIELD NOTES: Forages mainly on the ground. *G. c. superciliaris* (1b) occurs in Manipur. VOICE: A *cheek-cheurk* and a descending *treek-treek-treek*. Song is a mix of high-pitched, liquid, musical notes. HABITAT: Cultivations, damp grasslands with scattered trees and urban areas. DISTRIBUTION: Resident across much of the N, apart from the NW.

2 ASIAN GLOSSY STARLING *Aplonis panayensis* 20cm FIELD NOTES: Mainly arboreal. Gregarious. Juvenile dark above, grey-white below with dark streaking. White-eyed race *A. p. albiris* (2b) occurs on the Nicobars. VOICE: Calls consist of a series of metallic squeaks. HABITAT: Coconut plantations, forest edge and clearings. DISTRIBUTION: Resident on the Andamans, Nicobars and a summer visitor to the NE.

3 BANK MYNA *Acridotheres ginginianus* 23cm FIELD NOTES: Often tame. Gregarious. In flight shows ochre primary-patches and underwing. VOICE: A *wheek* and a harsh note when agitated. Song consists of tuneless gurgles and whistles. HABITAT: Agricultural and urban areas. DISTRIBUTION: Widespread resident across the C and N of the region.

4 COLLARED MYNA *Acridotheres albocinctus* 23cm FIELD NOTES: Forages mainly on the ground. In flight shows white primary-patches. VOICE: Undescribed. HABITAT: Tall grassland and cultivated areas. DISTRIBUTION: Resident in Manipur and Assam.

5 JUNGLE MYNA *Acridotheres fuscus* 23cm FIELD NOTES: Gregarious. Forms large groups at roosts; forages mainly on the ground. In flight shows white primary-patches. VOICE: A repeated *tiuck-tiuck-tiuck*; other calls and song similar to Common Myna. HABITAT: Open wooded areas, plantations and around villages. DISTRIBUTION: Resident in the Himalayas, the NE and SW.

6 COMMON MYNA *Acridotheres tristis* 23cm FIELD NOTES: Very tame. In flight shows white primary-patches. VOICE: A querulous *kwerrh* and many gurgling and chattering notes; when alarmed utters a harsh *chake-chake*. Song is a tuneless mixture of gurgling and whistled phrases. HABITAT: Around human habitations and cultivations. DISTRIBUTION: Widespread resident.

7 GREAT MYNA *Acridotheres grandis* 25cm FIELD NOTES: Forages mostly on the ground. In flight shows white primary-patches. VOICE: Song and calls similar to Common Myna. HABITAT: Grasslands and cultivated areas. DISTRIBUTION: Resident in the NE.

8 GOLDEN-CRESTED MYNA *Ampeliceps coronatus* 19–21cm FIELD NOTES: Arboreal. In flight shows yellow primary-patches. VOICE: Calls include a metallic bell-like note; otherwise said to be similar to Hill Myna, but higher-pitched. HABITAT: Lowland evergreen forest, moist deciduous woodland, open forest and clearings with tall relict trees. DISTRIBUTION: Resident in Manipur and Assam.

9 SRI LANKA HILL MYNA *Gracula ptilogenys* 25cm FIELD NOTES: Arboreal. In flight shows white primary-patches. VOICE: A variety of piercing whistles, croaking and guttural notes. HABITAT: Forests, well-wooded areas, plantations and gardens. DISTRIBUTION: Resident in Sri Lanka.

10 SOUTHERN HILL MYNA (LESSER HILL MYNA) *Gracula indica* 24cm FIELD NOTES: Arboreal, usually in pairs or small parties; larger flocks occur in flowering trees. In flight shows white primary-patches. VOICE: Similar to Hill Myna, but higher-pitched and less variable. HABITAT: Evergreen forest, well-wooded cultivations. DISTRIBUTION: Resident in the W Ghats and Sri Lanka.

11 HILL MYNA (COMMON HILL MYNA) *Gracula religiosa* 25–29cm FIELD NOTES: Arboreal, generally encountered in pairs or small groups. In flight shows white primary-patches. VOICE: Various *chip* notes, soft *um* sounds, whisper-whistles and many types of whistles, croaks and wails. HABITAT: Moist forest, forest edge and clearings; also plantations. DISTRIBUTION: Resident in the Andamans, the Nicobars, the Himalayan foothills, the hills of NE India and the E Ghats.

108 NUTHATCHES

1 CHESTNUT-VENTED NUTHATCH *Sitta nagaensis* 12.5–14cm FIELD NOTES: Climbs up, down and along trunks or branches in typical nuthatch fashion, but also regularly feeds on the ground. VOICE: A *sit* or *sit-sit*, a *quir* and a *tsit* or *tsit-tsit-tsit...* Song is a rapid *chichichichichi...*, or a slower *chi-chi-chi-chi-chi.....* HABITAT: Evergreen hill forest, pine forests and mixed light deciduous forest. DISTRIBUTION: Resident in the NE Indian hills.

2 KASHMIR NUTHATCH *Sitta cashmirensis* 14cm FIELD NOTES: Actions similar to Chestnut-vented Nuthatch, including foraging on the ground on fallen trees or rocks. VOICE: A *tsi-tsi*, a rapid *pee-pee-pee-pee* and a harsh *kraaa*. HABITAT: Various deciduous and pine forests. DISTRIBUTION: Resident in the NW Himalayas.

3 INDIAN NUTHATCH *Sitta castanea* 13cm FIELD NOTES: Actions as Chestnut-vented Nuthatch; usually forages in the upper parts of tall trees. Often considered conspecific with Chestnut-bellied Nuthatch. VOICE: A rapid, descending trill. Calls include a short *stit* that sometimes accelerates into a fast trill. HABITAT: Deciduous forest, groves and gardens. DISTRIBUTION: Resident in C and SW India.

4 CHESTNUT-BELLIED NUTHATCH *Sitta cinnamoventris* 14cm FIELD NOTES: Foraging actions much as Chestnut-vented Nuthatch. VOICE: Calls include a mellow *tsup*, a thin *sit* or *sit-sit*, and a screechy *chreet chreet chreet*. Advertising 'song' is a fast trilled *treeeee*. HABITAT: Mainly open deciduous forest. DISTRIBUTION: Resident in the Himalayas and the hills of NE India.

5 WHITE-TAILED NUTHATCH *Sitta himalayensis* 12cm FIELD NOTES: Forages mostly on mossy branches in the upper parts of trees. VOICE: Calls include a *nit*, *shree*, *tschak* and a *chak-kak* which may be repeated as *chic-kak-ka-ka-ka-ka*. Songs include a fast, rising *dwi-dwi-dwi...* or similar and a slower *tui-tui-tui-tui....* HABITAT: Mid-altitude oak and rhododendron forest; at higher altitudes favours mixed forests of pine, oak, maple and rhododendron. DISTRIBUTION: Resident in the Himalayas and the hills of NE India.

6 WHITE-CHEEKED NUTHATCH *Sitta leucopsis* 13cm FIELD NOTES: Shy, best located by call; forages mainly in the treetops. VOICE: Gives a constant, bleating *kner-kner* or similar. Song consists of prolonged, rapid, wailing squeaks. HABITAT: Coniferous forests or mixed forests. DISTRIBUTION: Resident in W Himalayas.

7 VELVET-FRONTED NUTHATCH *Sitta frontalis* 12.5cm FIELD NOTES: Very active; forages on trunks and branches from undergrowth to the canopy. VOICE: Song is a rattling *sit-sit-sit-sit...* Calls include a hard *chat*, *chit*, *chlit* or *chip*, also a thin *sip*, *sit* or tsit. HABITAT: Open forests and well-wooded areas. DISTRIBUTION: Resident in the Himalayas, Sri Lanka and the hills of the NE, E, C and SW.

8 EASTERN ROCK NUTHATCH *Sitta tephronota* 15cm FIELD NOTES: Forages with jerky hops, on cliff faces and boulders and in rock crevices; also makes aerial sallies to capture flying insects. VOICE: Loud trilling calls given all year round, also gives a *ch-ch-ch* when agitated. Song is a loud, trilling *iti-tit-tuit-tuit-tuit-tuit....* HABITAT: Rocky valleys, with broken cliffs and boulders. DISTRIBUTION: Resident in Baluchistan.

9 BEAUTIFUL NUTHATCH *Sitta formosa* 16.5cm FIELD NOTES: Elusive. Actions are more sluggish than other nuthatches, although still forages up, down and along branches, usually high up in tall trees that are well covered with epiphytes. VOICE: A soft liquid *plit*, an explosive *chit* that is sometimes lengthened to *chit-it chit-it chit-it....* or *chit-it-it chirririt*. 'Song' is a *chit it it it it it it........* HABITAT: Dense forests. DISTRIBUTION: Resident in the NE.

109 WALLCREEPER, TREECREEPERS, SPOTTED CREEPER, PENDULINE TIT, TITS

1 WALLCREEPER *Tichodroma muraria* 16.5cm FIELD NOTES: Wary. Forages on cliff faces and in crevices; regularly flicks wings open to reveal red and white markings. VOICE: A whistled *tseeoo*, a rapid twitter, a buzzing *zree*, a *tui* and a *chup*. Song a drawn-out, piping *tu-tuee-zreeeeeu* or *chewee-cheweeooo*. HABITAT: Cliffs and rock faces; in bad weather often forced lower to old buildings and rocky riverbeds. DISTRIBUTION: Resident in Himalayas; winters at lower elevations.

2 BAR-TAILED TREECREEPER *Certhia himalayana* 14cm FIELD NOTES: Forages by climbing up tree trunks and along branches; sometimes fly-catches or occasionally feeds on the ground. VOICE: A thin *tsui*, sometimes given as a descending series, also a *tsee* and a rising *tseet*. Song is a lilting *tsee tsu-tsu tsut tut tut li tee* or *ti ti tu-du-du-du-du*. HABITAT: Mainly coniferous forests. DISTRIBUTION: Resident in the NW.

3 RUSTY-FLANKED TREECREEPER *Certhia nipalensis* 14cm FIELD NOTES: Forages among mosses and plants on trunks and branches. VOICE: A thin *sit*. Song is a high-pitched, accelerating trill. HABITAT: Breeds in mixed forests; winters at lower elevations in broadleaved forests. DISTRIBUTION: Resident in the Himalayas.

4 BROWN-THROATED TREECREEPER (SIKKIM TREECREEPER) *Certhia discolor* 14cm FIELD NOTES: Typical of the genus, creeps up mossy trunks and branches. VOICE: An explosive *tchip*, a high *tsit* and a rattling *chi-r-r-it*. Song is a monotonous *chit-it-it-it-it-it-it-it-it-it.....* or similar. HABITAT: Mature broadleaved evergreen and deciduous forests. DISTRIBUTION: Resident in the Himalayas, from NW India eastwards.

5 MANIPUR TREECREEPER (HUME'S TREECREEPER) *Certhia manipurensis* 14cm FIELD NOTES: Once considered a race of Brown-throated Treecreeper; actions thought to be similar. VOICE: An explosive *chit* or *tchip* which sometimes turns into a rattle. Song is a monotonous, slow rattle, slower than that of Brown-throated Treecreeper. HABITAT: Moist evergreen hill forest, also pines when mixed with broadleaved trees. DISTRIBUTION: Resident in Nagaland, Manipur and Mizoram.

6 HODGSON'S TREECREEPER *Certhia hodgsoni* 11–12cm FIELD NOTES: Creeps up and around trees in jerky movements. Race *C. h. mandellii* (6b) occurs in C Himalayas. VOICE: A *tsree* or *tsree-tsree-tsree*. Song is a high-pitched *tzee-tzee-tzizizi*. HABITAT: Mixed conifer and birch forests. DISTRIBUTION: Resident in the Himalayas.

7 SPOTTED CREEPER (INDIAN SPOTTED CREEPER) *Salpornis spilonotus* 15cm FIELD NOTES: Forages on trunks and branches. VOICE: A strident, rising *tui-tui-tui*. Song is a short series of plaintive whistled notes. HABITAT: Open deciduous forest, well-wooded country and groves. DISTRIBUTION: Resident in C and N India.

8 WHITE-CROWNED PENDULINE TIT *Remiz coronatus* 11cm FIELD NOTES: Agile forager in trees and reeds. VOICE: A thin high-pitched *tsee*, *tseeuh* or *tee-tsee-tsee*. HABITAT: Reed-beds, riverside acacias and irrigated plantations. DISTRIBUTION: Winter visitor to the NW.

9 FIRE-CAPPED TIT *Cephalopyrus flammiceps* 10cm FIELD NOTES: Active and agile forager in tall trees and occasionally in bushes. VOICE: A high-pitched, constantly repeated *tsit*. Song is variable, with many phrases, such as a high-pitched *tink-tink-tink-tink*, a slow *pitsu-pitsu*, a quicker *pissu-pissu-pissu* and a vibrant *psing-psing-psing*; some individuals can have up to nine song types. HABITAT: Moist temperate mixed or deciduous forests, orchards and stands of poplars. DISTRIBUTION: Himalayas; breeds in the W, resident from Nepal eastwards; winters in C and NE India.

10 YELLOW-BROWED TIT *Sylviparus modestus* 10cm FIELD NOTES: Active and acrobatic forager in tree foliage. VOICE: Probable song is a shrill *zee-zi-zee-zi-zee-zi....* Calls include a *tsip*, *tchup*, a rapid, trilling *tszizizizizizizizizi....* and a metallic *pli-pli-pli-pli*. HABITAT: Mainly oak forests. DISTRIBUTION: Resident in the Himalayas and the NE.

mandellii

110 TITS

1 WHITE-CHEEKED TIT *Aegithalos leucogenys* 11cm FIELD NOTES: Typical tit; agile and acrobatic forager in trees and bushes, usually in pairs or small parties. Juvenile lacks the black bib. VOICE: A *si-si-si-si*, a fuller *see-see-see*, a *seeup*, and a buzzing *trrrp*. Song is a weak jumble of squeaky and piping notes. HABITAT: Open scrubby forest and riverside tamarisk bushes. DISTRIBUTION: Resident in W Himalayas and W Pakistan.

2 BLACK-THROATED TIT (BLACK-THROATED BUSHTIT) *Aegithalos concinnus iredalei* 10.5cm FIELD NOTES: Active and acrobatic; gregarious, often in flocks of 40 or so. Juvenile lacks the black throat. Paler-crowned race *A. c. manipurensis* (2b) occurs in the northeast, south of the Brahmaputra River. VOICE: Calls include a *si-si-si-si* and a rattling *churr-trrrt-trrrt*. Song is a repeated twittering combined with the odd single chirp. HABITAT: Broadleaved, cedar and pine forest edge, secondary growth and gardens. DISTRIBUTION: Resident in the Himalayas and NE Indian Hills.

3 WHITE-THROATED TIT (WHITE-THROATED BUSHTIT) *Aegithalos niveogularis* 11cm FIELD NOTES: Active and acrobatic, usually in pairs, with larger parties post breeding. VOICE: Song consists of a rapid chattering, combined with a *tsi-tsi-tsi* and a short warbling. Calls include a *tze-tze-tze* and a *wi*. HABITAT: Bushes in mixed conifer and birch forests and alpine shrubs. DISTRIBUTION: Resident in W Himalayas.

4 BLACK-BROWED TIT (RUFOUS-FRONTED TIT, RUFOUS-FRONTED BUSHTIT) *Aegithalos iouschistos* 11cm FIELD NOTES: Typically active and agile. White-bellied race *A. i. bonvaloti* (4b), sometimes treated as a full species, may occur in the high ranges of NE India. VOICE: A constant *see-see-see-see* and *tup* or *trrup*, and when alarmed a shrill *zeet* and *trr-trr-trr*. Song is a jumbled twittering. HABITAT: Forest undergrowth and low trees; occurs in dense evergreen forest post breeding. DISTRIBUTION: Resident in C and E Himalayas.

5 RUFOUS-NAPED TIT *Periparus rufonuchalis* 13cm FIELD NOTES: Agile forager in trees and bushes, and on the ground. VOICE: Calls include a *cheep*, a deep *chut-chut* and a squeaky *trip-ip-ip*. Two song types, a trilling and a whistled *tsi-tsi-peedduw*. HABITAT: Conifer and mixed forests; also poplars, willows and cultivations in NW Pakistan. DISTRIBUTION: Resident in W Himalayas and Baluchistan.

6 RUFOUS-VENTED TIT *Periparus rubidiventris* 12cm FIELD NOTES: Often in small parties. Race *P. r. beavani* (6b) occurs in E Himalayas. VOICE: Song is a rattle that includes some slurred whistles and trills. Calls include a high *seet*, a sharp *chit* and a scolding *chit-it-it-it*. HABITAT: High-altitude forest, including oak, birch, pine and rhododendron. DISTRIBUTION: Resident in the Himalayas and Nagaland.

7 SPOT-WINGED TIT *Periparus melanolophus* 11cm FIELD NOTES: Active, often in mixed-species flocks. Sometimes considered conspecific with Coal Tit. VOICE: Song transcribed as *want you - need you - deed you - kin-ka-jou...* Calls include a *te-tewy*, a plaintive, repeated *tyu-tyu* and a thin *zee-zee*. HABITAT: Mainly conifer forests. DISTRIBUTION: Resident in the Himalayas, from C westwards.

8 COAL TIT *Periparus ater aemodius* 11cm FIELD NOTES: Agile, active forager; gregarious in winter when occurs in mixed-species flocks. VOICE: Calls include a continual cheeping *tsi tsi* and a hoarse *szee*. Song is variable: includes a thin *chip-pe chip-pe....* or *peechoo-peechoo-peechoo* and a *wee-tsee wee-tsee wee-tsee*. HABITAT: Mainly coniferous forests. DISTRIBUTION: Resident in C and E Himalayas.

9 GREY CRESTED TIT *Lophophanes dichrous* 12cm FIELD NOTES: Shy; usually in pairs or small parties. VOICE: Song is a *whee-whee-tz-tz-tz*. Calls include a high *zai* and a rapid *ti-ti-ti-ti-ti*. HABITAT: Mainly oak or other broadleaved forests, also mixed and conifer forests. DISTRIBUTION: Resident in the Himalayas.

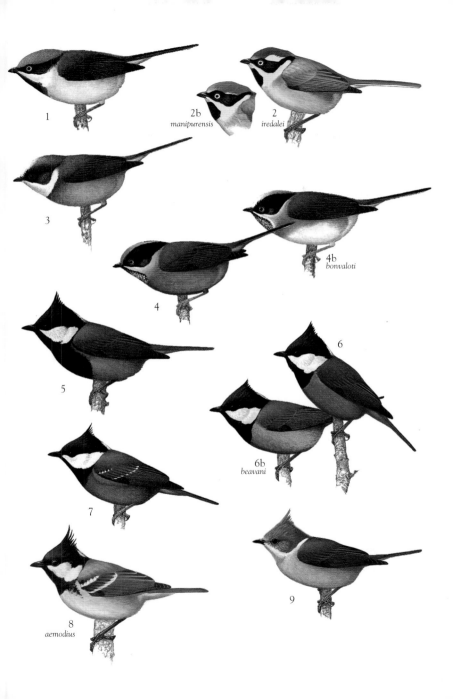

1

2b
manipurensis

2
iredalei

3

4

4b
bonvaloti

5

6

6b
beavani

7

8
aemodius

9

111 TITS

1 GREAT TIT *Parus major stupae* 14cm FIELD NOTES: Active and agile, but less acrobatic than the smaller tits. Usually encountered in pairs, in small scattered parties or in mixed-species flocks. Green-backed race *P. m. tibetanus* (1b) recorded from Sikkim. Some authorities treat these and other Asian forms as Cinereous Tit *P. cinereus*. VOICE: Calls include a *tsee tsee tsee* and a harsh churring when alarmed. Song very variable: includes a *weeter-weeter-weeter*, a repeated *wheet-chee-chee* and a clear *zwink zwink*. HABITAT: Forests and well-wooded country, orchards, groves and gardens. DISTRIBUTION: Widespread, mainly in hills.

2 GREEN-BACKED TIT *Parus monticolus* 12.5cm FIELD NOTES: Agile forager in shrub layer, understorey and canopy. Post breeding occurs in small flocks of up to 20 birds. VOICE: Song variable, including a *seta-seta-seta*, a *tu-weeh-tu-weeh*, a *hit-ee whit-ee....* Calls are like Great Tit but louder and shriller. HABITAT: Evergreen, deciduous and mixed forests. DISTRIBUTION: Resident in the Himalayas and the hills of NE India.

3 WHITE-NAPED TIT *Parus nuchalis* 12cm FIELD NOTES: Usually found in pairs or small family parties, foraging in the canopy and shrub layer. VOICE: Song is a thin, high-pitched *tiu-sut-sut-sut*. Calls include a repeated *ti pee-pee-pee* or *teep whee whee whee whee* and a bold *whew whew whew whew whew*, the last note higher-pitched. HABITAT: Thorn-scrub forest. DISTRIBUTION: Resident in NW and S India.

4 YELLOW-CHEEKED TIT *Parus spilonotus* 14cm FIELD NOTES: Actions similar to Great Tit. VOICE: Song is a ringing, rapidly repeated *chee-chee-piu chee-chee-piu chee-chee-piu....* or *dzi-dzi-pu dzi-dzi-pu.....* Calls similar to Great Tit; including a *sit* a *si-si-si*, a lisping *tsee-tsee-tsee* and a *witch-a-witch-a-witch-a* which is often combined with a harsh *churr-r-r-r-r-r*. HABITAT: Mainly light oak or pine forests, also rhododendrons and second growth with scattered trees. DISTRIBUTION: Resident in E Himalayas and NE Indian hills.

5 BLACK-LORED TIT *Parus xanthogenys* 13cm FIELD NOTES: Arboreal; forages in the canopy, occasionally makes fly-catching sallies after flying insects. When agitated raises crest and flicks wings and tail. Race *P. x. aplonotus* (5b) occurs in N and E peninsular India, *P. x. travancoreensis* (5c) in S peninsular India; together they are sometimes considered a full species with the name Indian Yellow Tit or Indian Black-lored Tit. VOICE: Song consists of repeated phases, such as *pui-pui-tee pui-pui-tee...*, *tsi-teuw tsi-teuw...* or *tsi-eheeah-wheeah...* Calls include a *si-si*, *tzee-tzee-wheep-wheep-wheep*, *tsi-tsi-pit-tui* and a rapid *ch-chi-chi-chi-chi*; when alarmed utters a *tst-reet*. HABITAT: Mainly light open subtropical forest and forest edge. DISTRIBUTION: Resident in the Himalayas and the hills of peninsular India.

6 AZURE TIT *Cyanistes cyanus* 13.5cm FIELD NOTES: Active forager in low bushes, usually in small parties. *C. c. flavipectus* (Yellow-breasted Tit) (6b) should probably be treated as a full species, although regular hybridisation still clouds the situation. VOICE: Calls include a slurred *tstirrup*, a nasal *tsee-tsee-dze-dze* and a scolding *chr-r-r-r-rit*. HABITAT: Thickets and bushes. DISTRIBUTION: Vagrant, recorded from Pakistan.

7 SULTAN TIT *Melanochlora sultanea* 20.5cm FIELD NOTES: Acrobatic forager in foliage of trees and bushes. Crest is raised when excited. VOICE: Song consists of a mellow, whistled *piu-piu-piu-piu-piu* or similar. Calls include a rattling *chi-dip tri-trip* and a fast, squeaky *tria-tria-tria*, *tcheery-tcheery-tcheery* or *squear-squear-squear*. HABITAT: Evergreen and deciduous forests, especially along paths and roads; also large trees near cultivations. DISTRIBUTION: Resident in C and E Himalayas and the NE hills.

1b
tibetanus

2

1
stupae

3

5b ♀
aplonotus

4

5c ♀

trancoreensis
♂

5

7
♀

6b
flavipectus

6

♂

112 MARTINS, SWALLOWS

1 SAND MARTIN *Riparia riparia* 12cm FIELD NOTES: Rapid light flight, usually low over water or ground; highly gregarious. VOICE: A harsh *tschr* or *brrtt*. HABITAT: On migration and post breeding open country, generally near water; often roosts in reed-beds. DISTRIBUTION: Winter visitor to Sri Lanka and probably in the NE.

2 PALE SAND MARTIN (PALE MARTIN) *Riparia diluta* 13cm FIELD NOTES: Very similar to Sand Martin, breast-band less well defined; wintering birds from SW China, *R. d. tibetana* (not shown), nearly as dark as Sand Martin. Fast fluttery flight, often in the company of other swallows. VOICE: A short grating twittering. Calls include a short *ret* or *brrit*. HABITAT: Mainly open country with nearby water; regularly roosts in reed-beds. DISTRIBUTION: Breeds in the NW; more widespread in the NW in winter, and in Sri Lanka.

3 PLAIN MARTIN (BROWN-THROATED MARTIN) *Riparia paludicola* 12cm FIELD NOTES: Variable: occurs in pale- and brown-throated forms. Weak, fluttering flight that can recall a small bat. VOICE: A soft twittering, often uttered in flight. Calls include a low *chrrr* and a harsh *svee-svee*. HABITAT: Rivers, streams and lakes; also forages over grasslands. DISTRIBUTION: Widespread resident across most of the N and C of the region.

4 DUSKY CRAG MARTIN *Ptyonoprogne concolor* 13cm FIELD NOTES: Flight slow with frequent periods of gliding; usually in pairs or small groups, with larger parties post breeding. Shows pale spots on spread tail. VOICE: A twittering song and a soft *chit-chit* contact call. HABITAT: Mountainous and hilly areas with cliffs, caves and gorges; also old buildings and urban areas. DISTRIBUTION: Widespread resident over much of India W of the E Ghats.

5 CRAG MARTIN (EURASIAN CRAG MARTIN) *Ptyonoprogne rupestris* 15cm FIELD NOTES: Powerful, slow but agile flight with much gliding. Shows pale spots on spread tail. Usually encountered in small parties; larger flocks occur post breeding. VOICE: A, quiet, throaty, rapid twitter. Calls include a *prrit*, a warning *zrrr*, a plaintive *whee*. HABITAT: Cliffs, gorges and old buildings. DISTRIBUTION: Resident in the Himalayas and NW, although leaves NW India post breeding; winters mainly in the W Ghats.

6 PALE CRAG MARTIN *Ptyonoprogne (fuligula) obsoleta* 13cm FIELD NOTES: Flight slow with regular gliding; white spots show when tail spread. Usually in small groups with larger flocks post breeding. Thought by some authorities to be a race of Rock Martin *P. fuligula*. VOICE: A low twitter. Calls include a high-pitched *twee*, a rapid *chir-chir-chir* and a low *chirp*. HABITAT: Cliffs, gorges and ravines in dry country. DISTRIBUTION: Resident in C and S Pakistan.

7 SWALLOW (BARN SWALLOW) *Hirundo rustica* 18cm FIELD NOTES: An agile, fast flier that twists and turns to capture flying insects. Post breeding often occurs in large flocks. Rusty race *H. r. tytleri* (7b) occurs as a winter visitor to the NE. VOICE: A melodious twittering interspersed with a grating rattle, given in flight or when perched. Calls include a *vit-vit*, a sharper *flitt-flitt* and a *chir-chir* when agitated. HABITAT: Open country and cultivations, usually not far from water. DISTRIBUTION: Breeds in the Himalayas and the NW; widespread throughout the region in winter.

8 PACIFIC SWALLOW (HILL SWALLOW) *Hirundo tahitica domicola* 13cm FIELD NOTES: Flight fast with glides and frequent swerving and banking. Slightly greener-looking race *H. t. javanica* (not shown), from the Andamans, is sometimes considered a full species. VOICE: A twittering song and a *titswee* call. HABITAT: Grassy hills near plantations; birds on the Andamans frequent open country along coasts and rivers. DISTRIBUTION: Resident in the SW Ghats, Sri Lanka and the Andamans.

7b
tytleri

7

8

dark-throated
form

pale-throated
form

113 SWALLOWS, HOUSE MARTINS

1 WIRE-TAILED SWALLOW *Hirundo smithii* 14–21cm FIELD NOTES: Flight fast, often low over water. Juveniles have a brown crown and lack the long, fine outer tail filaments. VOICE: Song is a twittering *chirrickweet-chrrickweet*. Calls include a *chit-chit* and, when alarmed, a *chichip-chichip*. HABITAT: Grassland, cultivations and urban areas, usually near water. DISTRIBUTION: Widespread resident.

2 STRIATED SWALLOW *Cecropsis striolata* 19cm FIELD NOTES: Flight is slow and buoyant, usually low over the ground or around cliffs. VOICE: Song is soft and twittering. Calls include a drawn-out *quitsch*, a *pin* and when alarmed a repeated *chi-chi-chi*. HABITAT: Open hilly country, river gorges, forest clearings and cultivations. DISTRIBUTION: Resident in the NE.

3 RED-RUMPED SWALLOW *Cecropsis daurica* 16–17cm FIELD NOTES: Flight slow and graceful with much gliding and soaring. At least six races recorded in the region, differing mainly in the strength of streaking on the underparts; Sri Lanka race *C. d. hyperythra* (3b) is sometimes considered a separate species. VOICE: A quiet twittering. Calls include a mewing, an aggressive *krr* and a *djuit* contact note. HABITAT: Open hilly country, lightly wooded areas, rocky gorges and cliffs; also open scrub, cultivations and paddyfields. DISTRIBUTION: Widespread resident and winter visitor.

4 INDIAN CLIFF SWALLOW (STREAK-THROATED SWALLOW) *Petrochelidon fluvicola* 11–12cm FIELD NOTES: Weak, fluttering flight. Often occurs in flocks and in the company of other swallows. VOICE: Twittering song and a sharp *trr-trr* call. HABITAT: Open country, foothills, cultivation and around human habitations; often near water. DISTRIBUTION: Widespread resident.

5 HOUSE MARTIN (EUROPEAN, NORTHERN or COMMON HOUSE MARTIN) *Delichon urbicum* 13cm FIELD NOTES: Flies with much gliding and soaring, often at a great height. Gregarious, often in the company of other swallows and swifts. VOICE: Song consists of a rapid twittering interspersed with a dry rattling. Calls include an abrupt *prrt*, a longer *pri-pit* and a *za-za-za*. HABITAT: Mountain valleys with cliffs and gorges, often near to cultivation and villages. DISTRIBUTION: Summer visitor to W Himalayas; passage migrant elsewhere.

6 NEPAL HOUSE MARTIN *Delichon nipalense* 13cm FIELD NOTES: Rump and underparts greyer and tail shallower-forked than House Martin. Flight includes much gliding and swooping at a great height or along cliffs and above treetops. Regularly joins with other swallows and swifts. VOICE: In flight utters a high-pitched *chi-i*. HABITAT: Wooded mountain ridges with cliffs and river valleys; also around mountain villages. DISTRIBUTION: Resident in the Himalayas and the hills of NE India.

7 ASIAN HOUSE MARTIN *Delichon dasypus* 12cm FIELD NOTES: Square-ended tail. Flight contains frequent gliding, swooping and banking, often at a great height. Gregarious, regularly foraging with other swallows or swifts. VOICE: A shrill flight call and a soft trilling song. HABITAT: Gorges, valleys and villages in hilly or mountain areas. DISTRIBUTION: Resident in the Himalayas; moves to lower areas in bad winters.

NA

hyperythra

114 BULBULS

1 CRESTED FINCHBILL *Spizixos canifrons* 22cm FIELD NOTES: Often in small parties. VOICE: A bubbling trill; issues a *purr-purr-prruit-prruit-prruit* call when agitated. HABITAT: Open woodland, secondary growth and overgrown forest clearings. DISTRIBUTION: Resident in NE Indian hills.

2 STRIATED BULBUL *Pycnonotus striatus* 23cm FIELD NOTES: Generally forages in tree-tops. VOICE: A series of pleasant warbling notes. Calls include a sharp, repeated *tyiwut* and a loud *pyik....pyik*. HABITAT: Broadleaved evergreen forest, moist oak–rhododendron forest and deciduous forest in NE India. DISTRIBUTION: Resident in C and NE Himalayas and the hills of NE India.

3 GREY-HEADED BULBUL *Pycnonotus priocephalus* 19cm FIELD NOTES: Forages at all levels, singly, in pairs or in small parties. VOICE: Calls include incessant, monosyllabic, shrill notes, a thin metallic wheezy *jzhwink* and a jarring *chraink*. HABITAT: Moist broadleaved evergreen forests with dense undergrowth and scrub in abandoned clearings. DISTRIBUTION: Resident in SW India.

4 BLACK-HEADED BULBUL *Pycnonotus atriceps* 18cm FIELD NOTES: Usually in pairs or small parties foraging in trees or bushes. Greyish form is rare. VOICE: Song is a disjointed series of rising and falling *tink* notes. Calls include an emphatic *chew* or *chewp*. HABITAT: Open forests and gardens. DISTRIBUTION: Resident in the NE.

5 ANDAMAN BULBUL *Pycnonotus fuscoflavescens* 14–17cm FIELD NOTES: Usually forages singly, in pairs or in small groups. VOICE: A short series of high-pitched *tsit-tsit-tsit* notes. Calls include a *tsit* and an upward-inflected *shrinkit*. HABITAT: Forest, forest edge and thick secondary growth. DISTRIBUTION: Resident on the Andamans.

6 BLACK-CRESTED BULBUL *Pycnonotus flaviventris* 22cm FIELD NOTES: Arboreal, generally seen singly or in pairs. VOICE: Song is a sweet *weet-tre-trippy-weet*. Calls similar to Flame-throated Bulbul. HABITAT: Forests with undergrowth, abandoned clearings, scrub around cultivations and orchards. DISTRIBUTION: Resident in the NE and the Himalayas.

7 BLACK-CAPPED BULBUL *Pycnonotus melanicterus* 19cm FIELD NOTES: Arboreal; usually in pairs or small groups. VOICE: Various sweet, mellow piping whistles and sharper notes. Calls include a rapid whipcrack note. HABITAT: Luxuriant forest, secondary growth and forest edge. DISTRIBUTION: Resident in Sri Lanka.

8 FLAME-THROATED BULBUL *Pycnonotus gularis* 18–19cm FIELD NOTES: Arboreal, generally in the canopy. VOICE: Utters a low, constant churring. Song consists of six or so tinkling notes. HABITAT: Evergreen forest edge, thickets and overgrown clearings. DISTRIBUTION: Resident in the W Ghats.

9 WHITE-EARED BULBUL *Pycnonotus leucotis* 20cm FIELD NOTES: Bold and confiding. VOICE: A brief, complex chatter. Calls include a harsh *nyuk-nyuk* and a mellow *pip-pip*. HABITAT: Semi-desert scrub, mangroves and gardens. DISTRIBUTION: Resident in the NW.

10 WHITE-CHEEKED BULBUL (HIMALAYAN BULBUL) *Pycnonotus leucogenys* 20cm FIELD NOTES: Bold and confiding; usually in small parties. VOICE: A melodious *tea-for-two*; when agitated issues a *pit-pit* or a *pititititit*. HABITAT: Wooded valleys and bushy hillsides. DISTRIBUTION: Resident in the Himalayas.

11 RED-VENTED BULBUL *Pycnonotus cafer* 20cm FIELD NOTES: Tame; usually in pairs or small parties. Darker race *P. c. bengalensis* (11b) occurs in the N and NE. VOICE: A cheery *be-care-ful*. Calls include a chattering *peep-a-peep-a-lo* and a rapid *pititititit*. HABITAT: Open deciduous forest, scrub and gardens. DISTRIBUTION: Widespread resident.

12 RED-WHISKERED BULBUL *Pycnonotus jocosus* 20cm FIELD NOTES: Usually seen singly, in pairs or in small parties. Juvenile lacks red cheek-patch. VOICE: Varied musical phrases. Calls include a rolling *prroop* and a harsh, raspy *bzeep*. HABITAT: Open forest, scrub, orchards and gardens. DISTRIBUTION: Widespread over much of the region, apart from the C and NE.

greyish
form

1

2

3

4

5

6

7

8

9

10

11

11b

bengalensis

12

115 BULBULS

1 YELLOW-THROATED BULBUL *Pycnonotus xantholaemus* 20cm FIELD NOTES: Skulking, but restless; in pairs or small groups. VOICE: A rich, low burbling and warbling. Calls include a brief *teetle-lerp* and a nasal *rhid-tu-tu*. HABITAT: Rocky wooded hillsides. DISTRIBUTION: Resident in S India.

2 YELLOW-EARED BULBUL *Pycnonotus penicillatus* 20cm FIELD NOTES: Shy; forages mainly in undergrowth, although higher if trees are in fruit. VOICE: An explosive, ringing *Swink-Swink-Swink* and a low *crr-crr*. HABITAT: Forests and nearby gardens. DISTRIBUTION: Resident in Sri Lanka.

3 FLAVESCENT BULBUL *Pycnonotus flavescens* 22cm FIELD NOTES: Shy; forages in foliage of trees and bushes. VOICE: A harsh churring. Song is a chuckling *srzk-bzeek zink-zenk-zink*. HABITAT: Forests with thick undergrowth, scrub jungle and dense bushes in abandoned cultivations. DISTRIBUTION: Resident in the hills of NE India.

4 WHITE-BROWED BULBUL *Pycnonotus luteolus* 20cm FIELD NOTES: Shy; more often heard than seen. Forages in thick cover. VOICE: A loud burst of lively, discordant, bubbling, spluttering notes. Calls include a *churr* and a *krr-kurr*. HABITAT: Dry open scrub, thickets, forest edge and clearings, also gardens. DISTRIBUTION: Resident in peninsular India and Sri Lanka.

5 WHITE-THROATED BULBUL *Alophoixus flaveolus* 22cm FIELD NOTES: Creeps and clambers about undergrowth in chattering parties. VOICE: A strident, nasal *nyak nyark nyark*, a higher-pitched *yap* and a shrill *shree-shree-shree*. HABITAT: Undergrowth in evergreen forests and secondary jungle. DISTRIBUTION: Resident in E Himalayas and the NE.

6 YELLOW-BROWED BULBUL *Acritillas indica* 20cm FIELD NOTES: Found in pairs or small parties. Race *A. i. guglielmi* (6b) occurs in Sri Lanka. VOICE: A low-toned, pleasant warble. Calls include a clear, mellow double whistle and a harsh jarring *chaink-chaink*. HABITAT: Evergreen forest edge, secondary forest, plantations and undergrowth. DISTRIBUTION: Resident in the W Ghats and Sri Lanka.

7 OLIVE BULBUL *Iole virescens* 19cm FIELD NOTES: Shy, forages mainly in the canopy. VOICE: A nasal, repeated *chwaa* or *jer-wee* and a mewing *whee-ik*. HABITAT: Well-wooded ravines, dense, humid evergreen forest and tall secondary growth. DISTRIBUTION: Resident in the NE.

8 MOUNTAIN BULBUL *Ixos mcclellandii* 24cm FIELD NOTES: Usually in pairs or small parties; forages mainly in the canopy. VOICE: A screechy *chirrut chewt chirrut chewt*. Calls include a downward inflected *tsiuc* or *chewp*. HABITAT: Forest and secondary growth. DISTRIBUTION: Resident in the Himalayas and the NE.

9 NICOBAR BULBUL *Ixos nicobariensis* 20cm FIELD NOTES: Often forages in noisy flocks. VOICE: A chattering babble. HABITAT: Forests and secondary growth. DISTRIBUTION: Resident on the Nicobars.

10 ASHY BULBUL *Hemixos flavala* 20cm FIELD NOTES: Arboreal; sociable, especially post breeding. VOICE: A metallic, perky *skrink-er rink-er-rink*. Calls include twangy buzzes and musical chatters. HABITAT: Broadleaved evergreen forest. DISTRIBUTION: Resident in the Himalayan foothills and the NE.

11 BLACK BULBUL *Hypsipetes leucocephalus* 25cm FIELD NOTES: Generally encountered in the tops of trees; post breeding may form large, noisy flocks. VOICE: Song consists of a series of notes that vary in tone and pitch, punctuated with a high bell-like note; foraging groups give a continual chattering babble. HABITAT: Tall forests of oak, pine and rhododendron, also gardens. DISTRIBUTION: Resident in the Himalayas and the NE.

12 SQUARE-TAILED BULBUL *Hypsipetes ganeesa* 22cm FIELD NOTES: Habits and actions similar to Black Bulbul, which is often considered conspecific. VOICE: Similar to Black Bulbul, but harsher and less nasal. HABITAT: Broadleaved evergreen forests and shade trees in plantations. DISTRIBUTION: Resident in the W Ghats and Sri Lanka.

116 BUSH WARBLERS

1 ASIAN STUBTAIL (ASIAN STUBTAIL WARBLER) *Urosphena squameiceps* 10–11.5cm FIELD NOTES: Skulks mainly on the ground; forages by hopping, similar to an accentor, among forest undergrowth. VOICE: A soft low *chip-chip-chip*. Song is a high-pitched, insect-like *see-see-see-see-see-see-see-see...*, final notes getting progressively louder. HABITAT: Coniferous and deciduous forests, with thick undergrowth, on mountain slopes. DISTRIBUTION: Vagrant, recorded from Nepal and Bangladesh.

2 PALE-FOOTED BUSH WARBLER *Cettia pallidipes* 11–12.5cm FIELD NOTES: Skulking, flits through bush or grass; more often heard than seen. Brighter race *C. p. osmastoni* (2b) occurs on the Andamans. VOICE: A quiet, sharp *chik-chik*. Song is an explosive, repeated *zip...zip-tschuk-o-tschuk*. HABITAT: Thickets, grass jungle and bushes at forest edge or glades. DISTRIBUTION: Resident in the Himalayas, the NE and S, and the Andamans.

3 ORIENTAL BUSH WARBLER (MANCHURIAN BUSH WARBLER) *Cettia canturians* 18cm FIELD NOTES: Secretive, often remaining immobile in thick foliage. VOICE: A dry ticking *chick-chuck* or *tyok-tyok*. HABITAT: Dense thickets or scrub, also secondary forest. DISTRIBUTION: Vagrant, recorded from India.

4 BROWNISH-FLANKED BUSH WARBLER (BROWN-FLANKED BUSH WARBLER) *Cettia fortipes* 12cm FIELD NOTES: Skulks in thick cover; more often heard than seen. Greyer race *C. f. pallidus* (4b) occurs in W Himalayas. VOICE: A loud, staccato *tyit tyu-tyu*, a churring *churrk* and a hard *tack*. Song consists of a sustained, rising *weeeee* followed by an explosive *chiwiyou*. HABITAT: Thick undergrowth in open forests, thickets and lush vegetation on swampy ground. DISTRIBUTION: Resident in the Himalayas and the NE.

5 CHESTNUT-CROWNED BUSH WARBLER (LARGE BUSH WARBLER) *Cettia major* 13cm FIELD NOTES: Shy and skulking, creeps on the ground. VOICE: A sharp *tzip* or *pseet*. Song consists of a short whistle followed by a rapid shrill warble. HABITAT: Forest undergrowth, forest bushes, rhododendron shrubberies; winters in tall grass and reed-beds. DISTRIBUTION: Resident in the Himalayas and the NE hills.

6 HUME'S BUSH WARBLER *Cettia brunnescens* 9.5–11cm FIELD NOTES: Skulks in thick cover, usually heard rather than seen. VOICE: A rasping *brr* and a sharp *tik*. Song is a high-pitched *see-saw see-saw see-saw......* HABITAT: Bamboo thickets. DISTRIBUTION: Resident in the Himalayas.

7 ABERRANT BUSH WARBLER *Cettia flavolivacea* 12cm FIELD NOTES: Skulking, sometimes inquisitive, and may come to the edge of cover; constantly flicks wings and tail. VOICE: A soft *brrrt-brrt* and a sharp *chick*. Song is a series of thin rising notes followed by a long whistle. HABITAT: Dense forest-edge thickets, forest undergrowth; also long grass and scrub in pine forests. DISTRIBUTION: Resident in the Himalayas and the hills of NE India.

8 GREY-SIDED BUSH WARBLER *Cettia brunnifrons* 10–11cm FIELD NOTES: Skulking, but sometimes ventures to the edge of cover; recorded singing in the open, on bush tops. VOICE: A sharp, metallic *tzip*. Song consists of a high-pitched *dzit-su-ze-sizu* followed by a nasal *bzeeuu-bzeeuu*. HABITAT: Subalpine bamboo and bushes in forest clearings, also dense thickets in open coniferous forests; winters at lower altitudes in scrub and forest undergrowth DISTRIBUTION: Resident in the Himalayas and NE India.

9 CETTI'S WARBLER *Cettia cetti* 14cm FIELD NOTES: Skulks, more often heard than seen, although sometimes sings in the open. VOICE: A sharp *chip*, a *tsuk* and when alarmed a rattling *twik-ik-ik-il*. Song is a loud and explosive *chee-weechoo-weechoo-weechoo* or similar. HABITAT: Reed-beds, tall grass and tamarisks. DISTRIBUTION: Winter visitor and passage migrant in the NW.

117 BUSH WARBLERS, GRASSHOPPER WARBLERS

1 SPOTTED BUSH WARBLER *Bradypterus thoracicus* 11–13cm FIELD NOTES: Secretive, especially in winter; generally keeps to thick cover. VOICE: Song transcribed as *trick-i-di....* HABITAT: Shrubbery in open grassy areas, pastures with scrub and bracken, also dwarf juniper and rhododendron around the tree line. DISTRIBUTION: Breeds in C and E Himalayas; winters in the Himalayan foothills and the NE plains.

2 WEST HIMALAYAN BUSH WARBLER *Bradypterus kashmirensis* 13cm FIELD NOTES: Often treated as a race of Spotted Bush Warbler. VOICE: Song consists of rhythmical, mechanical buzzing and clicking notes. HABITAT: Open grassy areas, low scrub and dwarf juniper. DISTRIBUTION: Breeds in W Himalayas.

3 LARGE-BILLED BUSH WARBLER (LONG-BILLED BUSH WARBLER) *Bradypterus major* 13cm FIELD NOTES: Very skulking; runs through vegetation like a small rodent, hard to flush. VOICE: A monotonous, rapid reeling. Calls include a quiet *tic* and grating *trrr.* HABITAT: Grassy slopes with bushes and waste areas, forest clearings and upland cultivation. DISTRIBUTION: Breeds in W Himalayas.

4 CHINESE BUSH WARBLER *Bradypterus tacsanowskius* 13cm FIELD NOTES: Very secretive; creeps about in tangled vegetation. VOICE: Call note is a *chirr-chirr.* Song consists of insect-like rasping or buzzing notes, *raaasp...raaasp...raaasp...raaaaasp...raaaaaaasp... raaasp........* HABITAT: Grasslands, reed-beds and paddyfields. DISTRIBUTION: Winter visitor to E Nepal and NE India.

5 BROWN BUSH WARBLER *Bradypterus luteoventris* 13–14cm FIELD NOTES: Skulking, but not shy, although more secretive post breeding; often sings from a prominent perch. VOICE: A reeling *tk tk tk tk tk tk tk......* Calls include a hard *tack* and a higher *tink-tink-tink.* HABITAT: Grassy and dense weedy areas. DISTRIBUTION: Resident in E Himalayas and the hills of NE India.

6 RUSSET BUSH WARBLER *Bradypterus mandelli* 13cm FIELD NOTES: Probably skulking like others of the genus. VOICE: A rapid *cre-ut cre-ut cre-ut cre-ut......* Call note a short, emphatic *shtuk.* HABITAT: Sparsely wooded slopes with forest clearings, thickets, tangles of brambles, grasses and willows, also cultivation margins. DISTRIBUTION: Resident in the NE.

7 SRI LANKA BUSH WARBLER (PALLISER'S WARBLER) *Elaphrornis palliseri* 16cm FIELD NOTES: Secretive; constantly on the move and continually flicking tail. Post breeding often forms loose flocks. VOICE: A low, explosive *quitz* or *queek.* Song consists of squeaky scattered notes. HABITAT: Dense undergrowth in damp forests. DISTRIBUTION: Resident in Sri Lanka.

8 GRASSHOPPER WARBLER (COMMON GRASSHOPPER WARBLER) *Locustella naevia* 13cm FIELD NOTES: Very secretive and skulking. VOICE: A sharp *thik* or *thik-thik* and a quieter *whit.* HABITAT: Waterside vegetation, thick grass, tamarisk scrub, paddyfields and grassy slopes with scattered bushes. DISTRIBUTION: Widespread winter visitor.

9 PALLAS'S GRASSHOPPER WARBLER (RUSTY-RUMPED WARBLER) *Locustella certhiola* 13–14cm FIELD NOTES: Skulks and creeps mouse-like among reeds and tall grass. VOICE: Calls include a thin *tik-tik-tik,* a sharp *chirk* or *chuck* and a trilling *chi-chirr,* similar to Lanceolated Warbler but less urgent and quieter. HABITAT: Reed-beds and paddyfields. DISTRIBUTION: Winter visitor to Sri Lanka, scattered records elsewhere in the region.

10 LANCEOLATED WARBLER *Locustella lanceolata* 12cm FIELD NOTES: Very secretive; tends to run through vegetation or along the ground in between roots, very reluctant to fly. VOICE: Calls include a loud, urgent *chirr-chirr* or *chi-chirr* and a low-pitched *chk.* HABITAT: Dense bush, reed-beds, tall grassy vegetation and paddy stubble. DISTRIBUTION: Winter visitor, mainly to the N lowlands.

118 PRINIAS

1 RUFOUS-VENTED PRINIA *Prinia burnesii* 17cm FIELD NOTES: Keeps low in grass clumps, best located by song. The Nepal race *P. b. nepalicola* (not shown) is generally greyer above and lighter rufous on the vent. VOICE: A loud, clear liquid warble. Calls include a wheezy *feez* and a quiet, rapid, nasal rattle. HABITAT: Tall grassland or tall grass mixed with scrub and reed-beds. DISTRIBUTION: Resident in Pakistan, N India and SE Nepal.

2 SWAMP PRINIA *Prinia cinerascens* 17cm FIELD NOTES: Usually in pairs or small parties; tends to stay well hidden while foraging on or near the ground. Sometimes considered a race of Rufous-vented Prinia. VOICE: A low *chisp chisp*. Song consists of a rising and falling, rich, mellow warble interspersed with short trills. HABITAT: Tall grass, especially in swamps. DISTRIBUTION: Resident in the NE.

3 STRIATED PRINIA *Prinia crinigera* 16cm FIELD NOTES: Usually skulking, but in breeding season sings from a prominent perch on trees or bushes. VOICE: A jaunty, wheezy *chitzereet-chitzereet-chitzereet-chitzereet-chitzereet-chitzereet*; the last few notes speed up, making a slight climax. HABITAT: Open grassy mountainsides or hillsides with scattered shrubs; also in rank herbage in cultivations. DISTRIBUTION: Resident in the Himalayas and the NE.

4 BLACK-THROATED PRINIA *Prinia atrogularis* 17cm FIELD NOTES: Active; forages in thick cover, constantly flicks tail. Chestnut-capped race *P. a. khasiana* (4b) occurs E and S of the Brahmaputra River; race *P. a. superciliaris* (Hill Prinia) (4c) occurs in E Arunachal Pradesh and may be given separate species status. VOICE: A scrapping, buzzing *szelik szelik szelik* or similar. Calls include a soft *tp-tp-tp* and a scolding *chrrr-chrrr-chrrr*. HABITAT: Grassy mountainsides and hillsides with scattered shrubs, scrub in forest clearings and thick vegetation in cultivations. DISTRIBUTION: Resident in the NE.

5 GREY-CROWNED PRINIA *Prinia cinereocapilla* 11cm FIELD NOTES: Shy and elusive; forages in thick tangles, constantly twitches tail. VOICE: A twittering *tweetoo-wee-too-weetoo-weeto* followed by a tinny *ti-ti-ti-ti-ti*. Call note is a repeated *tzit*. HABITAT: Bushes and scrub in forest clearings, secondary growth and scrub in cultivations. DISTRIBUTION: Resident, in isolated pockets, in the Himalayan foothills.

6 RUFOUS-FRONTED PRINIA *Prinia buchanani* 12cm FIELD NOTES: Active, tail constantly twitched; forages in tangled vegetation. VOICE: A musical, reeling *chid-le-weeest*, the last note with a rising inflection, followed by a repeated *chid-le-ee...* HABITAT: Semi-desert areas with scrub and coarse grasses; in C India also occurs in clearings in dry forests. DISTRIBUTION: Resident over much of the NW and C of the region.

7 RUFESCENT PRINIA *Prinia rufescens* 11cm FIELD NOTES: Very secretive, occasionally in small parties; tail regularly waved up and down or sideways. VOICE: A rhythmic *chewp-chewp-chewp-chewp*. Calls include a *chip chip chip* and a buzzy *peez-peez-peez*. HABITAT: Grassy areas in open forest, grassland with scattered trees. DISTRIBUTION: Resident in the NE.

8 GREY-BREASTED PRINIA *Prinia hodgsonii* 11cm FIELD NOTES: Active, moves quickly through bushes or undergrowth; often in parties post breeding. VOICE: A squeaky, warbling *chiwee-chiwee-chewi-chip-chip-chip*. Calls include a tinkling *zeee-zeee-zeee* and a thin *chew-chew-chew*. HABITAT: Scrub jungle, bushes in open forest or forest edge, also bushes in cultivations and gardens. DISTRIBUTION: Widespread resident.

9 GRACEFUL PRINIA *Prinia gracilis* 11cm FIELD NOTES: Constantly flicks wings and tail. Sings from a prominent perch or in display-flight. VOICE: A fast, wheezy, reeling warble. Calls include a *breep* or *tzeep* and a *trrt-trrt-trrt*. HABITAT: Tall grass and scrub, particularly by watercourses. DISTRIBUTION: Widespread resident in the N and NW.

119 PRINIAS, CISTICOLAS, REED WARBLERS

1 JUNGLE PRINIA *Prinia sylvatica* 13cm FIELD NOTES: Forages in low vegetation; sings from a prominent perch or during an undulating display-flight. Race *P. s. insignis* (1b), which has whiter tail sides, occurs in NW India, darker race *P. s. valida* (1c) occurs in Sri Lanka. VOICE: A loud, rapid *pit-pretty pit-pretty pit-pretty.......* Calls include a rapid chatter and a quickly repeated *pit pit pit.* HABITAT: Scrubby bush jungle mixed with boulders and grassland. DISTRIBUTION: Widespread resident in C and peninsular India and Sri Lanka.

2 YELLOW-BELLIED PRINIA *Prinia flaviventris* 13cm FIELD NOTES: Restless forager among grasses. Sings from a prominent perch or during a short display-flight. VOICE: Song is flute-like, starting with a *chirp* followed by a descending trill, repeated many times. Calls include a *chink chink....* and a plaintive *twee-twee.* HABITAT: Wet areas with tall grassland and small bushes, waterside reeds. DISTRIBUTION: Widespread across the N.

3 ASHY PRINIA *Prinia socialis* 13cm FIELD NOTES: Skulking but active forager low down in tall grass or scrub. Sings from prominent perch or during display-flight. VOICE: A loud, cheerful, wheezy *jimmy-jimmy-jimmy.* Calls include a sharp, nasal *tee-tee-tee* and a cracking *kit kit kit.* HABITAT: Tall grassland and scrub along wetlands, open scrub jungle, mangroves, cultivations and gardens. DISTRIBUTION: Widespread resident.

4 PLAIN PRINIA *Prinia inornata* 13cm FIELD NOTES: Unobtrusive, keeps low in vegetation. VOICE: An insect-like, wheezy *jirt jirt jirt jirt....* Calls include a buzzy *zzpink* or *bzzp* and a clear *clact.* HABITAT: Scrubby grassland, reed-beds, mangroves and cultivations. DISTRIBUTION: Widespread resident.

5 SCRUB WARBLER (STREAKED SCRUB WARBLER) *Scotocerca inquieta* 10cm FIELD NOTES: Mouse-like actions, usually difficult to see well, although can be quite inquisitive. VOICE: Variable, usually starting with a series of staccato piping notes followed by a scratchy warble. Calls include a high-pitched *te-he*, a short *drzip* and a scolding *prrt.* HABITAT: Dry stony hillsides with low scrub. DISTRIBUTION: Resident in Pakistan hills.

6 ZITTING CISTICOLA *Cisticola juncidis cursitans* 10cm FIELD NOTES: Best located while singing from an exposed perch or during bounding song-flight. The richly coloured race *C. j. salimalii* (6b) occurs in the Kerala region of SW India. VOICE: A simple *zit-zit-zit-zit-zit.....* Calls include a *tew* and a *tsipp-tsipp-tsipp.* HABITAT: Grasslands. DISTRIBUTION: Widespread resident.

7 BRIGHT-HEADED CISTICOLA (GOLDEN-HEADED CISTICOLA) *Cisticola exilis tytleri* 10cm FIELD NOTES: Sings from an exposed perch or during display-flight; forages low in thick grass. Brighter race *C. e. erythrocephalus* (7b) occurs in the SW. VOICE: Scratchy buzzy note, or notes, followed by a liquid *plook.* Call note is a scolding *squee.* HABITAT: Tall grassland and scrubby hillsides in the SW. DISTRIBUTION: Resident in the SW, N and NE.

8 MOUSTACHED WARBLER *Acrocephalus melanopogon* 12–13cm FIELD NOTES: Usually stays out of sight, often feeds among reed debris near water surface; cocks tail when alarmed. VOICE: A *lu-lu-lu-lu-lu* followed by a scratchy warble. Calls include a churring *trrrp* and a *tac-tac* contact note. HABITAT: Reed-beds and waterside scrub. DISTRIBUTION: Winter visitor, mainly to the NW.

9 SEDGE WARBLER *Acrocephalus schoenobaenus* 13cm FIELD NOTES: Furtive, but often shows well, especially if singing. VOICE: A medley of sweet and harsh phrases. Calls include a *tuc* or *tuc-tuc-tuc* when alarmed and a soft *churr.* HABITAT: Dense vegetation, usually near water. DISTRIBUTION: Vagrant, recorded in India.

worn
fresh
1
1b
insignis
worn
worn
1c
valida
2
3
4
fresh
worn
fresh
5
6
cursitans
fresh
worn
6b
worn
salimalii
7
tytleri
fresh
worn
7b
erythrocephalus
fresh
worn
8
9

120 REED WARBLERS

1 LARGE-BILLED REED WARBLER *Acrocephalus orinus* 13cm FIELD NOTES: Little recorded; actions probably much like others of the genus. VOICE: Song is variable, consisting of some short, scratchy *wjitchety-wjitchety-wjitchety*, or *we-chuck we-chuck* phrases as well as some beautiful bulbul-like notes. HABITAT: Breeds in waterside scrubby bush; post-breeding habitat not documented. DISTRIBUTION: Probable passage migrant.

2 BLACK-BROWED REED WARBLER *Acrocephalus bistrigiceps* 13cm FIELD NOTES: Elusive, usually keeps to thick cover. VOICE: Calls include a sharp *tuc* and a high-pitched *zit*. HABITAT: Thick vegetation and scrub, generally near water. DISTRIBUTION: Winter visitor, mainly to the NE.

3 PADDYFIELD WARBLER *Acrocephalus agricola* 13cm FIELD NOTES: Constantly cocks and flicks tail. Forages low in cover and sometimes on the ground. VOICE: A hurried series of melodious, chortled notes interspersed with mimicry. Calls include a sharp *chik-chik*, a harsh *chr-chuck* and a slurred *zack zack*. HABITAT: Waterside vegetation and paddyfields. DISTRIBUTION: Mainly a widespread winter visitor; has bred in W Baluchistan.

4 BLYTH'S REED WARBLER *Acrocephalus dumetorum* 13cm FIELD NOTES: Mainly arboreal, often fans and flicks tail. Short primary projection. VOICE: A clicking *thik*, a harsh *tchirr* and a hard *chack*. HABITAT: Forest-edge bushes, cultivated areas, overgrown watercourses, parks and gardens. DISTRIBUTION: Widespread winter visitor and passage migrant.

5 BLUNT-WINGED WARBLER *Acrocephalus concinens* 13cm FIELD NOTES: Skulking, although regularly calls while foraging in cover. VOICE: Repeated slurred whistles, clear and buzzing notes. Calls include a quiet *tcheck* and a soft *churr*. HABITAT: Reed-beds, rank vegetation and scrub in swamps and marshes; also drier open areas in mountain valleys. DISTRIBUTION: Breeds in W Himalayas, resident in Assam, winter visitor in Nepal.

6 REED WARBLER (EURASIAN REED WARBLER) *Acrocephalus scirpaceus* 13cm FIELD NOTES: Furtive while foraging in reeds or bushes. Long primary projection. Greyer race *A. s. fuscus* (6b) the most likely to occur in the region. VOICE: A *churr* and a harsh *tcharr*. HABITAT: Reed-beds or bushes near water. DISTRIBUTION: Vagrant, recorded in Pakistan.

7 GREAT REED WARBLER *Acrocephalus arundinaceus* 19cm FIELD NOTES: Clumsy actions while foraging often give away bird's presence. Long primary projection. VOICE: A harsh *tchack* and a croaking *churr*. HABITAT: Reed-beds. DISTRIBUTION: Vagrant, recorded from India and Pakistan.

8 ORIENTAL REED WARBLER *Acrocephalus orientalis* 18cm FIELD NOTES: Appearance and actions similar to Clamorous Reed Warbler, but shorter- and thicker-billed. VOICE: A hard *tack* and a croaking *churr*. HABITAT: Reed-beds. DISTRIBUTION: Winter visitor, mainly in the NE.

9 CLAMOROUS REED WARBLER *Acrocephalus stentoreus* 18cm FIELD NOTES: Clambers clumsily among reed stems and in bushes. Short primary projection and long slender bill. Dark race *A. s. meridionalis* (9b) occurs in Sri Lanka. VOICE: Variable: generally a loud combination of harsh grating, chattering, squeaky and sweet notes, transcribed as *karra-karra-kareet-kareet-kareet*, *skareet-skareet-skareet* or *prit-prit-pritik*. Calls include a harsh *chack* and a low *churr*. HABITAT: Reed-beds, waterside scrub and vegetation. DISTRIBUTION: Breeds locally in Pakistan and India, resident in Sri Lanka, otherwise a widespread winter visitor.

10 THICK-BILLED WARBLER *Phragamaticola (Iduna) aedon* 18–19cm FIELD NOTES: Elusive; clumsy while foraging in vegetation and bushes. VOICE: Calls include a *chok*, a longer *cheer-rrek-chok* and a *tick* or *click-click*. HABITAT: Tall grass, marshy areas with reeds and bushes. DISTRIBUTION: Widespread winter visitor, mainly to the SW and NE.

121 LEAF WARBLERS

1 CHIFFCHAFF (COMMON CHIFFCHAFF) *Phylloscopus collybita* 11cm FIELD
NOTES: Active; forages from ground level to tree canopy, nervously flicks wings and tail. Race
P. c. tristris (1b) is greyer above and whiter below. VOICE: A rhythmic *chiff-chaff-chiff-chaff-
chiff-chaff....* Song of *P.c. tristis* is more hesitant with less distinction between notes. Call is a
monosyllabic *hweet* or *peep*. HABITAT: Bushes, woodland, waterside vegetation, groves, crops
and gardens. DISTRIBUTION: Widespread winter visitor to the N of the region.

2 MOUNTAIN CHIFFCHAFF *Phylloscopus sindianus* 11cm FIELD NOTES: Actions
and habits similar to Chiffchaff. VOICE: A repeated *chit-chiss-chyi-chiss-chit-chiss-chyi-chip-
chit-chyi*. Calls include a disyllabic *tiss-yip* and a *pseeu* or *pee-oo*. HABITAT: Willow and
poplar groves along streams, scrub and orchards; winters in waterside trees and bushes.
DISTRIBUTION: Breeds in the NW, winters mainly in S Pakistan.

3 PLAIN LEAF WARBLER *Phylloscopus neglectus* 9–10cm FIELD NOTES: Active; forages
in trees and bushes, often hovering to glean insects from leaves. VOICE: A variable short
rising warble, including a *pt-toodla-toodla* or *chit-chuwich-chissa*. Calls include a harsh *churr* or
trrr trrr and a nasal *chit* or *chi-ip*. HABITAT: Juniper thickets, open oak woods; post breeding
occurs in tamarisk bushes, open woods and orchards. DISTRIBUTION: Breeds in W Pakistan,
more widespread in the NW in winter.

4 DUSKY WARBLER *Phylloscopus fuscatus* 11cm FIELD NOTES: Skulking but active
forager, generally low down in thick vegetation or on the ground. VOICE: Clear whistled
phrases and trills. Call is a sharp *chac*, *chack* or *chett*. HABITAT: Bushes and tall grass areas.
DISTRIBUTION: Winter visitor, mainly to the NE.

5 TYTLER'S LEAF WARBLER *Phylloscopus tytleri* 10–12cm FIELD NOTES: Arboreal,
acrobatic forager, best located by song. VOICE: An even-paced, high-pitched *pi-tsi-pi-tsu*. Call
is a plaintive *sooeet* or *tsee-it*. HABITAT: Coniferous forest, dwarf willow and birch; winters in
broadleaved forest. DISTRIBUTION: Breeds in the NW, winters mainly in the W Ghats.

6 TICKELL'S LEAF WARBLER *Phylloscopus affinis* 11cm FIELD NOTES: Skulking; forages
low down in thick vegetation. VOICE: A rapid *tchip-chi-chi-chi-chi-chi*. Calls include a sharp
chep and a rapid *tak-tak* when alarmed. HABITAT: Open bushy alpine scrub; winters in forest-
edge bushes and cultivations. DISTRIBUTION: Breeds in the Himalayas, more widespread in
winter.

7 SMOKY WARBLER *Phylloscopus fuligiventer* 11cm FIELD NOTES: Skulking, keeps to
low vegetation, often among rocks; nervously flicks wings and tail, the latter often cocked.
Greyer race *P. f. tibetanus* (7b) occurs in the NE. VOICE: Repetition of a single note, *tsli-tsli-
tsli-tsli-tsli....* Calls include a soft *stup*, a sharp *chek* and a *tzik* or *tsrr*. HABITAT: Rocky alpine
pasture, low alpine scrub; winters in dense scrub, usually near water. DISTRIBUTION: Resident
in the Himalayas; occurs at lower elevations post breeding.

8 SULPHUR-BELLIED WARBLER *Phylloscopus griseolus* 11cm FIELD NOTES: Usually a
ground forager, running or hopping over rocks; becomes more arboreal in winter. VOICE: A
short, rapid *tsi-tsi-tsi-tsi-tsi*. Call is a *quip* or *pick*. HABITAT: Stunted mountain shrubs on dry
stony slopes; winters in open forests, rocky open ground, old buildings. DISTRIBUTION: Breeds
in the NW and W Himalayas; in winter widespread over much of the central region.

9 BUFF-THROATED WARBLER *Phylloscopus subaffinis* 11cm FIELD NOTES: Active,
nervous forager, low down in thick vegetation or on the ground. VOICE: A soft, weak
trrup or *trrip*. HABITAT: Alpine scrub, dense scrub, bush jungle and cultivations.
DISTRIBUTION: Vagrant, recorded in India.

1b
tristris

1

2

3

4

5

6

7

7b
tibetanus

8

9

122 LEAF WARBLERS

1 RADDE'S WARBLER *Phylloscopus schwarzi* 12cm FIELD NOTES: Forages with quite slow, lumbering movements; frequently flicks wings and tail. VOICE: A clear trill, followed by one or two quiet notes. Calls include a soft *chek* and a nervous *pwit*. HABITAT: Dense undergrowth, bushy forest edge and clearings, waterside thickets. DISTRIBUTION: Vagrant, recorded from India and Nepal.

2 BUFF-BARRED WARBLER *Phylloscopus pulcher* 10cm FIELD NOTES: Forages mainly in tree canopy with typical nervous leaf-warbler actions. VOICE: Song consists of one or more call notes followed by a fast trill. Call is a *tsip* or *twick* which is often repeated. HABITAT: Coniferous forests, oak and birch woods, rhododendron and other high-altitude scrub; in winter also occurs in broadleaved and mixed forest. DISTRIBUTION: Resident in the Himalayas and NE Indian hills.

3 ASHY-THROATED WARBLER *Phylloscopus maculipennis* 9–10cm FIELD NOTES: Greyish crown stripe and yellow rump. Active forager, generally in the tree canopy; in winter also frequents bushes. VOICE: A thin, *sweet wee-ty-wee-ty-weet-ty* or *du-ze-zuu-ze-za*. Call is a repeated *zip* or *zit*. HABITAT: Open mixed forests with thick undergrowth; post breeding occurs in oak forests and secondary scrub. DISTRIBUTION: Resident in the Himalayas and NE Indian hills.

4 LEMON-RUMPED WARBLER *Phylloscopus chloronotus* 9–10cm FIELD NOTES: Distinct pale yellowish rump and crown stripe. Frequently flicks tail and wings; hovers to capture insects from foliage. VOICE: Two song types, a stuttering, endless *tsi-ts-tsi-tsi-tsu-tsu-tsi-tsi-tsu-tsi-tsi-tsididididididididi-tsi-tsi-tsu-tsu....* or a drawn-out rattle followed by rapid same-pitched notes, *tsirrrrrrrrrrrrrrrrr-tsi-tsi-tsi-tsi-tsi-tsi-tsi....* Call is a high *uist*. HABITAT: Mixed or coniferous forest with thick undergrowth; also favours secondary growth in winter. DISTRIBUTION: Resident in the Himalayas; winters at lower altitudes and in the NE Indian hills.

5 BROOKS'S LEAF WARBLER *Phylloscopus subviridis* 9–10cm FIELD NOTES: Indistinct yellowish rump and crown stripe. Restless forager, generally in tree canopy. VOICE: Series of single notes followed by a reeling *tr-r-r-r-r-r-r*. Call is a strident *chwee, chewy* or *psee*. HABITAT: Coniferous or mixed forests; after breeding in bushes, scrub, olive groves, orchards, plantations and gardens. DISTRIBUTION: Breeds in the NW, more widespread in the NW in winter.

6 YELLOW-BROWED WARBLER *Phylloscopus inornatus* 10–11cm FIELD NOTES: Active and agile, flicks wings and tail. Forages mainly in tree canopy, often part of mixed-species feeding parties. VOICE: Calls include a rising *suu-eet, swee-ooo, seweest* or *weest*. HABITAT: Open forests, woodland and plantations. DISTRIBUTION: Winter visitor, mainly in the NE.

7 HUME'S LEAF WARBLER *Phylloscopus humei* 10cm FIELD NOTES: Arboreal, active, restless forager, with much wing and tail flicking, mainly in the canopy, but also occurs in bushes and shrubs; post breeding often part of mixed-species feeding parties. Darker race *P. h. mandellii* (7b) occurs as a winter visitor in the NE; sometimes regarded as a separate species. VOICE: A drawn-out, descending *eeeeeeeeezzzzzzzzzzzz* or a repeated *wesoo*. Calls include a *wesoo, dsweet, chwee* and a *tiss-yip*, the latter given by *P. h. mandellii*. HABITAT: Subalpine forests; winters in forests, woodland, orchards and gardens. DISTRIBUTION: Breeds in the Himalayas; more widespread in winter.

8 ARCTIC WARBLER *Phylloscopus borealis* 12cm FIELD NOTES: Mainly arboreal; active, restless forager in cover; frequently flicks wings and tail. VOICE: Calls include a husky *dzik* or *dzit* and a disyllabic *zirik* or *tset-tset*. HABITAT: Mangrove swamps and mango groves. DISTRIBUTION: Vagrant, recorded on the Andamans.

7b
mandellii

123 LEAF WARBLERS

1 GREENISH WARBLER *Phylloscopus trochiloides* 10–11cm FIELD NOTES: Mainly arboreal; highly mobile, flitting among foliage or hovering to capture insects. VOICE: Song variable, consisting of high-pitched accelerating phrases that culminate in an abruptly ending trill. Calls include *ch-wee*, *chirree* and *chis-weet*. HABITAT: Deciduous, mixed and coniferous forests with rich undergrowth; in winter also in woodland, groves and gardens. DISTRIBUTION: Breeds in the Himalayas and the NE; widespread on passage and in winter.

2 GREEN WARBLER *Phylloscopus nitidus* 10–11cm FIELD NOTES: Restless, forages mainly in the upper canopy; flicks wings and tail. Often thought to be a race of Greenish Warbler. VOICE: Calls include a *che-wee*, a *chirr-ir-ip* and a longer *chi-ru-weet*. HABITAT: Dense forest, orchards, parks and gardens. DISTRIBUTION: Passage migrant; winters in the SW and Sri Lanka.

3 TWO-BARRED GREENISH WARBLER (TWO-BARRED WARBLER) *Phylloscopus plumbeitarsus* 11–12cm FIELD NOTES: Arboreal; forages mainly in the middle level of trees. Often considered a race of Greenish Warbler. VOICE: Call is a *tissheep* or *chi-ree-wee*. HABITAT: Forests. DISTRIBUTION: Vagrant, recorded in India.

4 PALE-LEGGED LEAF WARBLER *Phylloscopus tenellipes* 10–11cm FIELD NOTES: Forages in undergrowth and lower branches of trees. VOICE: Call is a metallic *tik-tik*, *til-tic* or a loud *peet*. HABITAT: Deciduous forest. DISTRIBUTION: Vagrant, recorded in India.

5 LARGE-BILLED LEAF WARBLER *Phylloscopus magnirostris* 12–13cm FIELD NOTES: Shy; arboreal, forages in the upper canopy along boughs rather than among foliage. VOICE: A descending *tee-ti-tii-tu-tu*. Calls include a *dir-tee* and an ascending *yaw-wee-wee*. HABITAT: Open areas and glades in mountain coniferous or mixed forests, usually near water; winters in evergreen sholas. DISTRIBUTION: Breeds in the Himalayas; winters in the NE, S and Sri Lanka.

6 EASTERN CROWNED WARBLER *Phylloscopus coronatus* 11–12cm FIELD NOTES: Very active forager from undergrowth to canopy. Single wing-bar. VOICE: Call is a *phit-phit*, *swe-zueee* or *zweet*. HABITAT: Mixed and evergreen forests, low trees and bushes. DISTRIBUTION: Vagrant; disputed record from Bangladesh.

7 WESTERN CROWNED WARBLER *Phylloscopus occipitalis* 11–13cm FIELD NOTES: Restless, flicks wings and tail. Two wing-bars, but median bar can be indistinct. VOICE: A rapid, piercing *stic-swee-swee-swee-swee-swee-swee*, *chwi-chwi-chwi-chwi-chwi-chwi* or *tityu-tityu-tityu-tityu-tityu-tityu*. Calls are a *chiwee*, *chip-wee* and a repeated *stic* or *stic-swick*. HABITAT: Well-wooded country; in winter also uses deciduous and conifer hill forests. DISTRIBUTION: Breeds in W Himalayas and N Pakistan; winters in India, Nepal and Bangladesh.

8 BLYTH'S LEAF WARBLER *Phylloscopus reguloides* 11cm FIELD NOTES: Acrobatic. When agitated slowly flicks one wing at a time. VOICE: Call is a *pit-chee* or *pit-chew-a*. Song is a trilling extension of the call notes. HABITAT: Broadleaved, conifer forest and mixed forest; winters in open forest and forest edge. DISTRIBUTION: Breeds in the Himalayas; winters in lower areas.

9 CLAUDIA'S LEAF WARBLER *Phylloscopus claudiae* 11–12cm FIELD NOTES: Actions as Blyth's Leaf Warbler; probably only separated by song. VOICE: Starts with one or two notes followed by a rapid single-note trill. HABITAT: Forests. DISTRIBUTION: Vagrant, recorded in India.

10 YELLOW-VENTED WARBLER *Phylloscopus cantator* 10cm FIELD NOTES: Active; forages in bushes or the lower to middle levels of trees. VOICE: A *seep seep seep si-chu-chu to-YOU*. Call a soft *see-chew*. HABITAT: Evergreen broadleaved forest; also in deciduous forest post breeding. DISTRIBUTION: Resident in the NE.

11 GREY-HOODED WARBLER *Phylloscopus xanthoschistos* 10cm FIELD NOTES: Agile forager in trees and shrubs; fans and cocks tail. VOICE: A repeated *tsi-tsi-tsi-weetee*. Call is a high *psit-psit* or a plaintive *tyee-tyee*. HABITAT: Forests and secondary growth. DISTRIBUTION: Resident in the Himalayas and the NE.

124 WARBLERS

1 GREY-CROWNED WARBLER *Seicercus tephrocephalus* 11–12cm FIELD NOTES: Agile forager in foliage or undergrowth; post breeding often in small parties or in mixed-species flocks. VOICE: Song generally starts with a few single notes followed by a trill. Call is a soft *trrup* or *turup*. HABITAT: Forest understorey. DISTRIBUTION: Resident in NE Indian hills.

2 GREEN-CROWNED WARBLER *Seicercus burkii* 11cm FIELD NOTES: Arboreal, forages from middle tree level down to undergrowth; flicks wings, cocks and fans tail. VOICE: Similar to Grey-crowned Warbler. Call is a high-pitched, soft *huit*. HABITAT: Forest understorey and secondary growth. DISTRIBUTION: Breeds in the Himalayas; winters at lower elevations and in the NE, scattered records elsewhere.

3 WHITE-SPECTACLED WARBLER *Seicercus affinis* 11–12cm FIELD NOTES: Active, forages in trees and undergrowth; often makes fly-catching sallies. Frequently flicks wings and cocks and fans tail. VOICE: Song starts hesitantly then accelerates, *uee-tiu uee-tiu-chu-weet-chu-chu-weet-chu-weet....* Calls variable, including a quick, rising *u-di-si* and a whistled *ty-tyy-sit*. HABITAT: Humid broadleaved evergreen forest; winters at lower elevations in mixed forests. DISTRIBUTION: Resident in the NE.

4 WHISTLER'S WARBLER *Seicercus whistleri* 11–12cm FIELD NOTES: Forages in the understorey and the canopy of low trees. VOICE: A simple, whistled *chu chu-weet-tu-chu-wee....chu chu-weet-tu-chu-wee.......* Call is a soft *chip* or *tiu-du*. HABITAT: Lush undergrowth in temperate forest. DISTRIBUTION: Resident in the Himalayas and the hills of the NE.

5 GREY-CHEEKED WARBLER *Seicercus poliogenys* 10–11cm FIELD NOTES: Forages in the understorey; flicks wings, cocks and fans tail. VOICE: Song consists of varied whistled phrases, often quick and trilling. Call is a high-pitched *ueest*. HABITAT: Bamboo jungle and dense undergrowth in evergreen hill forests. DISTRIBUTION: Resident in E Himalayas and the hills of the NE.

6 CHESTNUT-CROWNED WARBLER *Seicercus castaniceps* 9.5cm FIELD NOTES: Very active, forages in the outer foliage of upper canopy; continuously flicks wings and tail. VOICE: Song is a series of upward-inflected, thin, high-pitched, ethereal notes, *see see see-see-see-see-see*. Calls include a quiet *chik* and a *chee-chee*. HABITAT: Mainly oak forests. DISTRIBUTION: Resident in the Himalayas and the NE hills.

7 BROAD-BILLED WARBLER *Tickellia hodgsoni* 10cm FIELD NOTES: Very active; post breeding joins mixed-species parties. VOICE: A long series of very high-pitched notes; also a rapid metallic *witiwiwititw-chu- witiwitiwiti*. HABITAT: Undergrowth and bamboo thickets at the edge of broadleaved evergreen forest. DISTRIBUTION: Resident in E Himalayas and the NE hills.

8 RUFOUS-FACED WARBLER *Abroscopus albogularis* 8cm FIELD NOTES: Nervous and very active; flicks wings and occasionally fans tail. VOICE: A repetitive, high-pitched, drawn-out, plaintive whistle; also a shrill twittering. HABITAT: Undergrowth in evergreen forest, especially bamboo. DISTRIBUTION: Resident in E Himalayas and the NE hills.

9 YELLOW-BELLIED WARBLER *Abroscopus superciliaris* 9–11cm FIELD NOTES: Forages mainly in the understorey, gleans from foliage or makes fly-catching sallies. Frequently flicks wings. VOICE: A halting, tinkling high-pitched whistled *dee-dee-dir-rit-tit-deweet* that rises at the end; repeated three or four times, each time higher than the last; also a subdued twittering. HABITAT: Undergrowth in evergreen forest, especially bamboo. DISTRIBUTION: Resident in the NE and E Himalayas.

10 BLACK-FACED WARBLER *Abroscopus schisticeps* 9cm FIELD NOTES: Nervous and highly active; frequently flicks wings and tail. Grey-breasted race *A. s. flavimentalis* (10b) occurs in the NE. VOICE: A thin, high-pitched tinkling. Call is a subdued *tit*; when alarmed gives a high-pitched *tz-tz-tz-tz-tz-tz*. HABITAT: Moist hill and mountain forests with moss-covered trees, bamboo thickets and thick undergrowth. DISTRIBUTION: Resident in the Himalayas and the hills of the NE.

125 WARBLERS

1 WHITETHROAT (COMMON WHITETHROAT) *Sylvia communis* 14cm FIELD NOTES: Usually shy and skulking, unless singing. VOICE: A hurried, scratchy warble. Calls include a sharp *tac-tack* and a scolding *tcharr*. HABITAT: Scrub and crops. DISTRIBUTION: Passage migrant in the NW.

2 LESSER WHITETHROAT *Sylvia curruca* 13cm FIELD NOTES: Very skulking, often sings from within cover. Race *S. c. minula* (2b), with weaker face mask, occurs in the NW; sometimes considered a full species. VOICE: A quiet warble followed by a dry rattle; *S. c. minula* lacks the rattle. Calls are a hard *tac-tac* and a scolding *churr*. HABITAT: Deciduous woods and scrub. DISTRIBUTION: Widespread winter visitor.

3 HUME'S LESSER WHITETHROAT (HUME'S WHITETHROAT) *Sylvia althaea* 13cm FIELD NOTES: Shy and skulking. Often treated as conspecific with Lesser Whitethroat. VOICE: A ringing *tru-tru-tru-ee tru-eee*. Calls include a *tek*, a *wheet-wheet-wheet* and a scolding *churr*. HABITAT: Dry scrub; winters in deciduous woodland and scrub. DISTRIBUTION: Breeds in the NW; winters in peninsular India.

4 MÉNÉTRIES'S WARBLER *Sylvia mystacea* 13cm FIELD NOTES: Shy, restless, constantly waves tail from side to side and up and down; usually forages in thick cover, but sings from exposed perch or in display-flight. VOICE: A rich, chattering warble. Calls include a buzzing *trrrrrt*, a quiet *trt-tr-tr* and an *ouak* or *ouak-ouak*. HABITAT: Scrub in arid or semi-arid areas. DISTRIBUTION: Breeds in W Pakistan.

5 DESERT WARBLER (ASIAN DESERT WARBLER) *Sylvia nana* 11.5cm FIELD NOTES: Skulking, usually in thick scrub, although often seen on the ground, scuttling between patches of vegetation. VOICE: Rich trilled and whistling phrases preceded by a purring trill. Calls include a feeble *drrrrrrrrr* and a rapid *chee-chee-chee-chee*. HABITAT: Scrub in arid areas. DISTRIBUTION: Winter visitor to the NW.

6 BARRED WARBLER *Sylvia nisoria* 15cm FIELD NOTES: Usually skulking; lumbering foraging actions. VOICE: A *chak-chak* and a *tch-tchurr-tchurr*. HABITAT: Shrubby thickets. DISTRIBUTION: Vagrant, recorded in India and Pakistan.

7 EASTERN ORPHEAN WARBLER *Sylvia crassirostris* 15cm FIELD NOTES: Skulking, keeps to thick cover. VOICE: A loud thrush-like warble with rattling notes. Calls include a sharp *tak* and a scolding *trrrrrr*. HABITAT: Bushy hillsides; winters in scrub and groves. DISTRIBUTION: Breeds in W Pakistan; widespread winter visitor.

8 GARDEN WARBLER *Sylvia borin* 14cm FIELD NOTES: Very skulking, slow and deliberate foraging actions. VOICE: An abrupt *chack-chack* and a rasping *tchurr-r-r-r*. HABITAT: Forest undergrowth and thickets. DISTRIBUTION: Vagrant, recoded in India.

9 UPCHER'S WARBLER *Hippolais languida* 14cm FIELD NOTES: Clambers, often clumsily, while foraging through foliage, regularly stretches neck to reach food; tail often appears 'unhinged' when moved up, down or sideways. VOICE: A scratchy warble. Call said to resemble two stones being struck together, *chuk-chuk*. HABITAT: Open bushy hillsides. DISTRIBUTION: Breeds in W Pakistan.

10 SYKES'S WARBLER *Iduna rama* 12–13cm FIELD NOTES: Forages mainly in bushes, with brief visits to pick food from the ground; while moving about twitches tail upwards or sideways. VOICE: A rattling, scratchy warble. Calls are a *chek* and a fuller *tslek*. HABITAT: Arid areas with scattered bushes. DISTRIBUTION: Breeds in Pakistan; widespread winter visitor.

11 BOOTED WARBLER *Iduna caligata* 12cm FIELD NOTES: Actions and habits similar to Sykes's Warbler. VOICE: A dry *chek* and a short trilled *tr-r-rk*. HABITAT: Herbaceous plants and shrubs, often near water. DISTRIBUTION: Widespread winter visitor.

126 GRASSBIRDS, TAILORBIRDS

1 STRIATED GRASSBIRD (STRIATED MARSH WARBLER) *Megalurus palustris*
22–28cm FIELD NOTES: Forages in reeds and bushes, sometimes on the ground; early in the day often perches prominently on reeds or bush tops, when the tail is flicked up-and-down. VOICE: A strong, rich warble; also a subdued whistle followed by a loud *wheeechoo*. Calls include an explosive *pwit* and a harsh *chat* or *tzic*. HABITAT: Tall damp grasslands, reed-beds and tamarisks. DISTRIBUTION: Resident in lowlands of the N and NE.

2 BRISTLED GRASSBIRD *Chaetornis striata* 19–21cm FIELD NOTES: Generally elusive, forages through reeds and tall grass, sometimes on the ground; sings from prominent perch or during song-flight. VOICE: A repeated, rising then falling *trew treuw* or *ji-jee jee-ji*. Calls include a harsh *cha* and a sharp *zip*. HABITAT: Lowland grassland with scattered bushes; also paddyfields. DISTRIBUTION: Breeds in NE Pakistan and in scattered locations across the N and NE of the region; winter visitor to EC India.

3 RUFOUS-RUMPED GRASSBIRD (INDIAN GRASSBIRD) *Graminicola bengalensis*
18cm FIELD NOTES: Skulking; occurs low down in reeds or thick grass, best seen while in song from reed top or during song-flight. VOICE: A strong down-slurred note followed by a series of clipped, rhythmic notes; also includes rattles and short wheezy notes. Calls include a mewing and a nasal screech. HABITAT: Lowland wet grassland, reed-beds and other vegetation near water. DISTRIBUTION: Resident in N and NE India.

4 BROAD-TAILED GRASSBIRD *Schoenicola platyurus* 18cm FIELD NOTES: Skulking, forages low in thick tangled vegetation; best located while singing, either from a reed stem or during display-flight. VOICE: A high-pitched, metallic, piping *twink twink twink* ending in a rattling *cheep-cheep-cheep*; also a soft ringing *tseenk tseenk*. Calls include a repeated, trisyllabic *jur-jur-jur* and a harsh *chick*. HABITAT: Grass, reed-swamp and bracken-covered hillsides. DISTRIBUTION: Resident in the W Ghats.

5 MOUNTAIN TAILORBIRD (GOLDEN-HEADED TAILORBIRD) *Phyllergates cuculatus* 11–12cm FIELD NOTES: Elusive; forages in low thickets, also makes aerial sorties after flying insects. Juvenile has forehead olive-grey, concolorous with crown and nape. VOICE: A thin, high-pitched 4–6-note whistle, *pee-pee-peeeeeeeeee-pee-pee* or similar. Calls include a dry, descending trill, a low buzzy *kiz-ki*, a repeated, thin *trit* and a long nasal chatter. HABITAT: Bushy thickets and undergrowth in evergreen forest. DISTRIBUTION: Resident in the NE.

6 COMMON TAILORBIRD (INDIAN or LONG-TAILED TAILORBIRD)
Orthotomus sutorius 10–14cm FIELD NOTES: Forages in cover or on the ground under cover, often in pairs; males in the breeding season develop long central tail feathers. Various races populate the region: nominate occurs in Sri Lanka; *O. s. guzuratus* (6b) occurs in Pakistan and peninsular India; *O. s. luteus* (6c) occurs in the NE. VOICE: A rapid, repetitive, loud *pitchik-pitchik-pitchik* or *cheeyup-cheeyup-cheeyup*. Calls include a sharp *cheep cheep cheep cheep cheep* and a quickly repeated *pit-pit-pit-pit.....* HABITAT: Forest and cultivation edge, bushy cover in urban areas and mangroves. DISTRIBUTION: Widespread throughout the region.

7 DARK-NECKED TAILORBIRD (BLACK-NECKED TAILORBIRD) *Orthotomus atrogularis* 11–12cm FIELD NOTES: Shy; restless forager, low in the centre of undergrowth, more often heard than seen. VOICE: A repeated, high, shivery *pirra pirra pirra...* and a trilled *kri-kri-kri*. Also a *titrrrrrt-churrit* duet between partners. HABITAT: Heavy scrub and edges of evergreen forest. DISTRIBUTION: Resident in Bangladesh and NE India.

1

worn

fresh

2

worn

fresh

3

worn

fresh

4

worn

fresh

5

6c
luteus

♂

6b
guzuratus

♂

7 ♀

6 ♂

♀

♂

127 TESIAS, GOLDCREST, TIT-WARBLERS, WHITE-EYES

1 CHESTNUT-HEADED TESIA *Tesia castaneocoronata* 9–10cm FIELD NOTES: Forages, wren-like, in and around dense undergrowth or moss-covered logs and rocks. VOICE: A loud, explosive *cheep-cheeu-che-wit*. Calls include a sharp *whit* or *tit* and a high-pitched *pseet*. HABITAT: Undergrowth in high-elevation open forests. DISTRIBUTION: Resident in the Himalayas and the hills of the NE.

2 GREY-BELLIED TESIA *Tesia cyaniventer* 9–10cm FIELD NOTES: Restless forager, generally on or near the ground. Dances to and fro on branches, in the manner of a clockwork toy. VOICE: Begins with a few high-pitched notes, followed by a series of loud slurred phrases. Call is a loud, rattling *trrrrrrk*. HABITAT: Dense tangled undergrowth in thick forest, usually near streams; post breeding occurs at lower altitude in shady evergreen or deciduous forests. DISTRIBUTION: Resident in the C and E Himalayas; winters in the NE Indian hills.

3 SLATY-BELLIED TESIA *Tesia olivea* 9–10cm FIELD NOTES: Secretive, although can be inquisitive; forages on or close to the ground, often tossing leaf-litter into the air while searching for food. Said to act like a clockwork toy when jumping back and forth from the ground or branch. VOICE: Begins with 4–11 single whistled notes, followed by an explosive jumble of tuneless notes. Calls include a sharp *tchirik* spluttering *trrrrt trrrrt trrrrt....* HABITAT: Dense undergrowth in moist evergreen forests, often near water. DISTRIBUTION: Resident in E Himalayas; winters in the hills of the NE.

4 GOLDCREST *Regulus regulus* 9cm FIELD NOTES: Agile forager, always on the move; flicks wings and tail and frequently hovers to capture insects; often gives away presence by continual calling. Race *R. r. tristis* (4b) lacks the black lateral crown stripes; it is a straggler to the Ladakh region. VOICE: Mainly a rapid trill. Call is a high, persistent *tsi-tsi-tsi-tsi*. HABITAT: Mainly coniferous forests. DISTRIBUTION: Resident in the Himalayas.

5 WHITE-BROWED TIT-WARBLER (SEVERTZOV'S TIT-WARBLER) *Leptopoecile sophiae* 10cm FIELD NOTES: Acrobatic forager in thick undergrowth, often a member of mixed-species feeding flocks. Darker race *L. s. obscurus* (5b) occurs in the C Himalayas. VOICE: Calls include a sibilant, trilling *sirrrr*, a hissing *psee*, a drawn-out *pseee* and an abrupt, buzzy *psrit*. HABITAT: Montane scrub and thickets; winters at lower elevations in valley-bottom thickets. DISTRIBUTION: Resident in the W and C Himalayas.

6 CRESTED TIT-WARBLER *Leptopoecile elegans* 10cm FIELD NOTES: Usually forages high in tree canopy; very active, behaves much like a Goldcrest. VOICE: Calls include a thin *pseee* and a shrill wren-like chatter. HABITAT: Coniferous forest, dwarf alpine juniper and birch scrub above the tree line. DISTRIBUTION: Vagrant, recorded in India.

7 SRI LANKA WHITE-EYE *Zosterops ceylonensis* 11cm FIELD NOTES: Restless, agile forager in bushes, undergrowth and trees; generally found in pairs with larger, scattered, parties after breeding. VOICE: Jingling song, said to sound like the shaking of a bunch of keys. Calls include a constant *cheep* or a reedy *chisip*. HABITAT: Forests and nearby plantations and gardens. DISTRIBUTION: Resident in Sri Lanka.

8 ORIENTAL WHITE-EYE *Zosterops palpebrosus* 10cm FIELD NOTES: Arboreal; restless, agile forager among tree foliage and blossoms. VOICE: A tinkling jingle. Calls include a sibilant *cheuw cheuw cheuw* or *cheer cheer cheer*. HABITAT: Open broadleaved forests, plantations, mangroves, orchards, groves and gardens. DISTRIBUTION: Widespread resident.

1 ASHY-HEADED LAUGHINGTHRUSH *Garrulax cinereifrons* 24–25cm FIELD NOTES: Forages in flocks of 4–20 that keep up a constant flow of squeaks and chatters, usually found low in vegetation or on the ground. VOICE: Continuous high-pitched squeaky notes and harsh churring sounds interspersed with sharp *chit* notes or higher-pitched *pieu-pieu*. HABITAT: Dense humid forest undergrowth and bamboo thickets. DISTRIBUTION: Resident in Sri Lanka.

2 WHITE-THROATED LAUGHINGTHRUSH *Garrulax albogularis* 28–30cm FIELD NOTES: Gregarious; in winter often forms large flocks, also joins mixed-species feeding parties; forages in trees and undergrowth, and on the ground. VOICE: While feeding gives a constant, low *teh teh* combined with a subdued chattering. Other calls include shrill, wheezy whistles and a gentle *chrrr*. HABITAT: Broadleaved evergreen forest, deciduous forests, coniferous forests, open secondary growth and light jungle. DISTRIBUTION: Resident in the Himalayas.

3 WHITE-CRESTED LAUGHINGTHRUSH *Garrulax leucolophus* 28cm FIELD NOTES: Gregarious at all times, often in the company of other species; noisy, constantly uttering contact chuckles. Forages on the ground and in the lower and middle storeys. VOICE: A rapid, laughing, chattering cackle; also a subdued staccato *ker-wick-erwick*. HABITAT: Broadleaved evergreen forest, secondary growth and bamboo jungle. DISTRIBUTION: Resident in the Himalayas and the NE.

4 LESSER NECKLACED LAUGHINGTHRUSH *Garrulax monileger* 27cm FIELD NOTES: Gregarious, often in the company of other laughingthrushes; forages mainly on the ground. VOICE: A mellow, repeated *u-wi-uu*, a more subdued *ui-ee-ee-wu*, *wiu-wiu-wiu* or *ui-ui-ui* and a down-slurred *tieew ti-tiew.....* HABITAT: Broadleaved evergreen forest, deciduous forest and secondary growth. DISTRIBUTION: Resident in C and E Himalayas and the NE of the region.

5 GREATER NECKLACED LAUGHINGTHRUSH *Garrulax pectoralis* 29cm FIELD NOTES: Gregarious, often in the company of other laughingthrushes; forages mainly on the forest floor. VOICE: A repeated, clear, ringing *kleer-eer-eer-eer...* or an up-slurred, mellow *tu-tweetu-tweetu-twee...* also a clear, rapid *chit-it* or *chit-it-it-it*. HABITAT: Dense forest, secondary growth and bamboo jungle. DISTRIBUTION: Resident in the C and E Himalayas and the NE of the region.

6 STRIATED LAUGHINGTHRUSH *Garrulax striatus* 28cm FIELD NOTES: Arboreal, forages from undergrowth to the canopy; often encountered in fruiting trees. Race *G. s. cranbrooki* (6b) occurs in NE India. VOICE: A repeated, vibrant *prrit-you prrit-pri-prii-u* or *krrrrwhit kwit-kwit-wheeuuw*. Calls include a high, soft, nervous *wer-wer-wer-wer-wer*, a rising *wu-wiw* and a grumbling *greip-greip-greip*. HABITAT: Broadleaved evergreen forest, secondary forest, scrub jungle and thickets. DISTRIBUTION: Resident in the Himalayas and the NE.

7 RUFOUS-NECKED LAUGHINGTHRUSH *Garrulax ruficollis* 22–27cm FIELD NOTES: Forages on or near the ground. VOICE: A repeated, jolly, whistled *wiwi wi-whu whi-yi-ha*, and a clear, shrill *krkrkrkeeerkrookeerkoo*, which starts with a few quick notes and builds to a loud crescendo before falling at the end. Calls include a shrill *ch-yaa* or *cher*, a harsh *whit it*, also cheeping *sleeer* notes combined with short guttural trills. HABITAT: Forest and cultivation edge, scrub, secondary growth and bamboo jungle; also tall grass and reeds. DISTRIBUTION: Resident in E Himalayas and the NE.

8 CHESTNUT-BACKED LAUGHINGTHRUSH *Garrulax nuchalis* 23–26cm FIELD NOTES: Forages mainly on or near the ground, often with other laughingthrushes. VOICE: Mellow whistles, interspersed with short slurred notes. Calls include a soft *chip* and a *churr* uttered when alarmed. HABITAT: Thick scrub jungle, scrub-covered rocky ravines, forest edge and tall grass. DISTRIBUTION: Resident in the NE Indian hills.

129 LAUGHINGTHRUSHES

1 YELLOW-THROATED LAUGHINGTHRUSH *Garrulax galbanus* 23–25cm FIELD NOTES: Forages on or near the ground; usually encountered in pairs or small parties; often mixes with Rufous-necked Laughingthrush. VOICE: A feeble chirping. HABITAT: Tall grass with trees and shrubs, edge of dense broadleaved evergreen forest. DISTRIBUTION: Resident in the hills of the NE.

2 WYNAAD LAUGHINGTHRUSH *Garrulax delesserti* 23–26cm FIELD NOTES: Gregarious, in flocks of 6–40; forages mainly on the ground. VOICE: A strident *tseeurp*, a clanging *jhur-jhur-jheer-jheer-jheer-jheer* and a slower, piping *jheer-jheer-jheer*; also a nasal *tree-tree-true*, various squeaks and rattles, a rasping *churr* and low conversational notes. HABITAT: Humid rainforest with dense undergrowth, thorny cane-brakes and cardamom sholas. DISTRIBUTION: Resident in the W Ghats.

3 RUFOUS-VENTED LAUGHINGTHRUSH *Garrulax gularis* 23–26cm FIELD NOTES: Skulking; forages mainly on the ground; gregarious. VOICE: Sweet chiming whistles, up-slurred then down-slurred. Calls include harsh rattling churrs, interspersed with high-pitched whistled phrases. Flocks utter mellow squabbling and chattering notes. HABITAT: Broadleaved evergreen forest, secondary growth and scrub. DISTRIBUTION: Resident in the hills of the NE.

4 MOUSTACHED LAUGHINGTHRUSH *Garrulax cineraceus* 21–24cm FIELD NOTES: Generally in pairs or small parties; forages mostly on the ground. VOICE: A repeated, high-pitched, up-slurred *pr r r r ip* that may be interspersed with hard, chuckling staccato notes. HABITAT: Thick bushes in moist forest, thick scrub and secondary growth near cultivations. DISTRIBUTION: Resident in the NE Indian hills.

5 RUFOUS-CHINNED LAUGHINGTHRUSH *Garrulax rufogularis* 23–26cm FIELD NOTES: Skulking; forages on the ground or in low bushes. Rufous-eared race G. r. occidentalis (5b) occurs from NE Pakistan to W Nepal; G. r. rufitinctus (5c) has rufous lores and throat, and occurs in the Meghalaya region of NE India. VOICE: A repeated, clear, husky *whi-whi-whu-whi* or *whi-whi-whi-whi*; also short grating rattles, a low buzzing *jzzzzz* and a twangy *gshwee*. HABITAT: Dense undergrowth in subtropical forest. DISTRIBUTION: Resident in the Himalayas and the NE.

6 SPOTTED LAUGHINGTHRUSH *Garrulax ocellatus* 30–33cm FIELD NOTES: Forages on the ground or in bushes; usually in pairs or small parties. VOICE: A rich, mellow, fluty *wu-it wu-u wu-u wi-u wi-u w'you w'you uu-i w'you uu-i.....* or a *fuwit-fuwee fuwit-fuweet*, often mixed with a nasal *fu-u-uwheen*. Calls include a screechy *schuwee*. HABITAT: Undergrowth in high-elevation forest, open mixed forest with undergrowth and thick rhododendron scrub and bushes at the edge of fields. DISTRIBUTION: Resident in the Himalayas.

7 GIANT LAUGHINGTHRUSH *Garrulax maximus* 30–35cm FIELD NOTES: Secretive; mainly a ground forager; gregarious, often in the company of other laughingthrushes. VOICE: A jerky rattling, also some shrill notes. HABITAT: Dense, dry subalpine forest with undergrowth and glades. DISTRIBUTION: Vagrant, recorded from NE India; possible resident.

8 GREY-SIDED LAUGHINGTHRUSH *Garrulax caerulatus* 27–29cm FIELD NOTES: Forages on the ground or in bushes. G. c. subcaerulatus (8b) has white tips on outer tail feathers, it occurs in the Meghalaya region of NE India. VOICE: Clear, loud, spaced whistled phrases. Calls include a gruff *zhyurt-zhyurt*, a mewing *zhaow-zhaow* and a nasal rattle. HABITAT: Undergrowth in dense forest and bamboo thickets. DISTRIBUTION: Resident in the Himalayas and NE India.

9 SPOT-BREASTED LAUGHINGTHRUSH *Garrulax merulinus* 22cm FIELD NOTES: Skulking, noisy and gregarious; forages mainly on the ground. VOICE: Various rich, melodious phrases with some mimicry; also a repeated coughing chuckle. HABITAT: Dense undergrowth in damp forests, overgrown clearings and bamboo thickets. DISTRIBUTION: Resident in the NE Indian hills.

5b
occidentalis

5c
rufitinctus

8b
subcaerulatus

130 LAUGHINGTHRUSHES

1 WHITE-BROWED LAUGHINGTHRUSH *Pterorhinus sannio* 22–24cm FIELD
NOTES: Forages on the ground or in low bushes; occurs in small noisy parties after breeding.
VOICE: A harsh, shrill *tcheu...tcheu...tcheu*; also a harsh *tcheurrrr* and harsh buzzy *dzwee* notes.
HABITAT: Undergrowth in dense forest, secondary growth, bamboo thickets and hillsides
covered with bracken and bramble scrub. DISTRIBUTION: Resident in the NE Indian hills.

2 BLACK-CHINNED LAUGHINGTHRUSH *Trochalopteron cachinnans* 20cm FIELD
NOTES: Forages on the ground or in low vegetation. *T. c. jerdoni* (2b) occurs in NE Kerala
and SW Karnataka. VOICE: Includes a nasal *wi-yu wi-yu wi* followed by a low *dhu-dhu-dhu*,
a rising series of *aingk* notes, and a nasal *whur-whaink whur-whaink*; also a short *gruk* and
chittering *chink-chink-chink*. HABITAT: Shola forests, forest edge, thick scrub and plantations.
DISTRIBUTION: Resident in the W Ghats.

3 KERALA LAUGHINGTHRUSH *Trochalopteron fairbanki* 20cm FIELD NOTES: Forages
in bushes, undergrowth and occasionally on the ground. *T. f. meridionale* (3b) occurs in
S Kerala and S Tamil Nadu. VOICE: Short, mellow clear notes. Calls include a dry *ptr
trit* or *ptr tr tr trit*. HABITAT: Streamside thickets, plantations, scrub and secondary forest.
DISTRIBUTION: Resident in SW Ghats.

4 BHUTAN LAUGHINGTHRUSH *Trochalopteron imbricatum* 19–20cm FIELD
NOTES: Forages mostly on the ground, usually in pairs or small parties. VOICE: A rapid trill
followed by a ringing whistle. Calls include a buzzy *bzzrt-bzzrt*. HABITAT: Bushes, long
grass, thick scrub and thickets in open secondary forests and scrub bordering cultivations.
DISTRIBUTION: Resident in Bhutan and W Arunachal Pradesh.

5 STREAKED LAUGHINGTHRUSH *Trochalopteron lineatum* 18–20cm FIELD
NOTES: Forages on the ground, in the open or under cover. VOICE: Similar to Bhutan
Laughing Thrush but longer. Calls include a *tsip tsip tsip* and high-pitched buzzy notes.
HABITAT: Hillside scrub, bushes in open forest, forest edge and around human habitations.
DISTRIBUTION: Resident in the Himalayas and hills of the NW.

6 BROWN-CAPPED LAUGHINGTHRUSH *Trochalopteron austeni* 24cm FIELD
NOTES: Skulking, usually in pairs or small parties; forages on the ground or in low vegetation.
Pale-throated race *T. a. victoriae* (6b) occurs in SE Mizoram. VOICE: A repeated, clear, jolly
whit-wee-wi-weeoo. Calls include a harsh *grrrret-grrrret-grrrret* when alarmed. HABITAT: Oak
and rhododendron forest, secondary forest, forest edge, bushes in ravines and clearings,
bamboo thickets. DISTRIBUTION: Resident in the NE Indian hills.

7 STRIPED LAUGHINGTHRUSH *Trochalopteron virgatum* 23cm FIELD NOTES:
Skulking, generally singly or in pairs. VOICE: Includes a clear, hurried *chwi-pieu* and a rattling
cho-prrrrrrt. Calls are a harsh *chit* and *chrrrr*. HABITAT: Thick cover near broadleaved
evergreen forest, forest edge and secondary growth. DISTRIBUTION: Resident in the NE
Indian hills.

8 BLUE-WINGED LAUGHINGTHRUSH *Trochalopteron squamatum* 22–25cm FIELD
NOTES: Skulking; forages close to the ground, usually in pairs or small groups. VOICE: A rich
cur-white-to-go or *free-for-you*. Calls include a buzzy *jrrrrr-rrr-rrr*, a harsh *cher-cherrrru* and
a thrush-like *chuk*. HABITAT: Dense undergrowth in open broadleaved evergreen forest,
secondary growth, scrub and bush near forest, bamboo thickets. DISTRIBUTION: Resident in C
and E Himalayas and NE India.

9 SCALY LAUGHINGTHRUSH *Trochalopteron subunicolor* 23–25cm FIELD NOTES:
Forages on the ground or in tangled vegetation; forms post-breeding groups of 10–20 birds.
VOICE: A clear shrill 'wolf-whistle'. Calls include a squeaky chatter and a shrill alarm note.
HABITAT: Broadleaved evergreen forest with thick undergrowth, secondary growth, bramble
thickets and rhododendron shrubberies. DISTRIBUTION: Resident from C to E Himalayas.

131 LAUGHINGTHRUSHES, LIOCICHLAS

1 ELLIOT'S LAUGHINGTHRUSH *Trochalopteron elliotii* 26cm FIELD NOTES: Forages mostly on the ground, in pairs or small parties. VOICE: A wavering *whi-pi-piu*. Calls include a subdued, high-pitched chattering. HABITAT: Thickets, undergrowth and bamboo, at or above the tree line; also open broadleaved forest, mixed forests and juniper forests. DISTRIBUTION: Vagrant: disputed record from the NE.

2 VARIEGATED LAUGHINGTHRUSH *Trochalopteron variegatum* 24–26cm FIELD NOTES: Skulking, forages on the ground, in bushes and trees; generally in pairs, with larger parties post breeding. Grey-winged race *T. v. simile* (2b) occurs in W Himalayas. VOICE: A loud, musical, whistled *weet-a-weer* or *weet-a-woo-weer*. When alarmed utters muttering and squealing notes. HABITAT: Undergrowth, rhododendron and other bushes in open oak and mixed forests. DISTRIBUTION: Resident from W to C Himalayas.

3 BROWN-CHEEKED LAUGHINGTHRUSH *Trochalopteron henrici* 24–26cm FIELD NOTES: Forages mostly on the ground, usually in pairs or small parties. VOICE: A repeated, clear *wichi-pi-choo*, *wi-pi-choo* or *whi-choo-it*. HABITAT: Scrub and bushes bordering forests. DISTRIBUTION: Vagrant: disputed record from the NE.

4 BLACK-FACED LAUGHINGTHRUSH *Trochalopteron affine* 24–26cm FIELD NOTES: Forages on or near the ground, but also in trees; usually in pairs or small parties. VOICE: A repeated, shrill *wiee-chiweeoo*, *wiee-chweeiu* or *wiee-weeoo-wi*. Calls include a high rattle, a low chuckle and wheezy purrs and whines. HABITAT: Forest undergrowth, thickets and shrubberies above the tree line. DISTRIBUTION: Resident from C to E Himalayas.

5 CHESTNUT-CROWNED LAUGHINGTHRUSH *Trochalopteron erythrocephalum* 24–28cm FIELD NOTES: Skulking; forages on the ground or in low cover, usually in small parties. *T. e. nigrimentum* (5b) occurs in E Himalayas. VOICE: Various repeated short phrases, transcribed as *pearl-lee to-reaper to-real-year you-reap*. Calls include a *pheeou*, a loud *wee-ou-wee-whip* and a soft, musical *twi-ee-you*. When alarmed gives a grating *m-u-r-r-r*. HABITAT: Dense undergrowth, scrub in gulleys and by cultivation, forest edge and bamboo thickets. DISTRIBUTION: Resident in the Himalayas.

6 ASSAM LAUGHINGTHRUSH *Trochalopteron chrysopterum* 23–25cm FIELD NOTES: Forages on or near the ground, occasionally ascends moss- or lichen-covered tree branches; generally encountered singly, in pairs or small parties. VOICE: Similar to Chestnut-crowned Laughingthrush, but lower, mellower and more complex. Calls include a low purring *squar-squar-squar*. HABITAT: Understorey and bamboo in broadleaved evergreen, pine and mixed forest. DISTRIBUTION: Resident in the NE Indian hills.

7 CRIMSON-FACED LIOCICHLA (RED-FACED LIOCICHLA) *Liocichla phoenicea* 21–23cm FIELD NOTES: Unobtrusive; forages on the ground, in undergrowth and occasionally in trees; post breeding may form small parties of 4–5 birds. VOICE: Various clear, beautiful phrases, including *chewi-ter-twi-twitoo*, *chi-cho-choee-wi-chu-chooee* and *chiu-too-ee*. Calls include a rasping *chrrt-chrrt* and a buzzy, up-slurred *grssh grssh*. HABITAT: Dense undergrowth in broadleaved evergreen forest, dense thickets of secondary growth near cultivations or streams. DISTRIBUTION: Resident in E Himalayas and the NE.

8 BUGUN LIOCICHLA *Liocichla bugunorum* 22cm FIELD NOTES: Forages from ground to treetops, creeps through tangled vines and undergrowth and clambers on tree trunks; usually encountered in pairs or small groups. VOICE: Variable fluty phrases, including a descending *wieu-u-wee i-tuu i-tuu uw-tu oow* and a shorter *weee-keew* or *yu-weee-keew*; also utters an accompanying dry *trrrr-trii-trii*, which is presumed to be made by the female. HABITAT: Disturbed hillsides and ravines with dense shrubbery and small to medium-sized trees; also edge of primary forest. DISTRIBUTION: Resident in W Arunachal Pradesh in the NE.

132 WREN, WREN-BABBLERS

1 WREN (EURASIAN WREN) *Troglodytes troglodytes neglectus* 10cm FIELD NOTES: Restless; forages mouse-like amongst low vegetation, showing itself only in fleeting glimpses; more prominent when singing from an exposed perch. Dark race *T. t. nipalensis* (1b) occurs in the C and E Himalayas. VOICE: Very loud, a mixture of trills and rattling warbles. Calls include a harsh *tek* or *tac* and loud churrs. HABITAT: High-altitude forests of fir, birch or oak, low growth on rocky ground and stone walls surrounding cultivations. DISTRIBUTION: Resident in the Himalayas and W Pakistan.

2 LONG-BILLED WREN-BABBLER *Rimator malacoptilus* 11–12cm FIELD NOTES: Skulking; forages on the ground and in undergrowth, usually in pairs. VOICE: A short, clear, whistled *chiiuuh* or *fyeeer* that falls in pitch but rises in volume and is given every few seconds. HABITAT: Forest undergrowth and dense scrub in steep broken country. DISTRIBUTION: Resident in E Himalayas and the NE Indian hills.

3 STREAKED WREN-BABBLER *Napothera brevicaudata* 12cm FIELD NOTES: Forages in pairs or small groups, on the ground in low, tangled vegetation or among rocks and boulders. VOICE: Various loud, clear, melancholy ringing whistles, including a *chee-oo, peee-oo, pu-ee, chiu-ree, chewee-chui, pee-wi* or a single *pweee*. Calls include a hard *churk-urt-churk-urt* and when alarmed a buzzy *trrreeettt*. HABITAT: Moist and shady hill forest, broken up by rocky ravines and steep slopes. DISTRIBUTION: Resident in the NE Indian hills.

4 EYEBROWED WREN-BABBLER *Napothera epilepidota guttaticollis* 10cm FIELD NOTES: Forages on the ground, turning over leaves in search of insects; also creeps about in low vegetation and among mossy logs or rocks. *N. e. roberti* (4b) occurs south of the Brahmaputra River. VOICE: A thin, clear, falling *cheeeoo, cheeeeeu* or *piiiiiu*, repeated every few seconds. Calls include a loud, repeated *chyurk*, a low *pit pit pit* and a rattling *prrrt-prrrt-prrrt*. HABITAT: Dense, dark forests with natural openings, such as glades and streams, especially where strewn with mossy logs or boulders. DISTRIBUTION: Resident in the NE Indian hills.

5 SCALY-BREASTED WREN-BABBLER *Pnoepyga albiventer* 9–10cm FIELD NOTES: Nervously flicks wings while foraging in dense tangled undergrowth and among fallen mossy logs; usually in pairs, but generally solitary in winter. VOICE: A rapid, high-pitched, jumbled warble. Call is an explosive *tschik* or *tchik*. HABITAT: Undergrowth in damp, shady broadleaved, fir, hemlock and birch forests, forest edge; usually with nearby water. DISTRIBUTION: Resident in the Himalayas and the NE Indian hills.

6 NEPAL WREN-BABBLER *Pnoepyga immaculata* 10cm FIELD NOTES: Hops about in low herbage or about boulders. VOICE: A piercing *tsi-tsu-tsi-ts-si-tsu-tsi-tsi*. Call is a sharp *tchit tchit*. HABITAT: Vegetation and undergrowth with rocks and boulders near streams or rivers, open areas and edge of broadleaved evergreen forest, overgrown clearings, secondary growth and scrub in gulleys. DISTRIBUTION: Resident in C Himalayas.

7 PYGMY WREN-BABBLER *Pnoepyga pusilla* 9cm FIELD NOTES: Forages on or near the ground, in leaf litter, tangled vegetation and on mossy logs or branches. VOICE: A slow, drawn-out *se-e-e-s-w*, each syllable lasting a second with a two-second interval. Call is a repeated *tchit*. HABITAT: Undergrowth in broadleaved evergreen forest, dense vegetation in forest ravines, mossy rocks and fallen logs. DISTRIBUTION: Resident from C to E Himalayas and the NE of the region.

1 *neglectus*

1b *nepalensis*

2

3

4 *guttaticollis*

4b *roberti*

5
rufous morph
pale morph

6
rufous morph
pale morph

7
rufous morph
pale morph

133 WREN-BABBLERS, BABBLERS

1 RUFOUS-THROATED WREN-BABBLER *Spelaeornis caudatus* 9cm FIELD NOTES:
Very elusive, forages on the ground. VOICE: A powerful *witchu-witchu-witchu-witchu-witchu*;
when alarmed utters a low *birrh birrh birrh....* HABITAT: Dense thickets in broadleaved evergreen
forest, especially where ferns and mossy rocks occur. DISTRIBUTION: Resident in E Himalayas.

2 RUSTY-THROATED WREN-BABBLER *Spelaeornis badeigularis* 9cm FIELD
NOTES: Forages on or near the ground. VOICE: Variable; includes short three- or four-note
whistles and a combination of short warbles and trills. HABITAT: Dense undergrowth
in secondary broadleaved evergreen forest; in winter in moist subtropical forest.
DISTRIBUTION: Resident in E Arunachal Pradesh.

3 BAR-WINGED WREN-BABBLER *Spelaeornis troglodytoides* 10cm FIELD NOTES: More
arboreal than many wren-babblers; clambers on bamboo stems and mossy tree trunks.
VOICE: A 5–8-note, husky, rapid, rolling warble. HABITAT: Dense undergrowth and bamboo
in moist temperate forest. DISTRIBUTION: Resident in E Himalayas.

4 SPOTTED WREN-BABBLER *Spelaeornis formosus* 10cm FIELD NOTES: Actions
presumably similar to other wren-babblers. VOICE: A high, drawn-out tinkling. Call is a
spluttering trill. HABITAT: Dark rhododendron forest with thick fern cover, mossy logs and
rocks. DISTRIBUTION: Resident in E Himalayas and the NE.

5 GREY-BELLIED WREN-BABBLER *Spelaeornis reptatus* 10cm FIELD NOTES: Forages
in low, thick vegetation. VOICE: A loud, strident, accelerating trill that changes into
a descending warble. Contact call is a soft, repeated *pt.* HABITAT: Thick undergrowth
in broadleaved evergreen forest and wet, well-vegetated ravines and gulleys.
DISTRIBUTION: Probably resident in E Arunachal Pradesh.

6 NAGA WREN-BABBLER *Spelaeornis chocolatinus* 10cm FIELD NOTES: Active, often
forages in vegetation well off the ground. VOICE: Undescribed. HABITAT: Undergrowth in
montane broadleaved evergreen forest, steep hillsides with rocks covered with moss and
thick vegetation, also bushes and brambles at forest edge. DISTRIBUTION: Nagaland and N
Manipur, in NE India.

7 CHIN HILLS WREN-BABBLER *Spelaeornis oatesi* 10cm FIELD NOTES: Forages in low
vegetation. VOICE: A loud undulating warble that is quickly repeated: *chiwi-chiwi-chiwi-chew*
or *witchi-witchi-witchi-wu.* Calls include a soft *tuc tuc tuc,* a *chit-chit-chit* and a quiet *ik ik ik...*
HABITAT: Understorey of broadleaved evergreen forest, forest edge, secondary growth, scrub,
thickets and tangled vegetation on steep forested slopes. DISTRIBUTION: Resident in Mizoram
in NE India.

8 TAWNY-BREASTED WREN-BABBLER *Spelaeornis longicaudatus* 10cm FIELD
NOTES: Creeps and climbs in low vegetation and on rocks. VOICE: A loud, short, shrill
warble. HABITAT: Well-developed undergrowth in broadleaved evergreen forest and
secondary growth, also on steep hillsides with rocks and boulders. DISTRIBUTION: Resident
from E Meghalaya to NW Manipur, in NE India.

**9 BLACKISH-BREASTED BABBLER (HIMALAYAN or SIKKIM WEDGE-BILLED
BABBLER)** *Sphenocichla humei* 18cm FIELD NOTES: Relatively arboreal, often clambers on
tree trunks; also forages in thick undergrowth near streams. VOICE: Loud, piping and slurred
whistles, often given in duet. Calls include a strident set of whistles; when alarmed gives a
low *hrrrh hrrrh hrrrh hrrr it hrrrh hrrh....* HABITAT: Understorey of broadleaved evergreen forest
and bamboo brakes. DISTRIBUTION: Resident in E Himalayas.

**10 CHEVRON-BREASTED BABBLER (MANIPUR or CACHAR WEDGE-BILLED
BABBLER)** *Sphenocichla roberti* 18cm FIELD NOTES: Habits and actions similar to Blackish-
breasted Babbler. VOICE: A melodious, fluty *uu-wii-wuu-yu.* Calls similar to Blackish-
breasted Babbler. HABITAT: Evergreen forest and bamboo on the edge of dense jungle.
DISTRIBUTION: Resident in the NE Indian hills.

1 BLACK-HEADED BABBLER (DARK-FRONTED or BLACK-FRONTED BABBLER) *Rhopocichla atriceps* 13cm FIELD NOTES: Groups of 3–12 forage in undergrowth, often in the company of other species of babbler. Brown-crowned race *R. a. nigrifrons* (1b) occurs in Sri Lanka. VOICE: A rattling *kt t t t kt kt t t*, a subdued *chur-r chur-r*, used when on the move; also various squeaks and when alarmed a rattling *chur-r*. HABITAT: Sholas and thickets near streams, dense marshy and bamboo jungle, plantations, dense undergrowth and scrub. DISTRIBUTION: Resident in the W Ghats and Sri Lanka.

2 TAWNY-BELLIED BABBLER *Dumetia hyperythra* 13cm FIELD NOTES: Forages mainly among tall grasses or on the ground; also noted taking nectar from flowers of *Erythrina* trees. White-throated race *D. h. albogularis* (2b) is found in S and W India; white-faced race *D. h. phillipsi* (2c) occurs in Sri Lanka. VOICE: A clear, pleasant whistling that starts with a lark-like *psssi-yu* or *ssiiu* followed by a sunbird-like *tit-ut-swit-it*, *whit-it-it-it* or *whit-ut*. Calls include a feeble *tit* and a soft *tack-tack*. HABITAT: Open wooded areas, grassland with scattered scrub, bamboo clumps, thorn-scrub, deciduous scrub jungle and wasteland near forests. DISTRIBUTION: Widespread resident, apart from the N, NW and NE.

3 BROWN-CAPPED BABBLER *Pellorneum fuscocapillus* 16cm FIELD NOTES: Forages on or near the ground in pairs or small parties. VOICE: A monotonous, clear *tu-weee-deyuuu*. Calls include a sharp *wit*, a *quit-it-it* and a low *chr chrr chrr*. HABITAT: Dense thickets, undergrowth in and near evergreen broadleaved forest, scrub and overgrown areas near villages. DISTRIBUTION: Resident in Sri Lanka.

4 BUFF-BREASTED BABBLER *Pellorneum tickelli* 15cm FIELD NOTES: Skulking, forages close to the ground. VOICE: A loud, repeated *wi-twee*. Calls include a rattling *prrree* and an explosive *whit*. HABITAT: Scrub, bamboo thickets and forest undergrowth. DISTRIBUTION: Resident in the NE Indian hills.

5 SPOT-THROATED BABBLER *Pellorneum albiventre* 14cm FIELD NOTES: Very skulking, forages near the ground. VOICE: A rich mix of short whistles and hard ringing notes. Calls include a buzzing *chrr-chrrr-chrrr-chrrrit...* and a quickly repeated *tip* or *tchip*. HABITAT: Scrub in forest, bamboo jungle and heavy cut-over scrub. DISTRIBUTION: Resident in the NE.

6 MARSH BABBLER *Pellorneum palustre* 15cm FIELD NOTES: Very skulking, best located by call notes. VOICE: Variable; includes a *grgrgrgrgr chew-hwee chichi-chu-hee*. Calls include a loud *chi-chew*, an aggravated *chik-chik-tuwheeu* and clattery bursts combined with clear notes. HABITAT: Reeds and coarse grass alongside swamps and rivers, tall grass and bushes on marshy ground. DISTRIBUTION: Resident in the NE.

7 PUFF-THROATED BABBLER *Pellorneum ruficeps* 15cm FIELD NOTES: Forages on the ground, usually in pairs or small parties. *P. r. mandellii* (7b) occurs from Nepal E to NE India. VOICE: A repeated loud, shrill *whi-chu* or *wi-ti-chu*; peninsular birds give a *pre-tee-deer* or a shorter *tui-deer*. Calls include a nasal *chi* and a rasping *rrrrit*. HABITAT: Forest undergrowth, secondary growth, bamboo and thickets in ravines and by watercourses. DISTRIBUTION: Resident in the Himalayas and the hills of Bangladesh and India.

8 ABBOTT'S BABBLER *Malacocincla abbotti* 17cm FIELD NOTES: Forages on the ground, alone or in pairs. VOICE: A series of 3–4 rich, fluty whistled notes. Calls include a mewing, a purring trill and an explosive *cheu*. HABITAT: Tangled thickets in wet deep jungle, edge of forest along streams. DISTRIBUTION: Resident in the Himalayas and the NE.

1b *nigrifrons*

2c
phillipsi

2b
albogularis

7b *mandellii*

135 SCIMITAR BABBLERS

1 LARGE SCIMITAR BABBLER *Pomatorhinus hypoleucos* 28cm FIELD NOTES: Skulking, forages on or near the ground. VOICE: Three short, hollow notes. Calls include a grating rattle and a hard *puh*. HABITAT: Dense bamboo, scrub jungle, reeds and tall grass; also forest undergrowth. DISTRIBUTION: Resident in the NE hills.

2 SPOT-BREASTED SCIMITAR BABBLER *Pomatorhinus mcclellandi* 25cm FIELD NOTES: Forages mostly on the ground, but also in trees. VOICE: Duets, two fluty notes quickly followed with a sharp note: *wi-wru-pi* or *wi-wwu-jrr*. When alarmed utters a *wi-wi-chitit*. HABITAT: Forest undergrowth, scrub jungle and thickets in forest clearings. DISTRIBUTION: Resident in the hills of the NE.

3 RUSTY-CHEEKED SCIMITAR BABBLER *Pomatorhinus erythrogenys* 25cm FIELD NOTES: Skulks in long grass or dense scrub, sometimes in trees. VOICE: Similar to Spot-breasted Scimitar Babbler, but more hurried and broken. When alarmed utters a rattling *whih-whihihihihi* and a harsh *whit-it*. HABITAT: Forest-edge scrub, thickets and bushy hillsides. DISTRIBUTION: Resident in the Himalayas.

4 INDIAN SCIMITAR BABBLER *Pomatorhinus horsfieldii* 22cm FIELD NOTES: Forages on the ground or on mossy trunks and branches, in pairs or small parties. VOICE: A mellow, fluty *oo-pu-pu-pu* or *wot-ho-ho-ho*. Calls include various chirps and rattles, hoarse hoots and a guttural *woch-wohorro*. HABITAT: Forests, secondary growth, bamboo patches, thorn-scrub and dense bush jungle. DISTRIBUTION: Resident in the hills of peninsular India.

5 STREAK-BREASTED SCIMITAR BABBLER *Pomatorhinus ruficollis* 19cm FIELD NOTES: Forages in pairs or small groups, on the ground, in bushes or low in trees. VOICE: A fast, mellow *win-wun-wun*. Contact call is a raspy *wreep* or *wreep-wreep*; when alarmed gives a scolding rattle. HABITAT: Thick forest, open forest with thick undergrowth and hillside scrub. DISTRIBUTION: Resident in the Himalayas and the NE.

6 WHITE-BROWED SCIMITAR BABBLER *Pomatorhinus schisticeps* 22cm FIELD NOTES: Forages on the ground or in thick cover. VOICE: A short, low whistled *tji-u-u-u-u* or *woot-a-ah-hoot*. Calls include a *tjoo-tjoo* or *gouk-gouk* and some loud and shrill notes. HABITAT: Forest undergrowth, thick secondary growth and scrub jungle. DISTRIBUTION: Resident in the Himalayan foothills and the NE hills.

7 SRI LANKA SCIMITAR BABBLER *Pomatorhinus melanurus* 19–21cm FIELD NOTES: Only scimitar babbler in Sri Lanka. Often works up tree trunks like a woodpecker. VOICE: An *oop-oop-oop-oop* followed by a *kraa-kree kraa-kree*, the latter presumed to be uttered by the female. HABITAT: Moist deciduous and evergreen forest. DISTRIBUTION: Resident in Sri Lanka.

8 CORAL-BILLED SCIMITAR BABBLER *Pomatorhinus ferruginosus* 23cm FIELD NOTES: Elusive; forages on the ground. Brown-crowned *P. f. formosus* (8b) occurs in NE India. VOICE: A fluty *oo-pu-pu* or *oo-pu-pu-pu*. Calls include a grating *churr*, a *weeitch-oo* and a shrill *wheep-wheep*. HABITAT: Dense shrubbery, bamboo jungle, dense undergrowth and forest edge. DISTRIBUTION: Resident in E Himalayas and the NE.

9 RED-BILLED SCIMITAR BABBLER *Pomatorhinus ochraceiceps* 23cm FIELD NOTES: Forages in trees and bushes, and on the ground. VOICE: A hurried, piping *wu-wu-woi*, also a human-like whistle. HABITAT: Dense undergrowth in evergreen or mixed forest and bamboo jungle. DISTRIBUTION: Resident in the hills of NE India.

10 SLENDER-BILLED SCIMITAR BABBLER *Xiphirhynchus superciliaris* 20cm FIELD NOTES: Shy, restless and noisy; forages on or near the ground in pairs or small parties. VOICE: A rapid, hollow piping. Call is a harsh chattering. HABITAT: Bamboo, bushes on steep hillsides and bramble thickets. DISTRIBUTION: Resident in the C and E Himalayas and the NE.

136 BABBLERS

1 RUFOUS-FRONTED BABBLER *Stachyridopsis rufifrons* 12cm FIELD NOTES: Restless, forages through undergrowth and in tops of bamboo clumps; usually in pairs or small groups and often in the company of other babblers. VOICE: A monotonous, piping *per pe-pe-pe-pe-pe* or *tuh tuh-tuh-tuh-tuh-tuh*. Calls include a short rolling *wirrri*, given when alarmed, a fast *wu-yu-yu-yu-yu-yu-yi* and a soft *wit* or *wi* contact note. HABITAT: Thick undergrowth in open forests, dense forest in ravines, bamboo and scrub jungle. DISTRIBUTION: Resident in E Himalayas and the hills of the E and NE.

2 RUFOUS-CAPPED BABBLER *Stachyridopsis ruficeps* 12cm FIELD NOTES: Forages low in undergrowth, actions tit-like; post breeding often found with other small babblers. VOICE: Similar to Rufous-fronted Babbler, but lower in tone and without the space between the first and second note. When alarmed utters a harsh, scolding *trrrrt-trrrrt-trrrrt*. HABITAT: Dense bushes in forest clearings and bamboo jungle. DISTRIBUTION: Resident in E Himalayas and the hills of NE India.

3 BLACK-CHINNED BABBLER *Stachyridopsis pyrrhops* 10cm FIELD NOTES: Forages on or near the ground, in undergrowth; sometimes ascends trees. VOICE: A bell-like, mellow *wit-wit-wit-wit* repeated seven or eight times. Calls include a soft *chir*, a slow *pee-ve-ve* and a scolding *tchhirrirrr*, *irr-wir-wee* or *irr-wir-wir-wee*. HABITAT: Open and secondary forest with low undergrowth, forest edge, scrub jungle, thickets, bamboo and hedgerows. DISTRIBUTION: Resident in the Himalayas.

4 GOLDEN BABBLER *Stachyridopsis chrysaea* 10cm FIELD NOTES: Active, agile forager in tangled undergrowth and in tree foliage. *S. c. binghami* (4b) occurs in the E Mizoram area of NE India. VOICE: A level-toned *pee pi-pi-pi-pi-pi*, very like the song of Rufous-fronted Babbler. Calls include a soft twittering, a *chirik-chirik* and a scolding *chrrrr*. HABITAT: Dense bushes, bamboo, new undergrowth, thickets in moist secondary jungle and deserted, overgrown cultivations. DISTRIBUTION: Resident from C to E Himalayas and in the hills of the NE.

5 GREY-THROATED BABBLER *Stachyris nigriceps* 12cm FIELD NOTES: Very active, constantly on the move; usually encountered in small parties foraging in low growth. Rufous race *S. n. coltarti* (5b) occurs in Nagaland. VOICE: A high-pitched, quavering, rising *ti tsuuuuuuuueee*, or similar. Calls include a constant *chi chi chi* and a scolding *chrrrt* or *chrrrrr-rrr-rrt*. HABITAT: Secondary growth and bamboo in light or dense forest. DISTRIBUTION: Resident from C to E Himalayas and the NE hills.

6 SNOWY-THROATED BABBLER *Stachyris oglei* 13cm FIELD NOTES: Skulking, keeps to thick cover; forages in fast-moving parties of up to 25 birds. VOICE: A thin high-pitched rattling. HABITAT: Undergrowth in dense forest, adjacent secondary forest and scrub in ravines. DISTRIBUTION: Resident in the hills of extreme NE India.

7 YELLOW-EYED BABBLER *Chrysomma sinense* 18cm FIELD NOTES: Elusive; sometimes climbs to exposed perches, but soon dives back into cover. VOICE: A short, powerful whistled *tit-toowhee-twitchoo*, often mixed with trills or nasal notes. Calls include a dry trill and a subdued *stik*. HABITAT: Scrub, bush-covered grassy hillsides, secondary growth, bamboo and sugarcane fields. DISTRIBUTION: Widespread resident.

8 JERDON'S BABBLER *Chrysomma altirostre* 17cm FIELD NOTES: Highly skulking; best seen while singing from the top of a reed stem. Grey-throated race *C. a. griseigulare* (8b) occurs in S Nepal and the NE. VOICE: A weak *chi-chi-chi-chew-chew-chew*. Calls include a high-pitched *tic* or *ts-ts-tsik*. HABITAT: Tall grassland and reed-beds. DISTRIBUTION: Resident in the Indus Plains (Pakistan), S Nepal and NE India.

4b *binghami*

3

5b *coltarti*

4

5

6

8

7

8b
griseigulare

137 TIT-BABBLER, BABBLERS

1 PIN-STRIPED TIT-BABBLER (YELLOW-BREASTED BABBLER) *Macronus gularis* 11cm FIELD NOTES: Noisy, actions tit-like; post breeding often in parties of twelve or more foraging in bushes or trees. VOICE: A repetitive *chaunk-chaunk-chaunk...* Calls include a harsh *chrrrt-chrr* and a scolding *tseep*. HABITAT: Light and dense forest with bushes and undergrowth, bamboo jungle and long grass. DISTRIBUTION: Resident in Himalayan foothills and the hills of the NE, and in S and E India.

2 CHESTNUT-CAPPED BABBLER *Timalia pileata* 17cm FIELD NOTES: Elusive, threads its way through tangles of tall grass and bushes; usually in pairs or after breeding in groups of 6–8 birds. VOICE: Song consists of husky phrases ending with thin, metallic notes. Calls include a short *tzit*, a harsh *chrrt* and various chuntering notes. HABITAT: Tall grass, reed-beds and scrub jungle in swampy areas. DISTRIBUTION: Resident in S Nepal and N and NE India.

3 SPINY BABBLER *Turdoides nipalensis* 25cm FIELD NOTES: Forages mainly on the ground, under bushes; usually in pairs, with small groups post breeding. VOICE: Variable, including a rising *ter-ter-ter-ter-ter* and a descending *tee-tee-ker-chee-ker-chee-ker-chee*. Calls include musical *churr* and screaming notes. HABITAT: Dense secondary scrub, thick scrub and bracken on hillsides. DISTRIBUTION: Resident in Nepal.

4 COMMON BABBLER *Turdoides caudata* 23cm FIELD NOTES: Usually encountered in parties of up to 20 birds, hopping rapidly on the ground or scuttling rat-like under vegetation; regularly cocks tail. Grey race *T. c. huttoni* (4b) occurs in Baluchistan; sometimes considered a separate species. VOICE: Various loud, descending whistles and a squeaky *qwe-e-e qwe-e-e* or *qwee* given when alarmed. HABITAT: Thorn-scrub, scrub in plains and cultivations. DISTRIBUTION: Widespread resident.

5 STRIATED BABBLER *Turdoides earlei* 21cm FIELD NOTES: Clambers in reeds and grass; gregarious, usually in small parties. VOICE: A repeated *tiew-tiew-tiew-tiew*, interspersed with *quip-quip-quip* calls from other flock members. HABITAT: Tall grass and reed-beds in marshy areas. DISTRIBUTION: Resident in the plains across the N of the region.

6 SLENDER-BILLED BABBLER *Turdoides longirostris* 23cm FIELD NOTES: Skulking, gregarious and noisy. VOICE: Variable; includes a high-pitched series of shrill notes, a strident *chiu-chiu-chiu chiu*, a discordant *tiu-tiu-tit-tit-tu-tu* and a buzzy call that leads into an irregular rattle. HABITAT: Tall grassland, usually near water. DISTRIBUTION: Resident in the NE and the lowlands of C Nepal.

7 LARGE GREY BABBLER *Turdoides malcolmi* 28cm FIELD NOTES: Forages on the ground or in low vegetation; gregarious, often in quite large groups. VOICE: A monotonous, drawling *kay-kay-kay-kay*. Gives a noisy chatter when alarmed. HABITAT: Open dry scrub, cultivations and gardens. DISTRIBUTION: Resident in peninsular India, SW Nepal and NE Pakistan.

8 RUFOUS BABBLER *Turdoides subrufa* 25cm FIELD NOTES: Forages on or near the ground in thick cover; more often heard than seen; gregarious, usually in small parties. VOICE: A shrill, whistling *tree-tree-tree* interspersed with harsh squeaks. HABITAT: Dense undergrowth, especially when mixed with coarse grass and bamboo, forest edge and abandoned clearings. DISTRIBUTION: Resident in the hills of SW India.

9 JUNGLE BABBLER *Turdoides striata* 25cm FIELD NOTES: Very gregarious; forages mainly on the ground. *T. s. somervillei* (9b) occurs in the NW Ghats. VOICE: A harsh *ke-ke-ke* that may break into a squeaking and chattering. Calls include a nasal chortling and a low buzzy *churweeur*. HABITAT: Deciduous forests, cultivations and gardens. DISTRIBUTION: Widespread resident.

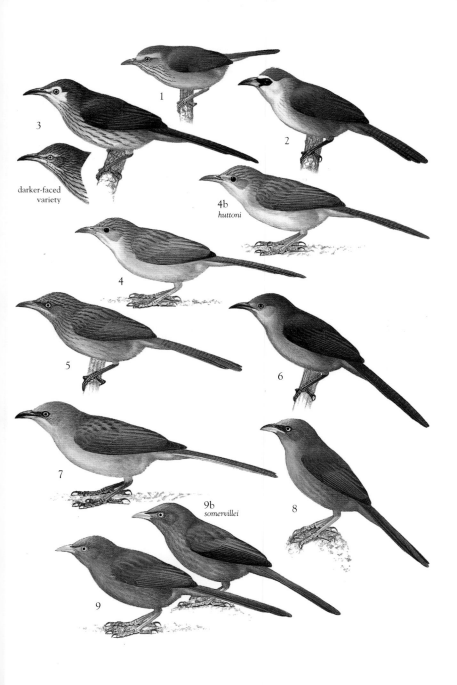

138 BABBLERS, BARWINGS

1 ORANGE-BILLED BABBLER *Turdoides rufescens* 25cm FIELD NOTES: Gregarious; forages in trees or undergrowth, gleaning insects from foliage and branches. VOICE: A constant chattering, squeaking and chirping. HABITAT: Broadleaved evergreen forest, thickets and bamboo scrub in well-wooded areas. DISTRIBUTION: Resident in Sri Lanka.

2 YELLOW-BILLED BABBLER *Turdoides affinis* 23cm FIELD NOTES: Forages mainly on the ground, but often gleans insects from tree branches and foliage. *T. a. taprobanus* (2b) occurs in Sri Lanka. VOICE: A high-pitched tinkly chittering that varies in pitch and volume. HABITAT: Open forest and secondary woodland, dry scrub, cultivations and gardens. DISTRIBUTION: Resident in S India and Sri Lanka.

3 CHINESE BABAX *Babax lanceolatus* 28cm FIELD NOTES: Skulking; forages on the ground or in low scrub, although will ascend trees to feed in the topmost branches, especially in mornings and evenings. VOICE: A wailing *ou-phee-ou-phee*, repeated several times; groups keep up a continual flow of soft musical notes interspersed with some harsher outbursts; also noted is a call that sounds like a creaky gate hinge. HABITAT: Thin scattered forest, open hillsides with a covering of bracken, brambles and grass. DISTRIBUTION: Resident in Mizoram (NE India).

4 GIANT BABAX *Babax waddelli* 31cm FIELD NOTES: Skulks in dense bushes; forages on the ground, turning over dead leaves in a search for food. VOICE: A series of quavering, whistled, thrush-like notes. Call is a harsh grating. HABITAT: High-altitude arid scrub and thickets. DISTRIBUTION: Vagrant: disputed records from NE Sikkim.

5 WHITE-HOODED BABBLER *Gampsorhynchus rufulus* 23cm FIELD NOTES: Forages mainly in the middle storey of trees or the canopy of bamboo; gregarious, often in parties of up to 20 birds. Juvenile has rufous crown and ear-coverts. VOICE: A loud, hollow cackling or an accelerating, hollow, laughing *khurk khurk khurk-khurk-khurk-khurk*. Contact call is a *wit*, *wet* or *wyee*. HABITAT: Bamboo, broadleaved evergreen forest, secondary growth, scrub and vegetation at forest edge. DISTRIBUTION: Resident in E Himalayas and the hills of NE India.

6 HOARY-THROATED BARWING *Actinodura nipalensis* 21cm FIELD NOTES: Arboreal; usually in small parties, foraging for insects on mossy branches and tree trunks. VOICE: Variable, including a whistled *tui-whee-er*, a clear quavering *wiu-iu* and *duit-duwee-duweer*, repeated every few seconds. When alarmed gives a repeated, rapid *je-je-je-je-je.....* HABITAT: Oak, mixed oak, conifer and rhododendron forest with rich mixed undergrowth. DISTRIBUTION: Resident in the Himalayas.

7 RUSTY-FRONTED BARWING *Actinodura egertoni* 23cm FIELD NOTES: Forages from undergrowth to the canopy, often among epiphytic growth; regularly joins mixed-species feeding parties. VOICE: A sweet, piping *tsit-tsit-seet-seeetsuut*, repeated every few seconds. Calls include a high-pitched rattle and a harsh, buzzy *gursh-gursh...* HABITAT: Dense undergrowth, forest edge, shrubbery and scrub in broadleaved evergreen forest. DISTRIBUTION: Resident from C to E Himalayas and in the hills of the NE.

8 STREAK-THROATED BARWING *Actinodura waldeni* 20–22cm FIELD NOTES: Clambers about mossy branches and tree trunks, pulling moss apart to find insects; often forms part of mixed-species foraging flocks. *A. w. daflaensis* (8b) is found in E Himalayas. VOICE: A strident, rising *tchrrrr-jo-jwiee*, *dddrt-juee-iwee* or a shorter *jorr-dwidu*. Calls include a nasal, grumbling *grrr-ut grrr-ut* and a *grr-grr-grr-grr-grr*. HABITAT: Mossy broadleaved evergreen and mixed forest. DISTRIBUTION: Resident in E Himalayas and the NE Indian hills.

2b *taprobanus*

8b
daflaensis

139 MESIA, LEIOTHRIX, CUTIA, SHRIKE-BABBLERS

1 SILVER-EARED MESIA *Mesia argentauris* 15–17cm FIELD NOTES: Acrobatic forager, mainly in bushes but also up to the canopy; post breeding often in parties of 6–30 individuals. VOICE: A cheerful, descending *che tchu-tchu che-rit* or *che-chu chiwi chwu.* Calls include a flat, piping *pe-pe-pe-pe-pe* and a harsh chattering. HABITAT: Scrub jungle, bush-covered open areas, secondary growth, bushes in and at the edge of evergreen forest. DISTRIBUTION: Resident in E Himalayas and the hills of the NE.

2 RED-BILLED LEIOTHRIX (PEKING ROBIN) *Leiothrix lutea* 14–15cm FIELD NOTES: Post breeding often encountered in small, noisy parties; regular member of mixed-species foraging groups; feeds mainly low down in undergrowth or on the ground. VOICE: A fluty warble of up to fifteen notes. Calls include a nasal *zhirk*, a *shreep* and a rattling *zhri-zhri-zhri...* When alarmed utters a buzzy *zhriti-zhriti-zhriti....* HABITAT: Undergrowth in open broadleaved evergreen, pine and mixed forests, forest edge, secondary growth and scrub. DISTRIBUTION: Resident in the Himalayas and the hills of the NE.

3 HIMALAYAN CUTIA *Cutia nipalensis* 20cm FIELD NOTES: Forages nuthatch-like; creeps along branches and tree trunks; post breeding forms small parties, often mixed with shrike-babblers and other babblers. VOICE: A long series of ringing notes. Calls include a light *chick-chick-chick....*, a loud *chip* and a low *jert.* HABITAT: Broadleaved evergreen forest, particularly larger trees festooned with moss and epiphytes. DISTRIBUTION: Resident in the Himalayas and NE Indian hills.

4 BLACK-HEADED SHRIKE-BABBLER *Pteruthius rufiventer* 18–20cm FIELD NOTES: Lethargic. Forages from low undergrowth to the canopy; regularly part of mixed-species feeding flocks. VOICE: A mellow *wip-wu-yu*, repeated every few seconds. Calls include a scolding *rrrrt-rrrrt-rrrrt...* and a quick *ukuk-wrrrrrii-yiwu.* HABITAT: Dense moss-covered oak and evergreen forest. DISTRIBUTION: Resident from C to E Himalayas and in the NE hills.

5 WHITE-BROWED SHRIKE-BABBLER *Pteruthius flaviscapis* 16cm FIELD NOTES: Forages slowly, shuffles sideways along branches to search mosses and lichens for insects; feeds mainly in the canopy, often in the company of other species. VOICE: A loud, far-carrying *chu-wip-chip-chip* or *cha-cha chip.* Calls include a quickly repeated harsh grating and a short *pink.* HABITAT: Montane forests of oak, rhododendron and conifer. DISTRIBUTION: Resident in the Himalayas and the hills of the NE.

6 GREEN SHRIKE-BABBLER *Pteruthius xanthochlorus* 13cm FIELD NOTES: Actions much like a sluggish leaf warbler; regular member of mixed-species feeding parties. *P. x. hybrida* (6b), which occurs in the hills S of the Brahmaputra River, has a whitish eye-ring. VOICE: A rapid, monotonous, repetition of a single note. Calls include a repeated *whit*, a nasal *nyeep nyeep* and a high *jerri.* HABITAT: Subalpine, mixed forests. DISTRIBUTION: Resident in the Himalayas and NE Indian hills.

7 BLACK-EARED SHRIKE-BABBLER *Pteruthius melanotis* 11cm FIELD NOTES: Arboreal, mainly in the canopy; regularly found among mixed-species foraging parties; actions sluggish and methodical. VOICE: A bright *tew wee tew we tew-wee.* Calls include a short *chid-it* and a high *t-cheer-cheer chee chee chee chee.* HABITAT: Broadleaved evergreen forest. DISTRIBUTION: Resident from C to E Himalayas and in the hills of the NE.

8 CHESTNUT-FRONTED SHRIKE-BABBLER *Pteruthius aenobarbus* 11cm FIELD NOTES: Actions similar to Black-eared Shrike-babbler. VOICE: A monotonous *chip-chip-chip...* Calls include a buzzy *jer-jer-jer...* and a sharp *pwit.* HABITAT: Open forest and evergreen forest edge. DISTRIBUTION: Resident in Meghalaya (NE India).

140 FULVETTAS

1 GOLDEN-BREASTED FULVETTA *Lioparus chrysotis* 11cm FIELD NOTES: Acrobatic, forages low in thickets. *L. c. albilineatus* (1b) occurs S of the Brahmaputra River. VOICE: A slightly descending, thin *si-si-si-si-suu*. Call is a staccato *witrrrit*, *wit* or *witit*, given in short bursts. HABITAT: Dense undergrowth, especially bamboo. DISTRIBUTION: Resident from C to E Himalayas and in the NE Indian hills.

2 YELLOW-THROATED FULVETTA *Pseudominla cinerea* 10cm FIELD NOTES: Very active; post breeding forms parties of up 30 birds which are often part of mixed-species flocks. VOICE: Thin, high notes that start slowly and end in a rapid jumble that often descends and tails off. Calls include rapid *tit* notes and a coarse rattle. HABITAT: Undergrowth in the glades and breaks of broadleaved evergreen forest. DISTRIBUTION: Resident in E Himalayas and the hills of NE India.

3 RUFOUS-WINGED FULVETTA *Pseudominla castaneceps* 10cm FIELD NOTES: Forages in undergrowth and over mossy trunks; often part of mixed-species feeding parties. VOICE: An undulating and slightly descending *ti-du-di-du-di-du-di*. Calls include a *tu-wee-we*, a wheezy *tsi-tsi-tsi-tsir* and a quiet *chip*. HABITAT: Thick evergreen undergrowth at forest edge, abandoned clearings and bamboo. DISTRIBUTION: Resident from C to E Himalayas and in the NE Indian hills.

4 MANIPUR FULVETTA *Fulvetta manipurensis* 11cm FIELD NOTES: Forages low down, sometimes in trees or on the ground. VOICE: A high-pitched *ti ti si-su*, *si-swu* or *see si-wu*. Calls include a low *tirrru* a high *swi-swi-swi-sw...* and a dry metallic rattle. HABITAT: Broadleaved evergreen forest, forest edge, bamboo and scrub. DISTRIBUTION: Resident in the NE Indian hills.

5 WHITE-BROWED FULVETTA *Fulvetta vinipectus* 11cm FIELD NOTES: Forages in low trees, bushes and undergrowth. *F. v. chumbiensis* (5b) occurs in E Himalayas; *F. v. perstriata* (5c) is found in E Arunchal Pradesh. VOICE: A faint *chit-it-it-or-key*. Calls include an incessant *chip-chip* and a *churr* when alarmed. HABITAT: Subalpine scrub and bamboo in forest. DISTRIBUTION: Resident in the Himalayas and the NE Indian hills.

6 LUDLOW'S FULVETTA (BROWN-THROATED FULVETTA) *Fulvetta ludlowi* 11cm FIELD NOTES: Usually in pairs or small parties; often part of mixed-species flocks. VOICE: A thin *see-see-spir r r*. HABITAT: Bamboo thickets and bushes in rhododendron forests. DISTRIBUTION: Resident in E Himalayas.

7 BROWN-CHEEKED FULVETTA *Alcippe poioicephala* 15cm FIELD NOTES: Forages from undergrowth up to canopy. VOICE: A pleasant, whistled *tui-tui-tui-tuwee-twee-tuee*. Call is a harsh, buzzy, spluttering rattle. HABITAT: Undergrowth in forests. DISTRIBUTION: Resident in the hills of India and Bangladesh.

8 NEPAL FULVETTA *Alcippe nipalensis* 12cm FIELD NOTES: Active, agile forager, mainly in undergrowth and the tops of low trees. VOICE: A simple *chu-chui-chiwi*. Call is a *chr-rr-r*. HABITAT: Forests, forest edge, secondary growth and bamboo. DISTRIBUTION: Resident in the Himalayas and the NE hills.

9 RUFOUS-THROATED FULVETTA *Schoeniparus rufogularis* 12cm FIELD NOTES: Skulks in deep cover near the ground, usually in small parties mixed with other babblers. VOICE: A loud, shrill *wi-chuw-i-chewi-cheeu*, repeated every few seconds. HABITAT: Evergreen forest undergrowth, bamboo and secondary growth. DISTRIBUTION: Resident in E Himalayas and NE Indian hills.

10 RUSTY-CAPPED FULVETTA *Schoeniparus dubius* 13cm FIELD NOTES: Forages in dense undergrowth, close to or on the ground; regularly occurs in small parties mixed with other babblers. VOICE: A short, sweet, fluty warble. Calls include a low rattle, buzzy trills and a quiet *peet-seet-seet*. HABITAT: Forest undergrowth. DISTRIBUTION: Resident in the NE Indian hills.

141 SIVA, MINLAS, SIBIAS

1 BLUE-WINGED SIVA (BLUE-WINGED MINLA) *Siva cyanouroptera* 15cm FIELD NOTES: Forages in the tops of bushes and in trees; regularly part of mixed-species feeding flocks. VOICE: A repeated, high-pitched *psii sii suuu*. Calls include a short *whit* or *bwik* and dry staccato buzzes. HABITAT: Bushes in evergreen or mixed deciduous forest and evergreen secondary growth. DISTRIBUTION: Resident in the Himalayas and the NE hills.

2 BAR-THROATED MINLA (CHESTNUT-TAILED MINLA) *Minla strigula* 14cm FIELD NOTES: Agile, forages in high bushes and medium-height trees. VOICE: A hoarse *tsi-tsu-ti-si* or *too-sweet-sweet*. Calls include a sharp *kip*, a soft, nasal *yeep* and a trilling buzz. HABITAT: Subalpine oak and rhododendron forest; winters in pine and mixed forest, bamboo and scrub jungle. DISTRIBUTION: Resident in the Himalayas and the NE hills.

3 RED-TAILED MINLA *Minla ignotincta* 14cm FIELD NOTES: Acrobatic, methodical forager in treetop branches and on mossy trunks; usually found in small parties or as part of large mixed-species feeding flocks. VOICE: A high-pitched, repeated *wi ti wi-wu* or a slurred, falling *si-swee-sweeeuuuu*. Calls include a harsh *wih-wih-wih-wih*, a short *wit* and a fast *witti-wi-wrrh*. HABITAT: Humid dense forest, especially oak and rhododendron. DISTRIBUTION: Resident in E Himalayas and hills of the NE.

4 RUFOUS-BACKED SIBIA *Leioptila annectans* 18cm FIELD NOTES: Forages in the canopy of tall trees, creeps and clambers on branches and trunks searching for insects among mosses and lichens. VOICE: A pretty, descending warble. Calls include a harsh chattering and a buzzy, chortling *fss-uss-uss-che-che-wee-whee-che-che-wee-whew*. HABITAT: Broadleaved evergreen forest, occasionally semi-deciduous forest. DISTRIBUTION: Resident in E Himalayas and the hills of NE India.

5 RUFOUS SIBIA (BLACK-CAPPED SIBIA) *Malacias capistratus* 21–24cm FIELD NOTES: Arboreal; forages in the canopy, on moss-covered tree trunks and occasionally in undergrowth. M. c. nigriceps (5b) occurs in the C and E Himalayas. VOICE: A fluty *tee-dee-dee-dee-dee-o-lu*. Calls include a rapid *chi-chi*, and when alarmed a harsh *chrai-chrai-chrai.....* HABITAT: Broadleaved evergreen forest, especially oak; also mixed oak and conifer forest. DISTRIBUTION: Resident in the Himalayas.

6 BEAUTIFUL SIBIA *Malacias pulchellus* 23cm FIELD NOTES: Actions and habits similar to Rufous Sibia. M. p. nigroauritus (6b) occurs N of the Brahmaputra River. VOICE: A strident, repeated *ti-ti-titi-tu-ti*. Calls with a continuous low rattling *chrrrrrrr* or *churrururr*, also utters a high trilling *tr rt-tr rt-tr rt....* HABITAT: Broadleaved evergreen forest. DISTRIBUTION: Resident in E Himalayas and the NE Indian hills.

7 GREY SIBIA *Malacias gracilis* 23–25cm FIELD NOTES: Forages in the canopy, among epiphytes and on mossy trunks, occasionally lower down in bushes and undergrowth. VOICE: A repeated loud, descending *tu-tu-ti-ti-ti-tu*, *ti-ti-ti-ti-tiu-tu* or *tiu-tiu-tiu-tiu-tiu*. Calls include a soft *ti-tew*, a squeaky *witwit-witarit* and a harsh, grating *trrit-trrit*. HABITAT: Broadleaved evergreen and deciduous forest, sometimes in pine and mixed forest. DISTRIBUTION: Resident in the NE Indian hills.

8 LONG-TAILED SIBIA *Heterophasia picaoides* 28–35cm FIELD NOTES: Forages mainly in the canopy, usually in pairs or small parties; post-breeding groups may number up to 30 birds; also a regular member of mixed-species feeding flocks. VOICE: A rich, six-note, whistled phrase. Calls include a high *tsip-tsip-tsip-tsip* which may be interspersed with a dry rattling or trilling. HABITAT: Broadleaved evergreen forest, forest edge, open scrub with large trees and forest clearings. DISTRIBUTION: Resident in E Himalayas and the hills of the NE.

142 YUHINAS, ERPORNIS, MYZORNIS

1 STRIATED YUHINA *Yuhina castaniceps* 13cm FIELD NOTES: Agile forager in the foliage of high bushes and low trees; often in parties of up to 30 birds. *Y. c. plumbeiceps* (1b) occurs from E Arunchal Pradesh south to Nagaland. VOICE: A series of high-pitched, shrill *tchu, tchi* or *tchi-chi* notes. Flocks utter an incessant twittering or cheeping; other calls include a dry trill and nasal peeps. HABITAT: Undergrowth, scrub and understorey in broadleaved evergreen forest. DISTRIBUTION: Resident in E Himalayas and the NE hills.

2 WHISKERED YUHINA *Yuhina flavicollis* 13cm FIELD NOTES: Actions tit-like, also fly-catches from bush tops; forages in small noisy parties, often mixed with tits, warblers, nuthatches and small babblers. *Y. f. albicollis* (2b) occurs from Himachal Pradesh east to W Nepal. VOICE: A repeated high-pitched *tzii-jhu ziddi* or *twe-tyurwi-tyawi-tyawa*. Calls include a thin squeaky *swii-swii-swii*, a buzzy *jhoh* or *fzee-tzzup jhoh*. HABITAT: Broadleaved evergreen forest, oak and open deciduous forest, also secondary growth. DISTRIBUTION: Resident in the Himalayas and hills of the NE.

3 STRIPE-THROATED YUHINA *Yuhina gularis* 14cm FIELD NOTES: Arboreal, actions tit-like but slower; usually encountered in small parties or in mixed-species foraging flocks. VOICE: A descending, nasal, mewing *mher* or *wher*, which is sometimes followed by a hurried *whu-whu-whu-whi-whi-whi*; also utters a short *wiht*. HABITAT: Temperate oak, birch and rhododendron forest or mixed rhododendron and conifer forest, also bamboo and low scrub. DISTRIBUTION: Resident in the Himalayas and the hills of NE India.

4 BLACK-CHINNED YUHINA *Yuhina nigrimenta* 11cm FIELD NOTES: Active, agile, noisy forager in the canopy of tall trees and in low shrubs; regularly occurs in parties of up to fifteen birds and in mixed-species feeding flocks. VOICE: A clear, thin sequence of ringing whistles. Calls include a staccato chattering and a metallic *pik pik pik* that is often mixed with other notes. HABITAT: Broadleaved evergreen forest, secondary jungle and overgrown clearings. DISTRIBUTION: Resident in the Himalayas and the hills of the NE.

5 RUFOUS-VENTED YUHINA *Yuhina occipitalis* 13cm FIELD NOTES: Forages in the canopy and on moss-covered trunks and branches; after breeding occurs in small parties along with other species. VOICE: A high-pitched *swi-si-si-su-su swi-si-si-si-si-sisu-su-su....* Calls include buzzy and nasal notes, *bee, beebee* or *bzzzee*. HABITAT: Broadleaved evergreen forest, especially oak and rhododendron. DISTRIBUTION: Resident from C to E Himalayas.

6 WHITE-NAPED YUHINA *Yuhina bakeri* 13cm FIELD NOTES: Forages in bushes and treetops in small parties; post breeding occurs in larger flocks, often alongside other small species. VOICE: A series of high thin notes, repeated every few seconds. Calls include a short metallic *tsit*, a falling *seep* and a *seet-chuut*. HABITAT: Broadleaved evergreen forest and secondary growth. DISTRIBUTION: Resident in E Himalayas and the NE hills.

7 WHITE-BELLIED ERPORNIS *Erpornis zantholeuca* 11cm FIELD NOTES: Agile, acrobatic forager in the lower canopy and higher bushes. VOICE: A high-pitched, trilling *si-i-i-i-i-i*, or a rising and falling *ss-ss-ss-se-se-se-se*. Calls include a loud, nasal *jeeer-jeeer-jeeer* interspersed with dry trills and chitterings. HABITAT: Broadleaved evergreen forest, rhododendrons and secondary growth. DISTRIBUTION: Resident in the Himalayas and the hills of the NE.

8 FIRE-TAILED MYZORNIS *Myzornis pyrrhoura* 12cm FIELD NOTES: Regularly visits rhododendron flowers for nectar; also climbs mossy tree trunks like a treecreeper. VOICE: A high, twittering *si-si-si-si-si*. HABITAT: Montane forests, mossy juniper and rhododendron scrub and bamboo thickets. DISTRIBUTION: Resident from C to E Himalayas.

1b
plumbeiceps

1

2b
albicollis

2

3

4

5

6

7

8 ♂

♀

1 BEARDED REEDLING (BEARDED TIT or PARROTBILL) *Panurus biarmicus* 14–17cm FIELD NOTES: Best located by pinging call; often feeds at the base of reeds. VOICE: Calls include a ringing *ping* or *pching*, a buzzing *tjipp* and a soft *pitt*. HABITAT: Reed-beds. DISTRIBUTION: Vagrant, recorded in Pakistan.

2 GREAT PARROTBILL *Conostoma aemodium* 28cm FIELD NOTES: Forages on or near the ground. VOICE: A loud, repeated *whip whi-uu* or similar. Calls with nasal wheezes, cackling, churring and squeals. HABITAT: Open evergreen forest, bamboo and rhododendron thickets. DISTRIBUTION: Resident in the Himalayas.

3 BROWN PARROTBILL *Cholornis unicolor* 21cm FIELD NOTES: Skulking; acrobatic, often hanging upside-down when foraging. VOICE: A loud, *ii-wuu-iiew* or *it ik ik - ii-wuu-iiew*. Calls include a shrill *whi-whi-whi*, a low *brrh* and a cackling *churrrh*. HABITAT: Dense bamboo thickets. DISTRIBUTION: Resident from C to E Himalayas.

4 BLACK-BREASTED PARROTBILL *Paradoxornis flavirostris* 19cm FIELD NOTES: Forages low down, but regularly sings from the top of reeds or grass stems; usually occurs in small parties. VOICE: A clear, high *woi-woi-woi-woi-woi-woi*, *whii-whii-whii-whii* or a huskier *jhor-jhor-jhor-jhor-jhor-jhor*. Calls include a *wu-wi-wi* and a nasal *uh-uh-uh-uh-uh-uh*. HABITAT: Reeds and tall grass. DISTRIBUTION: Resident in the plains of the NE.

5 SPOT-BREASTED PARROTBILL *Paradoxornis guttaticollis* 19cm FIELD NOTES: Noisy, usually in small parties, which may contain other species. VOICE: A staccato *whit-whit-whit-whit*… Calls include a low *ruk-ruk*, *ruk-uk-uk* or *rut-rut-rut-rut*. HABITAT: Secondary growth, scrub and tall grass. DISTRIBUTION: Resident in the NE Indian hills.

6 FULVOUS PARROTBILL *Suthora fulvifrons* 12cm FIELD NOTES: Active, lively forager; post breeding often forms large flocks. VOICE: Song includes a high-pitched *si-tsiiii chuu*, *si-sii juu* or *si-ti ti tituuuu-jhiiu*. Calls with a husky *chew-chew-chew* and a *cher-cher-cher-cher*, also a spluttering *trrrip*. HABITAT: Bamboo thickets. DISTRIBUTION: Resident from C to E Himalayas.

7 BLACK-THROATED PARROTBILL *Suthora nipalensis* 10cm FIELD NOTES: Generally acrobatic, active forager in small to large flocks. *S. n. poliotis* (7b) occurs in E Himalayas south to Manipur; *S. n. humii* (7c) is found from E Nepal to E Bhutan. VOICE: A wheezy, nasal *chu-irrr-diii-dirrr* or similar; contact calls are a soft *tu*, *ti*, *tit* or *tip*, which when given by flocks make up a constant twittering. HABITAT: Forest undergrowth, bamboo jungle with tangled undergrowth. DISTRIBUTION: Resident in the Himalayas and the hills of the NE.

8 LESSER RUFOUS-HEADED PARROTBILL (PALE-BILLED PARROTBILL) *Chleuasicus atrosuperciliaris* 15cm FIELD NOTES: Acrobatic forager, regularly in small parties or in larger mixed-species groups that often include Greater Rufous-headed Parrotbill and White-hooded Babbler. VOICE: A chirping *tik-tik-tik-tik-tik-tik*. Flocks give a chattering interspersed with harsh metallic notes. HABITAT: Bamboo, forest edge and forest undergrowth. DISTRIBUTION: Resident in E Himalayas and the NE hills.

9 GREY-HEADED PARROTBILL *Psittiparus gularis* 21cm FIELD NOTES: Forages from treetops down to undergrowth and occasionally on the ground. VOICE: A shrill *eu-chu-chu* or *eu-chu-chu-chu* and a high *wi-wuu* or *wi-wuu-wuu-wuu*. Calls include a harsh, slurred *jiew* and a scolding *chit-it-it-it-it-it-it*… HABITAT: Broadleaved evergreen forest, secondary growth, scrub and bamboo. DISTRIBUTION: Resident in E Himalayas and hills of the NE.

10 GREATER RUFOUS-HEADED PARROTBILL *Psittiparus ruficeps* 18cm FIELD NOTES: Clambers acrobatically among small twigs and branches; usually in pairs or small parties and in the company of other species. Race *P. r. bakeri* (not shown) is warmer buff below, and is sometimes considered a separate species. VOICE: A high, slightly descending *he-he-he-hew-hew*. Calls include a rattling *trrrrt trrrrrrrrt trrrrrrrrt* and a twangy *jhew*. HABITAT: Bamboo, forest edge and tall grass. DISTRIBUTION: Resident in E Himalayas and the NE hills.

1 SINGING BUSHLARK *Mirafra cantillans* 13–14cm FIELD NOTES: Forages on the ground, usually singly, in pairs or in small scattered parties. During song-flight, rises to about 30m before hovering over an extensive area, then drops to the ground or bush. VOICE: Various short chirps, whistles and buzzes that end in a buzzing trill; often includes mimicry; may utter a *chirrup* when flushed. HABITAT: Dry bush-covered plains, grassland, fallow cultivation and scrubby semi-desert. DISTRIBUTION: Resident in the foothills and plains in Pakistan, India and Bangladesh.

2 INDIAN BUSHLARK *Mirafra erythroptera* 14cm FIELD NOTES: Forages on the ground; regularly perches on bushes or posts. Sings from perch or song-flight, in the latter fluttering upward for about 10m before parachuting down to a nearby perch. VOICE: Clear whistles, alternating in length and pitch. Calls with drawn-out whistles and rattles. HABITAT: Arid, scrubby and rocky areas. DISTRIBUTION: Resident on the plains and plateaux of Pakistan and India.

3 JERDON'S BUSHLARK *Mirafra affinis* 14cm FIELD NOTES: Habits similar to Indian Bushlark. Sings mainly from a perch, on the ground or in a song-flight similar to that of Indian Bushlark. VOICE: A dry, drawn-out, rattling *zizizizezezezezezezezezezezezeze-zezezezeze*. Calls include a thin rattle and a thin, drawn-out whistle. HABITAT: Fallow fields edged with bushes or trees, scrub-covered rocky ground and scrubby areas of open forest. DISTRIBUTION: Resident in E and S India and Sri Lanka.

4 BENGAL BUSHLARK *Mirafra assamica* 15cm FIELD NOTES: Forages on the ground. Song-flight similar to Indian Bushlark. VOICE: A repeated, monotonous, squeaky disyllabic note. Call is an explosive series of high-pitched notes. HABITAT: Open grassy areas on plains and plateaux. DISTRIBUTION: Resident across much of the N.

5 BAR-TAILED DESERT LARK (BAR-TAILED LARK) *Ammomanes cinctura* 14cm FIELD NOTES: Forages on the ground; post breeding frequently encountered in small flocks. Song often given during undulating display-flight. VOICE: Repeated, thin fluty notes interspersed with a louder *see-oo-lee*. Calls include a harsh *bshee*, a nasal *chup* and a thin *peeyu*. HABITAT: Barren gravelly plains and low stony hills. DISTRIBUTION: Resident in SW Pakistan.

6 DESERT LARK *Ammomanes deserti* 17cm FIELD NOTES: Forages on the ground, generally in pairs or small parties; after breeding often in larger flocks. Song given from the ground or in a hesitating, undulating song-flight. VOICE: A trilled *trreooee*. Calls include a *chu* and a *chee-lu* flight note. HABITAT: Desolate, barren country, stony hill slopes, and fallow fields in desert-canal cultivations. DISTRIBUTION: Resident in Pakistan and NW India.

7 RUFOUS-TAILED LARK *Ammomanes phoenicura* 16cm FIELD NOTES: Forages on the ground; in song-flight, at about 30m, bird circles on deeply flapping wings before making steep, stepped dives to the ground. VOICE: A random *juu juuh tcherre tcherre tcherre...juuh... tchwerrwe...* sometimes mixed with short warbling notes. Call is a subdued *djup*. HABITAT: Dry open areas with sparse vegetation. DISTRIBUTION: NE Pakistan and widespread over much of peninsular India.

8 HOOPOE-LARK (GREATER HOOPOE-LARK) *Alaemon alaudipes* 18–20cm FIELD NOTES: Forages on the ground, runs about like a courser. In flight black and white wing-pattern is striking. VOICE: Characteristic desert sound; given during an acrobatic display-flight; melodious piping notes that start slowly, accelerate during climb, a short trill at peak of ascent, reverting to piping notes, lowering in tone and speed during descent. Call is a buzzing *zee*. HABITAT: Desert and semi-desert with low dunes or clay flats. DISTRIBUTION: Resident in Pakistan and the Rann of Kutch.

145 LARKS

1 BIMACULATED LARK *Melanocorypha bimaculata* 16–18cm FIELD NOTES: Forages on the ground, often in good-sized flocks. In flight shows greyish underwing and a white-tipped tail. VOICE: A harsh *churrup* or *chup*, also a liquid *plip*. HABITAT: Semi-desert, dry-grass areas, fallow fields, lake edges and coastal mudflats. DISTRIBUTION: Winter visitor to the N and NW.

2 TIBETAN LARK *Melanocorypha maxima* 21–22cm FIELD NOTES: Forages on the ground; sings in flight or from the ground. In flight tail shows much white on tips and outer tail feathers, and wing shows a white trailing edge. VOICE: A mix of slow-flowing phrases interspersed with grating notes and mimicry. Calls include low grating notes and loud whistles when disturbed. HABITAT: High-altitude grassy or marshy areas by lakes or rivers. DISTRIBUTION: Resident in Sikkim, breeds or resident in Ladakh.

3 SHORT-TOED LARK (GREATER SHORT-TOED LARK) *Calandrella brachydactyla longipennis* 14–15cm FIELD NOTES: Forages on the ground, runs around in typical zigzag jerky spurts, collects food with a crouched feeding posture; regularly seen in large, restless, wandering flocks. Warmer-toned *C. b. dukhunensis* (3b) occurs mainly in the S and E. VOICE: Calls include a dry *chirrup* or *dreet* and a *trlip*. HABITAT: Open stony grassland, semi-desert, fallow cultivation and dry coastal mudflats. DISTRIBUTION: Widespread winter visitor; *C. b. dukhunensis* probably breeds in Ladakh.

4 ASIAN SHORT-TOED LARK *Calandrella cheleensis persica* 13cm FIELD NOTES: Forages on the ground. Shows a long primary projection. *C. c. leucophaea* (4b) is said to be a vagrant to Pakistan. The taxonomic situation here is very complicated: some authorities regard all forms as races of Lesser Short-toed Lark *C. rufescens*, and others include both races as part of the 'split' Asian Short-toed Lark, or *C. c. leucophaea* as a race of the latter and *C. c. persica* as a race of Lesser Short-toed Lark. VOICE: A dry buzzing *pritt* or *chirrick*. HABITAT: Open sandy semi-desert and stony foothills. DISTRIBUTION: Winter visitor to the NW.

5 HUME'S SHORT-TOED LARK *Calandrella acutirostris* 14cm FIELD NOTES: Forages on the ground; restless; forms large winter flocks. Song given during wandering display-flight, when bird soars to about 50m, hovers, then dives to the ground. VOICE: A series of monotonous, faint, disjointed notes. Calls include a sharp *trree* and a rattled *dreep*. HABITAT: High-altitude semi-desert and rocky hills; winters in fallow cultivation. DISTRIBUTION: Breeds in the Himalayas and S and W Pakistan; winters mainly in N India and S Nepal.

6 SAND LARK *Calandrella raytal* 12cm FIELD NOTES: Forages on the ground; sings in flight or on the ground. During song-flight soars at about 30m, singing and flying aimlessly around with an intermittent series of rapid wing-flaps before parachuting to the ground in a series of steps. Race *C. r. krishnakumarsinhji* (6b) occurs in Gujarat. VOICE: Short with disjointed, dry rattling phrases. Calls include a low *chirr, cherr* or *chirr-de*. HABITAT: Sandy banks and islets of rivers or lakes, banks of tidal creeks and dry tidal mudflats with scanty vegetation. DISTRIBUTION: Resident across much of the N, along the Indus and in S Gujarat.

1

2

3
longipennis

3b
dukhunensis

4
persicus

4b
leucophaea

6b
krishnakumarsinhji

5

6

146 LARKS, SPARROW-LARKS

1 CRESTED LARK *Galerida cristata* 18cm FIELD NOTES: Forages on the ground, although regularly perches on bushes, posts and wires. Song is given mainly during a simple display-flight. Sandy-buff race *G. c. magna* (1b) occurs in NW Pakistan. VOICE: A clear pleasant warble mixed with call notes and mimicry. Calls include a liquid, plaintive *twee-tee-too*, *ti-ee* or *tee-urr*; in flight utters a *too-ee*. HABITAT: Desert, semi-desert, dry cultivated areas, often near villages; also dry coastal mudflats. DISTRIBUTION: Widespread in the N and NW.

2 MALABAR LARK *Galerida malabarica* 16cm FIELD NOTES: Actions similar to Crested Lark. Sings mainly from the ground or low perch, but also in flight. VOICE: A rich mixture of piping and melancholy notes along with some mimicry. Calls include a piping *chew-chew-you*, others similar to those of Crested Lark. HABITAT: Open sparse scrub, forest clearings, grass-covered stony hillsides, cultivations and grassy edges of coastal mudflats. DISTRIBUTION: Resident in W peninsular India.

3 SYKES'S LARK *Galerida deva* 14cm FIELD NOTES: Forages on the ground, usually alone, in pairs or small groups. Song delivered in a soaring, hovering and wandering flight. VOICE: Consists of various harsh and clear notes mixed with mimicry. Calls include high-pitched whistles and short guttural notes. HABITAT: Stony, sparse scrub areas and dry cultivations. DISTRIBUTION: Resident in WC and C India.

4 ORIENTAL SKYLARK *Alauda gulgula* 16cm FIELD NOTES: Forages on the ground. Shorter primary projection and shorter-tailed than Skylark. Sings from a low perch or more often in a very high display-flight, where on quivering wings delivers a beautiful song before dropping, in steps, to the ground. The greyer race *A. g. inconspicua* (4b) occurs in the NW. VOICE: A prolonged mix of warbling, twittering and short whistles. Calls include a buzzy *baz-baz* or *baz-terr* and a *twip*. HABITAT: Grassland, crop fields, grass bordering saltpans and coastal mudflats, also playing fields in urban areas. DISTRIBUTION: Widespread resident and winter visitor.

5 SKYLARK (EURASIAN or COMMON SKYLARK) *Alauda arvensis* 18cm FIELD NOTES: Forages on the ground, often in large flocks. Compared to Oriental Skylark has longer primary projection and longer tail. VOICE: Calls include a liquid *chirrup* and a shorter dry *prrylh* or *preet*. HABITAT: Grasslands and cultivated areas. DISTRIBUTION: Winter visitor to the NW.

6 HORNED LARK *Eremophila alpestris longirostris* 18cm FIELD NOTES: Forages on the ground; after breeding forms large flocks. *E. a. albigula* (6b) occurs in the NW. VOICE: A simple rippling trill followed by short warbling phrases mixed with long whistles. Calls include a short *eeh* or *eeh-ti* and a *tur-reep*. HABITAT: Barren stony steppe with scattered grass tufts, grassy pastures and, in winter, also fallow cultivation. DISTRIBUTION: Resident in the Himalayas.

7 ASHY-CROWNED SPARROW-LARK *Eremopterix griseus* 12cm FIELD NOTES: Forages on the ground. In spectacular display-flight, soars to about 30m, sings while hovering in wide circles, then dives toward the ground, pulls up with a few rapid wing-beats; this dive and pull-up may be repeated many times before landing. VOICE: Short fluty notes followed by a drawn-out whistle. HABITAT: Dry open areas with scattered low vegetation. DISTRIBUTION: Widespread resident.

8 BLACK-CROWNED SPARROW-LARK *Eremopterix nigriceps* 13cm FIELD NOTES: Forages on the ground. Sings from a low perch or during a low, drifting, wing-fluttering display-flight. VOICE: A repeated *wit-ti-weee* or similar. Calls include a *tchip* and a *zree* when alarmed. HABITAT: Sandy deserts. DISTRIBUTION: Resident in E Pakistan and NW India.

1b
magna

1

2

4b
inconspicua

3

4

5

6

♀

♂

6b *albigula*   ♂

7

♀

♂

8

♀

♂

147 FLOWERPECKERS

1 THICK-BILLED FLOWERPECKER *Dicaeum agile* 10cm FIELD NOTES: Restless, habitually twitches tail from side to side. Attracted to flowering or fruiting trees and shrubs, especially if infested with mistletoes. VOICE: 6–8 notes of differing pitches mixed with dry trills. Calls include a sharp *chik-chik-chik-chik*, a rattling *titititili* and a high-pitched *chit-chit*. HABITAT: Dry or moist deciduous or evergreen forest, orchards, groves and gardens. DISTRIBUTION: Widespread resident, apart from the NW.

2 YELLOW-VENTED FLOWERPECKER *Dicaeum chrysorrheum* 10cm FIELD NOTES: Active forager at all levels of vegetation; attracted to mistletoes and small figs. VOICE: Calls include a *zeet*, a repeated *chip-a-chip-tree* and a *zit-zit-zit*; also utters various soft squeaks. HABITAT: Open jungle, forest edge and orchards. DISTRIBUTION: Resident in E Himalayas and the hills of the NE.

3 YELLOW-BELLIED FLOWERPECKER *Dicaeum melanoxanthum* 12–13cm FIELD NOTES: Elusive, often sits upright; noted making fly-catching sallies from dead branches. VOICE: A harsh, agitated *zit-zit-zit-zit*. HABITAT: Tall trees in open forests and clearings in dense forest. DISTRIBUTION: Resident in the Himalayas and the NE hills.

4 LEGGE'S FLOWERPECKER (WHITE-THROATED FLOWERPECKER) *Dicaeum vincens* 10cm FIELD NOTES: Acrobatic forager, mainly in treetops. VOICE: Song said to consist of very high-pitched notes alternating in pitch. Calls include a *tchip tchip-twee-see*, a high *tee-too* and a *wheep-wheep-wheep*. HABITAT: Tall trees and creepers in rainforest, dry forest, plantations and occasionally gardens. DISTRIBUTION: Resident in Sri Lanka.

5 ORANGE-BELLIED FLOWERPECKER *Dicaeum trigonostigma* 9cm FIELD NOTES: Forages mainly in the tops of trees, favours flowering or fruiting trees. VOICE: A high-pitched *psee-psee-psee-psee-psee ptit-ptit-ptit-ptit-ptit tsi-si-si-si sew*. Calls include a continuous shrill *chirp*, a drawn-out *zeeee* and twittering and wheezy notes. HABITAT: Glades and edges of evergreen forests, also mangroves. DISTRIBUTION: Resident in SW and SE Bangladesh; may occur in NE India.

6 PALE-BILLED FLOWERPECKER *Dicaeum erythrorhynchos* 8cm FIELD NOTES: Restless, usually keeps to the tops of trees; attracted to mistletoe fruits. VOICE: A series of twittering notes or a reel. Calls include a repeated high-pitched *pit* and a sharp *chik-chik-chik*. HABITAT: Deciduous forest, plantations, groves, orchards and sometimes mangroves. DISTRIBUTION: Widespread resident, apart from most of the NW and NE.

7 PLAIN FLOWERPECKER *Dicaeum concolor* 8–9cm FIELD NOTES: Active agile forager, especially attracted to mistletoes. *D. c. olivaceum* (7b) occurs in the Himalayan foothills and the NE hills; *D. c. virescens* (7c) is the only flowerpecker on the Andamans; these latter two races are often given full species status. VOICE: A high-pitched trill; in SW India utters a short trilled *tse-e-e-ep*. Calls include twitterings and a *tik-tik-tik*. HABITAT: Broadleaved forests, forest edges and well-wooded areas. DISTRIBUTION: Resident in the W Ghats, foothills of the C and E Himalayas, the NE hills and the Andamans.

8 FIRE-BREASTED FLOWERPECKER *Dicaeum ignipectus* 9cm FIELD NOTES: Restless, agile forager, mainly in treetops; attracted to mistletoes. VOICE: A high-pitched *titty-titty-titty* or *see-bit see-bit see-bit see-bit*. Calls include a buzzing *zeeep*, a metallic *chip* and a rattling trill. HABITAT: Montane and hill forests. DISTRIBUTION: Resident in the Himalayas and the NE hills.

9 SCARLET-BACKED FLOWERPECKER *Dicaeum cruentatum* 9cm FIELD NOTES: Usually forages in the tops of trees among clumps of mistletoes. VOICE: Song includes a rising and falling *see-sip-see-sip-see-sip* and a ringing *chipi-chipi-chipi dzee-dzee-dzee*. Calls include various twitterings, a *chip-chip*, a clicking *tchik-tchik-tchik* and a high-pitched *chizee*. HABITAT: Open forests, forest edge, secondary forest and mangroves. DISTRIBUTION: Resident in E Himalayan foothills and the NE hills.

7b
olivaceum

7c
virescens

148 SUNBIRDS

1 RUBY-CHEEKED SUNBIRD *Chalcoparia singalensis* 11cm FIELD NOTES: Active forager around bushes and trees; post breeding sometimes forms small parties. Juvenile entirely yellow below. VOICE: A trilling *tirr-titi trirr tir tir*; flight calls are a chirping *seet-seet* or *tear-tear*. HABITAT: Open forest, forest edge, scrub jungle and mangroves. DISTRIBUTION: Resident in the C and E Himalayan foothills and the NE.

2 PURPLE-RUMPED SUNBIRD *Leptocoma zeylonica* 10cm FIELD NOTES: Active, acrobatic forager among flowers and foliage. Juvenile similar to female, but underparts entirely yellow. VOICE: A sharp, twittering *tityou tityou tityou trr-r-r-tit tityou...* a weak *sisiswee-sisiswee...* or a *sit-sit tseet-tseet-tseet tsut-tsut-tsut-tsut*. Calls include a constant *sweety-swee sweety-sweety-swee* and a high, metallic *tzip*. HABITAT: Open jungle, secondary jungle, cultivations and gardens. DISTRIBUTION: Widespread resident in Sri Lanka, C and S India and Bangladesh.

3 CRIMSON-BACKED SUNBIRD *Leptocoma minima* 8cm FIELD NOTES: Active, acrobatic forager among flowers and foliage; favours the blossoms of *Erythrina* and *Loranthus*. VOICE: A squeaky, repeated *see-see-whi-see-see-siwee....* or a tinkling *tseet-tsut-tseet*. Calls include a constant *chik*, a metallic ticking and a chittering. HABITAT: Evergreen forest, plantation shade trees, secondary growth and gardens. DISTRIBUTION: Resident in the hills of W India.

4 PURPLE-THROATED SUNBIRD *Leptocoma sperata* 10cm FIELD NOTES: Usually forages in treetops, active and agile; hovers to take insects or water from foliage. VOICE: A *psweet psweet psweet psweet psweet psweet ... psit-it pstit psweet psweet....* Calls include a weak *chip chip*, a sharp *si-si-si*, an up-slurred *psweeet*, a *fut-chit* and short, high trills. HABITAT: Forests and gardens. DISTRIBUTION: Resident in the plains of the NE.

5 OLIVE-BACKED SUNBIRD *Cinnyris jugularis* 11cm FIELD NOTES: Active, hovers to take insects and spiders; also takes nectar and small fruits. C. j. *klossi* (5b) has a blue forehead and is found on the Nicobars, apart from Car Nicobar, Katchal and Kondol. C. j. *proselius* (5c) occurs on Car Nicobar; it is like the latter but is smaller with a shorter bill. VOICE: A feeble twittering. Calls include a short *chup-chup-chup* or *trik-trik-trik*, usually uttered in flight, and a persistent *sweep*, given by the female. HABITAT: Forest, scrub and mangroves. DISTRIBUTION: Resident on the Andamans, the Nicobars and possibly SE Bangladesh.

6 PURPLE SUNBIRD *Cinnyris asiaticus* 10cm FIELD NOTES: Active, agile forager; very attracted to flowering trees and shrubs. Tends to sing from a high exposed perch. VOICE: An excited *cheewit-cheewit...cheewit-cheewit...cheewit-cheewit...cheewit-cheewit...* Calls include a *chip*, a *chweet*, a *sweep*, a hard *zik* and a crackling alarm note. HABITAT: Deciduous forests, thorn-scrub, cultivations and gardens. DISTRIBUTION: Widespread resident.

7 LOTEN'S SUNBIRD *Cinnyris lotenius* 13cm FIELD NOTES: Agile, active forager after insects, spiders and nectar. Juvenile male is much like adult female but with the addition of a blackish patch from throat to upper breast. VOICE: A quickly repeated *cheewit-cheewit-cheewit*, or *ti-ti-ti twink-it-twink*; also gives a *twink-it-tee*; in Sri Lanka utters a *titti-titu-weechi weechi weechi*. Calls include a metallic *chit-chit*, a clipped *twink-tuwink*, *cheerit* and a *chee-chee-teer*. HABITAT: Deciduous woodland, open country with trees, cultivations, tea plantations and gardens. DISTRIBUTION: Resident in Sri Lanka and W and S Peninsular India.

149 SUNBIRDS, SPIDERHUNTERS

1 BLACK-THROATED SUNBIRD *Aethopyga saturata* 10cm (male with tail 14–15cm)
FIELD NOTES: Active, agile forager from treetops to undergrowth; especially attracted to
flowering trees and shrubs. VOICE: Twittering, containing sharp, high-pitched notes mixed
with rapid metallic trills. Calls include a repeated high-pitched *tit tit-tit* or *ttiss-it* and a *tu-ti-
tee-tee*. HABITAT: Dense scrub and bushes in forests, secondary growth and open areas with
scattered bushes. DISTRIBUTION: Resident in the Himalayas and the NE.

2 GREEN-TAILED SUNBIRD *Aethopyga nipalensis* 10cm (male with tail 14–15cm)
FIELD NOTES: Typical active agile forager. During the winter, in Nepal, regularly seen in
the company of Fire-tailed Sunbird, Black-throated Sunbird and Crimson Sunbird feeding
among flowering trees and shrubs. Race in Mizoram *A. n. victoriae* (not shown) lacks maroon
on upper mantle. VOICE: A lively, twittering *swit-it-it-it-it-it-it* mixed with high notes and a
dry metallic trill. Calls include a sharp *dzii* or *reet*, a regularly repeated *tee-tzree-tzweeeet* and
a series of staccato *stip* notes. HABITAT: Forests, woodland, scrub jungle, secondary growth,
orchards and gardens. DISTRIBUTION: Resident in the Himalayas and the NE.

3 MRS GOULD'S SUNBIRD *Aethopyga gouldiae* 10cm (male with tail 14–15cm) FIELD
NOTES: Restless, agile forager, attracted to flowers of rhododendrons and *Loranthus*. Scarlet-
breasted race *A. g. dabryii* (3b) occurs in the extreme NE. VOICE: Described as a strong
seesawing sound. Calls include a *tzit-tzit*, a *squeeeee* that rises in the middle and a *tshi-stshi-ti-
ti-ti* given when alarmed. HABITAT: Forests and scrub jungle. DISTRIBUTION: Resident in the
Himalayas and the NE hills.

4 CRIMSON SUNBIRD *Aethopyga siparaja* 10cm (male with tail 12–14cm) FIELD
NOTES: Acrobatic forager among the blossoms of trees and shrubs. *A. s. nicobarica* (4b),
from the Nicobars, has forehead and tail purple and lacks elongated central tail feathers.
VOICE: A loud chirping trill. Calls include a *zit-zit* and a soft *siesiep-siepsiep*. HABITAT: Dense
evergreen forest, pine forest, open deciduous and scrub jungle, orchards and gardens.
DISTRIBUTION: Resident in the Himalayas and the NE.

5 VIGORS'S SUNBIRD *Aethopyga vigorsii* 11cm (male with tail 14–15cm) FIELD NOTES:
Active agile forager after nectar or small insects. VOICE: A sharp, harsh *chi-wee* and a *shwing*.
HABITAT: Evergreen and moist deciduous forest. DISTRIBUTION: Resident in the W Ghats.

6 FIRE-TAILED SUNBIRD *Aethopyga ignicauda* 10cm (male with tail 15–20cm) FIELD
NOTES: Very active around flowering bushes. VOICE: A series of descending high-pitched
notes. Calls include a repeated, high-pitched *dzdzi-dzidzidzidzi* and a rapid staccato twittering.
HABITAT: Open coniferous forest with rhododendron understorey; also in juniper scrub above
the tree line. DISTRIBUTION: Resident in the Himalayas and the hills of the NE.

7 LITTLE SPIDERHUNTER *Arachnothera longirostra* 16cm FIELD NOTES: Restless,
acrobatic forager, attracted to banana blossoms. VOICE: A monotonous metallic *which-which*,
given twice per second for about two minutes. Calls include a harsh *cheep*, *chee-chee-chee* or a
loud *sheep*, the latter repeated up to 25 times. HABITAT: Dense forest, forest edge and glades,
wild and cultivated banana patches. DISTRIBUTION: Resident in the NE and in SW India.

8 STREAKED SPIDERHUNTER *Arachnothera magna* 19cm FIELD NOTES: Noisy agile
forager from treetops to low levels. VOICE: Begins with a soft *vijvitte vij* that accelerates then
becomes rapid and monotonous. Calls include a chirruping *chiriririk* or *chirik chirik*; in flight
utters a loud musical trill. HABITAT: Dense evergreen forest, abandoned cultivations where
wild banana and plantain trees grow, gardens with flowering shrubs. DISTRIBUTION: Resident
in the Himalayas and the NE.

150 SPARROWS, PETRONIA

1 HOUSE SPARROW *Passer domesticus* 15cm FIELD NOTES: A common companion in and around urban areas; in winter occurs in large flocks that regularly forage away from urban areas. VOICE: An excited series of mostly call notes, *chirrup-chirrup-cheep-chirp-chirrup...* etc. Calls include a *chirrup*, *chirp* and *chissick*, also a soft *swee-swee* and a rolling *chur-r-r-it-it* given when alarmed. HABITAT: Urban areas, including towns and cities; post breeding also in cultivations and scrub jungle. DISTRIBUTION: Widespread resident.

2 RUSSET SPARROW *Passer rutilans* 14–15cm FIELD NOTES: Actions similar to House Sparrow. VOICE: A frequently repeated *cheep-chirrup-cheweep* or *chwe-cha-cha*. Calls include a *cheep* or *chilp*, also a *swee-swee* and a rapid *chit-chit-chit* given when alarmed. HABITAT: Mountain or upland forests, scrub near cultivation and villages; in winter also in grassland and fields. DISTRIBUTION: Resident in the Himalayas and the NE hills.

3 SIND SPARROW (SIND JUNGLE SPARROW) *Passer pyrrhonotus* 13cm FIELD NOTES: Sociable, usually in flocks of 20 or so, occasionally in the company of House Sparrow flocks. VOICE: House Sparrow-like, but softer with warbling twitters and a high wagtail-like note. Calls are also House Sparrow-like but softer and less strident. HABITAT: Bushes and trees alongside rivers and swamps. DISTRIBUTION: Resident in Pakistan and NW India.

4 TREE SPARROW (EURASIAN TREE SPARROW) *Passer montanus* 14cm FIELD NOTES: Black cheek spot. Usually in pairs; in winter forms larger flocks. VOICE: Song consists of a series of call notes interspersed with *tsooit*, *tsveet* or *tswee-ip* notes. Calls include a high *chip*, a sharp *tet* and a dry *tet-tet-tet* given in flight. HABITAT: Cultivations and around habitations. DISTRIBUTION: Resident in the Himalayas, W Pakistan, the NE and the E Ghats.

5 SPANISH SPARROW *Passer hispaniolensis* 15cm FIELD NOTES: Usually in very large flocks and often in the company of House Sparrows. VOICE: Similar to House Sparrow but more rhythmic. Calls include a *chweeng chweeng*, a squeaky *cheela-cheela*, a *chirrup* and a *chee-chee-chee*; all calls are higher and more metallic than those of House Sparrow. HABITAT: Cultivated areas, semi-desert, marshes and reed-beds. DISTRIBUTION: Winter visitor mainly to the NW.

6 DEAD SEA SPARROW *Passer moabiticus* 12cm FIELD NOTES: Forages on the ground or among foliage of bushes; usually in small flocks. VOICE: A rhythmic, high-pitched *tweeng-tweeng-tweeng* or *chilung-chilung-chilung*. Calls include a high *trrirp*, a *chet-chet-chet-chet* and the usual sparrow chirps, churrs and rattles. HABITAT: Tamarisks and other bushes near water. DISTRIBUTION: Winter visitor to SW Pakistan.

7 ROCK SPARROW *Petronia petronia* 14cm FIELD NOTES: Shy and wary; usually encountered in small flocks. In flight tail shows white subterminal spots. VOICE: Calls quite similar to those of the House Sparrow with some added metallic notes; in flight utters a *sup* or *doui*. HABITAT: Rocky or stony areas in mountains, also stubble fields. DISTRIBUTION: Winter visitor to the NW.

8 CHESTNUT-SHOULDERED PETRONIA (YELLOW-THROATED SPARROW) *Gymnoris xanthocollis* 14cm FIELD NOTES: Forages mostly on the ground; in winter forms large flocks, often in the company of House Sparrows and Black-headed Buntings. VOICE: A constantly repeated, rhythmic *chilp chalp cholp*. Calls include a *chilp*, a *chirrup* and harsh churring notes. HABITAT: Open country and low hills with trees, scrub jungle, groves and trees near cultivations and villages. DISTRIBUTION: Widespread over most of the region.

151 SNOWFINCHES, WEAVERS

1 ADAMS'S SNOWFINCH (TIBETAN SNOWFINCH) *Montifringilla adamsi* 17cm
FIELD NOTES: Forages on the ground, walks and runs in a lark-like fashion; in flight shows
much white on secondaries, secondary-coverts and sides of tail. Juvenile lacks the black bib.
VOICE: Song consists of a single note repeated monotonously. Call includes a sharp *pink-pink*
and a soft mewing; flocks utter a constant twittering. HABITAT: High stony plateaux, cliffs
and rocky slopes, cultivated fields near villages. DISTRIBUTION: Resident in the N Himalayas.

2 WHITE-RUMPED SNOWFINCH (MANDELLI'S SNOWFINCH) *Onychostruthus
taczanowskii* 17cm FIELD NOTES: Forages on the ground; often occurs in large winter
flocks. VOICE: A short, loud *duid-ai-duid duid-duid-ai*. Call is a sharp, resounding *duid duid*.
HABITAT: High stony plateaux. Regularly found around pika colonies; uses the burrows to
roost, breed and shelter. DISTRIBUTION: Resident in the Himalayas.

3 PÈRE DAVID'S SNOWFINCH (SMALL SNOWFINCH) *Pyrgilauda davidiana* 15cm
FIELD NOTES: Regularly flicks wings while perched atop a low stone or earth mound. Usually
occurs in large flocks post breeding. Juveniles lack the black head markings. VOICE: Flocks
utter a constant twittering. HABITAT: Stony mountains and semi-desert with sparse grass;
usually occurs among colonies of small burrowing animals. DISTRIBUTION: Vagrant: a
disputed record from N Sikkim.

4 RUFOUS-NECKED SNOWFINCH *Pyrgilauda ruficollis* 15cm FIELD NOTES: Forages
on the ground; during winter encountered in small flocks, often in the company of other
snowfinches. Juveniles lack the black facial markings. VOICE: Calls include a soft *duuid*
or *doooid* and a magpie-like chattering. HABITAT: High, barren, stony steppe and grassy
plateaux. DISTRIBUTION: Resident in the Himalayas.

5 BLANDFORD'S SNOWFINCH *Pyrgilauda blanfordi* 15cm FIELD NOTES: Runs around,
mouse-like, while foraging on the ground. In winter occurs in flocks, often in the company
of finches, sparrows and other snowfinch species. Juveniles lack the black head markings.
VOICE: A constant twittering. HABITAT: Dry, stony steppe and hillsides with stunted grass.
DISTRIBUTION: Resident in the Himalayas.

6 STREAKED WEAVER *Ploceus manyar* 14cm FIELD NOTES: Gregarious. Forages and
roosts in flocks, breeds in small scattered colonies. VOICE: A trill of high-pitched whistles
that ends with a wheezy note. Calls include a *re tre cherrer cherrer*, usually given by displaying
males, and a *chirt-chirt* given in flight. HABITAT: Reed-beds, reed swamps, tall grass and
seasonally flooded areas. DISTRIBUTION: Widespread local resident.

7 BLACK-BREASTED WEAVER *Ploceus benghalensis* 14cm FIELD NOTES: Variable face
pattern; intermediates occur with black ear-coverts and a white throat. Gregarious, often in the
company of other weavers, waxbills and starlings. VOICE: A soft series of sibilant notes ending
with a low buzzing; in flight utters a quiet *chit-chit*. HABITAT: Tall grass or reedy areas near water.
DISTRIBUTION: Resident, mainly in NE and SE Pakistan and across much of N India.

8 BAYA WEAVER *Ploceus philippinus* 15cm FIELD NOTES: Highly gregarious. Roosts
and forages in large flocks, often in the company of other weavers, waxbills, sparrows
and starlings. *P. p. burmanicus* (8b) occurs in the NE. VOICE: A chittering followed by a
wheezy whistle, a buzz and some chirps. HABITAT: Generally open areas with nearby water,
including grassland scrub with scattered trees, paddyfields, cultivated areas and mangroves.
DISTRIBUTION: Widespread resident.

9 FINN'S WEAVER *Ploceus megarhynchus* 17cm FIELD NOTES: Gregarious, often in
the company of other weavers. *P. m. salimalii* (9b) occurs in NE India. VOICE: A loud,
harsh chatter ending with a wheezy note; flight call is a *twit-twit*. HABITAT: Grassland with
scattered trees, paddyfields, tall grass and sugarcane. DISTRIBUTION: Resident in N and NE
India and SW Nepal.

1 DIPPER (WHITE-THROATED DIPPER) *Cinclus cinclus* 18–20cm FIELD NOTES: Swims and walks underwater, feeding on stream or river bottoms. Bobs whole body while perched. Juvenile grey above with pale scaling and mottling; grey below, scalloped and mottled darker; throat white. *C. c. leucogaster* (1b) has occurred in Gilgit. VOICE: A sustained rippling warble. Calls include a loud rasping *zink* or *zrets*. HABITAT: Fast-flowing mountain streams. DISTRIBUTION: Resident in the Himalayas.

2 BROWN DIPPER *Cinclus pallasii* 20cm FIELD NOTES: Actions similar to Dipper. Juvenile dark brown or dark grey mottled with pale spots. VOICE: Short and rich, more musical than Dipper. Calls include a buzzing *zzit-zzit* or *dzit-dzit*. HABITAT: Mountain streams and small lakes. DISTRIBUTION: Resident in the Himalayas and the NE.

3 FOREST WAGTAIL *Dendronanthus indicus* 16–18cm FIELD NOTES: Runs or walks rapidly; when flushed often flies into tree canopy. Sways tail and rear of body from side to side. VOICE: A repeated, high-pitched, squeaky *zlic-zhee zlic-zhee zlic-zhee....* Call is a hard, shrill *pick* or *pick-pick*. HABITAT: Tracks, clearings and edges of forests, plantations and bamboo jungle. DISTRIBUTION: Winter visitor, mainly to the NE, SW, Sri Lanka and the Andamans.

4 WHITE WAGTAIL *Motacilla alba* 17–18cm FIELD NOTES: Walks with a nodding head while wagging tail up and down. Agile forager, using running, jumping or acrobatic short fluttering flights to capture insects. Main illustration, *M. a. alboides*, breeds in the Himalayas, E from NE Pakistan, more widespread in winter. *M. a. personata* (4b) breeds in the NW and is more widespread in winter; *M. a. dukhunensis* (4c) widespread in winter; *M. a. leucopsis* (4d) winters in N India; *M. a. baicalensis* (4e) widespread in winter; *M. a. ocularis* (4f) uncommon visitor in the N and NE. VOICE: A twittering interspersed with call notes. Calls include a *ts-lee-wee*, *tslee-vit* or similar. HABITAT: Rocky streams, riverbeds and wet fields; winters in open areas near water. DISTRIBUTION: Breeds in the Himalayas; widespread winter visitor.

5 WHITE-BROWED WAGTAIL *Motacilla maderaspatensis* 21–24cm FIELD NOTES: Wags tail up and down. In winter sometimes forms flocks that roost in tamarisks or reeds. VOICE: A very simple *tchi-tchi-tchi-tchUU* or a mixture of harsh, shrill and melodious notes with some drawn-out harsh rolling notes. Calls include a loud *twee* or *tchit* and a metallic *tzweenk*. HABITAT: Embankments of watercourses; also villages and gardens with nearby water. DISTRIBUTION: Widespread resident.

6 CITRINE WAGTAIL *Motacilla citreola* 17–20cm FIELD NOTES: Actions much like White Wagtail, although tail-wagging less pronounced; regularly perches on vegetation, posts and wires. *M. c. calcarata* (6b) breeds in W Pakistan and in the Himalayas. VOICE: Song consists of call notes interspersed with warbling phrases. Calls include a *dzreeip* or *tzreep* and a soft *tslee*, *tselee* or similar. HABITAT: High-altitude wet grassland; winters in freshwater wetlands. DISTRIBUTION: Breeds in W Pakistan and the Himalayas; widespread in winter.

7 GREY WAGTAIL *Motacilla cinerea* 17–20cm FIELD NOTES: Constantly pumps rear body and tail. VOICE: A series of short notes, often with added high *si-si-si-siu* notes. Call is a high-pitched *zit-zit*. HABITAT: Mountain streams; winters by lowland waters. DISTRIBUTION: Breeds in W Pakistan and in the Himalayas.

8 YELLOW WAGTAIL *Motacilla flava* 16–18cm FIELD NOTES: Actions similar to Citrine Wagtail. Various races occur in the region, including *M. f. beema* (main illustration), *M. f. leucocephala* (8b), *M. f. thunbergi* (8c), *M. f. feldegg* (8d), *M. f. melanogrisea* (8e), *M. f. 'superciliaris'* (8f), *M. f. plexa* (8g), *M. f. taivana* (8h), *M. f. lutea* (8i). VOICE: Variable; calls include a loud *pseeu* and a *tsreep*. HABITAT: Damp grassland and pastures. DISTRIBUTION: Widespread winter visitor.

dark morph

1

1b
leucogaster

pale morph

2

3

4b

4d

4c

4e

4f

n-br ♂

♀

br

4 br
alboides

♂

5

6b
calcarata ♂

♀

6

n-br ♂

♂

br ♂

7

8

♀

8h

8g

8b

beema ♂

8e

8c

8d

8f

8i

153 PIPITS

1 RICHARD'S PIPIT *Anthus richardi* 17–20cm FIELD NOTES: Forages on the ground. When agitated often stands very upright with neck stretched. Flight powerful and undulating, with long dips; regularly hovers above grass before landing. VOICE: A harsh *schreep* or longer *sherrreeep*, given as bird rises from the ground; also a short *chup*, a subdued *chirp* and a *r-rump*. HABITAT: Damp grassland, stubble fields and bare hillsides. DISTRIBUTION: Widespread winter visitor.

2 PADDYFIELD PIPIT *Anthus rufulus* 15cm FIELD NOTES: Forages on the ground. Call note is the best way to distinguish from the similar but larger Richard's Pipit. Often stands more upright than shown, especially when alert. VOICE: Similar to Richard's Pipit, but faster and higher-pitched. Calls include a hard *chep* or *chep-chep*, a thin *pipit* and a harsh *chwist*. HABITAT: Open short grassland, paddyfields, stubble fields and cultivations. DISTRIBUTION: Widespread resident.

3 TAWNY PIPIT *Anthus campestris* 16–17cm FIELD NOTES: Forages on the ground, but often perches on bushes, posts or wires. Frequently pumps tail, especially when agitated. Juveniles have dark lores; otherwise can be very similar to Richard's and Paddyfield Pipit. VOICE: Calls include an explosive *chilp*, *chirlip* or *cherleep* and a loud *tseep* or *tseuc* given at take-off. HABITAT: Open, stony country with scattered scrub, semi-desert, fallow fields and pastures. DISTRIBUTION: Winter visitor, mainly to the NW.

4 BLYTH'S PIPIT *Anthus godlewskii* 16cm FIELD NOTES: Actions similar to the slightly larger Richard's Pipit, best distinguished from it by voice. Generally has back more heavily streaked than Paddyfield Pipit. VOICE: Calls include a loud *chup*, *chep* or *chep-chep* and a longer *pshee* or *pshee-chep-chep*. HABITAT: Grasslands, dry paddyfields and edges of cultivations. DISTRIBUTION: Widespread winter visitor, mainly in peninsular India and the NE.

5 LONG-BILLED PIPIT *Anthus similis* 17–20cm FIELD NOTES: Forages on the ground, tends to creep about; when flushed regularly lands on rocks, bushes or trees. Birds from W Pakistan generally slightly paler. VOICE: A series of monotonous, unmusical, well-spaced phrases, such as *tjup-threee-tjup-tjup-threee* or *chreep-shreep-chew-ee*. Calls include a *klup* or *klup-klup* and a loud *che-vlee*. HABITAT: Rocky hillsides with sparse cover; winters on grassy plains, sparsely scrubbed country, fields and sand dunes. DISTRIBUTION: Resident in the hills of Pakistan and India, and in the foothills of the W Himalayas; also in the N plains in winter.

6 UPLAND PIPIT *Anthus sylvanus* 17cm FIELD NOTES: Forages on the ground; when agitated stands upright, often on a rock, and twitches or flicks tail. VOICE: A repeated *seetyu-seetyu* or *tyu-see-tyu-ee*; also a more monotonous *weeeee-tch-weeeeee-tch* or *wichee-wiche-wichee*. Call, infrequently given, is a sparrow-like *chirp*. HABITAT: Steep rocky and grassy slopes with scattered bushes and boulders, abandoned terrace cultivations and open pine forest with abundant grass or clearings. DISTRIBUTION: Resident in the NW and the Himalayas.

7 NILGIRI PIPIT *Anthus nilghiriensis* 17cm FIELD NOTES: Forages on the ground; when disturbed usually flies to settle on the nearest bush or tree. Distinguished from Richard's, Paddyfield and Blyth's Pipit by dark lores and streaked flanks. VOICE: A feeble, hesitant, accelerating *tsip tsip tsip-tsip-sip-sip-sipsipsipsipsip*. Calls include a *dzeep*, a weak *see-see* and a repeated *tzip-tzip-tzip-tzip*. HABITAT: Hilltops and downs covered with short grass. DISTRIBUTION: Resident in the hills of extreme SW India.

1 OLIVE-BACKED PIPIT *Anthus hodgsoni* 14–15cm FIELD NOTES: Forages on the ground; when disturbed flies up to settle in a nearby tree. Eastern Palearctic race *A. h. yunnanensis* (not shown) has less streaking on the upperparts, it occurs as a widespread winter visitor. VOICE: Repeated trilled phrases and dry rattles. Calls include a loud *teaze*, a thin *teez* or *tseep*. HABITAT: Grass- and bracken-covered slopes, rocky ground and clearings in open forests, abandoned cultivation and scrub with isolated trees; in winter also in plantations and groves. DISTRIBUTION: Breeds in the Himalayas, more widespread post breeding.

2 RED-THROATED PIPIT *Anthus cervinus* 14–15cm FIELD NOTES: Forages on the ground, often encountered in small flocks. Red areas on head can be much less intense or lacking altogether. VOICE: Calls include a short *tew* and a longer, high-pitched *pseeeeu*. HABITAT: Marshes, grasslands and stubble fields. DISTRIBUTION: Winter visitor, mainly to the N, the Andamans and the Nicobars.

3 TREE PIPIT *Anthus trivialis* 15cm FIELD NOTES: Forages on the ground, walks with a more deliberate gait than vagrant Meadow Pipit; when disturbed usually flies to settle in a nearby tree. Greyer-backed race *A. t. haringtoni* (not shown) breeds in the NW. VOICE: A rapid *chikchikchik chia-chia-chia-wich-wich-wich... tsee-tsee-tsee-tsee...* the latter usually given as bird descends during display-flight. Calls include a drawn-out *tseep* or *teez* and a high-pitched *seet-seet-seet*. HABITAT: Breeds on grassy slopes with scattered trees or bushes; winters in open forests, groves of large trees, cultivations, open country with scattered trees and stubble fields. DISTRIBUTION: Breeds in the NW Himalayas; widespread winter visitor.

4 ROSY PIPIT *Anthus roseatus* 15–16cm FIELD NOTES: Forages on the ground, usually in pairs; forms small loose flocks post breeding. Song is mainly given during display-flight. VOICE: A monotonous *tree-tree-tree* mixed with some drawn-out notes, given as bird rises, and a *tsuli-tsuli-tsuli...* uttered during descent. Calls include a *tzeep* or *tzeep-tzeep-tzeep*. HABITAT: Breeds on alpine meadows and boulder-strewn grassy slopes; winters on short grassland, marshy areas and paddyfields. DISTRIBUTION: Breeds in the Himalayas; winters in foothills and plains in the N.

5 MEADOW PIPIT *Anthus pratensis* 15cm FIELD NOTES: Forages on the ground, often perches on low wires, fences or bushes when flushed. Overall colour may vary (mainly due to wear) from that shown; can be paler olive-buff above and whiter below. VOICE: Calls include a squeaky *seep* or *seep-seep-seep*, a *chutt* and a *sitt-it*. HABITAT: Grassland, fields, grassy lakesides. DISTRIBUTION: Vagrant, recorded from Pakistan.

6 BUFF-BELLIED PIPIT *Anthus rubescens* 15–17cm FIELD NOTES: Actions like Water Pipit, but gait tends to be quicker and lighter; often in flocks. VOICE: Calls include a high *sipit* or *sip*, a higher *tsweep*, and when flushed a *tsi-tsi-tsi-tsip*. HABITAT: Marshes, damp grassland, irrigated cultivation and wetland edges. DISTRIBUTION: Winter visitor across the N.

7 WATER PIPIT *Anthus spinoletta* 15–17cm FIELD NOTES: Forages on the ground, tends to be wary; usually encountered singly or in pairs, sometimes in small loose flocks. VOICE: Calls include a *pheet*, *tslp*, *wisst*, *tsi*, *tsiip*, *dzip*, *tsupi* or *chui*. HABITAT: Damp grassland, marshes, irrigated cultivations, grassy edges of watercourses. DISTRIBUTION: Winter visitor to the NW and N.

155 ACCENTORS

1 ALPINE ACCENTOR *Prunella collaris* 15.5–17cm FIELD NOTES: Forages on the ground, among rocks, stones and vegetation; generally in pairs, post breeding in small parties of up to 20. Song given from a rock or during a short display-flight. Juvenile duller and grey areas browner; dark streaking on underparts. VOICE: A variable warble consisting of low-pitched trills and ripples with fluty whistles, much like a Skylark. Calls include a rolling *chirrup* or *chirrirrip* and a low *chit-chittur*. HABITAT: Rocky mountain slopes with sparse vegetation; often descends in winter, when regularly occurs around upland villages. DISTRIBUTION: Resident in the Himalayas.

2 ALTAI ACCENTOR *Prunella himalayana* 15cm FIELD NOTES: Forages on the ground; gregarious, often encountered with other accentors and mountain finches. VOICE: Calls include a finch-like *tee-tee* and a low twitter. HABITAT: Grassy, rocky hillsides and valleys at lower altitudes. DISTRIBUTION: Winter visitor to the Himalayas.

3 ROBIN ACCENTOR *Prunella rubeculoides* 16–17cm FIELD NOTES: Forages on the ground, usually in open grassy areas; occurs in small flocks in winter. Juvenile generally like adult but duller, with dark streaking on underparts and head. VOICE: A sweet and short chirping *si-tsi-si-tsi - tze-e-you*. Call is a metallic trill. HABITAT: Dwarf scrub, sedge tussocks around lakes; in winter frequents stony and rocky ground and around upland villages. DISTRIBUTION: Resident in the Himalayas.

4 RUFOUS-BREASTED ACCENTOR *Prunella strophiata* 15cm FIELD NOTES: Skulking. Wing-twitching makes bird appear nervous as it forages, mouse-like under bushes. Juvenile much like a dull adult, but with more dark streaking below. VOICE: A long, melodious, wren-like warbling and trilling. Call is a fast *tr-r-r* or *trr-r-rit*. HABITAT: Forest and scrub near or above the tree line; in winter occupies scrub jungle and pastures at lower altitudes. DISTRIBUTION: Resident in the Himalayas.

5 RADDE'S ACCENTOR *Prunella ocularis* 15–16cm FIELD NOTES: Forages, with frequent wing-twitching, on the ground among rocks, scrub and low vegetation. In worn plumage may show a band of darkish spots across upper breast. VOICE: A gentle, sweet twittering or trembling. Calls include a slurred *tseer*, a *ti-ti-ti* and a *tseep*. HABITAT: Low scrub in dry rocky mountains; moves to slightly lower areas in winter. DISTRIBUTION: Vagrant, recorded from Pakistan.

6 BROWN ACCENTOR *Prunella fulvescens* 15cm FIELD NOTES: Often forages in the open; in winter frequently seen in small parties and regularly encountered feeding on village refuse or muck heaps. Juvenile generally duller, especially the head pattern; underparts show dark streaking. VOICE: A short low warble with trills. Call is a bunting-like *ziet-ziet-ziet*. HABITAT: Dry, rocky boulder-strewn hillsides with low scrub; in winter often around villages. DISTRIBUTION: Resident in W Himalayas and N Nepal.

7 BLACK-THROATED ACCENTOR *Prunella atrogularis* 15cm FIELD NOTES: Forages on the ground, singly, in pairs or sometimes in small parties. Juvenile duller, especially head pattern; throat white, speckled blackish; rest of underparts with dark streaks. VOICE: Call is a *teeteetee*. HABITAT: Sandy semi-desert near cultivation, damp valleys with dense vegetation, scrub jungle and cultivations. DISTRIBUTION: Winter visitor to W Pakistan and from W to C Himalayas.

8 SIBERIAN ACCENTOR *Prunella montanella* 15cm FIELD NOTES: Forages mainly on the ground, sometimes in bushes. VOICE: Call is a *tsee-ree-see*. HABITAT: Thickets along watercourses. DISTRIBUTION: Vagrant: disputed record from NW India.

9 MAROON-BACKED ACCENTOR *Prunella immaculata* 14–15cm FIELD NOTES: Secretive; forages on the ground under thick vegetation. Juvenile much duller, with dark streaking above and below. VOICE: Call is a weak, high-pitched *zieh-dzit* or *tzip*. HABITAT: Undergrowth in humid conifer and rhododendron forests; winters in secondary forest and forest edges. DISTRIBUTION: Resident in E Himalayas; winter visitor to the C Himalayas.

156 AVADAVATS, SILVERBILL, MUNIAS

1 RED AVADAVAT (RED MUNIA or STRAWBERRY FINCH) *Amandava amandava*
10cm FIELD NOTES: Forages on the ground or on grass-heads, often in small flocks; in winter flocks much bigger and may include other species. Roosts communally in reed-beds or sugarcane fields. VOICE: A weak, high-pitched warble combined with sweet twittering notes. Calls include a thin *teei* or *tsi*, also various chirps and squeaks. HABITAT: Swampy grassland, sugarcane fields, reeds and tall grass near marshes and watercourses, grass and scrub near cultivations; also gardens in the NW. DISTRIBUTION: Widespread resident, absent from much of the NW and the E.

2 GREEN AVADAVAT (GREEN MUNIA) *Amandava formosa* 10cm FIELD NOTES: Forages on the ground, usually near cover; gregarious, generally in small groups, with larger flocks post breeding. VOICE: A prolonged twitter that ends with a loud trill. Calls include a constant *seee* or *swee swee* and some *cheeps* or *chirps*. HABITAT: Tall grassland, sugarcane fields, boulder-strewn scrub jungle and open dry woodland. DISTRIBUTION: Widespread resident in C India.

3 INDIAN SILVERBILL (WHITE-THROATED MUNIA) *Euodice malabarica* 10–11cm FIELD NOTES: Forages on the ground or on grass seedheads; gregarious, breeds and roosts communally. White rump shows in flight. VOICE: A short series of rambling twittering notes. Calls include a *cheep*, a soft *seeip*, a harsh *tchwit* and a trilling *zip-zip*. HABITAT: Dry cultivated country, grassland and light secondary jungle. DISTRIBUTION: Widespread resident, apart from the NW, NE and the Himalayas.

4 WHITE-RUMPED MUNIA *Lonchura striata* 11–12cm FIELD NOTES: Forages on the ground or on seedheads; gregarious, usually in small parties, with larger flocks in winter. Rufous race *L. s. acuticauda* (4b) occurs in the Himalayan foothills and the NE. VOICE: A series of rising and falling twittering notes. Calls include a plaintive *peep* and a twittering *tr-tr-tr*, *prrrrit* or *brrt*. HABITAT: Lightly wooded areas, open dry scrub, forest edge and clearings, cultivations and gardens. DISTRIBUTION: Apart from the NW a widespread resident.

5 BLACK-THROATED MUNIA *Lonchura kelaarti* 12cm FIELD NOTES: Forages on the ground, usually in small groups, with larger flocks in winter. *L. k. jerdoni* (5b) occurs in SW and E India. VOICE: Calls include a high-pitched, nasal *tay* and a *chirp*. HABITAT: Scrub, grassland, forest clearings, plantations and gardens. DISTRIBUTION: Resident on the hills of Sri Lanka, SW and E India.

6 TRICOLOURED MUNIA *Lonchura malacca* 11–12cm FIELD NOTES: Forages on the ground, usually in pairs or small parties; bigger flocks, often mixed with other species, occur after breeding. *L. m. atricapilla* (6b) occurs in the N and NE and is sometimes treated as a separate species (Chestnut Munia). VOICE: Calls include a weak *peekt* or *pee-eet*, a *veet-veet* and a *chirp-chirp-chirp* given in flight. HABITAT: Edges of marshes or swamps, reed-beds, grasslands and cultivation edge. DISTRIBUTION: Resident over most of the region apart from the NW.

7 SCALY-BREASTED MUNIA (SPOTTED MUNIA or SPICE FINCH) *Lonchura punctulata* 10–12cm FIELD NOTES: Forages on the ground or on grass stems, usually in small groups with bigger flocks after breeding. VOICE: Contact calls are a repeated *tit-ti tit-ti* and a *kit-teee kit-teee*. HABITAT: Open country with scrub and trees, bushy hillsides, secondary growth with grass patches, cultivations and gardens. DISTRIBUTION: Widespread resident, apart from parts of C India and the NW.

8 JAVA SPARROW *Lonchura oryzivora* 15cm FIELD NOTES: Forages on the ground and clings to grass stems to feed on seedheads; usually in small flocks. Juvenile generally brownish with a pink-buff face and a dark crown. VOICE: Bell-like trilling and clicking notes ending with a drawn-out whistle. Call is a *tup*, *t'luk* or *tack*. HABITAT: Cultivations, reed-beds and gardens. DISTRIBUTION: Introduced in Sri Lanka, NW and W India.

157 FINCHES

1 CHAFFINCH *Fringilla coelebs* 15cm FIELD NOTES: Forages on the ground and in tree foliage; usually encountered in flocks, often in the company of other finches and buntings. VOICE: Calls include a loud *pink* or *pink-pink*, a loud *whit*, a wheezy *eeese* and a *tsup* flight note. HABITAT: Fields with nearby bushes and trees. DISTRIBUTION: Winter visitor to the N Himalayas and the hills of Pakistan.

2 BRAMBLING *Fringilla montifringilla* 15cm FIELD NOTES: In flight shows white rump. Non-breeding male similar to breeding female, but darker-headed. Forages on the ground, usually in flocks that often include other finches and buntings. VOICE: Calls include a nasal *tsweek* or *zweee* and a *chuk-chuk* flight note. HABITAT: Upland fields and forests. DISTRIBUTION: Winter visitor to the N Himalayas and the hills of Pakistan.

3 CROSSBILL (COMMON or RED CROSSBILL) *Loxia curvirostra* 16–17cm FIELD NOTES: Sociable, usually in small parties; regularly drinks at small pools. Often feeds acrobatically, even upside-down, to extract seeds from pine cones. Commonly sings from the topmost branch of a conifer. Juvenile like female but generally greyer with dark streaks above and below. VOICE: Song consists of a few call notes that run into a *cheeree-cheeree-choop-chip-chip-chip-cheeree* combined with various trills, twitters and more call notes. Call is a *chip-chip* or a quieter *chuk-chuk*, often given in flight. HABITAT: Conifer forests. DISTRIBUTION: Resident in the Himalayas.

4 ORANGE BULLFINCH *Pyrrhula aurantiaca* 14cm FIELD NOTES: Forages mainly on the ground at the base of trees, flying into trees when disturbed; white rump shows well in flight. Usually quiet and unobtrusive, often sitting motionless for long periods in bushes or trees. VOICE: Song consists of a loud *tew* followed by a rapid, repeated metallic *tyatlinka-tlinka*. Call is a soft, clear *tew*. HABITAT: Open fir, birch or mixed forest. DISTRIBUTION: Resident in W Himalayas.

5 BROWN BULLFINCH *Pyrrhula nipalensis* 16–17cm FIELD NOTES: Confiding, usually encountered in pairs or small parties foraging in the tops of trees or bushes. White rump-band during flight, which is fast and direct. VOICE: A hastily repeated mellow *her-dee-a-duuee*. Calls include a mellow *per-lee* and a soft whistling twitter given while feeding. HABITAT: Dense undergrowth or thick forests; favours oak, rhododendron or fir. DISTRIBUTION: Resident in the Himalayas and NE India.

6 RED-HEADED BULLFINCH *Pyrrhula erythrocephala* 17cm FIELD NOTES: Generally seen in pairs or small parties foraging on the ground or low down in bushes; often sits motionless in bushes for long periods. In flight shows prominent white rump. VOICE: A low, mellow *terp-terp-tee*. Call is a soft, plaintive *pew-pew*. HABITAT: Dense cedar, pine or juniper forests; also mixed forests that include fir, birch and rhododendron. DISTRIBUTION: Resident in the Himalayas.

7 GREY-HEADED BULLFINCH (BEAVAN'S BULLFINCH) *Pyrrhula erythaca* 17cm FIELD NOTES: White rump shows well in flight. Forages low down in bushes or on the ground in pairs or small parties; can be approachable or confiding. VOICE: A descending, then rising, mellow whistled warble mixed with some long slurred notes and short creaky notes. Call a slow *soo-ee* or *poo-ee*, frequently repeated or given as a triple whistle. HABITAT: Conifer and rhododendron forests, also willow and buckthorn thickets. DISTRIBUTION: Resident in E Himalayas.

1 RED-FRONTED SERIN *Serinus pusillus* 12cm FIELD NOTES: Forages on the ground, usually in small flocks that often include other finches. Female duller, with less red on forehead. Juvenile as female but with rusty-brown forehead, ear-coverts, throat and upper breast. VOICE: A series of long twittering phrases mixed with trills and wheezy notes. Calls include a rapid, ringing trill, a soft *dueet* and a twittering *bri-ihihihihi.* HABITAT: Rocky mountain slopes with grass and scrub, scattered junipers, stands of conifers and low rhododendrons. DISTRIBUTION: Resident in E to C Himalayas and the mountains of W Pakistan.

2 TIBETAN SERIN (TIBETAN SISKIN) *Serinus thibetanus* 12cm FIELD NOTES: Usually in small flocks foraging in treetops or on the ground under bushes. VOICE: A soft dry twittering and a twang; in flight utters a short twitters, trills and a *chut-chut-chut.* HABITAT: Hemlock, birch or mixed forest; winters in alders and hemlocks. DISTRIBUTION: Winters in C and E Himalayas; may breed.

3 YELLOW-BREASTED GREENFINCH (HIMALAYAN GREENFINCH) *Carduelis spinoides* 14cm FIELD NOTES: Forages in treetops or bushes, or on the ground; usually in pairs or small family parties, with larger flocks post breeding. VOICE: A *trit-it-it-tt* followed by a rapid trill, then a *trit-it-it-it er chip-chip-chip,* ending with a descending *tew-tew-tew be-e-e-e-ze ouu.* Calls include a twittering followed by harsh *dzwee* and a metallic *swee-tuu.* HABITAT: Open forest, forest edge, scrub, cultivations and gardens. DISTRIBUTION: Resident in the Himalayas and NE India.

4 BLACK-HEADED GREENFINCH (TIBETAN GREENFINCH) *Carduelis ambigua* 14cm FIELD NOTES: Forages in bushes, low vegetation and on the ground; in winter often feeds on fields in large flocks. VOICE: A drawn-out, wheezy *wheeeeeeuu wheeeeeeuu* mixed with metallic notes, high trills and a harsh *scree* or *treeee-tetrah.* Calls include a wheezy *twzyee* and a twittering *titutu titu-titu titritititit,* often interspersed with a harsher *chutut* or *chut-ut-ut.* HABITAT: Open conifer or deciduous forest, forest edge and clearings, open hillsides and scrub. DISTRIBUTION: Resident in extreme NE India, although records disputed.

5 SISKIN (EURASIAN SISKIN) *Carduelis spinus* 12cm FIELD NOTES: Forages acrobatically, mainly in trees; usually encountered in small parties. VOICE: Call is a plaintive *dlu-ee* or *dlee-u,* a dry *tet* or *tet-tet;* in flight utters a *twilit, tirrillili* or *titteree.* HABITAT: Conifer or mixed woods; during winter also in riverside trees, cultivation edge and thickets. DISTRIBUTION: Vagrant, recorded from Nepal and N India.

6 GOLDFINCH (EUROPEAN GOLDFINCH) *Carduelis carduelis caniceps* 13–14cm FIELD NOTES: Feeds on seedheads or on the ground; in winter often seen in small flocks. More colourful race *C. c. frigoris* (6b) is a rare vagrant. Juvenile plain buff-grey, streaked above and below; wing pattern as adult. VOICE: A liquid tinkling. Calls include a ringing *pee-uu* and a harsh *zeez.* HABITAT: Orchards, open conifer forest, scrub above the tree line; winters in lower-altitude foothills, valleys and plains. DISTRIBUTION: Resident and winter visitor, W to C Himalayas and Pakistan hills.

7 TWITE *Carduelis flavirostris* 13cm FIELD NOTES: Forages on the ground in bushes or on seedheads; often in large flocks in winter. *C. f. montanella* (7b) occurs in the extreme W Himalayas. VOICE: A *teet-sweet teedle-eu twee-teedle-ee teedl-eu.* Call is a *ditoo* or *didoo* combined with a twanging *twayeee,* in flight utters a *tweee or chweee.* HABITAT: High-altitude scree and stony hillsides with furze. DISTRIBUTION: Resident in the N Himalayas.

8 LINNET *Carduelis cannabina* 13cm FIELD NOTES: Forages on the ground or on seedheads; often perches on bush tops. White in wing shows well in flight. VOICE: Calls include a rapid *tett-tett-terret* and a soft *hoooi* or *tsooeet.* HABITAT: Upland meadows and open stony slopes. DISTRIBUTION: Winter visitor to the NW.

1

2 ♂

3 ♀

4 ♀ ♀

3 ♂

♂

5 ♂ ♀

6

6b
frigoris

7b
montanella

8

♀

♂

♂ n-br   7   ♂ br

159 FINCHES

1 SILLEM'S MOUNTAIN FINCH *Leucosticte sillemi* 15–17cm FIELD NOTES: Rump and outer tail feathers pale buff-white. Actions probably much as other mountain finches. VOICE: Unknown. HABITAT: High, barren plateaux. DISTRIBUTION: May be resident in the NW Himalayas.

2 BRANDT'S MOUNTAIN FINCH *Leucosticte brandti* 16–19cm FIELD NOTES: Forages on the ground, often at the edge of snow-melt or lakesides, readily perches on rocks and bushes; usually encountered in pairs or small parties, with much larger, compact flocks in winter, which wheel, circle, plunge and rise around cliffs. Nominate is a straggler to the extreme NW; *L. b. haematopygia* (2b) is resident in the Himalayas. VOICE: A short trill. Calls include a loud *twit-twitt*, *twee-ti-ti* or *peek-peek* and a harsh *churr*. HABITAT: High-altitude cliffs and crags, barren stony mountaintops. DISTRIBUTION: Resident in the Himalayas.

3 PLAIN MOUNTAIN FINCH *Leucosticte nemoricola* 15cm FIELD NOTES: Forages on the ground, flying into nearby treetops when disturbed; gregarious at all times, often flies in large wheeling, twisting flocks. VOICE: A sharp twittering *rick-pi-vitt* or *dui-dip-dip-dip* interspersed with twittering trills and sweet warbling notes. Calls include a soft twittering *chi-chi-chi-chi* and double-noted shrill whistle. HABITAT: Mountains, hillsides and alpine meadows; descends in winter to terraced fields, open forested slopes and cultivations. DISTRIBUTION: Resident in the Himalayas.

4 CRIMSON-WINGED FINCH (EURASIAN CRIMSON-WINGED FINCH)
Rhodopechys sanguineus 16cm FIELD NOTES: Forages mainly on the ground. In flight shows much pink on wings and rump. VOICE: Calls include a soft, musical *wee-tll-ee* or *wee-tell-er* and a harsh *chilip* that is often uttered in flight; other flight notes are a fluty *dy-lit-dy-lit* and a soft *chee-up*. HABITAT: Bare mountain slopes, boulder fields, cliffs and gorges with or without sparse scrub. DISTRIBUTION: Vagrant, recorded from Chitral in N Pakistan.

5 TRUMPETER FINCH *Bucanetes githagineus* 15cm FIELD NOTES: Gregarious at all times, with larger flocks in winter; forages on the ground, often visits small pools to drink. VOICE: A distinctive drawn-out, nasal, buzzing *cheeeeeu* interspersed with twittering, clicks and whistles. Calls include an abrupt *chee* or *chit* and a soft *weechp* or *dzit* given in flight. HABITAT: Desert or semi-desert areas, including stony plains and rocky hills. DISTRIBUTION: Resident in Pakistan, winter visitor to NW India.

6 MONGOLIAN FINCH *Eremopsaltria mongolica* 15cm FIELD NOTES: Forages on the ground, alone or in pairs or small parties; forms larger locks in winter; regularly makes evening or morning flights to drink at desert springs. VOICE: A slow *do-mi-sol-mi* or *towit-too whit-tu-tu-churrrh*. Calls include a soft *djou-voud* or *djouddjou*; feeding flocks keep up a constant twittering. HABITAT: Arid or semi-arid mountain areas, with crags, ravines and rocky slopes with low vegetation and scattered low bushes. DISTRIBUTION: Resident in the extreme NW; winter visitor to W Pakistan and Nepal.

7 DESERT FINCH *Rhodospiza obsoleta* 15cm FIELD NOTES: Forages on the ground, but regularly perches on bushes, trees and wires. Generally in pairs, with small flocks formed post breeding. VOICE: A repetitive jumble of twittering call notes, harsh trills and rolls. Calls include a soft purring, a harsh *turr* and in flight a sharp *shreep*. HABITAT: Dry plains with scattered trees and bushes. DISTRIBUTION: Resident in W Pakistan.

8 SPECTACLED FINCH *Callacanthis burtoni* 17cm FIELD NOTES: Forages on the forest floor or under bushes, retreats to sit in trees when disturbed; generally in pairs or small parties. VOICE: A loud trilling *il-til-til....* also a monotonous, repeated single note. Calls include a clear *tew-tew*, a loud *pwee* or *chew-we*, often followed by a *pweeu*, *pweuweu* or *chipeweu*; also utters a light *chip* and when alarmed a rising *uh-eh* or *twee-yeh*. HABITAT: Open mixed forest. DISTRIBUTION: Resident in the Himalayas.

2b *haematopygia*

160 ROSEFINCHES

1 BLANFORD'S ROSEFINCH (CRIMSON ROSEFINCH) *Carpodacus rubescens* 15cm FIELD NOTES: Little known. Sings from top of tree; forages on the ground, generally in pairs, with larger parties in winter. VOICE: A loud musical warbling that rises and falls in pitch, the last note down-slurred. Calls include a high, thin *sip* and a series of short rising and falling *pitch-ew*, *pitch-it*, *chit-it*, *chit-ew* notes which are also given individually. HABITAT: Open areas in coniferous or mixed conifer and birch forest. DISTRIBUTION: Resident in the C and E Himalayas.

2 DARK-BREASTED ROSEFINCH (DARK or NEPAL ROSEFINCH) *Carpodacus nipalensis* 15–16cm FIELD NOTES: Shy; feeds on the ground or in or under bushes, in pairs or small parties; often occurs in large, single-sex flocks mixed with other rosefinches. VOICE: A monotonous chirping. Calls include a plaintive, wailed double whistle, a twittering and a *cha-a-rr* alarm note. HABITAT: Mixed forests of oak, conifer and rhododendrons, also scrub, low bushes and weedy areas above the tree line; in winter also in forest edge and clearings. DISTRIBUTION: Resident in the Himalayas.

3 COMMON ROSEFINCH (SCARLET ROSEFINCH) *Carpodacus erythrinus* 15cm FIELD NOTES: Skulking, forages on the ground or in low vegetation, bushes and trees, generally alone, in pairs or small parties; in winter often in larger flocks mixed with other finches, sparrows or buntings. Nominate is a widespread winter visitor; *C. e. roseatus* (3b) breeds in NW Pakistan and the Himalayas. VOICE: A cheery *twee-twee-tweeou* or *ti-dew-di-dew* or similar. Calls include a rising *ooeet*, *ueet* or *too-ee*, and when alarmed a sharp *chay-eeee*. HABITAT: Streamside willows, rock and scrub, bush-covered slopes and open conifer forest; winters in open wooded country, scrub, bushes and cultivation. DISTRIBUTION: Breeds in the Himalayas and NW Pakistan; widespread winter visitor.

4 BEAUTIFUL ROSEFINCH (HIMALAYAN BEAUTIFUL ROSEFINCH) *Carpodacus pulcherrimus* 15cm FIELD NOTES: In flight shows a pink rump. Forages on the ground or low down in bushes and scrub, usually in pairs or small flocks. VOICE: Calls include a subdued *trip*, *trilp* or *trillip*, a tit-like twitter; in flight utters a harsh *chaaannn*. HABITAT: Steep hillsides with rhododendron and other bushes, near or above the tree line; winters on open scrub-covered hillsides and terraced cultivation with nearby bushes. DISTRIBUTION: Resident in the Himalayas.

5 PINK-BROWED ROSEFINCH *Carpodacus rodochroa* 14–15cm FIELD NOTES: Unobtrusive ground forager, flying up to perch in bushes if disturbed; usually in pairs or small loose flocks. VOICE: A loud, lilting *toowhi toowhi*. Calls include a loud *per-lee* or *chew-wee* and a canary-like *sweet*. HABITAT: Undergrowth in mixed fir and birch forest, willow bushes, rhododendrons and dwarf juniper; in winter also occurs in scrub jungle, open hillsides, grassy slopes and gardens. DISTRIBUTION: Resident in the Himalayas.

6 VINACEOUS ROSEFINCH *Carpodacus vinaceus* 15cm FIELD NOTES: Shows distinct whitish tips to tertials. Forages on the ground, in dense vegetation or in low bushes; usually in pairs or small parties. VOICE: A simple *pee-de - be - do-do*. Calls include a whiplash-like *pwit* or *zieh*, a high *tip* and a low *pink* or *zick*. HABITAT: Moist mixed or bamboo forests and scrubby open hillsides. DISTRIBUTION: Resident in C Himalayas.

7 DARK-RUMPED ROSEFINCH *Carpodacus edwardsii* 16cm FIELD NOTES: Paler-chinned than similar Vinaceous Rosefinch. Skulking, forages on the ground under bushes, usually alone or in small groups; post breeding may occur in larger flocks. VOICE: Calls include a metallic *twink* and a rasping *che-wee*. HABITAT: Breeds in rhododendron and silver fir forest; winters in open rhododendron or birch forest and mountainside bamboo and scrub. DISTRIBUTION: Resident in the C and E Himalayas.

161 ROSEFINCHES

1 THREE-BANDED ROSEFINCH *Carpodacus trifasciatus* 18cm FIELD NOTES: Lethargic, often sits immobile for long periods hidden in bushes or trees. Forages on the ground or in bushes, usually in pairs or small groups. VOICE: Generally silent. HABITAT: Orchards and hedges in cultivated fields. DISTRIBUTION: Vagrant, recorded from Bhutan.

2 SPOT-WINGED ROSEFINCH *Carpodacus rodopeplus* 15cm FIELD NOTES: Generally shy and retiring, although often perches prominently on bush tops; forages on the ground. VOICE: Usually silent, but occasionally gives a *chirp* or an up-slurred *churr-weee*. HABITAT: Rhododendron scrub and bushes on alpine slopes and meadows; descends to bamboo thickets, bushes and mixed forest in winter. DISTRIBUTION: Resident in the C Himalayas.

3 WHITE-BROWED ROSEFINCH (HIMALAYAN WHITE-BROWED ROSEFINCH) *Carpodacus thura* 17cm FIELD NOTES: Forages on the ground, usually in pairs or small parties; sometimes mixes with other rosefinches or grosbeaks. VOICE: Calls include a buzzing *deep-deep deep-de-de-de-de* or a bleating *veh ve ve ve ve ve ve*, a rapid piping *pupupipipipi* and a loud *pwit-pwit*. HABITAT: High-altitude open forest or forest edge, rhododendron, juniper and bamboo scrub above the tree line; winters on open hillsides with bushes and scrub. DISTRIBUTION: Resident in the Himalayas.

4 RED-MANTLED ROSEFINCH *Carpodacus rhodochlamys* 18cm FIELD NOTES: Usually secretive; forages on the ground or low down in bushes, generally in pairs; in winter alone or in small parties. VOICE: A feeble series of short, wheezy *chirp* and *twit* notes interspersed with occasional squeaky whistles. Calls include a plaintive, buzzing *kwee* or *squee* and a sharp *wir*. HABITAT: High-altitude juniper, briar and scrub; winters at lower levels in bushes, thorny scrub, cultivations and gardens. DISTRIBUTION: Resident in W Himalayas and Pakistan mountains.

5 GREAT ROSEFINCH (SPOTTED GREAT ROSEFINCH) *Carpodacus rubicilla* 19–21cm FIELD NOTES: Forages on the ground or in low bushes, wary; generally alone or in pairs; in winter forms small flocks, often in the company of other rosefinches. VOICE: A low *wreep* and a series of low chuckles. Calls include a rasping *jink*, a soft *jeweet* and a short twittering. HABITAT: High-altitude areas with boulders and sparse vegetation; in winter also in hillside scrub and fields. DISTRIBUTION: Resident in the Himalayas.

6 STREAKED ROSEFINCH (EASTERN GREAT ROSEFINCH) *Carpodacus rubicilloides* 19cm FIELD NOTES: Generally shy and retiring. Perches on rocks, bushes and trees, forages on the ground; flicks wings and tail when agitated. There is a record of large numbers (hundreds) roosting in willow groves. VOICE: A slow descending *tsee-tsee-soo-soo-soo*, usually repeated. Calls include a *twink*, *pink* or *sink*, a soft *sip* and a melancholic *dooid-dooid*. HABITAT: High-altitude rocky slopes, scree, plateaux and hillsides with scrub; winters in thickets. DISTRIBUTION: Resident in the N Himalayas.

7 RED-BREASTED ROSEFINCH (RED-FRONTED ROSEFINCH) *Carpodacus puniceus* 20cm FIELD NOTES: Forages on the ground among boulders, bushes or by melting snow, alone, in pairs or small parties. VOICE: A short *twiddle-le-de* with various melodious down-slurred whistles. Calls include a loud, cheery *are-you-quite ready*, a cat-like *maaau* and a *chirp* or *jeelp* uttered in flight. HABITAT: High-altitude boulder fields, rocky screes and slopes. DISTRIBUTION: Resident in the N Himalayas.

8 CRIMSON-BROWED FINCH (RED-HEADED ROSEFINCH) *Propyrrhula subhimachala* 19cm FIELD NOTES: Unobtrusive. Forages on the ground or in bushes and low trees, usually in pairs or small parties. VOICE: A bright variable warble, which may include a *ter-ter-ter* phrase. Call is a sparrow-like *chirp*. HABITAT: Dense, high-altitude scrub; winters in thick undergrowth in forests. DISTRIBUTION: Resident from C to E Himalayas; winter visitor to the NE.

162 FINCHES, GROSBEAKS

1 SCARLET FINCH *Haematospiza sipahi* 18cm FIELD NOTES: Often perches, prominently, on the end of a dead branch; forages in trees, bushes and on the ground, alone, in pairs or in scattered flocks; in winter often seen in single-sex flocks. VOICE: A clear, liquid *par-ree-reeeeee*. Calls include a loud *too-eee* or *pleeau* and a *kwee-i-iu* or *chew-we-auh*. HABITAT: Edges and clearings in montane coniferous forest; in winter also in oak and bamboo forest. DISTRIBUTION: Resident in the Himalayas and NE India.

2 HAWFINCH *Coccothraustes coccothraustes* 17cm FIELD NOTES: Forages in trees or on the ground beneath trees, in small scattered flocks of up to six individuals, occasionally up to 30. VOICE: Calls include an abrupt *tick* or *tzik*, also a thin *seep* or *sreee*. HABITAT: Wooded hills, wild olive forest and orchards. DISTRIBUTION: Winter visitor, mainly to Pakistan.

3 BLACK-AND-YELLOW GROSBEAK *Mycerobas icterioides* 22cm FIELD NOTES: Best located by ringing calls. Forages in treetop foliage, in bushes and on the ground in pairs or loose flocks. Male similar to Collared Grosbeak, but yellow less golden; black thighs. VOICE: A rich, clear *prr-trweeet-a-troweeet* or a *tookiyu tookiyu*. Calls include a high-pitched, whistled *pi-riu pir-riu pir-riu* or *tit-te-tew tit-te-tew* and a short *chuck* or *cluck*. HABITAT: Pine, silver fir and deodar forest, also oak woods and scrub at forest or woodland edge. DISTRIBUTION: Resident in W Himalayas.

4 SPOT-WINGED GROSBEAK *Mycerobas melanozanthos* 22cm FIELD NOTES: Shy. Usually sits and forages in treetops, also feeds low down or on the ground; generally in pairs or flocks of 50 or so individuals. VOICE: A loud, melodious *tew-tew - teeeu*, also some mellow *tyop-tiu* or *tyu-tio* whistles. Call is a rattling *krrr* or *charrarauk*, said to sound like the shaking of a matchbox containing only a few matches; feeding flocks keep up a constant cackling. HABITAT: Mixed conifer and broadleaved forest. DISTRIBUTION: Resident in the Himalayas and NE India.

5 WHITE-WINGED GROSBEAK *Mycerobas carnipes* 22cm FIELD NOTES: Forages mainly in the treetops, also in scrub and undergrowth; generally in pairs or small groups, with bigger flocks in winter. VOICE: A piping *add-a-dit - un-di-di-di-dit* or *dja-dji-dji-dju*. Calls include a nasal *shwenk* or *chwenk*, a strident *wit* or *wet*, a grating *goink* and a rapid, harsh *chet-et-et-et*. HABITAT: Dwarf juniper forest above tree line, mixed juniper and fir near tree line, at lower elevations mixed fir, juniper and rhododendron forest or fir forest with bamboo undergrowth. DISTRIBUTION: Resident in the Himalayas and the mountains of W Pakistan.

6 COLLARED GROSBEAK *Mycerobas affinis* 22cm FIELD NOTES: Forages in tree canopy, in bushes or low vegetation and on the ground, usually in pairs or small loose parties, in larger flocks in winter. Male similar to Black-and-yellow Grosbeak, but yellow more golden, especially on the nape; thighs yellow. VOICE: A loud, clear, piping *ti-di-li-ti-di-li-umm*, also a constantly repeated creaky phrase, interspersed with musical bulbul-like notes. Calls include a rapid, mellow *pip-pip-pip-pip-pip-pip-pip-ugh* and a sharp *kurr* given when alarmed. HABITAT: Oak, rhododendron or mixed conifer and deciduous forest, occasionally in dwarf rhododendron or juniper above the tree line. DISTRIBUTION: Resident in the Himalayas.

7 GOLDEN-NAPED FINCH *Pyrrhoplectes epauletta* 15cm FIELD NOTES: Secretive. Forages on the ground or in the interior of bushes and undergrowth; in winter occurs in small flocks, often in the company of rosefinches. VOICE: A rapid, high-pitched *pi-pi-pi-pi*, also a low piping. Calls include a thin, repeated *teeu*, *tseu* or *peeuu*, a *pur-lee* and a *plee-e-e*. HABITAT: Undergrowth in high-altitude oak and rhododendron forests. DISTRIBUTION: Resident from C to E Himalayas.

163 BUNTINGS

1 CRESTED BUNTING *Melophus lathami* 17cm FIELD NOTES: Forages on the ground, usually near cereal crops; regularly perches on rocks or bushes. In winter forms loose small flocks. Sings from a prominent perch such as an overhead wire, treetop or rock. VOICE: Starts with some subdued notes, followed by low mellow notes and ending with two or three descending notes, transcribed as *tzit dzit dzit see-see-suee* or similar. Call is a soft *tip* or *tup*, which is uttered more emphatically in flight. HABITAT: Dry rocky or grassy hillsides and terraced cultivation with rocky outcrops and scattered bushes. DISTRIBUTION: Resident in the Himalayas and the hills of C India and the NE of the region.

2 YELLOWHAMMER *Emberiza citrinella* 16.5cm FIELD NOTES: Usually gregarious, forages on the ground and regularly retreats to perch on bushes if disturbed. Hybridises with Pine Bunting, hybrids usually showing some amount of yellow on the throat or breast; there is an old record of a hybrid from Baluchistan. VOICE: Calls include a metallic *tsit*, a thin *see* and a clicking *tit-tit-tit-tit*. HABITAT: Upland agricultural land. DISTRIBUTION: Winter visitor to the Himalayas in India and Nepal.

3 GODLEWSKI'S BUNTING *Emberiza godlewskii* 17cm FIELD NOTES: Forages mainly on the ground, but often perches in trees; in winter occurs in small flocks. Often considered conspecific with Rock Bunting. VOICE: Similar to Rock Bunting but starting with higher-pitched notes. Calls include a thin *tzii* and a hard *pett-pett*. HABITAT: Bushy and rocky mountainsides, often near forests; regularly visits fields in winter. DISTRIBUTION: May be resident in N Arunachal Pradesh, although disputed by some authorities.

4 ROCK BUNTING *Emberiza cia* 16cm FIELD NOTES: Forages on the ground, among rocks or low vegetation, usually in pairs or small parties post breeding. Birds from the W Himalayas *E. c. stracheyi* (not shown) are generally more richly coloured, especially the rusty underparts. VOICE: Variable; starts hesitantly then accelerates into a clear twittering phase, transcribed as *tsiritt churr chu-chut chirrirri tsirr chu-tsirriritt*. Calls include a sharp *tsii*, a high-pitched *tseee* and when disturbed a rolling *trrr*; also utters a short *tup* in flight. HABITAT: Rocky mountain and hill slopes, usually with bushes and scattered trees, juniper forest, open pine forest and cultivation edge; in winter also in lowland fallow cultivation. DISTRIBUTION: Resident from C to W Himalayas and the Pakistan mountains; more widespread in lower areas of the NW during winter.

5 GREY-NECKED BUNTING *Emberiza buchanani* 15cm FIELD NOTES: Forages on the ground in sparse vegetation, usually in pairs or small parties; more gregarious on migration and in winter. VOICE: A *dzee-zeee-zeee-zee-zee-zee-deo*. Calls are a *tcheup* or *chep* and a soft *tsip* given in flight. HABITAT: Bare mountain slopes and foothills with sparse vegetation; in winter favours dry, stony cultivation and euphorbia-covered dry slopes. DISTRIBUTION: Breeds in SW Pakistan; winters mainly in C and W India and W Pakistan.

6 ORTOLAN BUNTING *Emberiza hortulana* 16cm FIELD NOTES: Forages on the ground, in bushes and trees; usually gregarious post breeding. VOICE: Calls include a dry *plet*, and a metallic *ziie*, often followed by a short *tew*. HABITAT: Grassy slopes with bushes and orchards. DISTRIBUTION: Vagrant, recorded from Pakistan and India.

7 PINE BUNTING *Emberiza leucocephalos* 17cm FIELD NOTES: Forages on the ground, usually in small to large flocks and often in the company of other buntings and finches. See Yellowhammer for hybrid note. Non-breeding males have head pattern and back obscured by pale fringes. VOICE: Calls very similar to those of Yellowhammer. HABITAT: Grassy slopes with bushes and fallow or stubble fields. DISTRIBUTION: Winter visitor to the Himalayas and the NW.

1 WHITE-CAPPED BUNTING *Emberiza stewarti* 15cm FIELD NOTES: Forages on the ground and in bushes; in winter forms small flocks, often in the company of other buntings and finches, especially at drinking sites. Non-breeding males have chestnut and black plumage areas obscured by pale feather edges. VOICE: A buzzy, metallic rattle ending with a single high-pitched note. Calls include a high-pitched *tit* and a squeaky, stacatto *tchirit*. HABITAT: Mainly grassy and rocky slopes with or without bushes and trees; in winter favours dry foothills, scrub jungle, agricultural land and the edges of plains with scattered bushes. DISTRIBUTION: Breeds in the mountains of Pakistan and the W Himalayas; winters in the foothills and valleys of Pakistan and C and N India.

2 LITTLE BUNTING *Emberiza pusilla* 13cm FIELD NOTES: Forages mainly on the ground, often in the company of other buntings and pipits; tends to sit on bare treetops on cold mornings with fluffed-out feathers. VOICE: Calls include a hard *tzik* or *pwick*. HABITAT: Grass, reeds, rice stubbles and scrub in cultivated open country. DISTRIBUTION: Winter visitor to the Himalayas and the NE.

3 CHESTNUT-EARED BUNTING *Emberiza fucata* 16cm FIELD NOTES: Forages on the ground, usually in pairs or small parties; post breeding often roosts in marshy reed-beds. Birds breeding in the Himalayas *E. f arcuata* (not shown) are generally darker, with more chestnut on the lower breast and flanks and a broader, blacker upper breast-band. VOICE: A rapid, twittering *zwee-zwizewezwizizi-triip-triip* or similar. Calls include an explosive *pzick*, a high-pitched *zii* or *zii-zii* and a lower-pitched *chutt*. HABITAT: Hillsides with bushes and scrub, especially near rivers; in winter favours wet stubbles, marshes, grassland and bushes. DISTRIBUTION: Breeds in W Himalayas, resident in C Himalayas and a winter visitor to NE India and Bangladesh.

4 STRIOLATED BUNTING *Emberiza striolata* 13cm FIELD NOTES: Forages on the ground, generally in pairs or small parties; in dry areas regularly drinks at water holes in the morning. VOICE: A simple, repetitive *trip trip te-tree-cha tre-tree-cha*. Calls include a nasal *dschu* and a sparrow-like *chielp* flight note. HABITAT: Dry rocky hills with sparse thorn or euphorbia scrub; in winter occurs on sandy plains, tamarisk scrub and grass areas by canals. DISTRIBUTION: Resident in Pakistan and NW India.

5 YELLOW-BREASTED BUNTING *Emberiza aureola* 15cm FIELD NOTES: Forages on the ground, when disturbed retreats to sit in nearby bushes or trees; usually in flocks, sometimes with 200 or so individuals. Non-breeding males have back and head pattern obscured by pale feather edges. VOICE: A sweet, twittering *tswit tsu ri tu tswee witt tsuri weee dee tswit tsuri tu*. Calls include a sharp *tsik* and an abrupt *chup* when flushed. HABITAT: Cultivation, grassland, hedgerows and gardens. DISTRIBUTION: Winter visitor mainly to the N and NE.

6 RUSTIC BUNTING *Emberiza rustica* 14–15cm FIELD NOTES: Forages on the ground and in low vegetation; on migration occurs in small flocks, generally in larger flocks in winter. Non-breeding male similar to breeding female. VOICE: Calls include a sharp *tzik*, often repeated, and a high-pitched *tsiee* occasionally given when alarmed. HABITAT: Winters in dry woodland, riverside scrub, rank vegetation, stubble fields, reed-beds and damp grassland. DISTRIBUTION: Vagrant, recorded from Nepal.

165 BUNTINGS

1 CHESTNUT BUNTING *Emberiza rutila* 14cm FIELD NOTES: Forages on the ground, retreats into bushes or trees when disturbed; usually in small flocks. Non-breeding adults have chestnut areas obscured by variable amounts of pale scaling. VOICE: Calls include a *zick* and a thin, high *tsweep*. HABITAT: Rice stubbles, bushes in cultivation and forest clearings. DISTRIBUTION: Winter visitor, mainly to the NE.

2 BLACK-HEADED BUNTING *Emberiza melanocephala* 16–18cm FIELD NOTES: Forages mainly on the ground, retreats into nearby bushes or trees when disturbed; often in large flocks in the company of Red-headed Buntings. In winter head and back colours of male are obscured by pale fringes. VOICE: A low-pitched *zrit zrit srutt srutt-sruttsutteri-sutt sutterrih* or similar. Calls include a *cheep* or *chlip*, a *dzuu* and in flight a *chuhp*. HABITAT: Cereal cultivations. DISTRIBUTION: Winter visitor to N, W and WC India; migrates through S Pakistan.

3 RED-HEADED BUNTING *Emberiza bruniceps* 16cm FIELD NOTES: Actions and habits similar to Black-headed Bunting. In winter head and back colours of male are obscured by pale fringes. VOICE: Song very similar to Black-headed Bunting. Calls include a *chip*, a *chuupp*, a *zrit*, a sharp *tsit* and a series of clicks; all calls very similar to those of Black-headed Bunting. HABITAT: Cereal cultivations. DISTRIBUTION: Winter visitor to NW and WC India; migrates through the NW.

4 BLACK-FACED BUNTING *Emberiza spodocephala* 15cm FIELD NOTES: Forages on the ground, usually in cover near water; generally in pairs or small parties. Non-breeding male has face pattern partly obscured by pale fringes, sometimes shows a faint supercilium and submoustachial stripe. VOICE: Call is a sharp *tzit* or *tzii*. HABITAT: Tall grass, bamboo and scrub jungle, hedges around village compounds, paddyfield and marsh margins. DISTRIBUTION: Winter visitor, mainly to the NE.

5 PALLAS'S REED BUNTING *Emberiza pallasi* 14cm FIELD NOTES: Forages on the ground, on grass-heads and in bushes; post breeding usually seen in flocks. Non-breeding male has black head markings browner, obscured by pale fringes; also shows a faint supercilium and generally buffier breast and neck-patch. VOICE: Calls include a sparrow-like *chleep* or *tsilip* and a slurred *dziu*. HABITAT: Reed-beds, grassy fields, paddyfields, arable land and shrubs near watercourses. DISTRIBUTION: Vagrant, recorded from Nepal; disputed by some authorities.

6 REED BUNTING (COMMON REED BUNTING) *Emberiza schoeniclus* 14–16cm FIELD NOTES: Forages on the ground and in low vegetation, regularly perches on reed stems; usually occurs in pairs or small parties. Non-breeding males have black head pattern browner with paler scaling. Larger, paler race *E. s. pyrrhuloides* (6b) is a rare vagrant. VOICE: Calls include a plaintive *seeoo* and a harsh *brzee*. HABITAT: Reed-beds, irrigated fields, scrub and bushes. DISTRIBUTION: Winter visitor, mainly to the NW.

7 CORN BUNTING *Emberiza calandra* 17–18cm FIELD NOTES: Forages on the ground, regularly perches on bushes, posts or overhead wires; generally occurs in flocks post breeding. VOICE: Song starts with a few chipping notes followed by a harsh jangling. Call is a hard, dry *tuk* or *bitt*, often rapidly repeated. HABITAT: Arable land and waste ground. DISTRIBUTION: Vagrant, recorded from Pakistan and India.

FURTHER READING

Ali, S. & Ripley, S. D. (1987) *Compact Handbook of the Birds of India and Pakistan*, 2nd edition. Oxford University Press.

Alström, P. & Mild, K. (2003) *Pipits and Wagtails of Europe, Asia and North America*. Helm.

Baker, K. (1997) *Warblers of Europe, Asia and North Africa*. Helm.

Beaman, M. & Madge, S. (1998) *The Handbook of Bird Identification for Europe and the Western Palearctic*. Helm.

Byers, C., Olsson, U. & Curson, J. (1995) *Buntings and Sparrows*. Helm.

Cheke, R. A., Mann, C. F. & Allen, R. (2001) *Sunbirds: a Guide to the Sunbirds, Flowerpeckers, Spiderhunters and Sugarbirds of the World*. Helm.

Clement, P., Harris, A. & Davis, J. (1993) *Finches and Sparrows*. Helm.

Clement, P. & Hathway, R. (2000) *Thrushes*. Helm.

Cramp, S., Simmons, K. E. L. & Perrins, C. M. (eds.) (1977–94) *The Birds of the Western Palearctic*, Vols 1–9. Oxford University Press.

del Hoyo, J., Elliott, A., Sargatal, J. & Christie, D. A. (eds.) (1992–2011) *Handbook of the Birds of the World*, Vols 1–16. Lynx Edicions.

Dickinson, E. C. (ed.) (2003) *The Howard and Moore Complete Checklist of the Birds of the World*. Helm.

Feare, C. & Craig, A. (1998) *Starlings and Mynas*. Helm.

Fry, C. H., Fry, K. & Harris, A. (1992) *Kingfishers, Bee-eaters and Rollers*. Helm.

Grimmett, R., Inskipp, C. & Inskipp, T. (2011) *Birds of the Indian Subcontinent*. Helm.

Hancock, J. & Elliott, H. (1978) *The Herons of the World*. London Editions.

Hancock, J., Kushlan, J. A. & Kahl, M. P. (1992) *Storks, Ibises and Spoonbills of the World*. Academic Press.

Harrison, P. (1983 & updates) *Seabirds: an Identification Guide*. Helm.

Harrop, S. & Quinn, D. (1996) *Tits, Nuthatches and Treecreepers*. Helm.

Hayman, P., Marchant, A. J. & Prater, A. H. (1986) *Shorebirds: an Identification Guide to the Waders of the World*. Helm.

Lefranc, N. & Worfolk, T. (1997) *Shrikes: a Guide to the Shrikes of the World*. Pica Press.

MacKinnon, J. & Phillipps, K. (2000) *A Field Guide to the Birds of China*. Oxford University Press.

Madge, S. & Burn, H. (1988) *Wildfowl: an Identification Guide to the Ducks, Geese and Swans of the World*. Helm.

Madge, S. & Burn, H. (1991) *Crows and Jays*. Helm.

Madge, S. & McGowan, P. (2002) *Pheasants, Partridges and Grouse: Including Buttonquails, Sandgrouse and Allies*. Helm.

Mullarney, K., Svensson, L., Zetterström, D. & Grant, P. J. (2009) *Collins Bird Guide*, 2nd edition. HarperCollins.

Olney, D. & Scofield, P. (2007) *Albatrosses, Petrels and Shearwaters of the World*. Helm.

Olsen, K. M. & Larsson, H. (2004) *Gulls of Europe, Asia and North America*. Helm.

Olsen, K. M. & Larsson, H. (1997) *Skuas and Jaegers: a Guide to the Skuas and Jaegers of the World*. Pica Press.

Olsen, K. M. & Larsson, H. (1995) *Terns of Europe and North America*. Helm.

Porter, R. F., Christensen, S. & Schiermacker-Hansen, P. (1996) *Birds of the Middle East*. Helm.

Porter, R. F., Willis, I., Christensen, S. & Neilsen, B. P. (1981) *Flight Identification of European Raptors*, 3rd edition. Poyser.

Robson, C. (2002) *Birds of South-east Asia*. New Holland.

Taylor, B. & van Perlo, B. (1998) *Rails: a Guide to the Rails, Crakes, Gallinules and Coots of the World*. Pica Press.

Turner, A. & Rose, C. (1989) *Swallows and Martins of the World*. Helm.

Vinicombe, K., Harris, A. & Tucker, L. (1989) *The Macmillan Field Guide to Bird Identification*. Macmillan.

Voous, K. H. (1988) *Owls of the Northern Hemisphere*. Collins.

Winkler, H., Christie, D. A. & Nurney, D. (1995) *Woodpeckers: a Guide to the Woodpeckers, Piculets and Wrynecks of the World*. Pica Press.

SPECIES DISTRIBUTION MAPS

Key to Maps

Breeding season
Non-breeding season
Resident season

Vagrants and most introduced species are not included in the distribution maps section. Species that spend most of their time at sea or occur only on islands, including Sri Lanka, are also not included in this section.

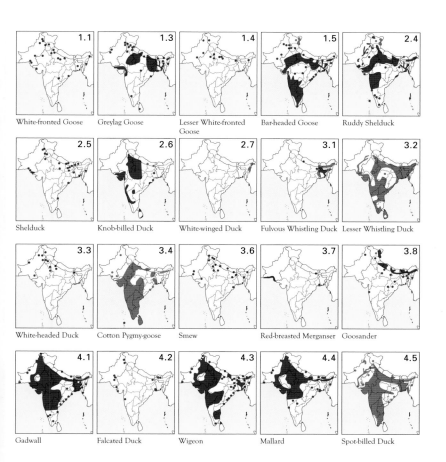

1.1	1.3	1.4	1.5	2.4
White-fronted Goose	Greylag Goose	Lesser White-fronted Goose	Bar-headed Goose	Ruddy Shelduck
2.5	2.6	2.7	3.1	3.2
Shelduck	Knob-billed Duck	White-winged Duck	Fulvous Whistling Duck	Lesser Whistling Duck
3.3	3.4	3.6	3.7	3.8
White-headed Duck	Cotton Pygmy-goose	Smew	Red-breasted Merganser	Goosander
4.1	4.2	4.3	4.4	4.5
Gadwall	Falcated Duck	Wigeon	Mallard	Spot-billed Duck

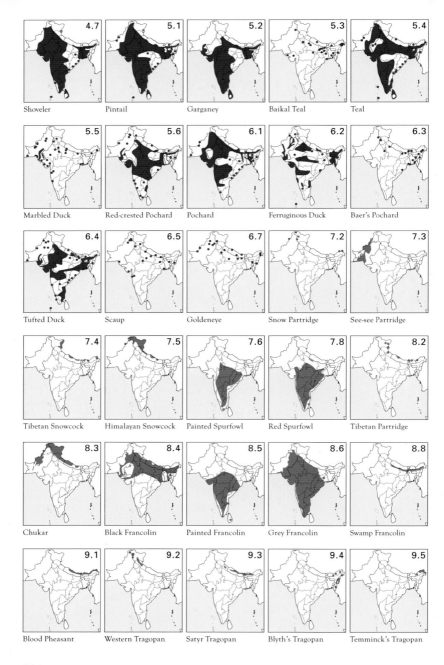

4.7 Shoveler	**5.1** Pintail	**5.2** Garganey	**5.3** Baikal Teal	**5.4** Teal
5.5 Marbled Duck	**5.6** Red-crested Pochard	**6.1** Pochard	**6.2** Ferruginous Duck	**6.3** Baer's Pochard
6.4 Tufted Duck	**6.5** Scaup	**6.7** Goldeneye	**7.2** Snow Partridge	**7.3** See-see Partridge
7.4 Tibetan Snowcock	**7.5** Himalayan Snowcock	**7.6** Painted Spurfowl	**7.8** Red Spurfowl	**8.2** Tibetan Partridge
8.3 Chukar	**8.4** Black Francolin	**8.5** Painted Francolin	**8.6** Grey Francolin	**8.8** Swamp Francolin
9.1 Blood Pheasant	**9.2** Western Tragopan	**9.3** Satyr Tragopan	**9.4** Blyth's Tragopan	**9.5** Temminck's Tragopan

344

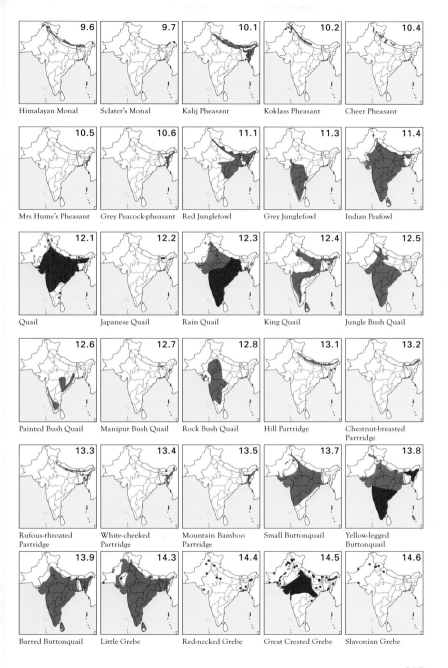

9.6	9.7	10.1	10.2	10.4
Himalayan Monal	Sclater's Monal	Kalij Pheasant	Koklass Pheasant	Cheer Pheasant
10.5	10.6	11.1	11.3	11.4
Mrs Hume's Pheasant	Grey Peacock-pheasant	Red Junglefowl	Grey Junglefowl	Indian Peafowl
12.1	12.2	12.3	12.4	12.5
Quail	Japanese Quail	Rain Quail	King Quail	Jungle Bush Quail
12.6	12.7	12.8	13.1	13.2
Painted Bush Quail	Manipur Bush Quail	Rock Bush Quail	Hill Partridge	Chestnut-breasted Partridge
13.3	13.4	13.5	13.7	13.8
Rufous-throated Partridge	White-cheeked Partridge	Mountain Bamboo Partridge	Small Buttonquail	Yellow-legged Buttonquail
13.9	14.3	14.4	14.5	14.6
Barred Buttonquail	Little Grebe	Red-necked Grebe	Great Crested Grebe	Slavonian Grebe

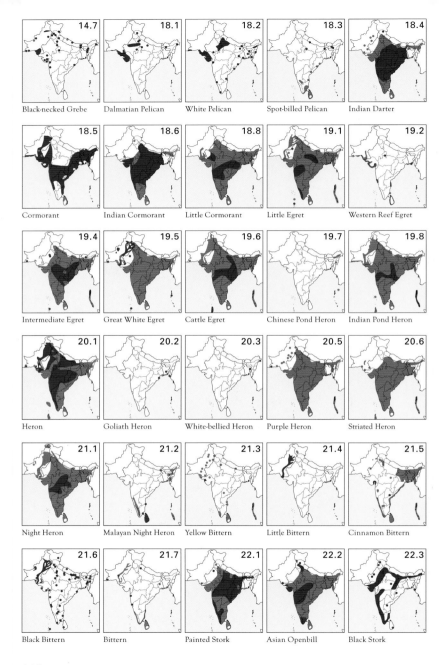

14.7	18.1	18.2	18.3	18.4
Black-necked Grebe	Dalmatian Pelican	White Pelican	Spot-billed Pelican	Indian Darter
18.5	18.6	18.8	19.1	19.2
Cormorant	Indian Cormorant	Little Cormorant	Little Egret	Western Reef Egret
19.4	19.5	19.6	19.7	19.8
Intermediate Egret	Great White Egret	Cattle Egret	Chinese Pond Heron	Indian Pond Heron
20.1	20.2	20.3	20.5	20.6
Heron	Goliath Heron	White-bellied Heron	Purple Heron	Striated Heron
21.1	21.2	21.3	21.4	21.5
Night Heron	Malayan Night Heron	Yellow Bittern	Little Bittern	Cinnamon Bittern
21.6	21.7	22.1	22.2	22.3
Black Bittern	Bittern	Painted Stork	Asian Openbill	Black Stork

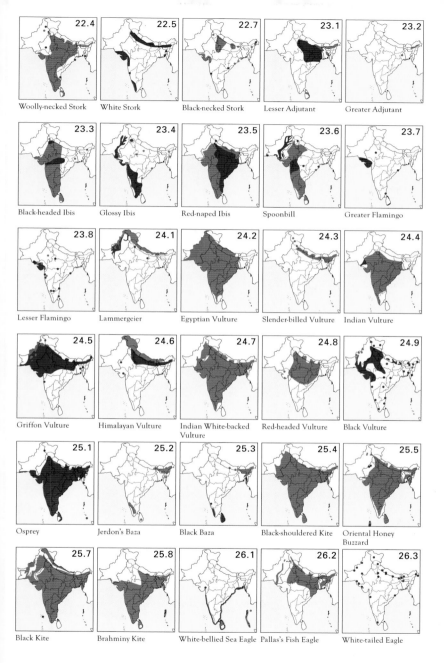

22.4 Woolly-necked Stork	**22.5** White Stork	**22.7** Black-necked Stork	**23.1** Lesser Adjutant	**23.2** Greater Adjutant
23.3 Black-headed Ibis	**23.4** Glossy Ibis	**23.5** Red-naped Ibis	**23.6** Spoonbill	**23.7** Greater Flamingo
23.8 Lesser Flamingo	**24.1** Lammergeier	**24.2** Egyptian Vulture	**24.3** Slender-billed Vulture	**24.4** Indian Vulture
24.5 Griffon Vulture	**24.6** Himalayan Vulture	**24.7** Indian White-backed Vulture	**24.8** Red-headed Vulture	**24.9** Black Vulture
25.1 Osprey	**25.2** Jerdon's Baza	**25.3** Black Baza	**25.4** Black-shouldered Kite	**25.5** Oriental Honey Buzzard
25.7 Black Kite	**25.8** Brahminy Kite	**26.1** White-bellied Sea Eagle	**26.2** Pallas's Fish Eagle	**26.3** White-tailed Eagle

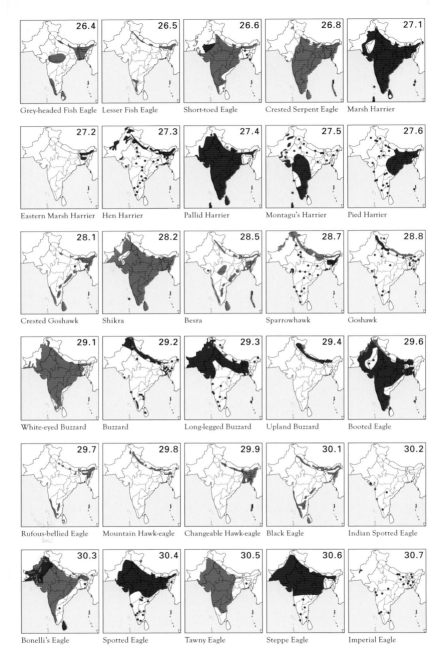

26.4 Grey-headed Fish Eagle	26.5 Lesser Fish Eagle	26.6 Short-toed Eagle	26.8 Crested Serpent Eagle	27.1 Marsh Harrier
27.2 Eastern Marsh Harrier	27.3 Hen Harrier	27.4 Pallid Harrier	27.5 Montagu's Harrier	27.6 Pied Harrier
28.1 Crested Goshawk	28.2 Shikra	28.5 Besra	28.7 Sparrowhawk	28.8 Goshawk
29.1 White-eyed Buzzard	29.2 Buzzard	29.3 Long-legged Buzzard	29.4 Upland Buzzard	29.6 Booted Eagle
29.7 Rufous-bellied Eagle	29.8 Mountain Hawk-eagle	29.9 Changeable Hawk-eagle	30.1 Black Eagle	30.2 Indian Spotted Eagle
30.3 Bonelli's Eagle	30.4 Spotted Eagle	30.5 Tawny Eagle	30.6 Steppe Eagle	30.7 Imperial Eagle

348

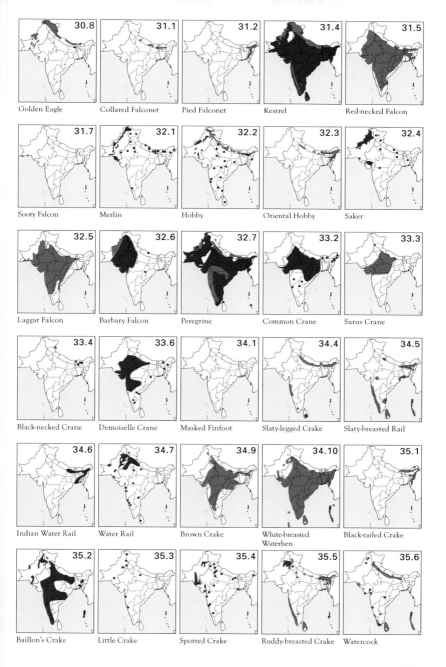

30.8 Golden Eagle	31.1 Collared Falconet	31.2 Pied Falconet	31.4 Kestrel	31.5 Red-necked Falcon
31.7 Sooty Falcon	32.1 Merlin	32.2 Hobby	32.3 Oriental Hobby	32.4 Saker
32.5 Laggar Falcon	32.6 Barbary Falcon	32.7 Peregrine	33.2 Common Crane	33.3 Sarus Crane
33.4 Black-necked Crane	33.6 Demoiselle Crane	34.1 Masked Finfoot	34.4 Slaty-legged Crake	34.5 Slaty-breasted Rail
34.6 Indian Water Rail	34.7 Water Rail	34.9 Brown Crake	34.10 White-breasted Waterhen	35.1 Black-tailed Crake
35.2 Baillon's Crake	35.3 Little Crake	35.4 Spotted Crake	35.5 Ruddy-breasted Crake	35.6 Watercock

349

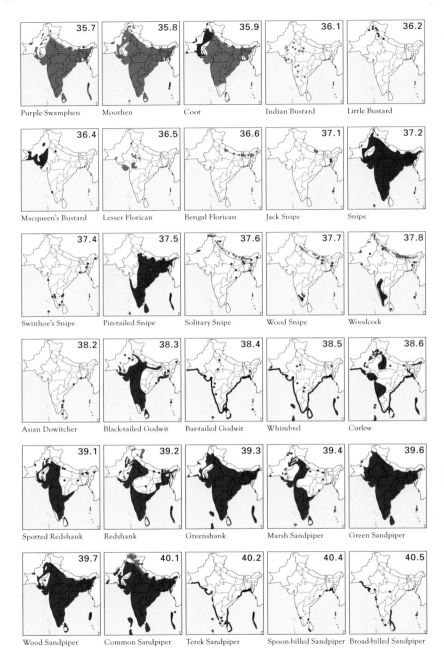

35.7 Purple Swamphen	35.8 Moorhen	35.9 Coot	36.1 Indian Bustard	36.2 Little Bustard
36.4 Macqueen's Bustard	36.5 Lesser Florican	36.6 Bengal Florican	37.1 Jack Snipe	37.2 Snipe
37.4 Swinhoe's Snipe	37.5 Pin-tailed Snipe	37.6 Solitary Snipe	37.7 Wood Snipe	37.8 Woodcock
38.2 Asian Dowitcher	38.3 Black-tailed Godwit	38.4 Bar-tailed Godwit	38.5 Whimbrel	38.6 Curlew
39.1 Spotted Redshank	39.2 Redshank	39.3 Greenshank	39.4 Marsh Sandpiper	39.6 Green Sandpiper
39.7 Wood Sandpiper	40.1 Common Sandpiper	40.2 Terek Sandpiper	40.4 Spoon-billed Sandpiper	40.5 Broad-billed Sandpiper

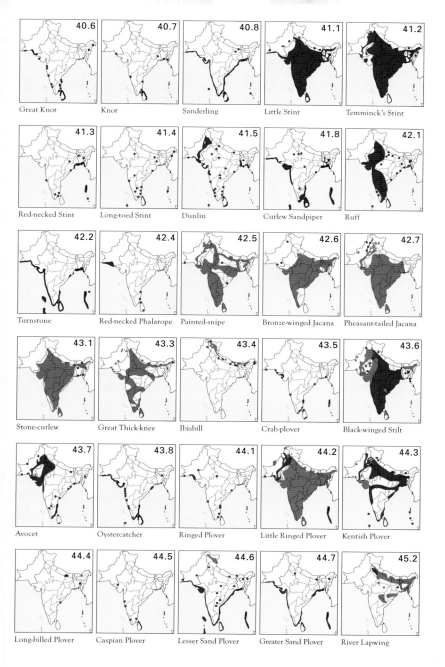

40.6	40.7	40.8	41.1	41.2
Great Knot	Knot	Sanderling	Little Stint	Temminck's Stint
41.3	41.4	41.5	41.8	42.1
Red-necked Stint	Long-toed Stint	Dunlin	Curlew Sandpiper	Ruff
42.2	42.4	42.5	42.6	42.7
Turnstone	Red-necked Phalarope	Painted-snipe	Bronze-winged Jacana	Pheasant-tailed Jacana
43.1	43.3	43.4	43.5	43.6
Stone-curlew	Great Thick-knee	Ibisbill	Crab-plover	Black-winged Stilt
43.7	43.8	44.1	44.2	44.3
Avocet	Oystercatcher	Ringed Plover	Little Ringed Plover	Kentish Plover
44.4	44.5	44.6	44.7	45.2
Long-billed Plover	Caspian Plover	Lesser Sand Plover	Greater Sand Plover	River Lapwing

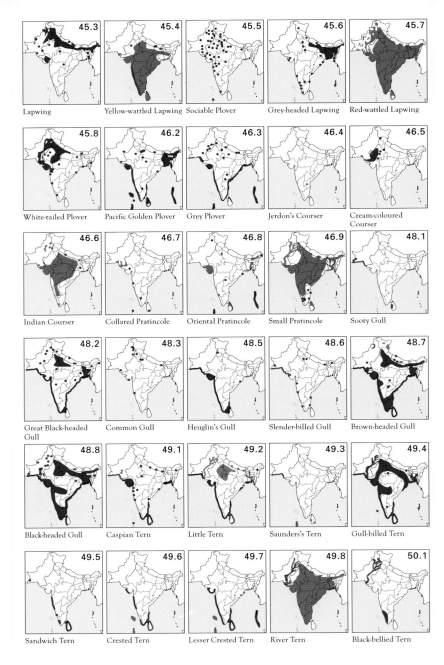

Lapwing   45.3

Yellow-wattled Lapwing   45.4

Sociable Plover   45.5

Grey-headed Lapwing   45.6

Red-wattled Lapwing   45.7

White-tailed Plover   45.8

Pacific Golden Plover   46.2

Grey Plover   46.3

Jerdon's Courser   46.4

Cream-coloured Courser   46.5

Indian Courser   46.6

Collared Pratincole   46.7

Oriental Pratincole   46.8

Small Pratincole   46.9

Sooty Gull   48.1

Great Black-headed Gull   48.2

Common Gull   48.3

Heuglin's Gull   48.5

Slender-billed Gull   48.6

Brown-headed Gull   48.7

Black-headed Gull   48.8

Caspian Tern   49.1

Little Tern   49.2

Saunders's Tern   49.3

Gull-billed Tern   49.4

Sandwich Tern   49.5

Crested Tern   49.6

Lesser Crested Tern   49.7

River Tern   49.8

Black-bellied Tern   50.1

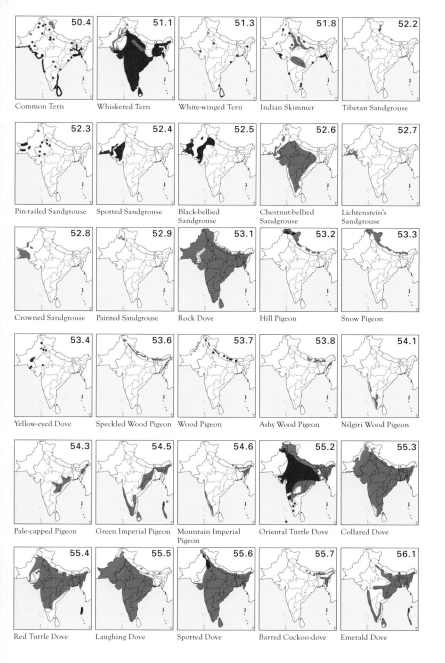

Common Tern 50.4

Whiskered Tern 51.1

White-winged Tern 51.3

Indian Skimmer 51.8

Tibetan Sandgrouse 52.2

Pin-tailed Sandgrouse 52.3

Spotted Sandgrouse 52.4

Black-bellied Sandgrouse 52.5

Chestnut-bellied Sandgrouse 52.6

Lichtenstein's Sandgrouse 52.7

Crowned Sandgrouse 52.8

Painted Sandgrouse 52.9

Rock Dove 53.1

Hill Pigeon 53.2

Snow Pigeon 53.3

Yellow-eyed Dove 53.4

Speckled Wood Pigeon 53.6

Wood Pigeon 53.7

Ashy Wood Pigeon 53.8

Nilgiri Wood Pigeon 54.1

Pale-capped Pigeon 54.3

Green Imperial Pigeon 54.5

Mountain Imperial Pigeon 54.6

Oriental Turtle Dove 55.2

Collared Dove 55.3

Red Turtle Dove 55.4

Laughing Dove 55.5

Spotted Dove 55.6

Barred Cuckoo-dove 55.7

Emerald Dove 56.1

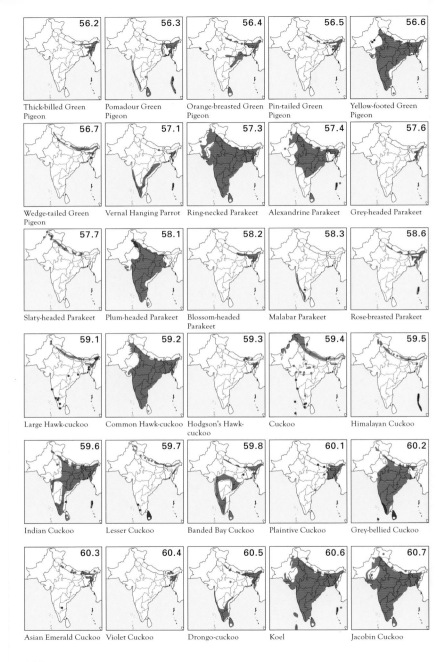

56.2 Thick-billed Green Pigeon	**56.3** Pomadour Green Pigeon	**56.4** Orange-breasted Green Pigeon	**56.5** Pin-tailed Green Pigeon	**56.6** Yellow-footed Green Pigeon
56.7 Wedge-tailed Green Pigeon	**57.1** Vernal Hanging Parrot	**57.3** Ring-necked Parakeet	**57.4** Alexandrine Parakeet	**57.6** Grey-headed Parakeet
57.7 Slaty-headed Parakeet	**58.1** Plum-headed Parakeet	**58.2** Blossom-headed Parakeet	**58.3** Malabar Parakeet	**58.6** Rose-breasted Parakeet
59.1 Large Hawk-cuckoo	**59.2** Common Hawk-cuckoo	**59.3** Hodgson's Hawk-cuckoo	**59.4** Cuckoo	**59.5** Himalayan Cuckoo
59.6 Indian Cuckoo	**59.7** Lesser Cuckoo	**59.8** Banded Bay Cuckoo	**60.1** Plaintive Cuckoo	**60.2** Grey-bellied Cuckoo
60.3 Asian Emerald Cuckoo	**60.4** Violet Cuckoo	**60.5** Drongo-cuckoo	**60.6** Koel	**60.7** Jacobin Cuckoo

354

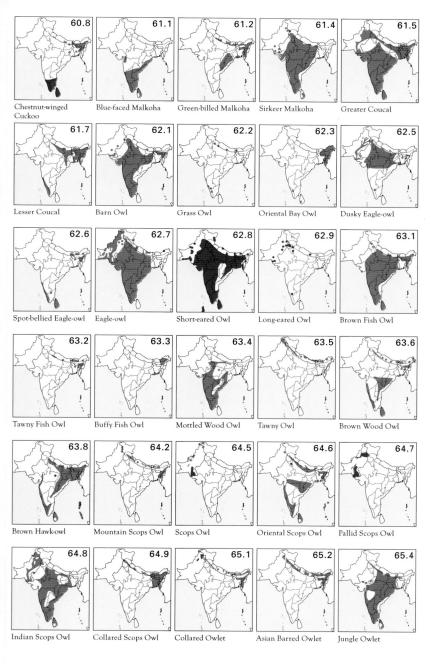

60.8 Chestnut-winged Cuckoo	61.1 Blue-faced Malkoha	61.2 Green-billed Malkoha	61.4 Sirkeer Malkoha	61.5 Greater Coucal
61.7 Lesser Coucal	62.1 Barn Owl	62.2 Grass Owl	62.3 Oriental Bay Owl	62.5 Dusky Eagle-owl
62.6 Spot-bellied Eagle-owl	62.7 Eagle-owl	62.8 Short-eared Owl	62.9 Long-eared Owl	63.1 Brown Fish Owl
63.2 Tawny Fish Owl	63.3 Buffy Fish Owl	63.4 Mottled Wood Owl	63.5 Tawny Owl	63.6 Brown Wood Owl
63.8 Brown Hawk-owl	64.2 Mountain Scops Owl	64.5 Scops Owl	64.6 Oriental Scops Owl	64.7 Pallid Scops Owl
64.8 Indian Scops Owl	64.9 Collared Scops Owl	65.1 Collared Owlet	65.2 Asian Barred Owlet	65.4 Jungle Owlet

355

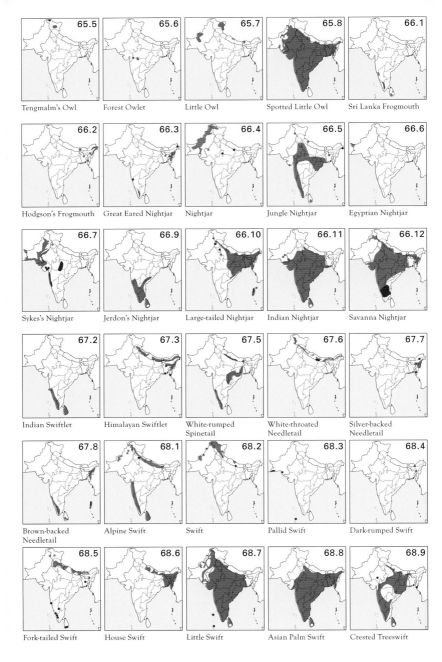

65.5	65.6	65.7	65.8	66.1
Tengmalm's Owl	Forest Owlet	Little Owl	Spotted Little Owl	Sri Lanka Frogmouth

66.2	66.3	66.4	66.5	66.6
Hodgson's Frogmouth	Great Eared Nightjar	Nightjar	Jungle Nightjar	Egyptian Nightjar

66.7	66.9	66.10	66.11	66.12
Sykes's Nightjar	Jerdon's Nightjar	Large-tailed Nightjar	Indian Nightjar	Savanna Nightjar

67.2	67.3	67.5	67.6	67.7
Indian Swiftlet	Himalayan Swiftlet	White-rumped Spinetail	White-throated Needletail	Silver-backed Needletail

67.8	68.1	68.2	68.3	68.4
Brown-backed Needletail	Alpine Swift	Swift	Pallid Swift	Dark-rumped Swift

68.5	68.6	68.7	68.8	68.9
Fork-tailed Swift	House Swift	Little Swift	Asian Palm Swift	Crested Treeswift

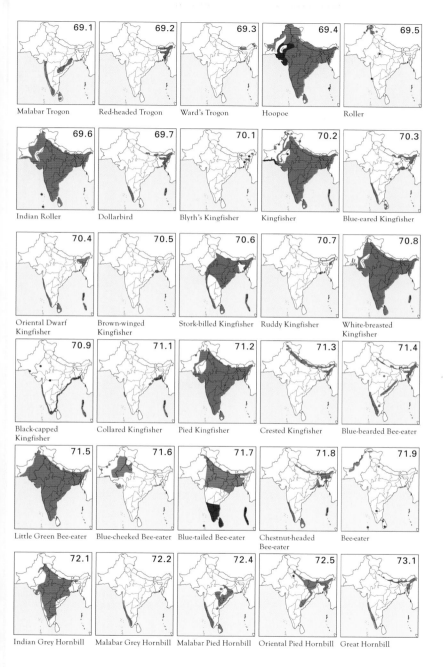

69.1	69.2	69.3	69.4	69.5
Malabar Trogon	Red-headed Trogon	Ward's Trogon	Hoopoe	Roller

69.6	69.7	70.1	70.2	70.3
Indian Roller	Dollarbird	Blyth's Kingfisher	Kingfisher	Blue-eared Kingfisher

70.4	70.5	70.6	70.7	70.8
Oriental Dwarf Kingfisher	Brown-winged Kingfisher	Stork-billed Kingfisher	Ruddy Kingfisher	White-breasted Kingfisher

70.9	71.1	71.2	71.3	71.4
Black-capped Kingfisher	Collared Kingfisher	Pied Kingfisher	Crested Kingfisher	Blue-bearded Bee-eater

71.5	71.6	71.7	71.8	71.9
Little Green Bee-eater	Blue-cheeked Bee-eater	Blue-tailed Bee-eater	Chestnut-headed Bee-eater	Bee-eater

72.1	72.2	72.4	72.5	73.1
Indian Grey Hornbill	Malabar Grey Hornbill	Malabar Pied Hornbill	Oriental Pied Hornbill	Great Hornbill

357

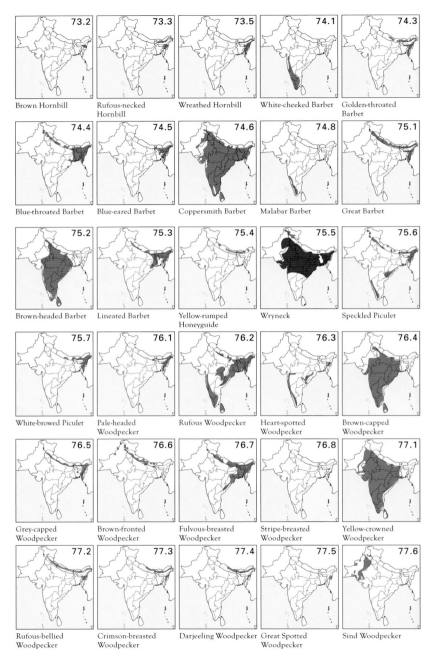

73.2 Brown Hornbill	73.3 Rufous-necked Hornbill	73.5 Wreathed Hornbill	74.1 White-cheeked Barbet	74.3 Golden-throated Barbet
74.4 Blue-throated Barbet	74.5 Blue-eared Barbet	74.6 Coppersmith Barbet	74.8 Malabar Barbet	75.1 Great Barbet
75.2 Brown-headed Barbet	75.3 Lineated Barbet	75.4 Yellow-rumped Honeyguide	75.5 Wryneck	75.6 Speckled Piculet
75.7 White-browed Piculet	76.1 Pale-headed Woodpecker	76.2 Rufous Woodpecker	76.3 Heart-spotted Woodpecker	76.4 Brown-capped Woodpecker
76.5 Grey-capped Woodpecker	76.6 Brown-fronted Woodpecker	76.7 Fulvous-breasted Woodpecker	76.8 Stripe-breasted Woodpecker	77.1 Yellow-crowned Woodpecker
77.2 Rufous-bellied Woodpecker	77.3 Crimson-breasted Woodpecker	77.4 Darjeeling Woodpecker	77.5 Great Spotted Woodpecker	77.6 Sind Woodpecker

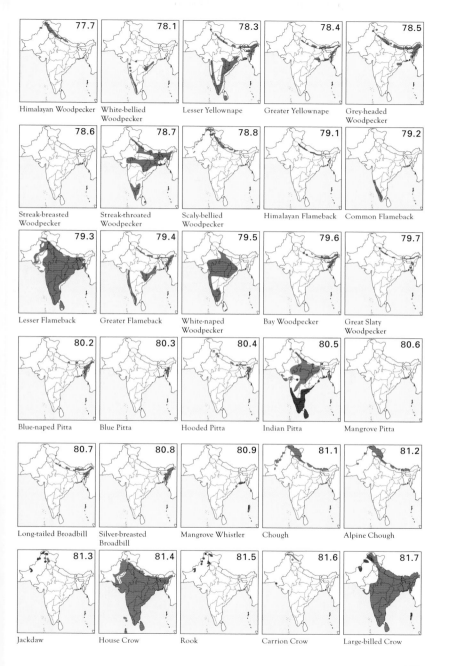

77.7	78.1	78.3	78.4	78.5
Himalayan Woodpecker	White-bellied Woodpecker	Lesser Yellownape	Greater Yellownape	Grey-headed Woodpecker
78.6	78.7	78.8	79.1	79.2
Streak-breasted Woodpecker	Streak-throated Woodpecker	Scaly-bellied Woodpecker	Himalayan Flameback	Common Flameback
79.3	79.4	79.5	79.6	79.7
Lesser Flameback	Greater Flameback	White-naped Woodpecker	Bay Woodpecker	Great Slaty Woodpecker
80.2	80.3	80.4	80.5	80.6
Blue-naped Pitta	Blue Pitta	Hooded Pitta	Indian Pitta	Mangrove Pitta
80.7	80.8	80.9	81.1	81.2
Long-tailed Broadbill	Silver-breasted Broadbill	Mangrove Whistler	Chough	Alpine Chough
81.3	81.4	81.5	81.6	81.7
Jackdaw	House Crow	Rook	Carrion Crow	Large-billed Crow

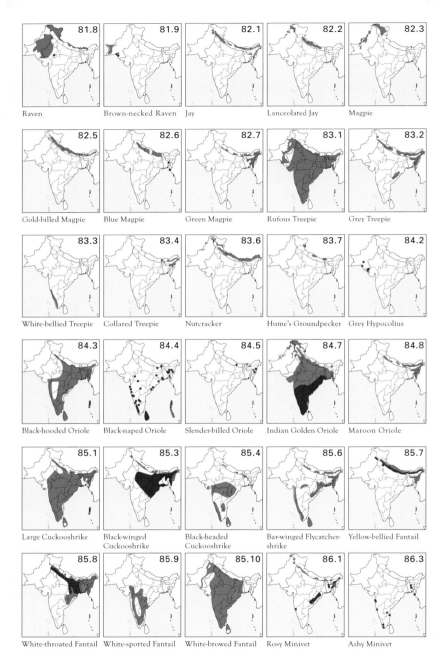

81.8	81.9	82.1	82.2	82.3
Raven	Brown-necked Raven	Jay	Lanceolated Jay	Magpie
82.5	82.6	82.7	83.1	83.2
Gold-billed Magpie	Blue Magpie	Green Magpie	Rufous Treepie	Grey Treepie
83.3	83.4	83.6	83.7	84.2
White-bellied Treepie	Collared Treepie	Nutcracker	Hume's Groundpecker	Grey Hypocolius
84.3	84.4	84.5	84.7	84.8
Black-hooded Oriole	Black-naped Oriole	Slender-billed Oriole	Indian Golden Oriole	Maroon Oriole
85.1	85.3	85.4	85.6	85.7
Large Cuckooshrike	Black-winged Cuckooshrike	Black-headed Cuckooshrike	Bar-winged Flycatcher-shrike	Yellow-bellied Fantail
85.8	85.9	85.10	86.1	86.3
White-throated Fantail	White-spotted Fantail	White-browed Fantail	Rosy Minivet	Ashy Minivet

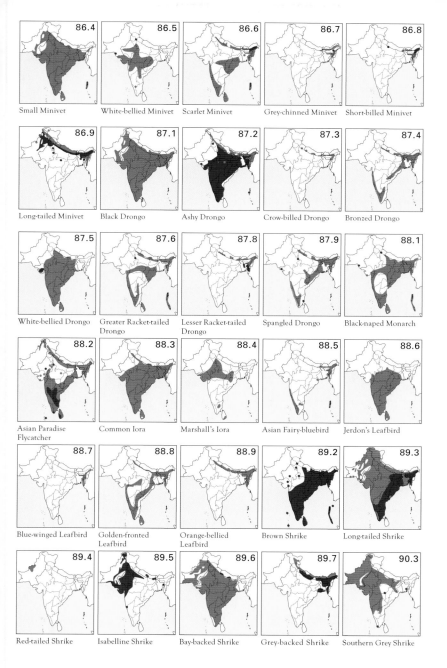

86.4	86.5	86.6	86.7	86.8
Small Minivet	White-bellied Minivet	Scarlet Minivet	Grey-chinned Minivet	Short-billed Minivet
86.9	87.1	87.2	87.3	87.4
Long-tailed Minivet	Black Drongo	Ashy Drongo	Crow-billed Drongo	Bronzed Drongo
87.5	87.6	87.8	87.9	88.1
White-bellied Drongo	Greater Racket-tailed Drongo	Lesser Racket-tailed Drongo	Spangled Drongo	Black-naped Monarch
88.2	88.3	88.4	88.5	88.6
Asian Paradise Flycatcher	Common Iora	Marshall's Iora	Asian Fairy-bluebird	Jerdon's Leafbird
88.7	88.8	88.9	89.2	89.3
Blue-winged Leafbird	Golden-fronted Leafbird	Orange-bellied Leafbird	Brown Shrike	Long-tailed Shrike
89.4	89.5	89.6	89.7	90.3
Red-tailed Shrike	Isabelline Shrike	Bay-backed Shrike	Grey-backed Shrike	Southern Grey Shrike

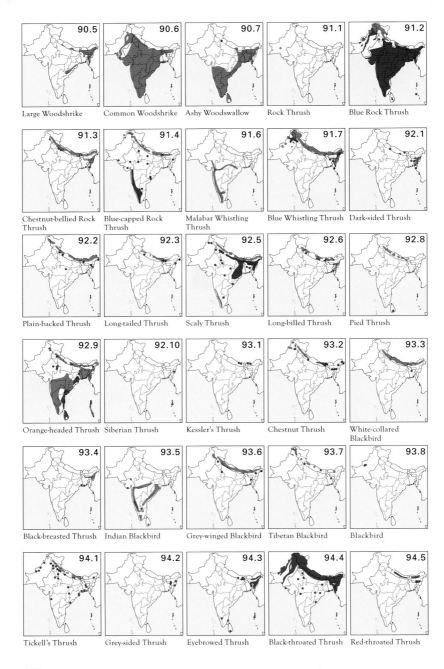

Large Woodshrike   90.5

Common Woodshrike   90.6

Ashy Woodswallow   90.7

Rock Thrush   91.1

Blue Rock Thrush   91.2

Chestnut-bellied Rock Thrush   91.3

Blue-capped Rock Thrush   91.4

Malabar Whistling Thrush   91.6

Blue Whistling Thrush   91.7

Dark-sided Thrush   92.1

Plain-backed Thrush   92.2

Long-tailed Thrush   92.3

Scaly Thrush   92.5

Long-billed Thrush   92.6

Pied Thrush   92.8

Orange-headed Thrush   92.9

Siberian Thrush   92.10

Kessler's Thrush   93.1

Chestnut Thrush   93.2

White-collared Blackbird   93.3

Black-breasted Thrush   93.4

Indian Blackbird   93.5

Grey-winged Blackbird   93.6

Tibetan Blackbird   93.7

Blackbird   93.8

Tickell's Thrush   94.1

Grey-sided Thrush   94.2

Eyebrowed Thrush   94.3

Black-throated Thrush   94.4

Red-throated Thrush   94.5

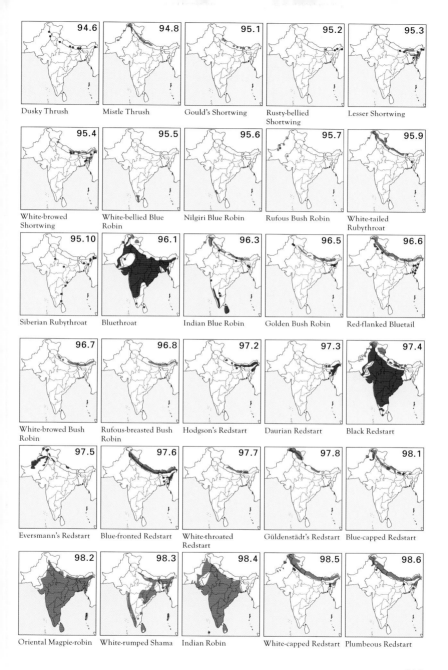

94.6 Dusky Thrush	94.8 Mistle Thrush	95.1 Gould's Shortwing	95.2 Rusty-bellied Shortwing	95.3 Lesser Shortwing
95.4 White-browed Shortwing	95.5 White-bellied Blue Robin	95.6 Nilgiri Blue Robin	95.7 Rufous Bush Robin	95.9 White-tailed Rubythroat
95.10 Siberian Rubythroat	96.1 Bluethroat	96.3 Indian Blue Robin	96.5 Golden Bush Robin	96.6 Red-flanked Bluetail
96.7 White-browed Bush Robin	96.8 Rufous-breasted Bush Robin	97.2 Hodgson's Redstart	97.3 Daurian Redstart	97.4 Black Redstart
97.5 Eversmann's Redstart	97.6 Blue-fronted Redstart	97.7 White-throated Redstart	97.8 Güldenstädr's Redstart	98.1 Blue-capped Redstart
98.2 Oriental Magpie-robin	98.3 White-rumped Shama	98.4 Indian Robin	98.5 White-capped Redstart	98.6 Plumbeous Redstart

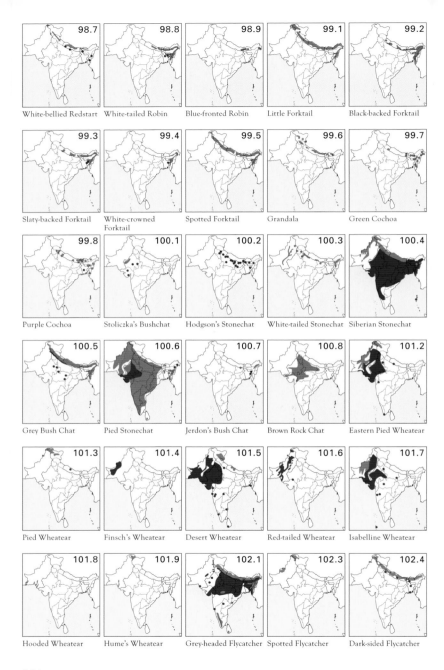

White-bellied Redstart   98.7

White-tailed Robin   98.8

Blue-fronted Robin   98.9

Little Forktail   99.1

Black-backed Forktail   99.2

Slaty-backed Forktail   99.3

White-crowned Forktail   99.4

Spotted Forktail   99.5

Grandala   99.6

Green Cochoa   99.7

Purple Cochoa   99.8

Stoliczka's Bushchat   100.1

Hodgson's Stonechat   100.2

White-tailed Stonechat   100.3

Siberian Stonechat   100.4

Grey Bush Chat   100.5

Pied Stonechat   100.6

Jerdon's Bush Chat   100.7

Brown Rock Chat   100.8

Eastern Pied Wheatear   101.2

Pied Wheatear   101.3

Finsch's Wheatear   101.4

Desert Wheatear   101.5

Red-tailed Wheatear   101.6

Isabelline Wheatear   101.7

Hooded Wheatear   101.8

Hume's Wheatear   101.9

Grey-headed Flycatcher   102.1

Spotted Flycatcher   102.3

Dark-sided Flycatcher   102.4

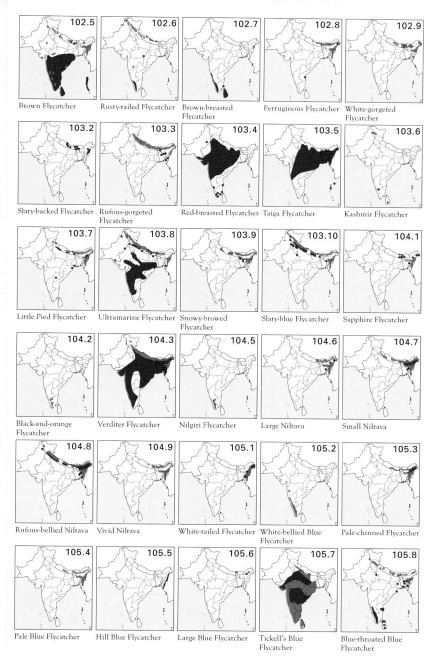

102.5 Brown Flycatcher	102.6 Rusty-tailed Flycatcher	102.7 Brown-breasted Flycatcher	102.8 Ferruginous Flycatcher	102.9 White-gorgeted Flycatcher
103.2 Slaty-backed Flycatcher	103.3 Rufous-gorgeted Flycatcher	103.4 Red-breasted Flycatcher	103.5 Taiga Flycatcher	103.6 Kashmir Flycatcher
103.7 Little Pied Flycatcher	103.8 Ultramarine Flycatcher	103.9 Snowy-browed Flycatcher	103.10 Slaty-blue Flycatcher	104.1 Sapphire Flycatcher
104.2 Black-and-orange Flycatcher	104.3 Verditer Flycatcher	104.5 Nilgiri Flycatcher	104.6 Large Niltava	104.7 Small Niltava
104.8 Rufous-bellied Niltava	104.9 Vivid Niltava	105.1 White-tailed Flycatcher	105.2 White-bellied Blue Flycatcher	105.3 Pale-chinned Flycatcher
105.4 Pale Blue Flycatcher	105.5 Hill Blue Flycatcher	105.6 Large Blue Flycatcher	105.7 Tickell's Blue Flycatcher	105.8 Blue-throated Blue Flycatcher

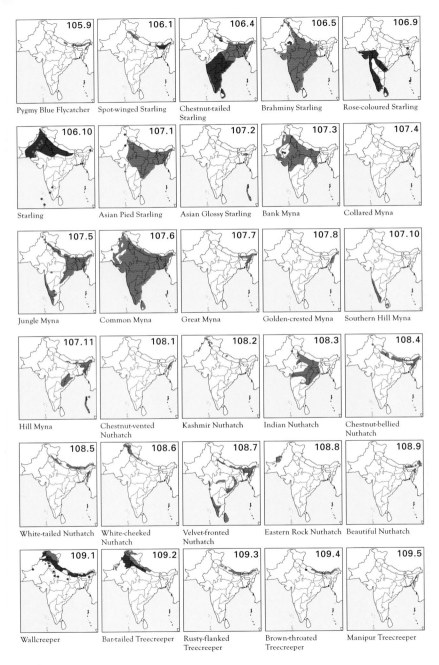

105.9 Pygmy Blue Flycatcher	106.1 Spot-winged Starling	106.4 Chestnut-tailed Starling	106.5 Brahminy Starling	106.9 Rose-coloured Starling
106.10 Starling	107.1 Asian Pied Starling	107.2 Asian Glossy Starling	107.3 Bank Myna	107.4 Collared Myna
107.5 Jungle Myna	107.6 Common Myna	107.7 Great Myna	107.8 Golden-crested Myna	107.10 Southern Hill Myna
107.11 Hill Myna	108.1 Chestnut-vented Nuthatch	108.2 Kashmir Nuthatch	108.3 Indian Nuthatch	108.4 Chestnut-bellied Nuthatch
108.5 White-tailed Nuthatch	108.6 White-cheeked Nuthatch	108.7 Velvet-fronted Nuthatch	108.8 Eastern Rock Nuthatch	108.9 Beautiful Nuthatch
109.1 Wallcreeper	109.2 Bar-tailed Treecreeper	109.3 Rusty-flanked Treecreeper	109.4 Brown-throated Treecreeper	109.5 Manipur Treecreeper

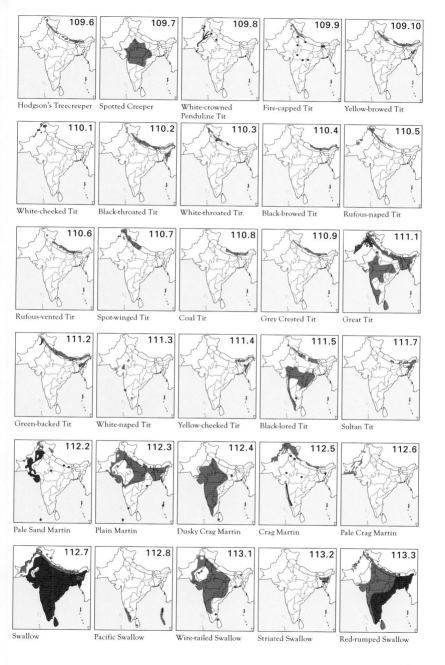

109.6 Hodgson's Treecreeper

109.7 Spotted Creeper

109.8 White-crowned Penduline Tit

109.9 Fire-capped Tit

109.10 Yellow-browed Tit

110.1 White-cheeked Tit

110.2 Black-throated Tit

110.3 White-throated Tit

110.4 Black-browed Tit

110.5 Rufous-naped Tit

110.6 Rufous-vented Tit

110.7 Spot-winged Tit

110.8 Coal Tit

110.9 Grey Crested Tit

111.1 Great Tit

111.2 Green-backed Tit

111.3 White-naped Tit

111.4 Yellow-cheeked Tit

111.5 Black-lored Tit

111.7 Sultan Tit

112.2 Pale Sand Martin

112.3 Plain Martin

112.4 Dusky Crag Martin

112.5 Crag Martin

112.6 Pale Crag Martin

112.7 Swallow

112.8 Pacific Swallow

113.1 Wire-tailed Swallow

113.2 Striated Swallow

113.3 Red-rumped Swallow

367

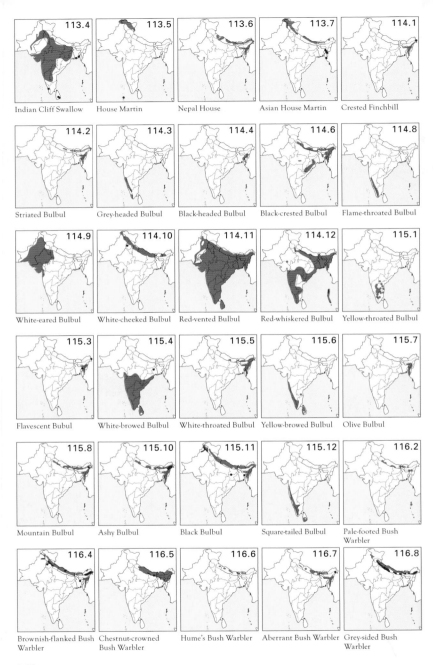

113.4 Indian Cliff Swallow
113.5 House Martin
113.6 Nepal House
113.7 Asian House Martin
114.1 Crested Finchbill

114.2 Striated Bulbul
114.3 Grey-headed Bulbul
114.4 Black-headed Bulbul
114.6 Black-crested Bulbul
114.8 Flame-throated Bulbul

114.9 White-eared Bulbul
114.10 White-cheeked Bulbul
114.11 Red-vented Bulbul
114.12 Red-whiskered Bulbul
115.1 Yellow-throated Bulbul

115.3 Flavescent Bulbul
115.4 White-browed Bulbul
115.5 White-throated Bulbul
115.6 Yellow-browed Bulbul
115.7 Olive Bulbul

115.8 Mountain Bulbul
115.10 Ashy Bulbul
115.11 Black Bulbul
115.12 Square-tailed Bulbul
116.2 Pale-footed Bush Warbler

116.4 Brownish-flanked Bush Warbler
116.5 Chestnut-crowned Bush Warbler
116.6 Hume's Bush Warbler
116.7 Aberrant Bush Warbler
116.8 Grey-sided Bush Warbler

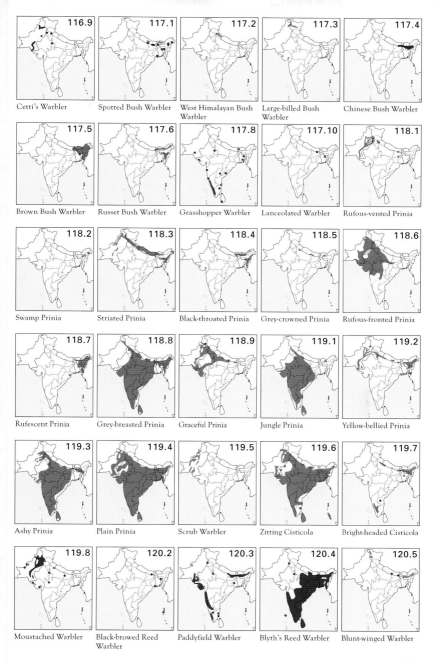

116.9 Cetti's Warbler	117.1 Spotted Bush Warbler	117.2 West Himalayan Bush Warbler	117.3 Large-billed Bush Warbler	117.4 Chinese Bush Warbler
117.5 Brown Bush Warbler	117.6 Russet Bush Warbler	117.8 Grasshopper Warbler	117.10 Lanceolated Warbler	118.1 Rufous-vented Prinia
118.2 Swamp Prinia	118.3 Striated Prinia	118.4 Black-throated Prinia	118.5 Grey-crowned Prinia	118.6 Rufous-fronted Prinia
118.7 Rufescent Prinia	118.8 Grey-breasted Prinia	118.9 Graceful Prinia	119.1 Jungle Prinia	119.2 Yellow-bellied Prinia
119.3 Ashy Prinia	119.4 Plain Prinia	119.5 Scrub Warbler	119.6 Zitting Cisticola	119.7 Bright-headed Cisticola
119.8 Moustached Warbler	120.2 Black-browed Reed Warbler	120.3 Paddyfield Warbler	120.4 Blyth's Reed Warbler	120.5 Blunt-winged Warbler

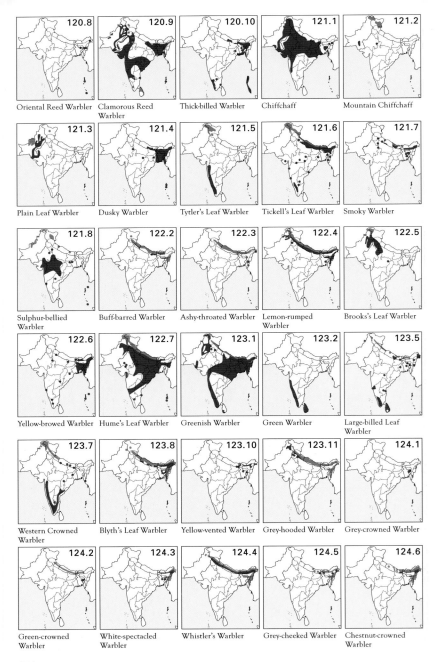

120.8 Oriental Reed Warbler	**120.9** Clamorous Reed Warbler	**120.10** Thick-billed Warbler	**121.1** Chiffchaff	**121.2** Mountain Chiffchaff
121.3 Plain Leaf Warbler	**121.4** Dusky Warbler	**121.5** Tytler's Leaf Warbler	**121.6** Tickell's Leaf Warbler	**121.7** Smoky Warbler
121.8 Sulphur-bellied Warbler	**122.2** Buff-barred Warbler	**122.3** Ashy-throated Warbler	**122.4** Lemon-rumped Warbler	**122.5** Brooks's Leaf Warbler
122.6 Yellow-browed Warbler	**122.7** Hume's Leaf Warbler	**123.1** Greenish Warbler	**123.2** Green Warbler	**123.5** Large-billed Leaf Warbler
123.7 Western Crowned Warbler	**123.8** Blyth's Leaf Warbler	**123.10** Yellow-vented Warbler	**123.11** Grey-hooded Warbler	**124.1** Grey-crowned Warbler
124.2 Green-crowned Warbler	**124.3** White-spectacled Warbler	**124.4** Whistler's Warbler	**124.5** Grey-cheeked Warbler	**124.6** Chestnut-crowned Warbler

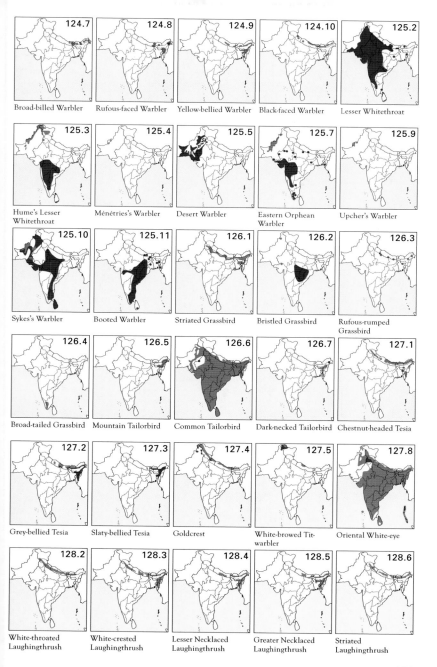

124.7 Broad-billed Warbler
124.8 Rufous-faced Warbler
124.9 Yellow-bellied Warbler
124.10 Black-faced Warbler
125.2 Lesser Whitethroat

125.3 Hume's Lesser Whitethroat
125.4 Ménétries's Warbler
125.5 Desert Warbler
125.7 Eastern Orphean Warbler
125.9 Upcher's Warbler

125.10 Sykes's Warbler
125.11 Booted Warbler
126.1 Striated Grassbird
126.2 Bristled Grassbird
126.3 Rufous-rumped Grassbird

126.4 Broad-tailed Grassbird
126.5 Mountain Tailorbird
126.6 Common Tailorbird
126.7 Dark-necked Tailorbird
127.1 Chestnut-headed Tesia

127.2 Grey-bellied Tesia
127.3 Slaty-bellied Tesia
127.4 Goldcrest
127.5 White-browed Tit-warbler
127.8 Oriental White-eye

128.2 White-throated Laughingthrush
128.3 White-crested Laughingthrush
128.4 Lesser Necklaced Laughingthrush
128.5 Greater Necklaced Laughingthrush
128.6 Striated Laughingthrush

371

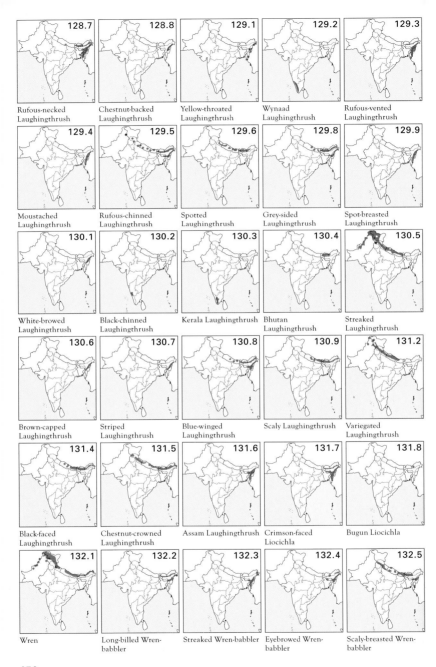

128.7 Rufous-necked Laughingthrush	128.8 Chestnut-backed Laughingthrush	129.1 Yellow-throated Laughingthrush	129.2 Wynaad Laughingthrush	129.3 Rufous-vented Laughingthrush
129.4 Moustached Laughingthrush	129.5 Rufous-chinned Laughingthrush	129.6 Spotted Laughingthrush	129.8 Grey-sided Laughingthrush	129.9 Spot-breasted Laughingthrush
130.1 White-browed Laughingthrush	130.2 Black-chinned Laughingthrush	130.3 Kerala Laughingthrush	130.4 Bhutan Laughingthrush	130.5 Streaked Laughingthrush
130.6 Brown-capped Laughingthrush	130.7 Striped Laughingthrush	130.8 Blue-winged Laughingthrush	130.9 Scaly Laughingthrush	131.2 Variegated Laughingthrush
131.4 Black-faced Laughingthrush	131.5 Chestnut-crowned Laughingthrush	131.6 Assam Laughingthrush	131.7 Crimson-faced Liocichla	131.8 Bugun Liocichla
132.1 Wren	132.2 Long-billed Wren-babbler	132.3 Streaked Wren-babbler	132.4 Eyebrowed Wren-babbler	132.5 Scaly-breasted Wren-babbler

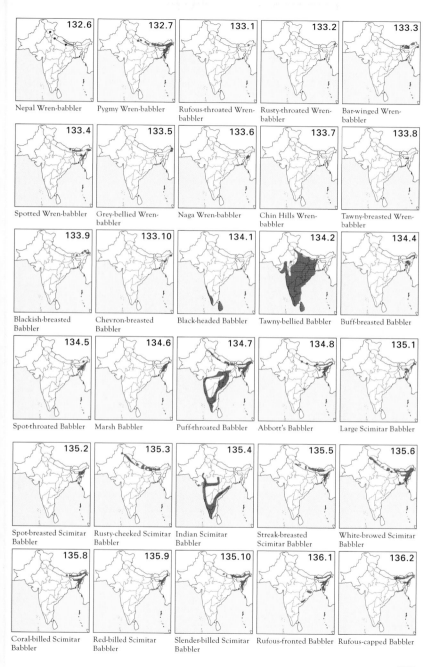

132.6	132.7	133.1	133.2	133.3
Nepal Wren-babbler	Pygmy Wren-babbler	Rufous-throated Wren-babbler	Rusty-throated Wren-babbler	Bar-winged Wren-babbler
133.4	133.5	133.6	133.7	133.8
Spotted Wren-babbler	Grey-bellied Wren-babbler	Naga Wren-babbler	Chin Hills Wren-babbler	Tawny-breasted Wren-babbler
133.9	133.10	134.1	134.2	134.4
Blackish-breasted Babbler	Chevron-breasted Babbler	Black-headed Babbler	Tawny-bellied Babbler	Buff-breasted Babbler
134.5	134.6	134.7	134.8	135.1
Spot-throated Babbler	Marsh Babbler	Puff-throated Babbler	Abbott's Babbler	Large Scimitar Babbler
135.2	135.3	135.4	135.5	135.6
Spot-breasted Scimitar Babbler	Rusty-cheeked Scimitar Babbler	Indian Scimitar Babbler	Streak-breasted Scimitar Babbler	White-browed Scimitar Babbler
135.8	135.9	135.10	136.1	136.2
Coral-billed Scimitar Babbler	Red-billed Scimitar Babbler	Slender-billed Scimitar Babbler	Rufous-fronted Babbler	Rufous-capped Babbler

373

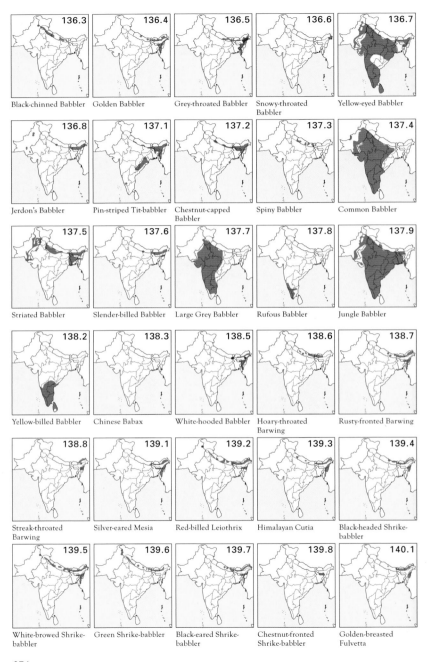

136.3 Black-chinned Babbler

136.4 Golden Babbler

136.5 Grey-throated Babbler

136.6 Snowy-throated Babbler

136.7 Yellow-eyed Babbler

136.8 Jerdon's Babbler

137.1 Pin-striped Tit-babbler

137.2 Chestnut-capped Babbler

137.3 Spiny Babbler

137.4 Common Babbler

137.5 Striated Babbler

137.6 Slender-billed Babbler

137.7 Large Grey Babbler

137.8 Rufous Babbler

137.9 Jungle Babbler

138.2 Yellow-billed Babbler

138.3 Chinese Babax

138.5 White-hooded Babbler

138.6 Hoary-throated Barwing

138.7 Rusty-fronted Barwing

138.8 Streak-throated Barwing

139.1 Silver-eared Mesia

139.2 Red-billed Leiothrix

139.3 Himalayan Cutia

139.4 Black-headed Shrike-babbler

139.5 White-browed Shrike-babbler

139.6 Green Shrike-babbler

139.7 Black-eared Shrike-babbler

139.8 Chestnut-fronted Shrike-babbler

140.1 Golden-breasted Fulvetta

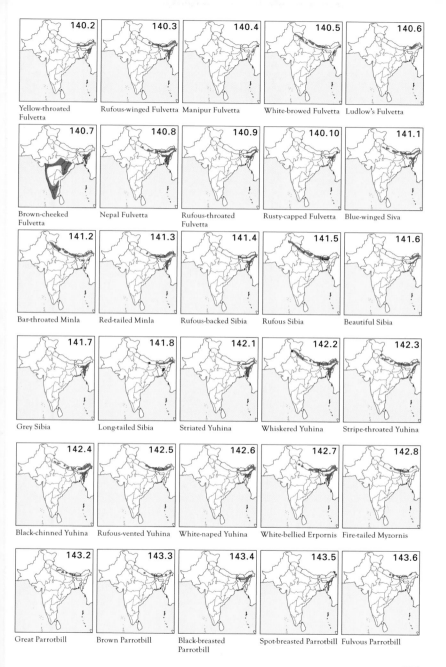

140.2 Yellow-throated Fulvetta

140.3 Rufous-winged Fulvetta

140.4 Manipur Fulvetta

140.5 White-browed Fulvetta

140.6 Ludlow's Fulvetta

140.7 Brown-cheeked Fulvetta

140.8 Nepal Fulvetta

140.9 Rufous-throated Fulvetta

140.10 Rusty-capped Fulvetta

141.1 Blue-winged Siva

141.2 Bar-throated Minla

141.3 Red-tailed Minla

141.4 Rufous-backed Sibia

141.5 Rufous Sibia

141.6 Beautiful Sibia

141.7 Grey Sibia

141.8 Long-tailed Sibia

142.1 Striated Yuhina

142.2 Whiskered Yuhina

142.3 Stripe-throated Yuhina

142.4 Black-chinned Yuhina

142.5 Rufous-vented Yuhina

142.6 White-naped Yuhina

142.7 White-bellied Erpornis

142.8 Fire-tailed Myzornis

143.2 Great Parrotbill

143.3 Brown Parrotbill

143.4 Black-breasted Parrotbill

143.5 Spot-breasted Parrotbill

143.6 Fulvous Parrotbill

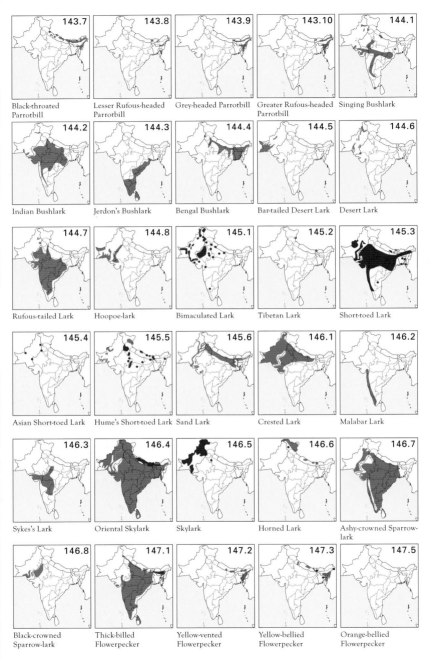

143.7 Black-throated Parrotbill

143.8 Lesser Rufous-headed Parrotbill

143.9 Grey-headed Parrotbill

143.10 Greater Rufous-headed Parrotbill

144.1 Singing Bushlark

144.2 Indian Bushlark

144.3 Jerdon's Bushlark

144.4 Bengal Bushlark

144.5 Bar-tailed Desert Lark

144.6 Desert Lark

144.7 Rufous-tailed Lark

144.8 Hoopoe-lark

145.1 Bimaculated Lark

145.2 Tibetan Lark

145.3 Short-toed Lark

145.4 Asian Short-toed Lark

145.5 Hume's Short-toed Lark

145.6 Sand Lark

146.1 Crested Lark

146.2 Malabar Lark

146.3 Sykes's Lark

146.4 Oriental Skylark

146.5 Skylark

146.6 Horned Lark

146.7 Ashy-crowned Sparrow-lark

146.8 Black-crowned Sparrow-lark

147.1 Thick-billed Flowerpecker

147.2 Yellow-vented Flowerpecker

147.3 Yellow-bellied Flowerpecker

147.5 Orange-bellied Flowerpecker

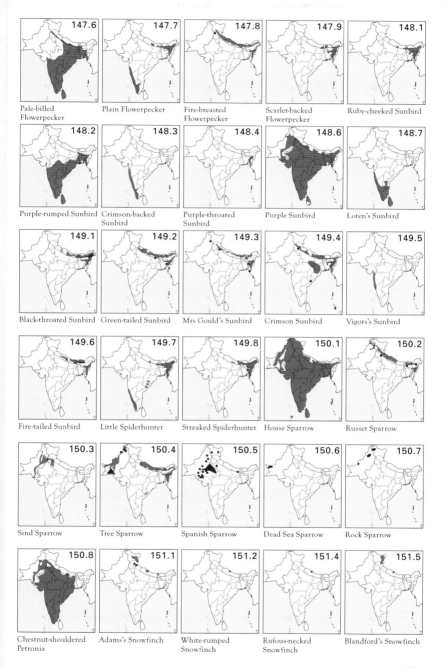

147.6 Pale-billed Flowerpecker

147.7 Plain Flowerpecker

147.8 Fire-breasted Flowerpecker

147.9 Scarlet-backed Flowerpecker

148.1 Ruby-cheeked Sunbird

148.2 Purple-rumped Sunbird

148.3 Crimson-backed Sunbird

148.4 Purple-throated Sunbird

148.6 Purple Sunbird

148.7 Loten's Sunbird

149.1 Black-throated Sunbird

149.2 Green-tailed Sunbird

149.3 Mrs Gould's Sunbird

149.4 Crimson Sunbird

149.5 Vigors's Sunbird

149.6 Fire-tailed Sunbird

149.7 Little Spiderhunter

149.8 Streaked Spiderhunter

150.1 House Sparrow

150.2 Russet Sparrow

150.3 Sind Sparrow

150.4 Tree Sparrow

150.5 Spanish Sparrow

150.6 Dead Sea Sparrow

150.7 Rock Sparrow

150.8 Chestnut-shouldered Petronia

151.1 Adams's Snowfinch

151.2 White-rumped Snowfinch

151.4 Rufous-necked Snowfinch

151.5 Blandford's Snowfinch

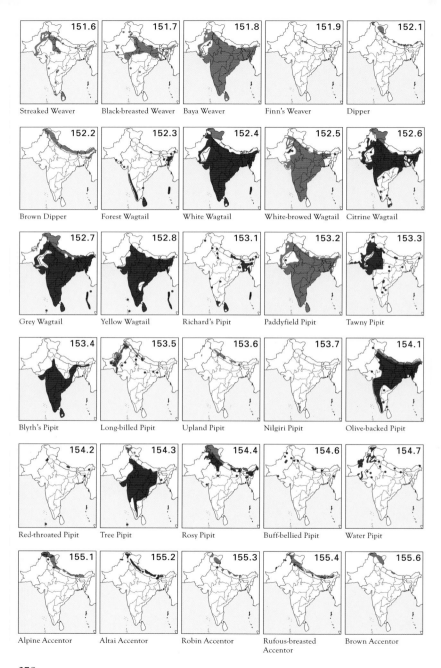

Streaked Weaver — 151.6
Black-breasted Weaver — 151.7
Baya Weaver — 151.8
Finn's Weaver — 151.9
Dipper — 152.1

Brown Dipper — 152.2
Forest Wagtail — 152.3
White Wagtail — 152.4
White-browed Wagtail — 152.5
Citrine Wagtail — 152.6

Grey Wagtail — 152.7
Yellow Wagtail — 152.8
Richard's Pipit — 153.1
Paddyfield Pipit — 153.2
Tawny Pipit — 153.3

Blyth's Pipit — 153.4
Long-billed Pipit — 153.5
Upland Pipit — 153.6
Nilgiri Pipit — 153.7
Olive-backed Pipit — 154.1

Red-throated Pipit — 154.2
Tree Pipit — 154.3
Rosy Pipit — 154.4
Buff-bellied Pipit — 154.6
Water Pipit — 154.7

Alpine Accentor — 155.1
Altai Accentor — 155.2
Robin Accentor — 155.3
Rufous-breasted Accentor — 155.4
Brown Accentor — 155.6

378

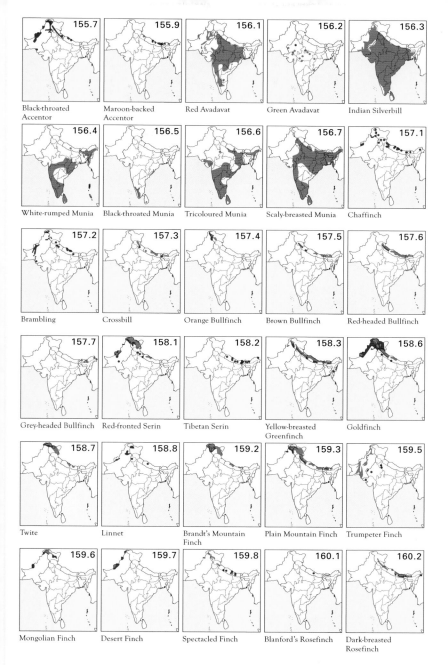

| 155.7 Black-throated Accentor | 155.9 Maroon-backed Accentor | 156.1 Red Avadavat | 156.2 Green Avadavat | 156.3 Indian Silverbill |

| 156.4 White-rumped Munia | 156.5 Black-throated Munia | 156.6 Tricoloured Munia | 156.7 Scaly-breasted Munia | 157.1 Chaffinch |

| 157.2 Brambling | 157.3 Crossbill | 157.4 Orange Bullfinch | 157.5 Brown Bullfinch | 157.6 Red-headed Bullfinch |

| 157.7 Grey-headed Bullfinch | 158.1 Red-fronted Serin | 158.2 Tibetan Serin | 158.3 Yellow-breasted Greenfinch | 158.6 Goldfinch |

| 158.7 Twite | 158.8 Linnet | 159.2 Brandt's Mountain Finch | 159.3 Plain Mountain Finch | 159.5 Trumpeter Finch |

| 159.6 Mongolian Finch | 159.7 Desert Finch | 159.8 Spectacled Finch | 160.1 Blanford's Rosefinch | 160.2 Dark-breasted Rosefinch |

379

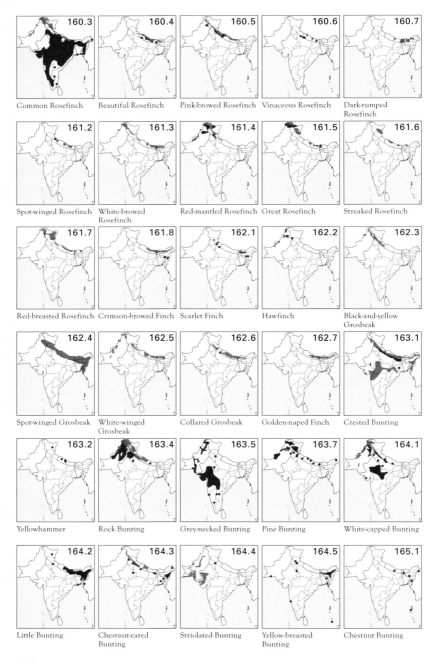

160.3 Common Rosefinch	160.4 Beautiful Rosefinch	160.5 Pink-browed Rosefinch	160.6 Vinaceous Rosefinch	160.7 Dark-rumped Rosefinch
161.2 Spot-winged Rosefinch	161.3 White-browed Rosefinch	161.4 Red-mantled Rosefinch	161.5 Great Rosefinch	161.6 Streaked Rosefinch
161.7 Red-breasted Rosefinch	161.8 Crimson-browed Finch	162.1 Scarlet Finch	162.2 Hawfinch	162.3 Black-and-yellow Grosbeak
162.4 Spot-winged Grosbeak	162.5 White-winged Grosbeak	162.6 Collared Grosbeak	162.7 Golden-naped Finch	163.1 Crested Bunting
163.2 Yellowhammer	163.4 Rock Bunting	163.5 Grey-necked Bunting	163.7 Pine Bunting	164.1 White-capped Bunting
164.2 Little Bunting	164.3 Chestnut-eared Bunting	164.4 Striolated Bunting	164.5 Yellow-breasted Bunting	165.1 Chestnut Bunting

380

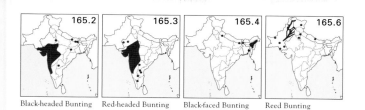

Black-headed Bunting   Red-headed Bunting   Black-faced Bunting   Reed Bunting